READER'S DIGEST
EXPLORE YOUR FAMILY'S PAST

READER'S DIGEST

EXPLORE YOUR

FAMILY'S PAST

Published by The Reader's Digest Association, Inc.
London • New York • Sydney • Montreal

Explore Your Family's Past Published in 2011 in the United Kingdom by
Vivat Direct Limited (t/a Reader's Digest), 157 Edgware Road, London W2 2HR

Explore Your Family's Past is owned and under licence from
The Reader's Digest Association Limited, Inc. All rights reserved.

Updated from **Explore Your Family's Past** reprinted with updates by
The Reader's Digest Association, Inc. in 2005. First published by
The Reader's Digest Association, Inc. in 2000.

We are committed to both the quality of our products and the service we
provide to our customers. We value your comments, so please do contact us on
0871 351 1000, or via our web site at: www.readersdigest.co.uk
If you have any comments or suggestions about the content of our books, you
can contact us at **gbeditorial@readersdigest.co.uk**

Concept code UK1223/IC
ISBN 978-1-78020-044-6
Book code: 400-565 UP0000-1

Colour origination FMG
Printed in China

FOR THIS EDITION

CONTRIBUTOR
David Hey

PICTURE RESEARCH
Wilf Matos

TECHNICAL ILLUSTRATIONS
Terry Burrows

PROOFREADER
Barry Gage

INDEXER
Marie Lorimer

FOR VIVAT DIRECT

EDITORIAL DIRECTOR
Julian Browne

ART DIRECTOR
Anne-Marie Bulat

MANAGING EDITOR
Nina Hathway

TRADE BOOKS EDITOR
Penny Craig

PICTURE RESOURCE MANAGER
Sarah Stewart-Richardson

PREPRESS TECHNICAL MANAGER
Dean Russell

PRODUCT PRODUCTION MANAGER
Claudette Bramble

PRODUCTION CONTROLLER
Jan Bucil

FOR FIRST EDITION

EDITORIAL CONSULTANT
Mark Herber

CONSULTANTS
Mary Casteleyn
Peter Christian
David Kynaston
Marjorie Moore
John Rowlands
Sheila Rowlands

CONTRIBUTORS
Paul Blake, Brian Brooks,
Colin Chapman, Else Churchill,
Jean Cole, Stella Colwell,
Sharon Floate, Tony Fuller,
Michael Gandy, Robert Gordon
Duncan Harrington, David Hawkings,
David Hey, Cecil Humphery-Smith,
Anthony Joseph, Roger Kershaw
Pauline Litton, Susan Lumas
Eve McLaughlin, Terry Morter
Mark Pearsall, Chris Pitt-Lewis
Colin Rogers, Jess Steele,
John Titford, Christopher Watts,
Michael Watts, Tom Wood

EDITORS
John Andrews
Justine Scott-Macnab

ART EDITOR
Neal Martin

DESIGNER
Kate Harris

SENIOR ASSISTANT EDITOR
Rachel Warren Chadd

ASSISTANT EDITORS
Alison Bravington, Julia Bruce
Celia Coyne, Caroline Knight
Cécile Landau, David Scott-Macnab
Miriam Sharland, Helen Spence

EDITORIAL ASSISTANT
Liz Edwards

DEVELOPMENT EDITOR
Ruth Binney

PICTURE RESEARCHER
Rosie Taylor

RESEARCHERS
Debbie Feldman
Fiona Hunter
Michael Paterson

CARTOGRAPHIC EDITOR
Alison Ewington

PROOFREADER
Barry Gage

STUDIO
Ian Atkinson

PHOTOGRAPHER
Jon Bouchier

ARTIST
Tom Meek

INDEXER
Laura Hicks

PICTURE RESOURCE MANAGER
Martin Smith

STYLE EDITOR
Ron Pankhurst

PRE-PRESS TECHNICAL ANALYST
Martin Hendrick

PRE-PRESS SUPPORT
Jim Lindsay

PRE-PRESS CONTROLLER
Byron Johnson

REGIONAL OPERATIONS MANAGER
Fiona McIntosh

GLOBAL PRE-PRESS MANAGER
Howard Reynolds

contents

THE
NEED
FOR
FIGHTING
MEN
IS
URGENT.

seeking your ancestors

Investigating your family history is like being a detective in a gripping drama—and all the more exciting because your own family is at the centre of the mystery. As you delve into the past you will sense the thrill of a treasure hunt, and with each discovery feel the glow of achievement.

Unknown to you, other members of your family may already be on the trail. One family historian was exploring her Gypsy heritage when she discovered distant cousins who had learnt that their mutual great-grandmother had been a fortune teller on Blackpool Beach (see pages 246–7).

We have brought together family historians and researchers to take you step by step through the processes involved in preparing a family tree. To start with, you will want to look at what you already have—your immediate family's birth or marriage certificates, the death certificate of a close relative, photograph albums, and perhaps a family Bible. Relatives are a valuable resource: you can learn a lot by asking questions of parents and grandparents.

Then there are census records. Since 1841, census returns have included the names of everyone who could be located and where they were on census night. Everything was handwritten, and inevitably there are spelling discrepancies. One researcher putting together his family tree found his surname spelt in 21 different ways (see pages 38–39).

the history of your family name

Surnames interest everyone, and *Explore your Family's Past* may help you to find out where yours came from. Some of the derivations are delightfully unexpected: Moody meant brave, for example, Lacy derives from the French town of Lassy, and Frobisher derives from an obsolete profession and meant restorer of armour. But you will undoubtedly want to find out much more about your ancestors than the origins of their names. After all, their story is your story, and family traits probably persist, as you will see when you unearth family photographs.

how to use this book

The book is divided into eight sections that broadly cover the records you will come across during your family history research.

GETTING STARTED explains how to gather clues from your family, explore archives, search the Internet, organise your notes and create a family tree.

MATTERS OF STATE explores the official documents—such as birth, marriage and death certificates or census returns—that record most people in the 19th to 21st centuries.

BLESSED RITES looks at parish records (some going back to the 16th century) and those of other denominations and faiths that mark those important rites of passage: baptism, marriage and burial.

THEIR PLACE IN SOCIETY is designed to help you to build up a picture of your ancestors' lives. It covers wills, education, employment, poor law and criminal records.

HOME GROUND will help you to visualise your ancestors' surroundings through maps, newspaper reports, property records and other local history.

JOINING UP delves into the documents that record information about the millions who served in the army, the merchant navy, the Royal Air Force and the Royal Navy.

ON THE MOVE will show you how to track down ancestors who moved around within

Family historians are often amazed at the striking likenesses that link different generations.

Photographs of people and places might inspire you to visit the towns or villages, or even the houses or cottages where your ancestors lived. You could find the churches they attended and hunt for their graves; and if one generation or more of your family lived in the same village—perhaps working as agricultural labourers on local farms—the chances are that their baptisms, marriages and burials will have been conducted in the same parish church and recorded in church registers.

If the family fell upon hard times—perhaps being given money or clothing by parish officials—this, too, will have been recorded in detail.

from heroes to highwaymen

Many of us have ancestors that played their part in major historical events. Did yours fight alongside Wellington, or in the trenches during the First World War? Did anyone go to sea? *Explore your Family's Past* can show you how to trace someone through the records of his regiment or ship. If he was awarded any medals, these may have been kept with other precious family memorabilia: a pocket watch with an inscription, a postcard from the Front, a book with a dedication on the flyleaf, a baby's first lock of hair, or even a family Bible with births, marriages and deaths carefully recorded in the margins.

Sometimes you will find marriages reported in newspapers, and *Explore your Family's Past* shows you how to make the most of this resource. Indeed, old newspapers contain all sorts of information, from lists of bankrupts to victims of disasters. Crimes often earned a mention, too.

Was your ancestor a highwayman or a pickpocket? Or was he hauled in front of the magistrates for poaching a rabbit to feed a starving family? If an ancestor fell foul of the law, *Explore your Family's Past* will help you to find out more from court records. Be warned, though: you may be horrified to learn that an ancestor ended his life on the gibbet.

Like any detective work, there will be blind alleys. But finding a missing piece of the jigsaw puzzle after weeks of hunting can be one of the most joyous and rewarding of discoveries. *Explore your Family's Past* will keep you company as you travel back in time. We hope that you will find it a guide and an inspiration.

the British Isles, settled abroad or migrated here from other parts of the world.

MEDIEVAL ROOTS looks at early documents, dating back from Tudor to Norman times, which might mention distant forebears. Could there be a title somewhere in your family? This section explores coats of arms and also explains how family names evolved. It is followed by a dictionary of a thousand surnames.

ON THE PAGE

♦ When DIRECTORY appears in the text after any source of information, look at the Directory of sources on pages 322–41 for addresses, telephone numbers and web sites.
♦ The KEY SOURCES OF INFORMATION box in most sections indicates where the most important records for this subject are found.
♦ TAKING IT FURTHER boxes list extra sources of information—in books, CDs and on the Internet. If the books mentioned are not available in your local library or high street bookshop, ask for advice in a good reference library. Family history books can be bought via the Internet; the Society of Genealogists and the Federation of Family History Societies (see DIRECTORY) have their own on-line bookshops.
♦ Web sites (in light print), listed throughout the book, reflect the fact that the Internet is a great research tool. Check out family history links at www.readersdigest.co.uk

the first steps

Whatever prompts you to explore your family's past, it can be the start of a wonderful adventure. But to ensure success, the exercise must be carefully planned step by step, as the following pages outline.

The search begins in the present with you and your relatives, then branches out to embrace the vast range of resources that help you to journey into the past to discover your ancestry and create a family tree.

start with yourself

Write an account of your life

♦ Begin by noting down your own personal details. Your children or grandchildren may become interested in your research, so they will need to know about you. Your details may also interest other relatives whom you contact for information. You should include:

♦ The important dates and events in your life, attaching copies of documents for future reference.

♦ The date and place of your birth and marriage.

♦ Where and when you went to school, college or university. Note your qualifications and the dates you obtained them.

♦ Your employment (where, when and what you did).

♦ Your children's names, dates of birth, dates of marriages, names of spouses and any children. Also note details of their education, employment and any other qualifications.

If you are starting the project when you already have children or grandchildren, this exercise provides a ready-made family tree that will interest other relatives and perhaps help their research.

Create your own archive

♦ The next step is to pull together all the valuable paperwork on your family that is close to hand. You may be amazed at what you find hidden away in drawers, boxes or chests in the attic.

You are the starting point of your family history—your close relations come next

Try to include the following:
♦ Your birth certificate, marriage certificate, and certificates of your educational achievements or other qualifications.
♦ Photographs of you at different ages, a wedding photograph and photographs of your children.
♦ Documents about jobs you have had or places in which you have lived.

Look at all the material you have gathered. With luck and persistence you will be able to find similar facts about many of your ancestors.

decide who to research

Start from what you know
♦ Begin by gathering information about close relatives. You will know much about your parents and something of your four grandparents.

♦ As you go back farther the possibilities increase. Your grandparents each had two parents, giving you eight great grandparents.
♦ Another generation on and you have 16 great-great-grandparents. The chart below will help you to work out family relationships.

Which family lines to pursue
♦ Most people start with their father's ancestral line because it is the one that gave them their surname.
♦ But you may want to try the line with the most unusual surname, as it could prove the easiest to trace, although there is no guarantee of this.
♦ If you are feeling ambitious and have the time, why not research as many as possible—mother, father, two grandmothers, two grandfathers and so on back through time?

BONUSES OF RESEARCH
There are advantages to following many different leads. For instance, whenever you research one ancestral line, you are likely to get stuck at some point as you hunt for an elusive baptism or marriage.

At such a time, you can develop other lines, which may provide fresh clues to solve your original problem.

The more you research, the more likely you are to encounter a range of fascinating characters—perhaps a noble family, a highwayman or other criminal, or the very poor who had to live on charity from the parish.

The level of detail to include
♦ The choice is yours. You can gather brief details on many ancestors such as dates of birth, marriage and death, occupations and where they lived.

WORKING OUT FAMILY RELATIONSHIPS

my great-grandparent		
my great uncle/aunt		my grandparent
my first cousin once removed	my parent	my uncle/aunt
my second cousin	me — my brother/sister	my first cousin
my second cousin once removed	my nephew/niece	my first cousin once removed
my second cousin twice removed	my grandnephew/niece	my first cousin twice removed

You and your relations
You know about yourself, your spouse, your children and probably your cousins too. But what relation to you are your cousins' children or their children's children? This chart should help.

A poignant record of their lives
Your search for clues and documented evidence of your ancestors' lives may at times take you away on trips of discovery to explore places where they lived and often their final resting place. If your forebears lived in a particular parish for a long time, one churchyard may reveal many family names.

♦ Or you can delve further into one line that you find interesting and learn about your ancestors' education, careers and how they fitted into the society of their day.

♦ Once you start researching beyond your immediate family, this sort of material will not be readily available and you will have to look for it, often in record offices.

how easy will it be to track down my ancestors?

Social status is significant

♦ The success of your research will depend, to a large extent, on how well your ancestors were recorded. For instance:

♦ Noble families are easily located in records because of the part they may have played in politics or because they owned land. Many land records date back to the Middle Ages.

♦ Professional men such as clergy and lawyers are often well recorded.

♦ Army or naval officers are usually better documented than the ranks.

♦ Labourers and their families are harder to find. But some documents record the poorest in society. A parish kept records of those who were given parish funds, clothes or firewood to support them in old age or in periods of unemployment.

♦ Parish registers—dating from the 16th century—record the baptisms, marriages and burials of people in all classes of society.

Ancestors high and low

♦ In the course of your research you may find forebears throughout society. Many ancestors of the rich were poor but rose in social status as successive generations used their skills and gained influence. Thus:

♦ The son of a labourer might progress to blacksmith, his son to clerk, and his son to merchant. The merchant's son might study and become a lawyer. And his son might be an army officer who received land and a title for military achievements.

♦ Families could equally slide down the social scale. Thus:

♦ A duke's youngest son has a poor army career. His son becomes a clergyman with a poor living. One of his sons turns to farming. This man's eldest son inherits the farm but the younger brothers have to work as labourers on other people's land.

Family roots and skills

♦ Your ancestors may have moved more than you think, making some difficult to trace. But other families lived in one place for generations and their baptisms, marriages and burials may appear in one parish register.

The fortunes of your family may have changed dramatically over the centuries

A family trade or an unusual name can help you to pick out your ancestors in the records

♦ Your ancestors may have worked in the same trade for generations. Your great-grandfather, his father and his father before him may each have been a shoemaker in Exeter.

Even if they moved around the city between different parishes, that continuity of occupation is likely to assist your research.

A distinctive surname

♦ The surname of your ancestors may influence the success of your research. It is obviously easier to check all references to an unusual surname for a particular record than it is to search for all mentions of a common name, then try to decide which was your ancestor.

♦ A rare Christian name can also assist your research. While any number of John Smiths may have lived in London in 1739, there might have been only one Cornelius Smith. The chances are that such a distinctive name was bequeathed from an earlier generation.

1 **Work backwards in time**

Start with yourself and work back to your parents, their parents and so on. Try to resist the temptation of attempting to find a link between you and a famous person with the same surname as yourself; you could well find yourself following a false trail.

2 **Note every clue that may help you later**

Organise your research and your time efficiently, doing as much spadework as possible by telephone, mail or on the Internet before making special trips.

3 **Tackle the home front first**

Dig out your personal papers and gather information and documents from family members.

4 **Research more than one family name**

You may make more progress with some ancestral lines than others, which keeps the research interesting. Aim to find your 16 great-great-grandparents and then choose which lines to extend back in time.

5 **Start drawing up family trees**

This helps you to see the gaps in your knowledge that you can aim to fill. It also allows you to show your relatives how far you have progressed.

6 **Find out what others have discovered about your family**

Are cousins also undertaking research? Does the Society of Genealogists (see page 31) or a local family history society (see page 22) have any information? Is there information relevant to your family on the Internet (see pages 34–37)?

7 **Interview as many relatives as you can**

Ask them about all members of the family and whether they have any documents or photographs.

8 **Visit your local library and the nearest reference library**

Local libraries and archives may have many books on family history as well as published records, indexes or reference books on particular aspects of genealogical research.

9 **Go on-line**

In recent years, millions of documents have been made available on the Internet. It is now possible to get back very quickly to early Victorian times, using census returns and birth, marriage and death records. Every few months, new sources of information appear on-line.

10 **Start exploring documents held in record offices**

Begin with birth, marriage and death certificates since 1837 (see pages 50–61), census records (see pages 62–75), parish registers (see pages 86–99), wills (see pages 120–31) and directories (see pages 174–5). But do not forget that a local library, family history society or one of the Family History Centres (see DIRECTORY) established around the British Isles by the Mormon Church (see pages 100–1) may have copies or indexes of this material that you can use without travelling far from home.

tackling the home front

The personal documents and photographs you have collected at home will have helped you to compile a fairly comprehensive history of yourself. But already there may be gaps in what you know about your parents' or grandparents' lives.

filling in the background

Talk to close relatives

♦ The memories of aunts, uncles and other older relatives will now become very valuable, particularly if your parents are no longer alive.

♦ Contact as many relations as possible as some may know facts and stories that others do not. Women often know more about the family than men as they are often responsible for family correspondence, such as birthday and Christmas cards, and all the news that goes with them.

Draft a simple family tree

♦ Include as many family members as possible. It may be easier, even at this early stage, to draw a pedigree for each main family; one tree for your mother's side of the family and one tree for your father's family. See Creating a family tree, pages 38–39.

♦ Ask relatives to check your information. See if they can fill in any further details about anyone who appears on the family tree.

meeting distant relatives

Carefully plan the interview

♦ How you make an initial approach will depend on how well acquainted you are. Some people prefer to send out questionnaires and ask for written answers. But it is usually better to meet each relative to talk about the family.

♦ It may help to send a relative a copy of the draft family tree before a meeting. It may revive old memories and help your relative to think about other family members.

♦ List the information you need so as not to forget important questions.

♦ A relative may provide detailed information about family members without prompting. But sometimes you may have to ask many questions in order to obtain useful information.

What to ask and how to ask it

♦ Tailor questions to the individual, based on that person's knowledge and willingness to help.

♦ If the relatives enjoy talking about the family, let them talk freely, merely interjecting with a question or two at convenient intervals.

♦ Try to frame questions so as to elicit either detailed answers or a

general indication. A relative may not remember exact dates and places for a birth or marriage but may recall that a birth took place 'before the Great War' or recall the details of certain weddings. If so, ask who was present, who was not there and why.

♦ Make the relative feel part of the research—make it clear how important their memories are to you and try to make the meeting interesting.

♦ Consider the gaps in your knowledge and think about what you want to ask and how it will help your research. Then try to direct the discussion towards these subject areas.

♦ Be ready to change the line of questioning if a relative can tell you about matters of which you were completely unaware, or if the relative knows little about the family members you asked about but knows much about other family members.

♦ Take detailed notes of everything that is said, as information that appears unimportant at first may later prove vital for your research.

♦ If a relative is clearly uncomfortable about discussing certain issues, do not press him or her. See if other relatives can help you first or try to find the answer in record archives.

♦ Use a tape recorder only if you are confident it will not make your relative uncomfortable. You may learn far more about the family without it. Every family has its scandals. Some relatives may not wish to speak about certain matters if they know they are being recorded.

♦ Many relatives will tell you about matters in confidence, which is a condition you should respect.

♦ Keep a note of the date and where each interview takes place.

documents in the family

Gathering more evidence

♦ If relatives share your interest in the research, ask them to look for any old documents that might help.

♦ They may hold birth, marriage or death certificates of ancestors. They

Contact your older relatives first as their memories are of key importance to your early research

TWENTY QUESTIONS

The most important questions are:

1 Where and when were you born?

2 What was your father's full name? Did he have a nickname?

3 What was your mother's full name? Did she have a nickname?

4 Where and when did your parents marry?

5 What work did your father do? Did you ever visit his workplace?

6 Did your father serve in the army, Royal Navy or Royal Air Force?

7 Did he receive any medals? Who has those medals?

8 Do you have any photographs of your parents?

9 Did your parents ever talk about their own parents, perhaps their names, places of origin, or their fathers' jobs?

10 When did your parents die and where are they buried?

11 Do you have copies of your parents' birth, marriage or death certificates?

12 Did either parent leave a will?

13 What were the names of your brothers and sisters?

14 Where and when were they born?

15 Did any of them die young?

16 Can you remember the family home when you were a child?

17 What schools did you and your brothers and sisters attend?

18 Did the family attend a church, and if so which church?

19 Do you have childhood memories of other relatives?

20 Do you remember any family weddings when you were young? Who was there and who was absent?

using the family Bible

As you pursue your search for family memorabilia and talk to more relatives about your project, you may be fortunate enough to come across an old family Bible or other religious book, which records generations of your ancestors.

Whoever undertook this task would record the names of each immediate family member, the date (and sometimes the time) of birth, and dates of baptisms, marriages and deaths. To discover generations of family entries (and details that may not appear in church or civil records) is particularly exciting if they include children (especially those who died young) of whom you were unaware.

Look in the Bible or other book for its year of publication. If any information precedes it, it should be verified as it would have been written from memory. If possible, try to check all the dates against official records.

might be able to unearth a copy of an old will, or they may have kept a newspaper obituary or report of an event involving a family member.

♦ Somewhere perhaps they may still have certificates of an ancestor's professional qualifications or his papers of discharge from the armed forces.

♦ They may also be able to show you memorabilia such as medals, which may tell you much about an ancestor's military career (see Memories of service and valour, pages 222–3).

♦ Family correspondence, books, inscribed watches or other jewellery may help you to confirm dates and events and add to your knowledge and feeling for the family's heritage.

the value of photographs

Annotate your collection
♦ You are likely to have many family photographs. Make sure they are properly labelled for the benefit of future generations but do not write on the back as that may damage them.

♦ If you cannot identify everyone in a group picture, ask as many relatives as possible and compare the answers.

♦ When you meet a new relative, such as a distant cousin, ask if he or she has any old photos of your immediate ancestors or other relatives that would illustrate the family tree.

Take your own family photos
♦ Add to this collection by taking your own photographs of relatives, or subjects that illustrate the family tree. For example:

♦ If you visit a house in which your ancestors once lived, take a picture of it as you may not find a photo taken at the time your ancestors lived there.

♦ If you find an ancestor's gravestone, take photographs of the stone, the church or cemetery chapel, and record the inscription. See In memoriam, pages 112–17.

♦ Take photographs of the places in which your ancestors worked or general views around a village in which they lived.

Add to your picture archive
♦ At fairs or postcard markets, you may find photographs or postcards of the churches in which your ancestors worshipped or were married, the streets in which they lived, schools they attended or their place of work.

♦ Most county record offices (see pages 28–29) have many photos of the area they serve. Their archives may also include material donated by schools, colleges or businesses, which may include group photos of past students or employees.

♦ Visit specialist archives such as the National Maritime Museum's huge catalogued collection of photographs of old ships (see page 219).

♦ Look for books that contain old photographs. For example, Sutton Publishing (see DIRECTORY) has produced the series *In Old Photographs*. Each book covers a town, village or part of a city in the 19th and early 20th centuries and may include photos relevant to your ancestors, such as the street in which they lived.

what old photographs can tell you

This is a daguerreotype (on copper), an early technique used mainly in the 1840s. At the same time, calotypes (on paper) were being made. These images were less sharp but had subtler degrees of shading.

Glass plate negatives superseded both calotypes and daguerreotypes in the 1850s. They allowed for multiplication of prints.

Daguerreotypes were costly and tended to mark special occasions: this one of Egerton Cleeve (1827–50) was taken before a trip to Montevideo, where he died of yellow fever.

The high collar and neat dress suit are typical of the mid 19th century; the slicked hair (probably with fashionable macassar oil) hints at a sophisticated, possibly moneyed lifestyle.

Few of us have any idea of what our ancestors looked like before the advent of portrait photography in the 1840s. Richer families might have portrait paintings or sculptures; sometimes there are silhouettes; but with a photograph comes the thrill of seeing someone who is related to you, but whose eyes looked out on a very different world.

The earliest portraits involved several minutes of sitting still with one's head held in a clamp; hardly surprising, then, that few Victorians are smiling. But technology evolved rapidly, and by 1900 Kodak's Box Brownie was selling for 5s.

The study of family photos can be very rewarding; for help in unlocking the secrets, see *Family Photographs and How to Date Them* (Jayne Shrimpton, Countryside Books, 2008).

You can look for clues to help you to narrow the search for the person whose eyes are gazing out of that old photograph

LOOKING FOR CLUES

1 Portraits for the masses

Most photography before 1900 was studio based. Cartes-de-visite (portraits on visiting-card size mounts) were popular from the 1850s—in 1862 alone, 105 million were made.

2 Where was the studio?

A studio name and location could help with dating: studios were often short-lived and local trade directories (see pages 174–5) list who was working where and when. From the early 1900s snaps grew popular as cameras became widely available and cheap.

3 Do not rely on fashion

Country folk in 'Sunday best' might be 20 years out of date; the elderly often preferred 'old-fashioned' clothes. A uniform says more, be it army, navy, police or postman.

4 Props and paraphernalia

Guns, hats or medals (see pages 222–3) can narrow the timescale—local museums or libraries might be able to help with identification.

5 Special places, familiar faces

Compare mysterious snaps with known faces or places—in a holiday album, for example. It is surprising how often you can spot a match.

6 Location, location

If there is a church, a house, a garden or a beach in the background, see whether family members recognise it; is there a car, shop sign or other clue to a date?

7 Follow the paper trail

Try matching photographs and documentation: you may have a marriage certificate that corresponds to an unidentified wedding photograph, or the record of a baptism for a baby in a dated but unnamed picture.

help from other sources

ALL THE LATEST NEWS

Four monthly magazines – *Family History Monthly*, *Family Tree Magazine*, *Your Family Tree* and *Who Do You Think You Are?* – are devoted to family history. They contain articles on all aspects of the subject, answers to readers' queries, reviews of books and CDs, updates on the Internet, news of events and advertisements from publishers, manufacturers of specialist equipment, and professional researchers. For details see DIRECTORY under Magazines.

Researching your family tree can prove challenging at times, but you are not on your own. There are several organisations dedicated to family history research that can help you, as well as the thousands of individuals currently undertaking their own research.

people who can help

Plug into the network

♦ Do contact other researchers by post (enclose a stamped addressed envelope) or on-line, as sharing information can speed up your research and make it much more fun. You may even find that someone has already researched part of your family tree, although you should not assume that all the details are correct.

♦ A family history society (see page 22) or the Society of Genealogists (see page 31) may hold research relating to your family; genealogists sometimes deposit their research for safekeeping and for the benefit of others. Members often advertise the names of the families they are researching in the societies' journals so you can find out if anyone else is pursuing the same ancestral lines.

♦ You can advertise the names you are researching in the journals of the local family history societies (see page 22) that you have joined so that others can contact you.

♦ The annual *Genealogical Research Directory* lists the surnames of families being researched by thousands of family historians all over the world, the county and place in which they lived and contact details for the researcher. It is edited and published by K.A. Johnson and M.R. Sainty in book and CD format. *The British Isles Genealogical Register* (Big R), published and periodically updated by the Federation of Family History Societies (FFHS—see DIRECTORY), is similar in format and sold complete or county by county.

Using the Internet

♦ In recent years the use of computers and the Internet has made it far easier to make a start on a family tree and to make rapid progress back into the Victorian era. Birth, marriage and death certificates from 1837 to the present day and census records from 1841 to 1911 are now available on the Internet, mainly from commercial companies, and these are easy to search. It is not as easy to get back further, but millions of records, ranging from parish registers to passenger lists have become available and many more are promised in future years.

♦ The essential guide is *The Genealogist's Internet* (P. Christian, The National Archives, 4th ed., 2009), though many more records have been added since its publication.

But you need to be aware that information derived from the Internet can be flawed:

♦ Do not take on trust the information on family trees supplied by other researchers. Check original sources.

♦ Be aware that the transcriptions of census returns on commercial sites, which were usually made by amateurs, may contain errors.

♦ Remember also that the census enumerators themselves made slips of the pen.

♦ Using the Internet can give a false sense that genealogy is easy. It is still necessary to spent a lot of time at record offices if you want to discover more about the lives of your ancestors and if you want to get back further.

SURNAME STUDIES

Your surname may be among the many thousands being studied by a growing number of researchers who look for all recorded information of a name in a bid to establish family links.

Many belong to the Guild of One-Name Studies. Its register of more than 8000 surnames and variants is available on-line, with contact details for the member studying each name, at www.one-name.org

You will also find surname lists by county together with the names and email addresses of the researchers at www.genuki.org.uk/indexes/SurnamesLists.html

Most 'one-name' researchers you contact will enjoy sharing their interest. You may exchange useful information, and they might give you new leads. You may even meet new relatives, if only distant cousins.

family history societies

Once you start delving into your family's past you will find that you share your interest with many thousands of others. This is reflected in the number of family history societies: more than 160 are currently members of the Federation of Family History Societies (FFHS)—most of them in the British Isles.

The main aim of these societies is to assist and promote the study of genealogy in their local area. Some cover a county; others are specific to a city or a particular part of a county. A few appeal to special areas of interest—such as the Catholic FHS, the Quaker FHS or the Railway Ancestors FHS. Most produce journals and other publications, and

provide a forum for guest speakers. They often have their own libraries, indexes of local genealogical information and copies of local registers. Some societies organise trips to venues such as The National Archives (see page 26).

The membership fee for such societies is usually in the region of £10 a year. It is a good idea to join your nearest society to gain access to its reference facilities. You might also consider joining the society for any area in which your ancestors lived for more than a couple of generations.

County and city record offices (see pages 28–29) can usually direct you to local family history societies. Or you can ask the FFHS as most local

family history societies are members. Send a stamped addressed envelope to: The Federation of Family History Societies, PO Box 8857, Lutterworth, LE17 9BJ.

Twice yearly the FFHS publishes the *Family History News and Digest*, which contains useful articles and lists all FFHS members, with contact details for membership secretaries. A full list of member societies and details of its publications are also displayed on the FFHS web site, www.ffhs.org.uk

Links to societies of genealogical interest are also available on-line at http://ww.genuki.org.uk/Societies/

visiting archives

YOUR RIGHT TO INFORMATION

Once you have pulled together all your own documents and photographs, and collected information from your living relatives, you will need to visit archives to use the records that they hold. Most sections in this book list the key sources of information for records relevant to the particular subject.

doing the groundwork

Locating a record office
♦ Most British archives are listed in *The Oxford Companion to Family and Local History* (ed. D.Hey, Oxford University Press, 2010).
♦ You will also find details of British archives on the web site www.nationalarchives.gov.uk/a2a.
♦ A web-based directory listing the family history resources held in public libraries throughout Britain and the Republic of Ireland is available on the Internet at www.earl.org.uk

Before you go
♦ Decide which documents you need and find out where they are.
♦ Get in touch with the archive to ensure that the material is available.
♦ Find out if advance notice is necessary or whether the material can be produced at the time of your visit.
♦ Find out how to get to an archive, check the opening hours and whether there is an entrance fee. To use most archives you need to obtain a reader's ticket and book a seat, especially if you want to use a computer terminal or a microfiche reader.
♦ If you want to use a laptop computer, check first with the record office. Many now permit their use, usually in designated areas where you can plug into power points.

Not all records relevant to genealogical research are openly available. In general, public records are closed for 30 years after the last entry to the file, some even longer.
♦ Army personnel records, census records and those containing highly sensitive or classified information relating to national security are often closed for 50, 75 or 100 years.

Rather than being deposited at the TNA, some of these records are kept by government departments, and access varies according to the department. Even if you are allowed to see them, you may have to observe restrictions about the use of information retrieved from the files.
♦ Anyone who wishes to look at closed or retained records should write to the Departmental Record Officer of the department responsible, stating the document references. The TNA has details of restricted records and the officers' addresses.
♦ Local record offices, hospitals and military departments also hold sensitive documents closed for up to 100 years. Contact the individual archive for advice about access.

Further information about record offices and restricted documents can be found in *Record Repositories in Great Britain* (ed. I. Mortimer, Public Record Office, 12th ed., 2000).

To get the best out of any archive, first make sure it is the one you require and that the information you need is available to the public

start here

A HEARTY WELCOME TO ALL

Tips on note taking

♦ If you record information from a document, copy it exactly as it appears. If some text is illegible, use a dotted line to make that clear in your notes, or place that text in brackets with a question mark.

♦ If you want to add a comment or further information—perhaps from other documents—distinguish it from the text of the original document by, for instance, using square brackets, or, if working on computer, by using a different typeface.

♦ Note the source of any information that you extract; name the document, its date, its reference (if it has one) and where the original is held.

at the National Archives

General procedure

♦ Take a notebook and a pencil; pens are rarely allowed in archives.

♦ If you need to order a document, you will probably have to consult an index to find a document reference

for the page or pages you require. For instance, at The National Archives a reference usually includes the government department or function that transferred the document (such as HO for Home Office), and a number to indicate the batch of records with which it was transferred.

using abbreviations

Abbreviations are useful. They appear in many source documents, indexes and transcripts, and you are likely to use them yourself.

♦ In a family tree you will usually see the abbreviation 'b.', meaning born

In most archives, historic material has been carefully stored, indexed and allotted reference codes that will take you to the specific document you require

or 'd.', for died, followed by a date, as there is insufficient space to repeatedly write out 'born' or 'died'.

♦ Be careful which abbreviations you use as they can cause confusion. For example, always use 'b.' for 'born', and if you are referring to a baptism, use 'bap.', 'bapt.' or 'bp.', and for a burial use 'bur.'

♦ The names of counties are usually abbreviated. The so-called Chapman county codes (three-letter codes for each British county that existed until the 1974 reorganisation of local government) now form the basis of a British Standard used by most family historians. For example, 'NFK' is the code for Norfolk. For a full list see Appendix III of *Ancestral Trails* (M.D. Herber, Sutton, 2nd ed., 2004).

using the professionals

At some stage you may need experienced help. You might, for instance, want someone to search a distant archive, or you might need help with a Latin document.

♦ A number of family historians—some professionals—advertise their services in family history magazines (see page 20), family history society journals and the annual *The Family and Local History Handbook* (Robert and Elizabeth Blatchford, Robert Blatchford Publishing, 2011).

♦ Where possible, work on personal recommendation. Try to obtain quotations for the cost of the research before you go ahead, or agree an hourly rate and limit the time, until you can see the first results.

♦ Many researchers are members of the Association of Genealogists and Record Agents (AGRA), which aims to ensure a high standard of competence. For a list of AGRA members, their web site is found at www.agra.org.uk

A similar Irish body, the Association of Professional Genealogists in Ireland (APGI), has a web site at www.apgi.ie

COMMONLY USED ABBREVIATIONS

.Ø.	unnamed issue	d.s.p.	died childless	o.s.p. (ob.s.p.)	died childless
afsd.	aforesaid	d.s.p. legit.	died without legitimate offspring	o.t.p.	of this parish
bach.	bachelor	d.s.p.m.	died without male issue	ob.	died
bap. or bp.	baptised	d.v.p.	died during father's lifetime	ob.v.p.	died during father's lifetime
b.	born	g.f.	grandfather	pr.	(will) proved
b.o.t.p.	both of this parish	g.m.	grandmother	s.	son
bur.	buried	g.g.f.	great-grandfather	s. and h.	son and heir
By Lic.	married by licence	g.g.m.	great-grandmother	spin.	spinster
c.	about	inf.	infant	temp.	in the time of
co.	county	lic.	licence	unm.	unmarried
cod.	codicil	m. or marr.	married	wdr.	widower
coh.	coheiress	ML.	marriage licence	wid.	widow
dau.	daughter	MI.	monumental inscription	w.	wife
d.	died	ob.s.p. legit.	died without legitimate offspring		

the national archives

The Public Record Office at Kew reflected in the tranquil waters of its ornamental lake

The National Archives (TNA) is the official archive for England and Wales, and for national government records of the United Kingdom. Magna Carta, William Shakespeare's will and Guy Fawkes' confession are among the hundreds of thousands of documents it holds.

♦ There is much of interest to family historians, including wills, records of apprentices, convicts, the armed forces, merchant seamen, emigrants and immigrants, nurses, the London Metropolitan Police and railwaymen.

♦ Check by phone or consult the TNA's on-line catalogue to make sure it holds the records you require.

♦ Access is free but proof of identity is required to obtain a reader's card (valid for three years) and there are charges for photocopying.

♦ Information leaflets and family fact sheets are available on-line or at the PRO to help your search and may provide reference codes for the documents you need. *Tracing Your Ancestors in the National Archives* (A. Bevan, TNA, 7th ed., 2006) is a useful guide.

♦ Save time by requesting up to three documents in advance through the DocumentsOnline service.

♦ The TNA is closed on Mondays. It is open 9am–5pm on Wednesdays, Fridays and Saturdays and 9am–7pm on Tuesdays and Thursdays.

♦ Ruskin Avenue, Kew, Surrey TW9 4DU Tel. 020 8876 3444 (enquiries) www.nationalarchives.gov.uk

National Library of Wales

♦ The archive holds most printed material relating to Wales and has an on-line catalogue. Its holdings include many parish registers, all the diocesan records for Wales, pre-1858 wills, the post-1858 calendars of probate, a full set of Welsh census returns (1841–91), newspapers, maps and photos. Proof of identity is required to obtain a reader's ticket.

♦ Opening hours are Mon–Fri 9.30am–6pm and Sat 9.30am–5pm (closed first week of October).

♦ Penglais, Aberystwyth, Ceredigion SY23 3BU

Tel. 01970 632 800 www.llgc.org.uk

From Domesday Book onwards, the PRO's records mention millions of people from all walks of life

If your ancestors were Welsh, Scottish or Irish, you will probably have to consult national record offices in Aberystwyth, Edinburgh, Belfast or Dublin

National Archives of Scotland

♦ Formerly the Scottish Record Office, the archives are housed at General Register House in Edinburgh. They hold records of Scottish governments before the union with England in 1707 as well as later Scottish department records. Other holdings include court records, registers of sasines (land transactions), property deeds, records of local authorities, and private and business papers.

♦ Contact the archives before you visit as some records are stored at other premises and in certain cases a few days' notice is required in order to retrieve them. Access is free but a charge is made for photocopying.

♦ Open Mon–Fri 9am–4.45pm.

♦ HM General Register House, Princes Street, Edinburgh EH1 3YY Tel. 0131 535 1314
www.nas.gov.uk

General Register Office for Scotland

♦ The archive holds birth, marriage, death and adoption records, old parish registers and census returns for Scotland. There is a search fee and you should book a seat in advance.

♦ Open Mon–Fri 9am–4.30pm. For an on-line database of records see www.ogro-scotland.gov.uk

♦ New Register House, Edinburgh EH1 3YT Tel. 0131 3340380
www.gro-scotland.gov.uk

Public Record Office of Northern Ireland (PRONI)

♦ PRONI holds the records of the Northern Ireland government from 1922 to 1972, those of the Northern Ireland Office from 1972 and earlier records of government departments from the 19th century. Other records include those of courts and local authorities and collections deposited

by individuals, businesses and institutions. Proof of identity is required for a reader's ticket, valid for life.

♦ Open Monday, Tuesday, Wednesday and Friday 9am–4.45pm and Thursday 10am–8.45pm.

♦ 2 Titanic Boulevard, Belfast, BT3 9HQ. Tel. 028 9025 5905
www.proni.gov.uk

National Archives of Ireland

♦ The archives contain Irish government records. It also holds the 1901 and 1911 census returns for Ireland, indexes to wills and marriage licence bonds, records of courts and convict transportation, collections of manuscripts and private papers, church documents, and records of hospitals, schools and businesses. It is advisable to request records in advance. Proof of identity is required for a reader's ticket, valid for a year.

♦ Open Mon–Fri 10am–5pm.

♦ Bishop Street, Dublin 8 Tel. 00353 1 407 2300
www.nationalarchives.ie

Preserving old documents

TNA, like other national archives, must safeguard its many original documents; a fragile book, for instance , must be read on a lectern. At TNA pens and Biros are banned but you may take pencils to record your notes or use a lap-top computer in designated areas where electrical sockets are available.

county and city record offices

As your research expands beyond the home front, one of your first ports of call is likely to be a county or city record office in the area you are researching. For contact details see DIRECTORY under the county or city name.

You will find a wealth of local material, some dating back to the Middle Ages, that can tell you much about your ancestors.

visiting record offices

Where to find them
♦ All English and Welsh counties and most metropolitan districts have established record offices for their civil records. See their catalogues on the Access to Archives website at www.nationalarchives.gov.uk/a2a
♦ For Ireland, most sources of genealogical information are available centrally in Belfast or Dublin. But local material can also be found in a variety of locations such as heritage centres and local history

The local record office in the area where your ancestors once lived is likely to hold documents that mention them or key events in their lives

collections at county libraries. To find libraries, research sources and local societies, see *Irish Records: sources for family and local history* (J.G. Ryan, Flyleaf Press, 2nd ed., 1997).

♦ Local Scottish archive offices cover broader areas than those in England and Wales. See DIRECTORY by place name and also *Tracing Scottish Local History* (C. Sinclair, Scottish Record Office, reprinted 1996).

♦ On-line links to county record offices and other archives throughout the British Isles can be found at www.genuki.org.uk/big

using a record office

Carrying out your research

♦ Most record offices provide clear instructions on how to search for documents and use their material. They also have staff experienced in advising family historians.

♦ Check the opening times and whether you will need formal identification, such as a driver's licence, to obtain a reader's ticket and also whether the records should be ordered in advance.

♦ Begin by consulting the catalogues or indexes to decide which records you wish to see, then fill in a request slip. A member of staff will usually bring the records to your desk—and may supply gloves for handling delicate documents. Some record offices charge for viewing records, and you should expect to pay for photocopying and computer print-outs.

♦ If you cannot visit in person, a member of staff may be able to carry out research for you—although you will need to provide basic information, such as an ancestor's year and place of birth. Whether or not the search produces results, you should expect to be charged an hourly fee (often more than £20) as well as any costs incurred for administration, photocopying and postage.

The records you may find

The information held varies from one office to another, so find out if the office has what you are looking for before you visit. Some records may be held elsewhere, at a local study centre, library or museum.

Many record offices now produce books or leaflets describing their holdings. The material will often include the following:

♦ Parish registers, which record centuries of local baptisms, marriages and burials. Other parish, diocesan and local council records.

♦ Local census returns and civil registration indexes of births, marriages and deaths in the area.

♦ Workhouse records, school records, wills and papers relating to court cases and disputes.

♦ Copies of the records of manors and estate documents, which may include details of staff and wages.

♦ Business papers, photographs, maps, newspapers and even collections of private letters.

Local records can cover the whole spectrum of family history, and experienced staff are usually on hand to make your search a success

Society of Genealogists

The Society of Genealogists (SoG) is Britain's principal family history organisation. It organises courses, lectures and visits, and promotes annual family history fairs.

Its extensive collection of material is particularly valuable for research before the start of civil registration in 1837 and the first useful census return in 1841.

the society's archive

♦ Its library contains more than 11,000 parish register copies, Britain's largest collection, together with many Nonconformist registers. Most cover the period from the 16th century to 1837.

♦ See the index on www.soc.org.uk/prc/, which gives the dates for each parish for which there are transcripts and indexes, together with local histories, copies of monumental inscriptions, poll books, trade directories and census indexes. The county names are those in use before the 1974 local government reorganisation.

♦ Indexes for births, marriages and deaths for Scotland (1855 to 1920), for England and Wales, and for many Britons overseas (1837 to 1920), are also available, as are indexes of wills and marriage licences.

♦ Percival Boyd's marriage index of more than 7 million names was compiled from 4,300 churches from the beginning of registration in 1538 to the start of civil registration in 1837. The entries are copied mainly from printed registers, so the coverage is not complete. The Index is particularly useful for researching East Anglian ancestry, as more than 95 per cent of the ancient parishes are included.

♦ The Bernau Index is a microfilm collection of about four and a half million slips (sorted by surname only) relating to unindexed material in The National Archives, mainly Chancery and Exchequer Court Depositions and Proceedings, compiled by C. A. Bernau.

♦ Apprenticeship records. The collection of about 18,000 apprenticeship indentures between 1641 and 1888 provides the name, place of residence, and occupation of the master, the boy's name, and the name, residence, and occupation of his father. Indexes of the 'Apprenticeship Books' in class IR 1 at The National Archives, dating from 1710 to 1811, record the names, addresses, and trades of the masters, the names of the apprentices, and the dates of the indentures. Until 1752 the name, residence, and occupation of the father of the apprentice are also given.

♦ The society has a wide collection of miscellaneous manuscripts, printed and typescript family histories, and 'birth briefs' submitted by researchers, which set out the names of all their known ancestors.

becoming a member

♦ If you expect to be carrying out extensive research on British or Irish ancestors then membership is probably well worth while, although nonmembers can make enquiries and use the library for a small fee.

♦ Membership, currently £45 a year, confers a number of privileges, including borrowing rights and use of the library, free copies of the quarterly *Genealogists' Magazine* and various discounts on publications, lectures, courses and postal searches.

♦ Applications or requests for more information should be made to: The Society of Genealogists, 14 Charterhouse Buildings, Goswell Road, London EC1 M 7 BA

Tel. 020 7251 8799
Fax. 020 7250 1800
or by email to Info@soc.org.uk

Publications

♦ *The National Index of Parish Registers.* Volumes for each pre-1974 county list the location and time periods of Anglican, Roman Catholic and Nonconformist registers, together with information on bishops' transcripts, modern copies and marriage licences. If a volume is out of print, a full set of these titles can be accessed in the SoG library.

♦ *The My Ancestor Was ...* series gives advice on how to trace ancestors who worked at particular jobs, such as agricultural labourer, coal miner or railwayman, or who belonged to groups such as Londoners, gypsies or Jews.

♦ The society's shop has an enormous range of other books, maps and computer software. These are also available on-line at www.soc.org.uk

On-line resources

♦ In 2011 the Society of Genealogists, in partnership with a major commercial company, celebrated its centenary by making more than nine million family history records available on-line at www.findmypast.co.uk. Anyone with a full subscription to findmypast.co.uk can access all the records within their existing package. Otherwise they can be viewed with PayAsYouGo credits. Members of the Society of Genealogists can view the records for free via the Society of Genealogists own Members Area at www.sog.org.uk.

♦ These records include:
• Boyd's Marriage Index containing over seven million names from 1538–1840.
• Boyd's London Burials 1538–1872 containing 240,000 names.
• Faculty Office Marriage Licence Allegations 1701–1850.
• St Andrew's Holborn Marriage Index 1754–1812.
• Vicar-General Marriage Licences Allegations 1694–1850.
• St Leonard Shoreditch Burials 1805–58 and Workhouse Deaths 1820–28.
• Prerogative Court of Canterbury Wills Index 1750–1800.
• Bank of England Wills Extracts containing 60,500 names, and images.
• Apprentices of Great Britain containing 350,000 names.

♦ Earlier projects were Civil Service Evidence of Age and Great Western Railway Shareholder records.

♦ Searchable indexes and transcripts have been added to the web site, and customers can order copies of the originals for some of the records from the Society of Genealogists.

Founded in 1911, the Society of Genealogists has some 15,000 members around the world and is now making a selection of its records and indexes available on-line

how to read old handwriting

Many of the documents that you consult, such as parish records, wills, old letters or deeds, will have been written by hand centuries ago.

A range of handwriting styles was used for different purposes. Legal documents were often written in 'court hand' or 'chancery hand' with many variations, until the clearer hand 'copperplate', introduced in the 18th century, came into general use.

Do not be put off by the handwriting in old documents. If they are in archives, photocopy them so that you can work on them at home. The sources in Taking it further (right) will help you to make a transcription.

A step-by-step approach

♦ Build up an alphabet of letters from words you can read and use it to decipher more difficult words.

♦ Look for letters that were written differently, such as an 's' that looks like an 'f' (often the first 's' of 'ss'), or 'y' instead of 'th'. 'I' and 'J' are often interchangeable.

♦ Punctuation and spelling was often arbitrary; apostrophes indicate that letters have been missed out.

♦ Numbers such as '1' and '7' may look similar. Look for a date; it may help you to identify other figures.

TAKING IT FURTHER

♦ *The Handwriting of English Documents* (L.C. Hector, Kohler and Coombes, 2nd ed., 1980).

♦ *Examples of English Handwriting 1150–1750* (H.E.P. Grieve, Essex Record Office, 2nd ed., 1978).

♦ *Reading Tudor and Stuart Handwriting* (L. Munby, British Association for Local History, 1988).

♦ *Paleography for Family and Local Historians* (H. Marshall, Phillimore, 2004)

♦ www.dundee.ac.uk/archives/paleography

♦ Borthwick Institute for Archives (see DIRECTORY) produces handwriting packs for different eras.

Boarcote, 5th March 1799

Dear Mother

It is with the greatest pleasure I write to inform you that I received the parcel safe for which I am much oblig'd I have sent a Coat Waistcoat and a pair of Shoes to be mended — Mr and Mrs Cox present Compliments — Please to accept of duty to self the same to Father Love to Brother and proper respects to all Friends, I remain your Dutiful and Affectionate Son

John Lawley

P.S The proprietors of the inclos'd will be much oblig'd by your letting our servant deliver them at her leisure.

Writing home in the 18th century

The document above is a letter home from John Lawley to his mother, written in copperplate script. It is surprisingly easy to read but has a few unusual spellings, such as 'inclos'd' where we would use 'enclosed'. An apostrophe indicates a missing letter and was used because some combinations of letters were hard to form with a quill. Note how in the date the 'th' is superscripted (written above the line). Superscript letters were another way of showing that letters had been omitted. The abbreviations still used—'Mr' for Master and 'Mrs' for Mistress—originally appeared as they do here with the 'r' and 'rs' superscripted. The punctuation and capitalisation is typically arbitrary. There is no address because the original letter was sealed and hand-delivered.

A document from Cromwell's time

It looks daunting but the legal document on the left (though slightly damaged) is reasonably legible, especially if read in conjunction with the alphabet on the right. It concerns the changing ownership of the manor of Newton in Cleveland in 1653. Note the modified 'p' in 'present' on the first line, variant spellings such as 'tearme' for term, and the form of the 's' in 'person'. A large seal of the Commonwealth would have been attached to the document, as it dates from the rule of Oliver Cromwell.

Not quite as simple as ABC

The alphabet below shows how the form of a letter could vary in 16th and 17th-century documents. It is taken from *Court Hand Restored* (A. Wright, Reeves & Turner, 8th ed., 1846), which illustrates a range of styles used from the 11th to the 17th centuries. If you know the period of the document, use such an alphabet to compare letter styles with what you are trying to read. First try to identify common words, names or words that are repeated. Some of the words may be obsolete, in which case the *Oxford English Dictionary* can be useful. For difficult legal terms that appear in property or legal records, use a reference work such as *Mozley & Whiteley's Law Dictionary* (E.R.H. Ivamy, Butterworths, 12th ed., 2001).

A general Alphabet of the Old Law Hands.

using the Internet

Computers can make family history research much easier. The Internet is becoming a powerful genealogical tool. You can use it to:
♦ Find information.
♦ Keep in touch with others with shared interests.
♦ Publish your research.

Throughout this book you will see web sites (picked out in a lighter type) quoted for specialist organisations, sources of records and background information that will help you with your research.

the world wide web

♦ The world wide web, often called simply the web, is a collection of billions of linked pages of information held on computers all over the world, which are permanently connected to the Internet. If you have access, you can follow links on each page to find related information.

While you may not yet find many actual records on-line, most organisations involved with family history have web sites outlining what they

offer, and often provide indexes and searchable on-line catalogues. Such groups and organisations include:
♦ The TNA and other national record offices (see pages 26–27).
♦ The Society of Genealogists (see page 31).
♦ County and city record offices (see pages 28–29).
♦ Family history societies (see page 22).
♦ Many major public libraries, including the British Library and Guildhall Library in London.

As you browse you will also find sites that provide pages containing collections of links to other web sites of genealogical interest.

a pick of the best sites

GENUKI for Britain
♦ The best starting point on the web for British genealogy is GENUKI, the 'Genealogical Information Service for the UK and Ireland', at www.genuki.org.uk

Electronic mail – email – allows you to get in touch with other people around the world quickly and cheaply

Run by volunteers, it provides:

◆ Basic general information about family research in the British Isles.

◆ Information on every county in the British Isles, including record offices and surname lists.

◆ Comprehensive links to every other significant web site relating to British and Irish family history.

Cyndi's List for global links

◆ Cyndi's List on the web at www.cyndislist.com offers more than 64,000 worldwide links in over 120 categories. It includes:

◆ Links to country indexes and many personal family history sites.

◆ Links to software suppliers.

FamilySearch

◆ FamilySearch offers world-wide information at www.familysearch.org. Run by the Mormon Church, it is freely available to all.
The web site carries:

◆ Tips on getting started.

◆ A variety of free classes on-line.

The home page for GENUKI

The Cyndi's List web site

FamilySearch, for world-wide information

The site for Wales's national archives

◆ A free collection of family history articles written by enthusiasts.

◆ News about family history events, records and resources from many parts of the world.

communicating by email

◆ Email is cheaper and quicker than using the post. It allows you to:

◆ Send messages on the Internet to anywhere in the world.

◆ Send and receive computer files, so you can exchange word-processed documents, genealogical data files, or scanned photographs or maps.

◆ Join one of the thousands of specialised mailing lists—discussion groups devoted to some particular aspect of family history. There are mailing lists for every county or region of the British Isles, as well as lists for many surnames. You can even start your own mailing list for a surname you are researching.

WEB STARTING POINTS

- For GENUKI
www.genuki.org.uk
- Cyndi's List
www.cyndislist.com
- Family history societies
www.cs.ncl.ac.uk/genuki/
societies
- Genealogy mailing lists
www.rootsweb.com/
~jfuller/gen_mail.html
- Genealogy newsgroups
www.rootsweb.com/
~jfuller/gen_use.html
- County surname lists
www.genuki.org.uk/indexes/
surnameslists.html
- BT on-line phone directory
www.thephonebook.bt.com
- Roots Surname List
rsl.rootsweb.com/
cgi-bin/rslsql.cgi
- Surname resources
www.CyndisList.com/surname.
htm
- Yahoo!—a general web directory,
which lists sites by subject
www.yahoo.com
- Altavista, to search for web pages
containing a name or phrase
www.altavista.com
- Google, which is a vast web
directory, again based on key words
www.google.co.uk
- The best guide is P. Christian, *The
Genealogist's Internet* (The National
Archives, 3rd expanded ed., 2005).

discovering newsgroups

- Newsgroups are electronic bulletin boards. They are not web sites, but they can be found by using search engines such as Yahoo! or Altavista. Newsgroups are like mailing lists; but you do not need to join a group—anyone can post or read messages.

There are just over two dozen English-language newsgroups devoted to family history, each with a fairly large subject area, for example:

- The newsgroup for all British genealogy is soc.genealogy.britain
- For anything to do with using computers for family history, try soc.genealogy.computing

To make sure that you are able to access newsgroups, or for help sorting out any difficulties, consult your Internet service provider (ISP)—the company that provides your connection to the Internet—which will be able to explain how you should set up your software.

surnames on-line

- The Internet can also help you to find out who is interested in the same surnames as you and to locate other people with your surname.
- For every county in Britain there is a surname list—a web page that lists surnames being researched for that county and gives the email addresses of the contributors. See left, Web starting points.
- You can publicise which surnames you are interested in by submitting them to the relevant county lists.
- You can search specific areas of Britain using BT's on-line telephone directory, see Web starting points.

publish on the Internet

- Publishing your family history on the web is easy and cheap and the information is immediately accessible to everyone on the Internet.
- Most Internet service providers will give you enough web space to

Publishing your research on the Internet may generate a useful response and allows others to benefit from your hard work

creating a family tree

Most people undertaking family research want to draw a family tree.

To begin with, you need to assemble the basic building blocks: yourself, your children, your brothers and sisters and their children, your parents and grandparents. Ask everyone in the family what they remember; write it down; carry a notebook.

Collect and label old and new photographs so you can put faces to names. And do not forget that you are doing this for fun, for yourself.

types of chart

The simplest descent chart, called a pedigree or birth brief (see across), shows only your direct ancestors. If you go back to your great-great-grandparents (of whom there are 16) this is a 'seize quartiers' chart; another generation back gives you 'trente-deux [32] quartiers'.

A full family tree starts with one ancestor and shows all known descendants. This can become complicated and you may wish to concentrate on one branch of the family—perhaps by following the male line only—or design a tree to show connections between certain families. There are many options.

drop line chart

The most familiar layout is called a drop line chart (see inside), which uses the following conventions:

♦ Descent runs from the top down. Women are given their maiden names and spouses are linked by ══ or 'm'.

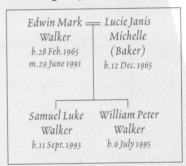

George Plant ══ Catherine
Rilett   (Perry)
bap. 31 Jan. 1830   b. (c.) 1840
m. 27 Feb. 1869   d. 1904
d. 1871

Catherine Sarah
Rilett
b. (c.) 1870
ob. inf. 1872

♦ A vertical line links children of a marriage to the marriage symbol, and horizontal lines link siblings. Children are normally listed chronologically from left to right.

Edwin Mark ══ Lucie Janis
Walker   Michelle
b. 28 Feb. 1965 (Baker)
m. 29 June 1991 b. 12 Dec. 1965

Samuel Luke   William Peter
Walker   Walker
b. 11 Sept. 1993 b. 6 July 1995

♦ Second spouses are placed on the other side of the partner's name, and each is numbered.

Levi ¹══ Hannah ══² Henry
Brighton   Mary   Rilett
Burgess   Beckett   m. 1 Oct. 1852
m. 26 Feb. 1848

♦ People of the same generation appear on the same horizontal level, which can cause problems when lines of descent cross. In the

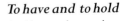

To have and to hold

An old group photograph can be a great springboard for research into your family tree. Armed with this, and pencil and paper, visit relations and old family friends, and ask them what they remember. Who were those little girls? And why was that man wearing a black armband? (To find out, see the full family tree.)

The blossoming of a typical family tree

Any family researching its ancestry will unearth a few surprises. The Riletts were no different, discovering unsung heroes and a share of tragedy

Elizabeth Rilett
bap. 10 May 1801

Mary Rilett
bap. 22 Nov. 1802
ob. inf. 1803

George Plant Rilett
bap. 31 Jan. 1830
m. 27 Feb. 1869
d. 1871

Catherine (Perry)
b. (c.) 1840
d. 1904

Sarah Rilett
b. 1832

Thomas Rilett
b. 1833

Henry Rilett
b. 1836

James Rilett
b. 1838

Catherine Sarah Rilett
b. (c.) 1870
ob. inf. 1872

Lilian Rilett

Charles Benjamin Rilett with WW1 medal

James 'Snowball' Smith

The records tell of a sad life
At just 27, **Hannah Mary Beckett** had been married and widowed twice, and had borne five sons, only two of whom survived. The third of 11 children, she ran away from her home in Bungay, Suffolk, at the age of 16. By the time of the 1851 census she was married with one son. By the 1861 census, Hannah had been widowed, remarried and been widowed again. She now worked as a bootbinder and, with her two surviving sons, James, 12, and Henry, 7, shared a house in London's East End with three other families.

Ronald Ivory

Bareback rider
Charles Benjamin Rilett's father, Henry, was in the army in India. When Charles was just three weeks old, Henry died. Lilian and her two babies would have been made homeless unless she found another army husband quickly. This she did, and within a year James 'Snowball' Smith had become the boys' stepfather. He was tough: Charles remembered breaking horses bareback at 12. Though severely wounded in 1914, Charles had a distinguished 23 year army career.

Interpreting the chart
You will need to use several symbols and abbreviations in your chart, and draw up a key. If you prepare a key early on, it will help you to remain consistent and allow others to interpret your chart. You can devise symbols for most eventualities. Commonly used codes include:
bur. (buried), ob. (obiit, or died), nat. (natural, ie illegitimate), m. (married), unm. or a horizontal zigzag, or ═══ (unmarried union), zigzag vertical (adopted child), w. (will), div. (divorced), k. (killed).

Abbreviations and symbols
bap.	baptised
b.	born
bur.	buried
d.	died
d.s.p.	(decessit sine prole) died childless
ob. inf.	(obiit) died in infancy
(c.)	(circa) approximately
═══	married
═════	unmarried

Stories and pictures
Stories and memorabilia have been gathered as this family tree has grown. We have drawn box-frames round those mentioned or pictured.

Edwin Mark Walker
b. 28 Feb. 1965
m. 29 June 1991

Lucie Janis Michelle (Baker)
b. 12 Dec. 1965

James John Walker
b. 15 June 1967
m. 16 June 1990

Samuel Luke Walker
b. 11 Sept. 1993

William Peter Walker
b. 6 July 1995

Freddie Henry Charles Walker
b. 10 May 2000

Jacob Harris Walker
b. 20 Apr. 1994

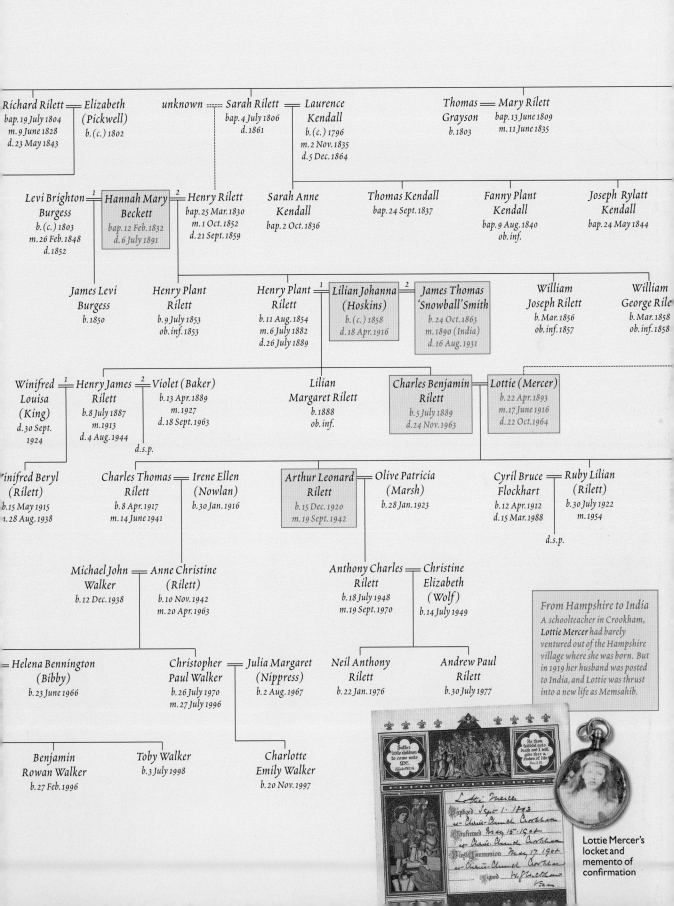

Richard Rilett
bap. 19 July 1804
m. 9 June 1828
d. 23 May 1843
═══ Elizabeth (Pickwell)
b. (c.) 1802

unknown ═════ Sarah Rilett
bap. 4 July 1806
d. 1861
═══ Laurence Kendall
b. (c.) 1796
m. 2 Nov. 1835
d. 5 Dec. 1864

Thomas Grayson
b. 1803
═══ Mary Rilett
bap. 13 June 1809
m. 11 June 1835

Levi Brighton Burgess
b. (c.) 1803
m. 26 Feb. 1848
d. 1852
—1— Hannah Mary Beckett
bap. 12 Feb. 1832
d. 6 July 1891
—2— Henry Rilett
bap. 25 Mar. 1830
m. 1 Oct. 1852
d. 21 Sept. 1859

Sarah Anne Kendall
bap. 2 Oct. 1836

Thomas Kendall
bap. 24 Sept. 1837

Fanny Plant Kendall
bap. 9 Aug. 1840
ob. inf.

Joseph Rylatt Kendall
bap. 24 May 1844

James Levi Burgess
b. 1850

Henry Plant Rilett
b. 9 July 1853
ob. inf. 1853

Henry Plant Rilett
b. 11 Aug. 1854
m. 6 July 1882
d. 26 July 1889
—1— Lilian Johanna (Hoskins)
b. (c.) 1858
d. 18 Apr. 1916
—2— James Thomas 'Snowball' Smith
b. 24 Oct. 1863
m. 1890 (India)
d. 16 Aug. 1931

William Joseph Rilett
b. Mar. 1856
ob. inf. 1857

William George Rile[tt]
b. Mar. 1858
ob. inf. 1858

Winifred Louisa (King)
d. 30 Sept. 1924
—1— Henry James Rilett
b. 8 July 1887
m. 1913
d. 4 Aug. 1944
—2— Violet (Baker)
b. 13 Apr. 1889
m. 1927
d. 18 Sept. 1963
d.s.p.

Lilian Margaret Rilett
b. 1888
ob. inf.

Charles Benjamin Rilett
b. 5 July 1889
d. 24 Nov. 1963
═══ Lottie (Mercer)
b. 22 Apr. 1893
m. 17 June 1916
d. 22 Oct. 1964

Winifred Beryl (Rilett)
b. 15 May 1915
d. 28 Aug. 1938

Charles Thomas Rilett
b. 8 Apr. 1917
m. 14 June 1941
═══ Irene Ellen (Nowlan)
b. 30 Jan. 1916

Arthur Leonard Rilett
b. 15 Dec. 1920
m. 19 Sept. 1942
═══ Olive Patricia (Marsh)
b. 28 Jan. 1923

Cyril Bruce Flockhart
b. 12 Apr. 1912
d. 15 Mar. 1988
═══ Ruby Lilian (Rilett)
b. 30 July 1922
m. 1954
d.s.p.

Michael John Walker
b. 12 Dec. 1938
═══ Anne Christine (Rilett)
b. 10 Nov. 1942
m. 20 Apr. 1963

Anthony Charles Rilett
b. 18 July 1948
m. 19 Sept. 1970
═══ Christine Elizabeth (Wolf)
b. 14 July 1949

═ Helena Bennington (Bibby)
b. 23 June 1966

Christopher Paul Walker
b. 26 July 1970
m. 27 July 1996
═══ Julia Margaret (Nippress)
b. 2 Aug. 1967

Neil Anthony Rilett
b. 22 Jan. 1976

Andrew Paul Rilett
b. 30 July 1977

Benjamin Rowan Walker
b. 27 Feb. 1996

Toby Walker
b. 3 July 1998

Charlotte Emily Walker
b. 20 Nov. 1997

From Hampshire to India
A schoolteacher in Crookham, *Lottie Mercer* had barely ventured out of the Hampshire village where she was born. But in 1919 her husband was posted to India, and Lottie was thrust into a new life as Memsahib.

Lottie Mercer's locket and memento of confirmation

hold your pages of family history and make them available to other people.

♦ Many genealogy software packages have facilities for turning your data into web pages, or you can download one of many freeware or shareware programs to create family history web pages. For details of genealogy software see pages 42–43.

getting connected

♦ To connect to the Internet from your computer you may use a dial-up service, which makes use of your phone line, or broadband, which allows you to be on the phone and the Internet at the same time. Broadband is also speedier than dial-up services,

so that you can download files from the Internet more quickly.

♦ You will need a modem (a device that links the computer to the phone system) and a nearby phone socket. The computer can be connected to the phone socket by a special cable, or via a wireless system.

♦ You also need to choose an Internet Service Provider (ISP), which will provide you with a disk and give you instructions on how to set up the software.

♦ There are numerous ISP packages on the market and the best option will depend on your pattern of usage. Some ISPs have a monthly flat-rate fee for unlimited on-line time (and you may or may not be paying call

charges). There are now also free ISPs, including Reader's Digest and ISPs that include a certain amount of free call-time.

If you don't have a computer
♦ Go to a public library. Many libraries provide access to the web.
♦ Go to a cybercafé or internet café.

further information

♦ *Finding Genealogy on the Internet* (P. Christian, David Hawgood, 1999).
♦ *Web Publishing for Genealogy* (P. Christian, David Hawgood, 1999).
♦ *Genealogy On-line for Dummies* (M. Helm and A. Helm, IDG Books Worldwide, 1998).

family tree featured here, we decided to avoid crossing lines, or 'bridging', in the interest of clarity, even if it meant going against convention and putting a line of siblings out of chronological order. The alternative, as shown below, is to enter step-siblings, Thomas Clement and Elizabeth Smith, in strict birth order. This has caused the Smiths' birth line to bridge Thomas's. The final version of the tree (see inside) avoids this convention—after all, the children's dates of birth or baptism clarify the chronology. In the same way, Lottie Mercer is placed before her older sister, Minnie, in order to show Lottie's marriage to Charles without any crossed lines.

For future generations

Once you have completed your chart, consider making copies for interested family members, and to lodge with your local family history society to help future researchers.

Computer software

You can buy computer programs to help you to organise and store data and draw your chart (see pages 42–43). Computer-generated charts are invaluable during the drafting stages as they are far easier to update and edit than hand-drawn versions. Their drawback is their functional appearance, but you can always use the final print-out as a template for a hand-drawn version.

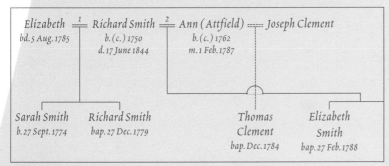

A simple birth brief

A birth brief or pedigree (right and below) is the simplest form of chart. It begins with one person and goes backwards, naming parents, grandparents and so on, but omitting siblings, aunts and uncles. In a horizontal arrangement, the subject of the brief is placed to the far left of the chart.

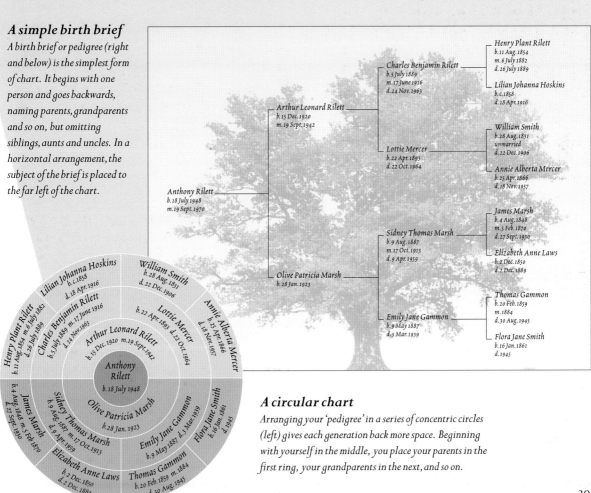

A circular chart

Arranging your 'pedigree' in a series of concentric circles (left) gives each generation back more space. Beginning with yourself in the middle, you place your parents in the first ring, your grandparents in the next, and so on.

39

The doll-maker who lived in a pub
In a booklet about 19th-century Old Fleet and Crookham, Arthur Rilett read: 'Old Mrs Smith of the pub, the North Horns, sells bread, groceries and wooden dolls'. He guessed that this Mrs Smith was **Ann Attfield**. The 1841 census return confirmed his hunch: Ann lived at the North Horns (left) with her son Stephen Smith, recorded as 'farmer and innkeeper', and his family. The pub is still there, but is now called the Tweseldown.

Richard Smith ⎯²⎯ Ann (Attfield) ┄┄┄ Joseph Clement
b.(c.) 1750   b.(c.) 1762
d. 17 June 1844   m. 1 Feb. 1787

Henry Smith   Sophia Smith   James Smith   Stephen Smith ⎯ Elizabeth   Thomas
bap. 27 Jan. 1793   bap. 31 May 1795   bap. 28 Jan. 1798   bap. 15 June 1800   (French)   Clement
bd. 31 May 1795   m. 3 May 1828   bap. 3 Oct. 1802   bap. Dec. 1784
ob. inf.   d. 8 Aug. 1876   d. 26 Mar. 1879

William Smith ┄┄┄ Annie Alberta ⎯ Henry Philip
b. 28 Aug. 1831   (Mercer)   Potter
d. 22 Dec. 1906   b. 25 Apr. 1866   b. Oct. 1861
               d. 18 Nov. 1957   m. 19 Feb. 1917
                             d. 1919
                   d.s.p.

John Charnley ⎯ Amelia Alberta   Albert Mercer ⎯ Josephine
b. 16 Sept. 1901   (Mercer)   b. 14 Aug. 1902   (Cooke)
d. 20 Jan. 1971   b. 6 June 1899   m. 23 Oct. 1926   b. 7 Aug. 1902
             m. 12 Oct. 1945   d. 1972   d. 10 Nov. 1990
             d. 21 Mar. 1997
       d.s.p.

Elizabeth Mercer   John Mercer
b. 15 Jan. 1928   b. 15 Apr. 1929
m. 20 June 1965
d. 16 Mar. 1994

A grandfather's gift to his family

Since retiring in 1980, Arthur Rilett has enjoyed an absorbing hobby. It all began when he discovered that his maternal grandmother's maiden name was Mercer—the same surname as his mother and her five brothers and sisters... Who was their father, and why did prim, proper Grandma and this mystery man never marry? The trail has taken Arthur back some 230 years, and resulted in a stunning family tree that, so far, stretches back nine generations.

The name's the same—or is it?
When searching through records in one Lincolnshire parish, Arthur Rilett found two main variants of his family name. It turned out that baptisms and marriages were conducted by the vicar, and spelt 'Rilett', while burials, the curate's responsibility, were entered as 'Rylatt'. Arthur has now come across no fewer than 21 spellings of the name.

When infant mortality was high, the same name was often re-used for a baby whose older brother or sister had died. It happens in this family tree (top left). Hannah Mary Beckett and Henry Rilett's firstborn, Henry Plant, died in infancy, but 13 months later another boy was born and given his names. This baby was Arthur Rilett's grandfather, although he died more than 30 years before Arthur's birth.

Children with their mother's name
People frequently discover ancestors whose parents were not married, the children often being given their mother's surname. **Annie Alberta Mercer**'s six children, born between 1891 and 1902, were all Mercers. Five are pictured, with nanny (below); Annie is pregnant with the sixth, Albert. The children's father was **William Smith** (below right). It is thought that he could not marry Annie because he was already married, and unable to obtain a divorce as his wife was in an asylum.

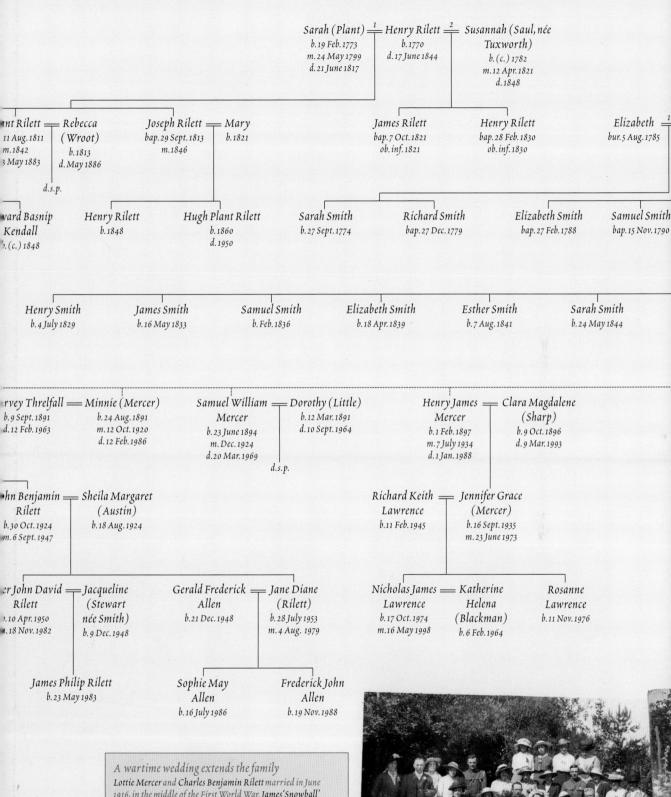

Sarah (Plant)
b. 19 Feb. 1773
m. 24 May 1799
d. 21 June 1817
═¹ Henry Rilett
b. 1770
d. 17 June 1844
═² Susannah (Saul, née Tuxworth)
b. (c.) 1782
m. 12 Apr. 1821
d. 1848

...nt Rilett
...11 Aug. 1811
...m. 1842
...3 May 1883
═ Rebecca (Wroot)
b. 1813
d. May 1886

d.s.p.

Joseph Rilett
bap. 29 Sept. 1813
m. 1846
═ Mary
b. 1821

James Rilett
bap. 7 Oct. 1821
ob. inf. 1821

Henry Rilett
bap. 28 Feb. 1830
ob. inf. 1830

Elizabeth ═¹
bur. 5 Aug. 1785

...ward Basnip Kendall
...b. (c.) 1848

Henry Rilett
b. 1848

Hugh Plant Rilett
b. 1860
d. 1950

Sarah Smith
b. 27 Sept. 1774

Richard Smith
bap. 27 Dec. 1779

Elizabeth Smith
bap. 27 Feb. 1788

Samuel Smith
bap. 15 Nov. 1790

Henry Smith
b. 4 July 1829

James Smith
b. 16 May 1833

Samuel Smith
b. Feb. 1836

Elizabeth Smith
b. 18 Apr. 1839

Esther Smith
b. 7 Aug. 1841

Sarah Smith
b. 24 May 1844

...rvey Threlfall
b. 9 Sept. 1891
d. 12 Feb. 1963
═ Minnie (Mercer)
b. 24 Aug. 1891
m. 12 Oct. 1920
d. 12 Feb. 1986

Samuel William Mercer
b. 23 June 1894
m. Dec. 1924
d. 20 Mar. 1969
═ Dorothy (Little)
b. 12 Mar. 1891
d. 10 Sept. 1964

d.s.p.

Henry James Mercer
b. 1 Feb. 1897
m. 7 July 1934
d. 1 Jan. 1988
═ Clara Magdalene (Sharp)
b. 9 Oct. 1896
d. 9 Mar. 1993

...hn Benjamin Rilett
b. 30 Oct. 1924
m. 6 Sept. 1947
═ Sheila Margaret (Austin)
b. 18 Aug. 1924

Richard Keith Lawrence
b. 11 Feb. 1945
═ Jennifer Grace (Mercer)
b. 16 Sept. 1935
m. 23 June 1973

...r John David Rilett
...10 Apr. 1950
...18 Nov. 1982
═ Jacqueline (Stewart née Smith)
b. 9 Dec. 1948

Gerald Frederick Allen
b. 21 Dec. 1948
═ Jane Diane (Rilett)
b. 28 July 1953
m. 4 Aug. 1979

Nicholas James Lawrence
b. 17 Oct. 1974
m. 16 May 1998
═ Katherine Helena (Blackman)
b. 6 Feb. 1964

Rosanne Lawrence
b. 11 Nov. 1976

James Philip Rilett
b. 23 May 1983

Sophie May Allen
b. 16 July 1986

Frederick John Allen
b. 19 Nov. 1988

A wartime wedding extends the family
Lottie Mercer and Charles Benjamin Rilett married in June 1916, in the middle of the First World War. James 'Snowball' Smith wears a black armband for his wife Lilian who died two months earlier. Annie Alberta Mercer (front row left, seated in black) met Henry Potter (standing, second from left) at this wedding, and married him in 1917. She would always be known to her grandchildren as Grandma Potter.

putting it all together

As soon as you start collecting information and obtaining family documents and photographs, it is essential to find an efficient way to store your records and notes.

organising your material

Be methodical
♦ Devise a way of keeping your records that allows you to find information quickly. Do not keep too many loose paper sheets that could be lost or inadvertently destroyed. Use:
♦ A document filing system.
♦ A computer software package.
♦ Or a combination of the two.

♦ When you jot down information from documents or make notes of your conversations with relatives:
♦ Make sure your notes are legible.
♦ Type them up as soon as possible.
♦ Indicate the source of the information you have gathered and the date you obtained it.
♦ If you use documents, note where the originals or copies are kept in your collection and from which relative or archive they were obtained.
♦ Keep a file for each family that you investigate, or a number of files for each family. You may find you collect enough information on one ancestor to dedicate a whole file to him or her.

♦ Divide a file into sections; each should contain a different type of information or document.
♦ One might hold copies of birth, marriage and death certificates and notes about your searches into those records.
♦ A second section might include extracts from census records.
♦ A third might include details from church registers of baptisms, marriages and burials.
♦ Further sections might include information that you obtain from churchyards, cemeteries, trade directories and other types of record described in this book.

PUBLISHING YOUR RESEARCH

Interest in your work may extend beyond your immediate kith and kin; it could be of use to other family historians researching the same lines of ancestry. Consider lodging copies of your research with the Society of Genealogists (see page 31), a family history society or a record office. This keeps your research safe and allows other people to consult it. Some family historians decide to publish their work. *Writing Up Your Family History* (J. Titford, Countryside Books, 2005) is a practical guide.

♦ Prepare a separate document for each person who appears on the family tree.

♦ You could use a card index system.

♦ Make out a card for each ancestor or relative. Record on it key dates and information with cross-references to other relevant documents.

♦ At the front of each family file, include any family trees that you prepare and your notes as to how you pulled that information together. This is your analysis of all the evidence that you have located.

looking after documents

Avoid poor storage

♦ Take care of your documents and photographs. Light, humidity, heat, pollution and attack by insects, moulds or vermin can all damage them if they are poorly stored.

♦ Keep photographs and papers in good-quality clear plastic sleeves that are free from the damaging additives used in cheaper products.

♦ Store them in files to protect against dirt, wear and direct sunlight.

♦ Try not to fold documents as this weakens the paper.

♦ If you are storing heavy volumes on shelves, lay them on their sides to prevent sagging, and dust regularly to discourage mould and infestation.

♦ Consider using specialist archive boxes made from acid-free materials.

♦ Store photographs in good-quality albums to prevent discoloration.

♦ Never glue photographs into albums. It may damage them and it also prevents you from rearranging them later or having them copied.

♦ Label every photograph: identify the subject, the person who gave it to you, and its approximate date.

♦ To learn more about the best way of storing your archives, consult *Caring for Books and Documents* (A. D. Baynes-Cope, British Library Publishing, 1989).

playing the detective

Search the records for clues

♦ As you gather snippets of information, you should compare them with material you have already collected to corroborate your findings and extend your research. One record can lead to others. Thus:

♦ Birth certificates note addresses at which you may find your ancestors in census records.

♦ Census records note ancestors' ages, places of birth and occupations, leading you to new areas of research.

♦ Gravestones should note the deceased's age at death. This gives you an approximate birth date to start searching for birth certificates or for baptisms in church registers.

♦ An ancestor's will may refer to a property that he held. You may be able to find this on a map and then search for records of that property.

Your family documents are likely to interest many people. Take care of them so that future generations can benefit from your research

A computer helps you to store, organise and print out your material. It also enables you to scan in portraits to embellish your family tree

why use a computer?

To store information

♦ Although you can keep information on paper and record cards, there are many advantages in using a computer to keep track of your research:

♦ You can use a word-processing program to type up your notes. It is then quick and easy to correct old information and add new. It is also easy to print copies to send to family members or to make into a booklet.

♦ You can use genealogy software to store information about your ancestors and to print out family trees.

♦ You can use a database or spreadsheet to store individual entries extracted from original sources.

For images and the Internet

♦ There are other things you simply cannot do with pencil and paper:

♦ You can use a scanner to scan family photographs and documents into your computer. You can then print copies when you need them and also use the images to add interest to your printed family tree.

♦ If any of your old photographs are damaged, you can use graphics software to create undamaged versions.

♦ You can get information from the many records and indexes now published on CD.

♦ You can connect to the Internet (see pages 34–37) to find information or contact other researchers.

genealogy software

Tailored to family history

♦ Specialised software for genealogy allows you to store all your research in a systematic way.

♦ Using a genealogy database, you can print out reports such as family trees, pedigrees and even a complete narrative history of your family.

♦ Some programs can even spot errors you have made when typing in data, such as a burial date before a birth date or accidental duplications.

HOW TO CHOOSE SOFTWARE

A standard genealogy package, costing between £30 and £99, will satisfy most requirements, enabling you to chart family trees, scan in pictures, record sources of information, create web pages and display stored data in a variety of ways.

The following are comprehensive and simple packages for a beginner:
♦ *Brother's Keeper 4*
♦ *Family Historian 4*
♦ *Family Origins 10*
♦ *Family Tree Maker 2011*
♦ *Roots Magic 3*
The above all run on Windows.
♦ *Reunion 9* is a program which is designed for Mac users.

The genealogy database *Personal Ancestral File* is available on CD for a nominal fee from the Mormon Church (see DIRECTORY), or can be downloaded free of charge from www.familysearch.org (look under 'Order Family History Resources' on the web site).

Review the software options

♦ The best way to decide on a package that is right for you is to read reviews, discuss your needs with a specialist genealogy software supplier (see DIRECTORY under Software) and look at the web sites of the software companies.

♦ Reviews of genealogy software appear in the monthly family history magazines (see page 20).

♦ For an on-line supplier and reviews of genealogy books, family tree software, data discs and archive binders see www.my-history.co.uk

♦ Most of the genealogy software is designed for PCs running the Windows operating system or, less frequently, the Apple Macintosh. For other types of computer there is much less choice. Many CDs can be read only on a PC.

♦ A quick guide to Windows genealogy packages is available at www.genealogysupplies.com/index

♦ If you have Internet access, look at the web sites of software publishers for detailed descriptions of their products; some offer demo versions that you can download. For links see 'Software and Computers' under www.cyndislist.com.

♦ Some software is available as 'shareware'. You download it from the Internet free of charge, then pay to register your copy if you keep using it.

data on CD

Information on tap

♦ An increasing amount of family history data is published on CD. A single disk can hold up to 650 million characters of text, and it can also store images and sound.

♦ The sort of material now on CD includes census information, reprints of rare 18th or 19th-century books such as trade directories, photographs of places and family trees. Many individuals transcribe and publish records in this format.

♦ The advantage of CDs is that the computer can search through all the information and select what you want quickly and accurately.

♦ You can search collections of CDs at record offices, the Society of Genealogists and other specialist libraries. Try to book a place in advance as the computers are often in great demand. You will be able to copy information to a floppy disk to take away and use at home.

sharing information

Using GEDCOM

♦ All genealogy software uses a standard way of storing information called GEDCOM (Genealogical Data Communication). This makes it easy to share your information with others who have different software and also means you can upgrade your program without retyping data.

Software packages such as these enable you to assemble a family tree on your computer, create charts and reports, and add photos, documents, videos and other multimedia. You can then share everything you have discovered with your family and friends.

common hurdles—be prepared

During your research you are likely to come across many kinds of document. Each type of record has its own particular problems, and these are explained in the relevant sections of the book. But some of the hurdles you will face apply to many documents and it is worth knowing about them before you begin.

Check the spelling

♦ When searching for a particular name, you should consider a range of possible spellings. For example, if you are looking for someone called Clough, you should also search indexes or registers for Cluff.

♦ Spelling errors may also have been introduced when handwritten texts were transcribed (it is common for the letters 'in' to be mistaken for an 'm'), or when a church minister misheard the name he was recording—a poorly pronounced letter 'b', for example, can be mistaken for a 'p'.

♦ Be aware of these possibilities and always note down the name exactly as it is found in a particular record. Explain in your notes why you think, for example, that the John Cluff you found in the records is the John Clough for whom you are searching.

Unexpected names

♦ Children would sometimes take their mother's surname, and often when a baby died in infancy the next born was given the same first name. Also note that foreign names may have been Anglicised as people found them difficult to spell (see page 303).

Difficult handwriting

♦ Many of the documents that you use will be manuscripts and perhaps written in an unfamiliar style. Most handwriting of the 19th and 20th centuries can be read fairly easily with a little patience. In earlier centuries, however, there were particular forms of script, especially for legal or official documents, that take some practice to read. See How to read old handwriting, pages 32–33.

Obsolete words

♦ Old documents may contain words that are no longer used, such as 'cordwainer' (a shoemaker) or 'yeoman' (a farmer or a farm tenant). Books such as *The Local Historian's Encyclopaedia* (J. Richardson, 3rd ed., Phillimore, 2003) will help you to determine the meanings of unfamiliar words.

Latin text

♦ Many early documents (and some legal records up to 1732) were written in Latin. Some have been transcribed into English, but you may come across Latin in original records such as parish registers. See Parish records, page 96.

You may find the Latin form of Christian names being used, such as Henricus for Henry or Jacobus for James. If you come across a document in Latin, make a copy of the part you need. You can then review it at your leisure with a guide such as *Simple Latin for Family Historians*

Keep a clear record of any misspelt name and where you found it—this will help to avoid any confusion at a later stage

(E. McLaughlin, FFHS, 2nd ed., 1994). For complex Latin documents, such as property records, you may need expert assistance.

Know your dates

♦ From about 1190 until 1752, the English used the Julian calendar, in which the year began on 25 March and finished on the following 24 March. Thus January to March 1710 came *after* April to December 1710. The Gregorian calendar (that we now use) came into effect in 1752. So 1751 began on 25 March and ended on 31 December. The year 1752 then commenced on 1 January.

♦ To add to the confusion, you need to be aware that some people started to use the Gregorian calendar before 1752. The Scots, for example, had been using it since 1600.

♦ People transcribing or indexing registers or other documents since 1752 have 'adjusted' the dates to our modern style. January, February and March were sometimes written in the style January 1709/10. This indicated that they were officially the last three months of 1709, in the 'old style' or Julian calendar, but the first three months of 1710 in the 'new style' Gregorian calendar.

Feast days

♦ Some documents, particularly medieval, note a date with reference to a feast day. For example, the fourth day after Easter. The date of Easter varies, but you can find it out, in any year, from *Dates and Calendars for the Genealogist* (C. Webb, Society of Genealogists, reprinted 1998).

Regnal years

♦ Another common method of dating documents, particularly legal records, was by reference to regnal years, such as in 'the 3rd year in the reign of King George II'. A regnal year began on the date of a monarch's accession to the throne. George II became king on 11 June 1727. His first regnal year, therefore, ran from that date to 10 June 1728 and his second regnal year began on 11 June 1728. The timeline on pages 322–41 includes the reigns of English and British monarchs.

Old currency

♦ Britain did not convert to decimal currency until 1971. Before then, £1 was divided into 20 shillings, each shilling equalling 12 pence. If you find a sum of money noted in a document, you can discover its equivalent value today in books such as *How Much is That Worth?* (L. Munby, Phillimore, 2nd ed., 1996).

Unfamiliar units

♦ Units of measurement have changed many times over the years. Britain now uses the metric system, although some imperial measures remain (such as miles or acres). If you find an unusual unit in an old document, try looking it up in *How Heavy, How Much and How Long?* (C. P. Chapman, Lochin Publishing, 1995).

UNDERSTANDING ROMAN NUMERALS

In Latin a number was represented by one or more letters. Add together the numbers represented by each letter, except where a letter in the sequence precedes a letter representing a larger figure. Thus XI is 11, but IX is nine. MM is 2000 and MCMXIX is 1919. This ancient way of writing numbers is still in use today.

I, i or **j**	1
V	5
X	10
L	50
C	100
D	500
M	1000

Research into your family's past can bring your present family together, as happened when Dr Jill Roberts had a phone call from Wendy Low, one of the 'Australian contingent' of her family. Wendy lives in Sydney; other family members live in Melbourne, and together they have been tracing their ancestry back to the aristocratic Blayneys. Wendy was now tracking down relations in Britain. Jill had such fun helping Wendy that she decided to try to arrange a get-together at Gregynog, the ancient family seat in the Welsh Marches.

A FAMILY REUNION

One woman's inspiration brings a family together

In spring 1997, some 50 Blayney descendants—in Britain, Australia, Canada, Italy and Majorca—received invitations from Jill Roberts to join her for a family gathering over the 1998 May bank holiday. With a year's notice, there was a good chance that many would make it. When the time came, 35 people, aged from five to 77, converged on Gregynog and had a weekend to get to know one another and swap stories. But the highlight was an informal exhibition of family memorabilia (left). People had brought portraits, photo albums, newspaper cuttings, letters and diaries; those who could not come had sent photographs and life-stories.

An English eccentric

This Edwardian lady was known as 'Granny-on-wheels' because she used to glide around in full-length gowns and her grandchildren (who are now in their 60s) couldn't believe that she actually had feet. Florence Ada Wright was born in 1869. She was the granddaughter of Elizabeth Blayney, the 12th and final Lord Blayney's older sister—he had died a bachelor, thereby ending the peerage. Florence married Edward Barnett in 1894 and bore five sons, but she was so desperate for a daughter that the boys were all dressed in frocks until they were six years old. One day, a Gypsy called on the Barnett household with a small flaxen-haired girl in tow. 'What a dear little girl,' Florence said. 'You can have her if you like,' replied the Gypsy, and so Winifred Janet Coleman came to be adopted. Edward was so outraged that he did not speak to his wife for three years. Although they continued to live in the same house, they communicated through their footman or by written notes.

'What a dear little girl,' Florence said. 'You can have her if you like,' replied the Gypsy, and so Winifred Janet Coleman came to be adopted.

'To its tables laden with wine may come bards and armies of people...'

There has been a hall on the site of Gregynog, five miles north of Newtown, Powys, since the 12th century, and by the middle of the 15th century it was the Blayney, or Blaenau, family seat. Much of Gregynog (from 'grug', the Welsh for heather) has been rebuilt since Moses Griffith painted this watercolour in 1750. However, the Blayney Room, lined with richly carved panelling, is dated 1636; the family coat of arms (top left) is carved above the stone fireplace. Medieval bards wrote in eulogistic praise of Gregynog's generous hospitality—a tradition it continues. Fortunately for the Blayney descendants, Gregynog is now owned by the University of Wales and hosts conferences, courses and a music festival every summer, so it was ideal for a large family gathering.

matters of state

The birth, marriage and death certificates that mark our life stages are the starting point for the family historian. What these easily obtained **civil records** reveal about family members can take you back to the early 19th century, when the records began. Armed with names and addresses you can then search **the census**, the decade-by-decade population count, which from 1841 lists the names, age, occupation and other details of everyone on census night. Tracking down members of **broken families**, such as foundlings or foster children, is a tougher challenge. But documents such as parish registers, foundling hospital records and adoption papers provide vital clues.

Busy starlet Julie Wilson finds time to fill in her census form in 1951

civil records
registering life's journey

The information disclosed by certificates of birth, marriage and death can take you back to 1837, although some families slipped through the net in the early years

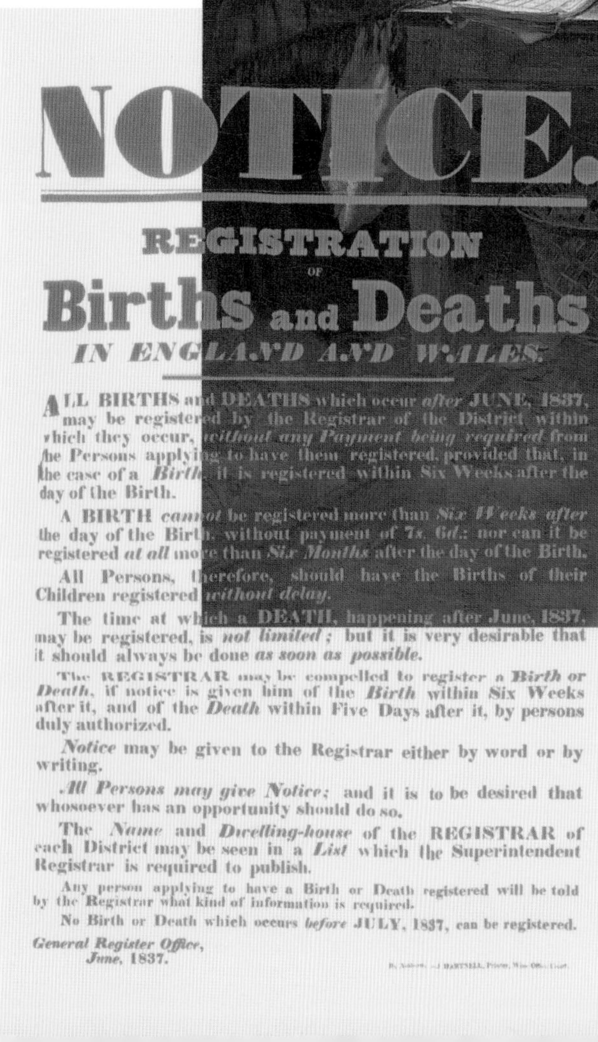

NOTICE.

REGISTRATION
OF
Births and Deaths
IN ENGLAND AND WALES.

ALL BIRTHS and DEATHS which occur *after* JUNE, 1837, may be registered by the Registrar of the District within which they occur, *without any Payment being required* from the Persons applying to have them registered, provided that, in the case of a *Birth*, it is registered within Six Weeks after the day of the Birth.

A BIRTH *cannot* be registered more than *Six Weeks after* the day of the Birth, without payment of *7s. 6d.*; nor can it be registered *at all* more than *Six Months* after the day of the Birth.

All Persons, therefore, should have the Births of their Children registered *without delay.*

The time at which a DEATH, happening after June, 1837, may be registered, is *not limited;* but it is very desirable that it should always be done *as soon as possible.*

The REGISTRAR may be compelled to register a *Birth* or *Death*, if notice is given him of the *Birth* within Six Weeks after it, and of the *Death* within Five Days after it, by persons duly authorized.

Notice may be given to the Registrar either by word or by writing.

All Persons may give Notice; and it is to be desired that whosoever has an opportunity should do so.

The *Name* and *Dwelling-house* of the REGISTRAR of each District may be seen in a *List* which the Superintendent Registrar is required to publish.

Any person applying to have a Birth or Death registered will be told by the Registrar what kind of information is required.

No Birth or Death which occurs *before* JULY, 1837, can be registered.

General Register Office,
June, 1837.

Entering a birth in the civil register

In 1837, posters (left) were used to publicise the new legislation covering the registration of births and deaths. In the early years some people did not register their children's births because they were under the impression that the recording of a child's baptism in a church register was sufficient.

The official records of births, marriages and deaths—gathered under the civil registration system—are of key importance to family research. They should enable you to trace your relatives back to around the mid 19th century and discover clues that can take you back farther.

A birth certificate allows you to prove a person's parentage and when and where that person was born. A marriage certificate proves that a marriage took place and that any offspring are legitimate. A death certificate allows you to bury or cremate a body and to wind up the deceased's affairs. It states the cause of death.

In some parts of England, particularly Essex, Middlesex, Shropshire, Surrey and Sussex, historians estimate that up to 15 per cent of births were not registered between 1837 and 1875.

The starting dates In England and Wales, civil registration began on 1 July 1837 and in Scotland on 1 January 1855. In Ireland non-Catholic marriages were registered from 1 April 1845, and births, deaths and all marriages from 1 January 1864. (There were also independent British systems of civil registration on the main Channel Islands from the 1840s and on the Isle of Man from 1858.) Events were registered locally and copies were sent to central repositories every quarter where they were nationally indexed.

how civil registration began

In 1538 the Church had been given the responsibility of registering baptisms, marriages and burials (see Parish records, pages 86–99). But two centuries later, the Industrial Revolution began to erode old patterns of rural life, and new religious movements, such as the Baptists and Quakers (see Nonconformists, pages 102–6), were coaxing people away from the established Anglican Church.

As the number of dissenters grew, so the number of people excluded from the Anglican registers increased (even though from 1754 all marriages, unless Jewish or Quaker, had to take place in an Anglican church). Nonconformists, Roman Catholics (see pages 107–9) and Jews (see pages 110–11) all kept their own registers.

Concern as population grows By the end of the 18th century, there was mounting concern that records of church baptisms, burials and marriages no longer presented a true picture of the population. In 1800 the Census Act was passed and the first official British census (a headcount only) took place in 1801 (see Counting people, pages 62–64).

The Registration Act In the early 1830s a parliamentary select committee investigated the problems of under-registration in parochial records and concluded that there should be a statutory system of civil registration of births, marriages and deaths. The Registration Act and Marriage Act were both passed in 1836, and the system was established in England and Wales the following year.

The Marriage Act This introduced civil marriage ceremonies by marriage certificate in register offices, or under the supervision of a registrar in a Nonconformist church or chapel, in addition to traditional weddings by banns or licence in Anglican churches. It also affirmed the rights of Jews and Quakers to hold their own ceremonies.

a developing system

To operate the new system of civil registration a Registrar General was appointed in London, with overall responsibility. England and Wales were divided up into administrative districts with central register offices staffed by a superintendent registrar and a complement of registrars. Each registration district was divided into subdistricts with a registrar appointed to record births and deaths. Today many of the original districts have been abolished, often as a result of local government boundary changes.

The system was so effective that similar arrangements were introduced in Scotland and Ireland.

At first local registrars had to travel round their subdistricts and record births within six weeks and deaths within five days. The public did not have to report either event, but once a registrar had been told of a birth or death, informants could be prosecuted if they refused to answer his questions.

The Births and Deaths Registration Act of 1874 removed the onus from registrars and made it the responsibility of the public to report births or deaths at local register offices. Fines were introduced for late and non-registration, but some parents avoided paying a late registration penalty fee by giving a later, incorrect date of birth for a child.

From 1875, you can also find out the cause of an ancestor's death. The Act required all death registrations to be supported by a medical certificate signed by a doctor and stating the cause of death. Unusual deaths had to be reported to the coroner by the police, medical authorities or registrars. The certificate will indicate if a coroner was involved.

the British way of divorce

In England and Wales divorce was impossible before 1858 except by costly private parliamentary bills. See the National Archives guides on divorce before and after 1858 at www.nationalarchives.gov.uk/records/research-guides.

Divorce through the courts From 1 January 1858, following the Matrimonial Causes Act of 1857, husbands could obtain a divorce through the civil courts because of a wife's adultery. A wife, however, had to be able to prove her husband's cruelty towards her as well as his adultery. This did not change until 1925. The Divorce Reform Act of 1969 made the irretrievable breakdown of marriage the sole ground for divorce in Britain.

Where the records are kept Indexed divorce files—decrees absolute—for England and Wales 1858–1937 are at the TNA (see DIRECTORY) in classes J 77 and J 78. Divorce records are closed for 75 years, but permission to consult individuals' case papers from more recent divorces may be obtained from the Divorce Registry at the Principal Registry of the Family Division (see DIRECTORY). This registry also has custody of divorce records since 1938.

Divorce in Scotland Before the 19th century, the only place in Britain where ordinary people could obtain divorces was Scotland, where it had been possible since 1560. Cases involving marriage dissolution were heard by the Commissary Court of Edinburgh up to 1830, and then by the Court of Session. The records for both are at the National Archives of Scotland (see DIRECTORY).

From 1855 to 1984, divorces were recorded by the words 'Divorce RCE' against the entry in marriage registers, RCE referring to the Register of Corrected Entries. The General Register Office for Scotland (see DIRECTORY) holds a microfiche index of divorces granted since 1984.

Divorce in Ireland Church courts retained all responsibilities for separations until 1870, when they passed to the Irish High Court. The court continued to grant decrees of nullity and divorce was only possible by Act of Parliament.

The Matrimonial Causes Act of 1939 extended divorce for the first time to Northern Ireland. In the Republic various Acts forbade dissolutions of marriage until 1995, when civil divorce became available to couples who had lived apart for four of the previous five years.

The Act also tightened up birth registration. It stated that the father of an illegitimate child could only be named on the birth certificate if he was present when the child was registered.

From 1899, for the first time, Nonconformist marriages could be solemnised without a registrar present and recorded in the church or chapel's own marriage register. Traditional Anglican, Jewish and Quaker ceremonies were unaffected.

Age of consent In England, Wales, Scotland and Northern Ireland the minimum age for marriage was raised to 16 years in 1929. The Republic of

Ireland maintained the former minimum ages of 12 for a girl and 14 for a boy until 1975.

In Scotland, the Marriage Act of 1939 finally abolished most of the forms of irregular marriage (see page 98) that had survived since the Middle Ages. In the same year civil marriages in a register office first became legal.

Today notifications of all marriages have to be made to the district registrars, who issue a marriage schedule authorising a church or register office ceremony, providing there are no impediments. As in England and Wales, Jews and Quakers in Scotland may conduct their own ceremonies.

The end of the affair

When the Hon. John Russell, heir to the Ampthill peerage, sought a divorce in 1923 it was on the grounds that Mrs Russell, an 'unconventional, lively woman', had committed adultery with Mr Mayer. Mr Russell also claimed that he and his wife had never consummated their marriage and that her son was the result of another adulterous liaison with an unknown man. After various testimonies, Mrs Russell was found guilty of adultery with a man unknown, but not with Mr Mayer.

Mrs Russell with her mother

Mr Mayer

Detectives were employed to watch witnesses before the trial

civil records
in England and Wales

Civil records reveal dates, names and family relationships. They can now be searched on the Internet

Millions of names at your fingertips
Record offices throughout the land (see DIRECTORY) nowadays offer not only original documents for you to see, but also online facilities, and copies of millions of records in the form of microfilm or microfiche. They often provide specialist advice on how to use these resources.

indexes and registers

National indexes of births, marriages and deaths recorded in England and Wales since 1 July 1837 are kept in bound volumes on open shelves in The National Archives at Kew, where births, marriages and deaths are arranged chronologically in different sections. These indexes are now available on various sites on the Internet (see p. 55). There are also copies of these indexes, or parts of them, on microfilm or microfiche in many county archives, large reference libraries, and some Family History Centres (see DIRECTORY)—the genealogical libraries run by the Mormon Church.

All the indexes are in alphabetical order of surnames, then first names. From 1837 to 1894 the index information for each year is divided into quarters: March quarter—events registered in January, February and March; June quarter—April, May, June; September quarter—July, August, September; and December quarter—October, November, December. The earliest index is for September quarter, 1837. After 1984 the indexes are organised by year only. Each entry in the indexes

Finding the birth, marriage and death certificates for your ancestors is one of the first steps in building a family tree. The information they contain will take you back generation by generation into the Victorian age and beyond, and help you to discover when and where members of your family lived. The details of the mother and father found on a birth certificate help you to search for their marriage certificate; the information on the marriage certificate, such as ages or names of fathers, can be used to search for the bride and groom's birth certificates. This process can often be repeated for several successive generations.

records also the name of the registration district where the event was registered and the entry's references. All this information is needed when ordering a certificate.

Civil partnership Records start December 2005 and are listed by surname, together with the surname of partner, year of formation, registration authority and registration entry number.

Obtaining certificates For a fee, a copy of a certificate can be ordered at the General Register Office or from the relevant local register office. You should always buy full birth certificates; the cheaper 'short' birth certificates contain little family history information.

using the registers

Birth registers Birth registrations do not always appear in the quarter in which a baby was born, because a period of six weeks was allowed in which to register births. So a birth that occurred late in one quarter may not have been registered until the next quarter. From the September quarter of 1911, the mother's maiden surname is shown in the indexes.

DETAILS REVEALED
The information found on birth certificates includes when and where the child was born. When the time of birth is noted it usually implies a multiple birth, although in some register offices in the early days of civil registration this was standard practice for all births.

Next are listed the child's given name(s), its sex, the father's full name and occupation (often left blank if the child was illegitimate), the mother's full name and her maiden surname, prefixed by 'formerly'. (The surname from a previous marriage would be prefixed by 'late'.)

This is followed by the name, address and signature of the person reporting the birth, the date

of registration and the signature of the registrar. On the extreme right-hand side is a column, nearly always blank, for any alterations to the given name(s) made within 12 months.

Marriage registers Marriage registrations are indexed twice—under the surnames of both bride and groom. If you know the other partner's name, check the indexes to make sure you have the right event. From the March quarter of 1912 the surname of the spouse is shown against separate entries for both bride and groom.

Poor handwriting and incorrect indexing of the original records can slow down your search. For example, the surname Milton in bad handwriting could be mistakenly indexed under Hilton or Wilton.

DETAILS REVEALED Marriage certificates show the date and place of the wedding and if it took place by banns, licence or certificate. The full names of bride and groom are shown along with their ages, although actual ages may be replaced by 'full age', which means 21 or over (18 or over from 1969).

Pre-marriage marital status ('bachelor', 'spinster', 'widow' and so on) are recorded together with the occupations of the bride and groom and their residences. If these addresses are the same, it does not necessarily mean that the bride and groom were already living together. Giving one address had an advantage, since it meant that the couple did not have to pay for banns in two different parishes.

The fathers of the couple and their occupations should be shown. Occasionally, in cases of

THE MANY NAMES OF MARIE LLOYD

Civil records plot a person's life and help to distinguish fact from fiction. Take Marie Lloyd, the music-hall star—a name known across the world. Her birth certificate (top left) reveals her humble origins as Matilda Alice Victoria Wood, born in London's East End on 12 February 1870. By the age of 16 she had become a public idol but her private life was less successful. At 17, she married Percy Courtenay, a betting man whom she left. The marriage certificate middle left reveals a second marriage, to Alec Hurley, a lesser music-hall star. That marriage failed when she fell in love with Bernard Dillon, a jockey 18 years her junior. They married in 1914. It was a far from happy union, and he beat her. But Marie Lloyd was still Mrs Dillon when she died in 1922, as her death certificate (bottom left) shows.

illegitimacy, this area was left blank or a false name was used to avoid embarrassment. Named fathers were not always living. Sometimes they are helpfully listed as 'deceased'.

Marriage certificates also show the name of the officiating clergyman or registrar, the signatures of the bride and groom and those of the witnesses, usually the minimum of two people 'of credible age' (over 14 years old). These original signatures do not appear on the marriage certificates issued by the Office for National Statistics as only copies of the documents were sent to the Registrar General. But they can be found in the actual church or chapel registers. Deposited original registers can often be seen in the appropriate county record office or at the register office within the registration district where the marriage took place.

Death records British death certificates, apart from those in Scotland, do not contain a great deal of useful information. But once a death has been found, other records, such as newspaper obituaries and funeral reports (see People in newspapers, pages 168–73), can be goldmines of family history information. There may be a will (see Legacies, pages 120–31), which could identify many other relations. The person's age at death will also simplify the search for his or her birth registration.

Deaths were always recorded where they took place and therefore not necessarily where the person lived or was buried. Recorded age at death appears in the indexes from the March quarter of 1866 but may be unreliable. From the June quarter of 1969 it was replaced by a record of the full date of birth of the deceased, which may also be inaccurate.

DETAILS REVEALED Death certificates show when and where a person died, his or her name in full, the age at death, sex, occupation, the medical cause(s) of death, which may be unreliable up to 1875 (see page 52), the name, address and signature of the informant (usually a close relative), the date of registration and the signature of the registrar. Deaths of children should include the father's name.

Sometimes death registrations of married women include their husband's name.

From 1 April 1969, the date and place of birth of the deceased (if known) were recorded and from 1 April 1982, the maiden surnames of married women. More recently, registrars have requested other personal details of the deceased for statistical purposes—these do not appear on certificates.

SUSPICIOUS DEATH If the death was not due to natural causes and the certificate indicates that a coroner's order was made, it may be worth while following up this lead and looking for reports of an inquest or inquiry in the local newspaper. Some coroners' records may be found in county record offices, but they are closed for at least 75 years. Although many coroners deposit their records, they are not legally bound to do so, and once the records are 15 years old, they may be destroyed.

further indexes

Microfiche copies of miscellaneous indexes of births, marriages and deaths, mostly of England and Wales, are sometimes available and researchers should make local enquiries to establish their availability at county record offices, large libraries or other sources. The indexes cover adoptions and stillbirths since 1927; marine and air records; regimental/army records from overseas (1761–1965); and service deaths for periods that include the Boer War (1899–1902), the First World War (1914–21) and the Second World War (1939–48).

TAKING IT FURTHER

♦ www.nationalarchives.gov.uk/records/ birthmarriagedeathcertificates.htm
♦ www.genuki.org.uk/big/eng/civreg/GROInd exes.html Index to the General Register Office's registration districts.

civil records
using Scottish archives

Anyone researching Scottish ancestors is lucky because in Scotland civil registration records are more detailed than elsewhere in Britain

Scottish civil registration records contain much more family history information than other British certificates. Registration began in 1855, and records for that year are particularly extensive. In subsequent years the amount of information recorded was curtailed but remained superior to that in the rest of Britain. The records can be searched at the General Register Office for Scotland (see DIRECTORY). You can pay for a daily or weekly search; book your place well in advance.

indexes and registers

The indexes of Scottish births, marriages and deaths from 1 January 1855 to 2006 are searchable on the official Scottish genealogy resource www.scotlandspeople.gov.uk (a pay-site). You can order an extract of an entry from the registers from this website or by one of the following options:
♦ Apply in person at New Register House (see DIRECTORY) or in the ScotlandsPeople Centre. If the priority service is used before 1pm the extract will be ready for collection by 4pm that day; after 1pm it will be ready by 11am the next working day. Or it can be sent by post within 5 working days.
♦ Apply in writing and the extract will be sent within 10 working days. The priority service dispatches the extract within 1 working day by first-class mail or air-mail. The downloadable version of Form SU3 can be used.
♦ Apply by telephone on 131 314 4411, from Monday to Friday 9am to 4.30pm. You will need to quote credit or debit card details.
♦ Official extracts from the Scottish records may

also be obtained from local registrars of births, marriages and deaths, etc.

Birth certificates These carry the full name of the child and its sex, the date and time of birth, the address where the birth occurred and the father's full name and occupation. The name of the mother, including her maiden surname (m.s.) and any previous married names, are also shown, together with the date and place of the parents' marriage (not recorded from 1856 to 1860).

The name, address and signature of the informant are recorded, and the date of registration together with the signature of the registrar. Additional information on 1855 birth certificates includes the ages and birthplaces of the parents, and the numbers (alive and dead) and sex of other children of the marriage, but not their names.

Marriage certificates There are separate indexes for brides and grooms. From 1855 to 1863 brides are indexed by their maiden surname and their married surname(s), from 1864 to 1928 by their maiden surname only, and from 1929 again by maiden and married surnames. Marriage certificates show the date and place of the wedding, as well as the type of ceremony and whether the marriage was regular or irregular (without banns). The full names, signatures, marital status, addresses and occupations of the bride and groom are also noted.

You will also find details of the names and occupations of both fathers and mothers (including maiden surnames), the marriage witnesses and the name of the officiating minister or, from 1940, the registrar. Marriage certificates for 1855 show the places of birth of the bride and groom, details of any previous marriages and numbers of any resulting children. If a marriage ended in divorce the details will be annotated, up to 1984.

Death certificates The indexes from 1866 note the age of the deceased and from 1974 the maiden surname of the deceased's mother. From 1855 to 1858 deaths of Scottish married women are indexed only under their married surname, and from 1859 under both maiden and married surname(s).

Death certificates record the full names of the deceased, sex and age, the date, time and place of death, his or her occupation and marital status. The name of any spouse is included in the 1855 records and from 1861 onwards.

The deceased's parents and the mother's maiden surname are also recorded. Medical causes of death and the name of any medical attendant are shown with the date of registration, the informant's signature and relationship to the deceased, and the signature of the registrar. Certificates from 1855 to 1860 include the place of burial. The certificates of 1855 also note the birthplace of the deceased, how long he or she had lived in the district, the names and ages of any children and whether they are alive.

At the General Register Office for Scotland you will also find indexes to Scottish adoptions since 1930, stillbirths since 1939, divorces since 1984, marine and air registers, and some HM Services records overseas since 1881.

Making connections
Web sites enable you to search through records in your own home. Some sites, such as Scotlands People, which is run by the General Register Office for Scotland, are regularly updated and allow searches by surname, event, sex, first name or initial, year or range of years and age. You may have to pay to access some sites.

civil records
using Irish archives

When looking for Irish civil registration records, remember that in 1922 Ireland was divided into two. As a consequence, the records were also segregated

A full system of civil registration, based on that of England and Wales, began in Ireland in 1864. Births, marriages and deaths were registered in local register offices. Copies were passed on to Dublin where they were nationally indexed.

indexes and registers

In 1922 Ireland was divided into Northern Ireland and the Irish Free State (Eire from 1937 and the Republic of Ireland from 1949). Since 1922 each has had its own separate system of civil registration.

Republic of Ireland's records The General Register Office in Dublin (see DIRECTORY) holds national indexes and microfilm of the registers of births, marriages and deaths in any part of Ireland from 1 January 1864 to 31 December 1921 (non-Catholic marriages from 1 April 1845). It also has records for the Republic of Ireland from 1 January 1922 to date. You can search the indexes for a fee and buy uncertified photocopies of them or certified copies of certificates in person or by post.

Northern Ireland's records Since 1922 the registers and indexes for births, marriages and deaths in the six counties of Northern Ireland have been held by the General Register Office for Northern Ireland in Belfast (see DIRECTORY). Also held there are original registers from 1864 onwards for births (which are indexed) and deaths. Searches are by appointment and for a fee; a staff-assisted search is available for a higher fee. Pre-payment is required when ordering certificates by post.

KEY SOURCES OF INFORMATION

♦ Indexes and registers for the whole of Ireland to 1921 and for the Republic of Ireland from 1922 at the General Register Office in Dublin.

♦ Indexes and registers for Northern Ireland for births and deaths from 1864 and marriages from 1922 at the General Register Office for Northern Ireland.

♦ Microfilm indexes and sometimes early registers at some Family History Centres.

SEE DIRECTORY ➤

Searching Irish indexes See wiki.family search.org for background information. Irish civil registration indexes can be searched for at www.familysearch.org/search. Certificates can be obtained on-line from The General Register Office, Dublin (www.hse.ie/lifeevents) and The General Register Office for Northern Ireland (www.nidirect.gov.uk). You can also visit in person.

BIRTHS The indexes list the child's given name(s) and surname and registrar's district. From 1903 the mother's maiden surname is listed. From 1903 to 1921 in Northern Ireland, and from 1903 to 1927 in the Republic of Ireland, birth indexes show the child's date of birth.

MARRIAGES Registrations are indexed twice, under the surnames of bride and groom.

DEATHS Indexes include the age at death.

Other registration records at Dublin and Belfast include marine, consular and army registers and indexes relating to Irish subjects at sea or abroad.

CIVIL RECORDS—A TROUBLESHOOTING GUIDE

When registering events, people were required to be truthful, and there were penalties for deliberate falsehoods. But it was impossible for officials to check every registration, so all indexes may contain errors or omissions.

♦ The most common reason for failure to find an event is that a surname was spelt differently and appears in an unexpected part of an index. For example, 'Coalman' will be some distance in the indexes from 'Coleman'. In the 19th century many ordinary people did not know how their surnames should be spelt.

♦ Sometimes clerks misread surnames, so that the name 'Fowler' might be indexed under 'Towler', or 'Sawyer' under 'Lawyer'. In Ireland a name such as 'O'Kelly' was often registered as 'Kelly'.

♦ Common surnames linked to equally common first names such as John Smith, Ann Taylor and William Williams can cause difficulties unless you are certain of the registration district where family events would have been registered. In densely populated urban areas, people would only have to move a few miles to find themselves in a different registration district.

♦ During the 19th century a child might be given the mother's maiden name (or the surname of some other female relation) as a second name. Later it may have been hyphenated to the surname, leading to a different surname at marriage or death.

♦ People occasionally became known by a particular name just because they used it long enough. So Tom Brown could become John Edwards.

♦ First names may also present problems. People may have swapped them around or dropped ones they did not like. Some may even have used nicknames such as 'Peggy' for Margaret or 'Pip' for Philip when they married.

♦ Couples did not always marry before children arrived, or at all, possibly because one partner was only separated from a previous spouse and was not permitted, by law, to re-marry.

♦ Illegitimate children should be listed under the mother's maiden surname unless there was a pretence of marriage, when they may occur under the father's surname. In the early days of registration many illegitimate children were never registered.

♦ Ages given on certificates and in indexes may be inaccurate. For deaths it was sometimes guesswork, while minors who married without parental consent would often add a few years to appear older. Some people might also knock a few years off their age when marrying younger spouses.

♦ Some quarterly returns from local register offices were lost en route to national repositories.

The latest addition

Large families were common in the early years of the 20th century. The Terry family all lived in the same terraced house in Greenwich, south London. With so many mouths to feed it is not surprising that parents occasionally forgot to register their children. The family portrait is actually incomplete: the Terrys had 19 children in all.

the census
counting people

Since the early 19th century the population of Britain has been surveyed every ten years. The exercise has produced a treasure trove of genealogical information for family historians

Doing the rounds

The enumerator, an educated man, had to visit every household in his district. His task was to distribute and later collect the census forms, sometimes helping the illiterate to complete them to ensure that the details of every inhabitant were clearly listed.

Britain's 19th-century census returns, the decade-by-decade review of its inhabitants, are a boon to family historians because of the personal information they contain. The first count (of England, Wales and Scotland) took place in 1801 and revealed a total of 10.8 million people. Ireland's first full census was in 1821.

The early returns were just a headcount but as the government realised the census' potential as a tool for assessing the nation's needs, more information

was collected. From 1841, the returns included names, addresses, ages, occupations and, from 1851, relationships and place of birth too—which are vital to further genealogical research. Because of their personal content, census returns for England,

Wales and Scotland are closed for 100 years. So the 1911 census records are the latest available.

The 1911 Irish census returns are the earliest complete sets for Ireland as most of the returns before that date were either routinely destroyed or lost in 1922 in a fire at the Public Record Office in Dublin.

how the census was taken

All over Britain the week before census night, an army of enumerators delivered the census forms to the homes in their designated area.

It was the householders' duty to complete them correctly and the enumerator's responsibility to collect the completed forms the morning after census night. The enumerator also had to make a note of any uninhabited houses on his route.

He then took the schedules home and copied them into his 'enumerator's book', which he took to his supervisor to be checked. Finally the books were sent to an office in London, where census clerks did the counting before the statistics were published.

the structure of the records

The records served their intended official purpose and, like other government papers, were later archived and released into the public domain. For those now researching them it helps to understand the structure of the original census-taking exercise because this is reflected in the way the returns are now arranged—by place and administrative districts rather than by surname, for instance.

Registration districts To organise the statistics census administrators divided Britain into manageable units. In England, Wales and Scotland, they used registration districts, also used for registering births and marriages. These were based on the boundaries of the poor law unions (see Poor and destitute, page 150). A county was divided into numbered registration districts according to the density of the population. Each registration district

was then further divided into subdistricts. When searching for your ancestors by place name at the TNA, which holds all the English and Welsh census returns, you will discover that towns and villages are grouped by a number that corresponds to their registration district. Street indexes and some surname indexes are also arranged by registration district.

Enumeration districts Once you look at a census return on film, another division becomes apparent—the enumeration districts, which appear on film and are occasionally mentioned in the street indexes that help you to search large towns.

Subdistricts were further divided into several enumeration districts, areas that one enumerator could reasonably cover in a day. They tended to be larger in the countryside, where the enumerator

Dividing up London
A section of an 1870 map of London shows the boundary of a registration district to the west of the city outlined in green and subdistricts within it outlined in pink. Kensington, a pink spot circled in green, gives its name to a registration district and subdistrict; other subdistricts are indicated by large pink spots.

covered fewer households but more ground. When you look at the documents on microfilm, you will see that a new enumeration book is marked by a break in style; it begins with a new title page and the next enumerator's description of the area to which he had been assigned and its number.

Comments on the work Some enumerators added their own remarks about the type of houses they had to cover and the people they had met. Some also included complaints about how badly paid they were for the enumeration work.

After the title page there are pages explaining what the enumerator was meant to do and a summary page for him to total up the number of people on the forms he had collected, which he signed. After that the personal particulars begin.

In Wales, from 1841, householders were given a Welsh translation of the schedule. From 1871 the enumerator could indicate if the schedule had been completed in Welsh by marking 'W' in the first column. When writing up their books, enumerators occasionally let a Welsh word slip through.

census records for Ireland

The 1901 and 1911 Irish censuses follow the English format. But in 1901 people were asked their religion and in 1911 wives were asked how long they had been married, how many children they had borne and the total living at the time of the census. Both years are organised by county and district electoral division (rather than by registration district).

To consult the Irish census, you need a street address if your ancestor lived in a large town or city; for country addresses the name of the townland (a small administrative district) is usually sufficient. *The Townland Index for 1901*, held by major reference libraries, the TNA and other national record offices, will supply the name and number of the district electoral division in which each townland lies.

Because of the loss of earlier Irish census material, other sources such as tithe applotment books and Griffith's Valuation are used instead, as these have been name-indexed for each county (see Property records, page 185). Surviving census material is listed in books such as *Tracing Irish Ancestors* (P. Gorry and M. MacConghail, HarperCollins, 1997).

WHERE TO FIND CENSUS RECORDS

Census records are now fully available on-line. See page 69 for more information.

FOR ENGLAND AND WALES
♦ A full set of English and Welsh census returns (1841–1911) is held at The National Archives at Kew, where free access to its reading rooms is available.

FOR SCOTLAND
♦ Census returns for 1841–1911 can be consulted at the General Register Office for Scotland.
♦ Copies of local returns are available at many libraries and county record offices.

FOR IRELAND
♦ The 1901 and 1911 census returns are held in the National Archives of Ireland.
♦ The 1901 and 1911 returns for the six Northern Ireland counties are also available from the Public Record Office of Northern Ireland.
♦ Copies of surviving local returns can be found in most Irish county libraries.
SEE DIRECTORY ➤

the census
finding your ancestors

Armed with some basic facts about your forebears, you will be able to use the many street, place name and surname indexes, compiled to help you to search the census

Before you begin to search the census try to find out a few basic details about the ancestors you hope to find in the returns. Overleaf we explain how the information helps you to track down English and Welsh returns at the Family Records Centre.

Whichever record office you visit for your census search (see left), it is worth noting that:

☞ To search most years you need to know a place of residence, a surname, and also first names if the surname is common. The 1881 census is easy to search as it has been fully name indexed for England, Wales and Scotland. It is available on CD.

☞ For other years, a street address is essential for London and other large towns and cities.

☞ You can find addresses for your ancestors from birth, marriage or death certificates (see Civil records, pages 50–61). They may also be listed in street or trade directories (see pages 174–5) or electoral registers (see page 173).

understanding document references

The document number gives you the reference you need to take a microfilm from the cabinets, and helps you to find the correct place on film.
In order to identify the documents they hold, all record centres have a numbering system, applied to the documents when they arrive.

The original census returns are held in paper-bound books, each covering around five or six enumeration districts. With the exception of the 1841 and 1851 censuses, each book was given a document reference. For 1841 and 1851, boxes of books rather than individual books were grouped together, so that more enumeration districts are included under one document reference.

The number of the document always has a prefix made up of the group code and class number. A 'group' of documents generally comes from one government department or court. In the case of the census, that is HO (1841 and 1851), which stands for Home Office, or RG (1861 onwards), which stands for Registrar General. The class numbers are simply a numerical system for identifying each different type of document coming from the same source. Thus the document reference for the 1861 census returns for Marsh Street, Walthamstow, London, is RG 9 / 1062 f 19v, consisting of:

- ☞ its group code—RG
- ☞ its class number—9
- ☞ the document number—1062
- ☞ the folio number—f 19v

For security and identification purposes, the folio number was stamped on the top left-hand corner of each folio or sheet of the document. Adding 'r' for recto indicates the front of the sheet; 'v' for verso indicates the back.

The complete document reference will take you directly to the entry on film. It is unique and cannot be confused with any other in the entire archive.

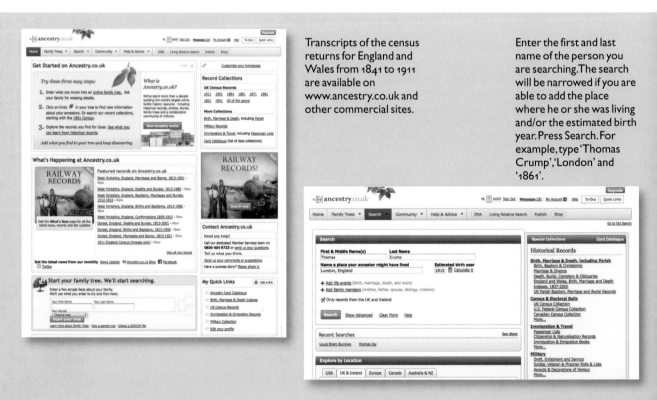

Transcripts of the census returns for England and Wales from 1841 to 1911 are available on www.ancestry.co.uk and other commercial sites.

Enter the first and last name of the person you are searching. The search will be narrowed if you are able to add the place where he or she was living and/or the estimated birth year. Press Search. For example, type 'Thomas Crump', 'London' and '1861'.

the 1911 census

As well as supplying the same information as in the previous censuses, the 1911 returns were the first to keep the details that were completed by the householders themselves. We can now see an ancestor's handwriting and sometimes supplementary information that had not been asked for.

Other details include:
- The length of the present marriage and how many children (living or deceased) were born to that marriage.
- Detailed occupational data.
- Infirmity (this and some other sensitive information remains closed until 2012).

using the 1911 census

The information contained in the census returns can narrow the search for vital events amongst other records. Charles Sandy (see photograph page 200),

a New Forest labourer who had moved to Poole to work as a builder, lost his first wife, Elizabeth, in 1907. An old photograph shows him with his second wife, Olive, a widow. In the column headed, 'Completed years the present Marriage has lasted', the 1911 census provided the information that they had been married for one year, so this enabled the quick discovery of their marriage certificate amongst civil registration records on 26 March 1910.

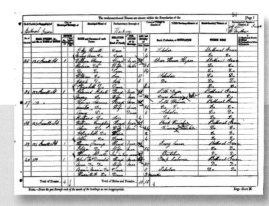

View the full transcript of the census return for the individual you have named. This will include all other members of the household. Remember that the transcribers often made mistakes. If in doubt, pay to view the photocopy of the original return.

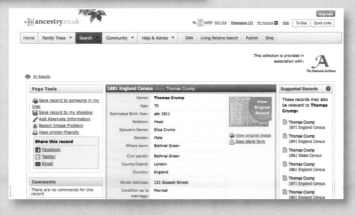

Click on the census return that you wish to search. This will bring up the most promising matches. Click on the most likely one (and others if this is unconvincing). Our Thomas Crump is the first of Matches 1-10.

CANNOT FIND THE FAMILY

If your family are not where you expect to find them on census night, they may have been visiting friends. Some men will have been working away from home; other families may have simply moved house.

STAYING WITH FRIENDS If people were on a night shift the night the census was taken, they had to be recorded where they would have slept had they not been working. Those who were genuinely staying away from home with relatives or friends in another part of the country would be recorded at the place they slept on the census night, rather than at their home.

ADDRESS MISSING Some people complain that the address they are looking for has been missed from the census. This is unlikely. But check the year of your address as a street or road name might have changed. If the family were away from home and the building was empty, the enumerator would write 'building uninhabited' and the address would not be written down. He would also make a note of any buildings on his route that were under construction.

MOVED HOME The majority of 19th-century people rented rather than bought their homes so moved house regularly. They may have stayed in the area but not at the same address. When you take an address from a civil registration document, try to find a certificate for a birth or marriage in the family that occurred close to the census date and year.

In 1841, the census date was 6 June; in 1851 it was 30 March. In 1861 it was 7 April, in 1871 it was 2 April, in 1881 it was 3 April, in 1891 it was 5 April, in 1901 it was 31 March and in 1911, it was 2 April.

SOMETHING LOST FROM THE DOCUMENT Occasionally a folio of the returns may be missing. Generally this occurs at the back of an enumerator's book where the last page has become detached. As only one set of returns was ever created, there is no alternative but to search in another census year.

However, if just one page of information is missing from the film, you know that part of the document exists because the reverse side is there. In this case the probable cause is an oversight during filming. Where this has been identified, it has been corrected but there may still be a few instances that have not yet been reported.

A hasty urban move
Poor families throughout Britain changed home frequently. Property was often let short-term and they also moved in order to find employment or to escape debt.

TAKING IT FURTHER

Census records are such an important source of information for family historians that many reference works, CDs and web sites have been created to assist your search or help you to do some homework before you visit a record office.

REFERENCE WORKS
Reference books include:
♦ *Tracing Your Ancestors in the National Archives* (A. Bevan, The National Archives, 7th ed., 2006).
♦ *Census: The Expert Guide* (P. Christian and D. Annal, The National Archives, 2008).
♦ *Making Sense of the Census* (E. Higgs, The National Archives, 2005).
♦ *Using Census Returns: Pocket Guides to Family History* (D. Annal, Public Record Office, 2002).
♦ *Making Use of the Census* (S. Lumas, Public Record Office, 4th ed., 2002)
♦ www.nationalarchives.gov.uk/records/research-guides/census-returns.htm
♦ The Society of Genealogists (see DIRECTORY) has a large collection of surname indexes, listed in *Census Copies and Indexes in the Library of the Society of Genealogists* (SoG, 1997). Collections of surname indexes are also held at the Family Records Centre, Guildhall Library, county record offices and family history societies (see DIRECTORY).

CENSUS RECORDS ON-LINE
The National Archives has co-operated with commercial sites to make the census returns for England, Wales, the Channel Islands and the Isle of Man searchable on-line. All the returns from 1841 to 1911 are available on the commercial sites, www.ancestry.co.uk, www.findmypast.co.uk, www.thegenealogist.co.uk and www.genesreunited.co.uk. The free site www.freecen.org.uk is currently engaged in transcribing the census returns for 1841-91.

The Scottish census records for 1841-1911 are searchable at the ScotlandsPeople site, www.scotlandspeople.gov.uk.

The Irish census records for 1901 and 1911 are searchable at The National Archives of Ireland's site, www.census.nationalarchives.ie. The returns for 1901 and 1911 are arranged by townland (the smallest division of land) or, in urban areas, by street. See also www.censusfinder.com/ireland.htm.

The commercial site, www.findmypast.ie/Census, has the 1901 and 1911 census returns for Ireland. The 1911 census records are also available at www.genesreunited.co.uk/1911_Census.

WORKING AWAY ON CENSUS NIGHT
Before the census returns were made available on websites, those of our ancestors whose work took them away from home were difficult to find. For example, in 1841 George Wakefield was a young boy in Lincolnshire, but he became a groom and moved long distances as a servant with aristocratic families. In 1851 he was a servant in Hampshire, in 1861 he was back in Lincolnshire working as a groom, in 1871 he was a groom in Cumberland, and in 1881 he was a servant in Devon, while his wife and children were at home in London. The ages and birthplace recorded on the census returns confirm his identity.

REAL LIVES
census figures and the lives behind them

For Allen David Williams the chance sighting of a census return sparked a passionate interest in his own family history. He was visiting South Marston in Wiltshire in 1987 when a centenary exhibition at the local school caught his eye. Inside he examined a copy of local returns from the 1881 census.

Prominent among the names was his great-grandfather, Elias Williams—a carpenter—listed with his wife and seven children. Among them was Alfred Owen Williams, who became a writer and poet.

From a biography of Alfred published in 1945, Allen knew a little of his family history. But the 1881 census supplied a missing link that was to help him to explore his Welsh roots. It revealed that Elias had been born not in Conwy, north Wales, as stated in the biography, but nearby in a place that came under a different administrative district.

Armed with this information, Allen set off for Wales. At the Caernarfon record office, he scoured local returns of the 1851 census and finally found details of his great-great-grandparents—David and Ann Williams, farming 20 acres—and Elias, their youngest son.

Allen went on to find the farm where his great-grandfather Elias had lived as a child. Since then he has met distant relatives, uncovered a family biography in Welsh, and found another ancestor, John Jones, who was in his time the most prominent preacher in north Wales.

Great-grandparents—soon to part
Allen discovered that Elias Williams (below right) had abandoned his family two years after the 1881 census, leaving his wife Elizabeth (below left) heavily in debt. To support her children she took in needlework, sold newspapers and helped with the local haymaking.

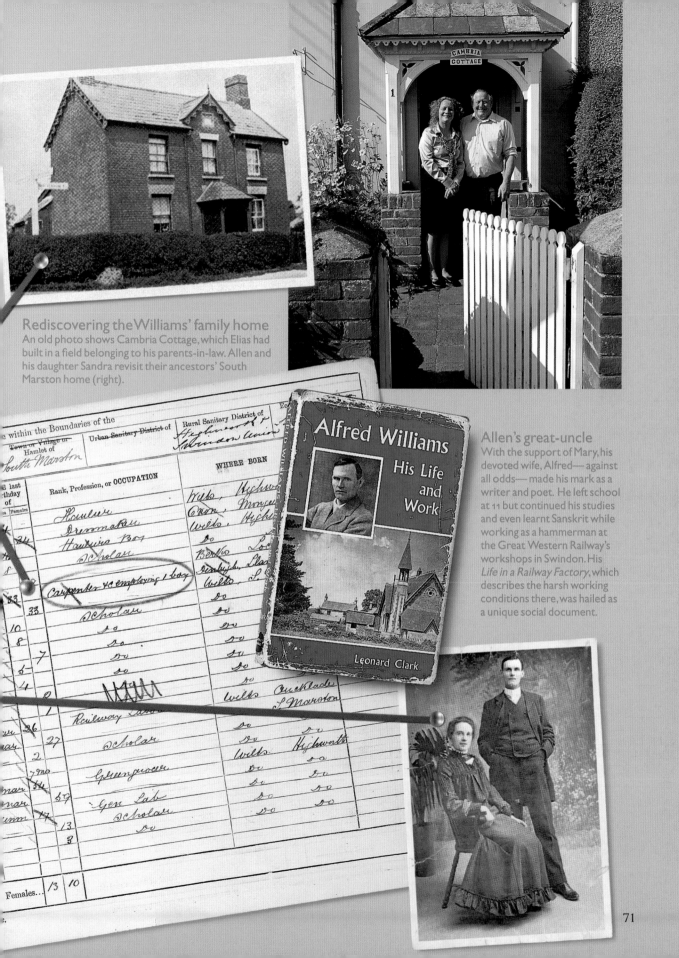

Rediscovering the Williams' family home

An old photo shows Cambria Cottage, which Elias had built in a field belonging to his parents-in-law. Allen and his daughter Sandra revisit their ancestors' South Marston home (right).

Allen's great-uncle

With the support of Mary, his devoted wife, Alfred— against all odds— made his mark as a writer and poet. He left school at 11 but continued his studies and even learnt Sanskrit while working as a hammerman at the Great Western Railway's workshops in Swindon. His *Life in a Railway Factory*, which describes the harsh working conditions there, was hailed as a unique social document.

the census
interpreting information

If you can recognise the clues, a page of census returns will add much to your knowledge of 19th-century ancestors and can extend your family research back one or more generations

What you see on a page of returns varies according to the census year. The returns for 1841, the first full census, differ most as the information is much less specific than in later census years.

In rural areas you may see minimal addresses such as 'top of the hill' or 'by the church'. This may be enough, as you can usually look through the returns of a small place quite quickly to find the family you need and the search may prove useful if you happen to discover related families at the same time.

Town addresses can be puzzling, especially if you are not familiar with the area. As towns expanded, more houses were built, street names changed and houses were renumbered. To further complicate

a page of the returns

On screen the census return for your forebears will probably look much like this 1871 page— reference RG 10/5159 f14r—for a small Northumberland community. Among the boxed headings at the top, you will see the town or village where your family lived. The enumerator had to note the civil parish and the township, village or hamlet. Ecclesiastical divisions are not particularly relevant to a census search. Stamped on the top right-hand side of every other microfilmed page is the folio number (in this case, 14), which forms the last part of the reference 'f14r' that guides you to this particular place in the returns. The printed number (here 'Page 7') merely denotes a page of the original enumeration book.

Name
The surname may appear to be misspelt as people unused to writing spelt their names in different ways. Enumerators also made mistakes and some residents who refused to give names were listed as 'unknown'.

* Civil Parish [or Township] of	City or Municipal Borough of	Munic

Corsenside Parish

No. of Schedule	ROAD, STREET, &c., and No. or NAME of HOUSE	HOUSES		NAME and Sur Perso
		In-habit-ed	Unin-habited (U.), or Building (B.)	
24	Woodburn			Robert
25	Woodburn	1		John Ga
				Elizabeth
	Woodhouse		1(u)	
26	Woodhouse	1		Nicholas
				Elizabeth
				Annie
27	Woodhouse	1		James
				Elizabeth
				Margaret
				George

Address
House numbers were often omitted and others changed between censuses as many streets were renumbered to a new system of 'odds' and 'evens' in the late 19th century. As a result, you may have to search an entire road or street to find a family.

matters, the enumerator did not necessarily record a street of houses in house number order. He had to make sure he did not miss out houses but he could choose his own route and decide, perhaps, to cover part of a long street and then go up and down a side street before continuing with the long street.

what was an 'institution'?

Some of your ancestors may be found in what the census calls an 'institution'. This could be any large establishment such as a barracks, a prison, a hospital or a workhouse that contained sufficient people (roughly 200) to make it large enough to be an enumeration district in its own right. The inmates

of these establishments are listed—sometimes only by their initials—together with their guardians, such as officers, warders or medical staff. The entries appear on special pages without an address column.

Institutions are always put at the end of the district in which they lie, and in a large town there will be several of them. This may be the place to look if you cannot find your ancestors elsewhere.

your ancestors' work

An occupation may seem to differ from census to census because people sometimes had several jobs or may have described their work in a different way. In the first full census, in 1841, occupations were

Age
A standard cartoon joke of Victorian times was the lady lying about her age. To verify ages, you should compare them with civil registration documents. For 1841 ages were rounded down to the nearest five years for those over 15.

Where born
This is crucial information that may extend a search back a further generation. In 1841, a code was used—'Y' for yes, the county of current residence; 'N' for no, but elsewhere in England or Wales; 'I' for born in Ireland; 'S' for born in Scotland; and 'F' for born abroad. From 1851 exact place names were listed in the 'where born' column, as in this example.

Disabilities
This information appears from 1851. 'Imbecile or Idiot' and 'Lunatic' are listed from 1871. The final column was not always completed even if the residents were infirm.

...mentioned Houses are situate within the Boundaries of the

Page 7

14

Parliamentary Borough of		Town of	Village or Hamlet, &c, of	Local Board, or [Improvement Commissioners District] of	Ecclesiastical District of
County of South North'd			Woodburn		

RELATION to Head of Family	CON-DITION	AGE of Males / Females	Rank, Profession, or OCCUPATION	WHERE BORN	Whether 1. Deaf-and-Dumb 2. Blind 3. Imbecile or Idiot 4. Lunatic
			Part 1		
Lodger	Unm	36	Station Agent	North'd North Shields	
Head	Mar	56	Miner	Do Whitton	
Wife	Mar	57		Do Corsenside	
Head	Mar	60	Shepherd	Do Elsdon	
Wife	Mar	59		Do Falstone	
Daur	Unm	20	Dressmaker	Do Throckrington	
Head	Mar	35	Stone Mason	Do Chollerton	
Wife	Mar	38		Do Elsdon	
Daur	Unm	9	Scholar	Do Kirkharle	
	Unm	7	Do	Corsenside	

Relation
From 1851 the column indicating the occupant's relationship to the head of household may extend your knowledge of the family by revealing names of visiting relatives or members of a different generation who were living in the home.

Occupation
In the 1841 census occupations were vague and generalised but became more specific, as can be seen from the above 1871 return. Children were usually listed as 'scholars', and a range of obsolete trades appear such as 'mercer' or 'washerwoman'.

generalised into categories such as 'agricultural', 'industrial' or 'independent' (of independent means). Later, more occupations were listed and an employer had to say how many people he employed.

all members of the household

Each household was defined by a new schedule number. The enumerator also indicated the last name in a household with one diagonal penstroke on the vertical line before the name column, and the last name in a building with a double penstroke.

At one address you may find several households, including family members, guests, servants, lodgers and boarders. Boarders differed slightly from lodgers; both paid rent but only boarders took their meals with the family.

relation to head of family

Within each household you will find only one head of household; everyone else is described by their relationship to him or her. Changes of name do not always indicate a separate family as the children listed may be from an earlier marriage of their mother; although not listed as such, other people living in the house may be related.

In the 1841 census there is no relationship column. Although names and ages provide clues, you should confirm how household members were related from later censuses and other records.

the place of birth

Birthplaces (noted precisely from 1851 onwards) are of key importance. They can take your research back a generation and may also tell an intriguing story. A wife might simply have left the family home to stay with her mother for the birth. But if, for instance, the birthplace for every child differs and one is a recognisable army town such as Aldershot,

it may be that the father was at one time in the army and posted to different barracks around the country or even abroad, taking a growing family with him.

Born abroad In the 1841 census the only clue to an overseas birthplace is an 'F' for foreign parts. In 1851 you will be given the country of birth and 'B.S.' if the person was a British subject. In 1861 and later you will get a place, and country of birth and, if the person is British, 'B.S.' and whether they were British at birth or naturalised—abbreviated to 'NAT'—which should not be misread as 'NOT'.

If the birthplaces of a man and his wife reveal that he was British and she was foreign, the birthplaces of the children can tell you much about the movement of the family and may indicate where the couple met

ONE FAMILY—TWO ADDRESSES

The 1881 census page for Queen Head Street in Islington, London, produces interesting clues about the inhabitants of two adjacent households at nos. 18 and 20.

The names Bastard and Brown appear at both addresses. At no. 18 William Bastard is head of household and has three stepchildren whose surname is Brown, which suggests that his wife, Emma, had been married before.

At no. 20, Jane and Sarah Brown and Lizzie Bastard, who are older than the other children, are listed as lodgers. It seems that no. 18 was not big enough to house all five Brown stepchildren as well as William Bastard's two sons and one daughter. As a result, two of the Brown girls and the eldest Bastard daughter lodged next door with the Norths, close enough to take meals with their family.

and married. If a man and his wife have a foreign surname but were born in Britain, one or both may be descendants of earlier immigrant families.

Changing foreign names Early foreign origins may be masked, as many immigrants altered surnames that were difficult to pronounce or simplified them to sound English. Others were translated to the English equivalent such as the German *Schwartz* to 'Black'. See Regional & foreign names, page 303.

Links to occupation Changing birthplaces may also indicate that economic need had forced the family to move in search of work. This can be mapped by looking at birthplaces and occupations within the family in different censuses.

A man's occupation may also explain why a couple were born far apart. If, for instance, your ancestor was a London man and a basketmaker and his wife was born in Norfolk, they probably met when he went there to get his wicker supplies.

A mobile workforce If a married couple from different parts of Britain are listed far from their birthplaces, both may have left home to find employment. In the 19th century both men and women travelled widely in search of work.

By comparing census years you may find that, for instance, a couple met while in domestic service in the same neighbourhood. It can be intriguing to figure out how your ancestors might have met by piecing together census clues.

Expanding population
Urban areas were growing fast during the 19th century. Between 1841 and 1891 the population of Greater London rose from 2.2 million to 5.6 million, while Birmingham's population more than trebled, and Leeds, Manchester and Newcastle all doubled their numbers. The government calculated that more than 3 million people lived in overcrowded city tenements in 1891. The most densely packed cities were London, Newcastle and Sunderland; Westmorland was the least populated area of England.

75

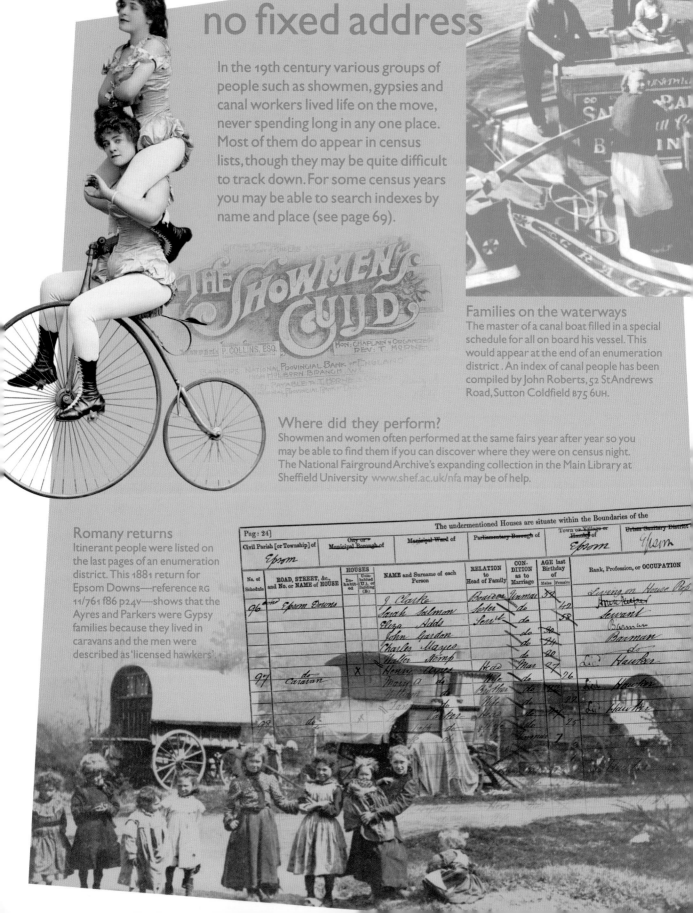

no fixed address

In the 19th century various groups of people such as showmen, gypsies and canal workers lived life on the move, never spending long in any one place. Most of them do appear in census lists, though they may be quite difficult to track down. For some census years you may be able to search indexes by name and place (see page 69).

Families on the waterways

The master of a canal boat filled in a special schedule for all on board his vessel. This would appear at the end of an enumeration district. An index of canal people has been compiled by John Roberts, 52 St Andrews Road, Sutton Coldfield B75 6UH.

Where did they perform?

Showmen and women often performed at the same fairs year after year so you may be able to find them if you can discover where they were on census night. The National Fairground Archive's expanding collection in the Main Library at Sheffield University www.shef.ac.uk/nfa may be of help.

Romany returns

Itinerant people were listed on the last pages of an enumeration district. This 1881 return for Epsom Downs—reference RG 11/761 f86 p24v—shows that the Ayres and Parkers were Gypsy families because they lived in caravans and the men were described as 'licensed hawkers'.

broken families
discovering lost links

The footsteps of some ancestors grow faint where family ties have been severed. But look in the right places and you may pick up the trail

One child too many

Before cheap, reliable birth control became widely available in the mid 20th century, many parents found themselves struggling to feed their large broods. This mother and father in the East End of London contemplate the effect on family life of another baby. With four mouths to feed already, the baby's father looks dolefully at a handful of pawn tickets. Tickets were issued by a pawnbroker for goods left as security against a loan of money. An extra baby could drive parents into debt or destitution; sometimes acute poverty meant that a child had to be given away to foster parents or to other branches of the family to be cared for.

War, abandonment, divorce, illegitimacy, adoption, fostering and simply losing touch can all pull family members apart. Your search may reveal ancestors whose origins have been hidden for religious, legal or social reasons, or because records are not centralised, indexed or easily accessible. With persistence, and some good fortune, you may be able to piece together enough information to reforge that broken link.

It should be possible to trace a fairly recent family 'fracture' as family matters are now recorded in an array of official documents. But finding them may need much research, and the emotional, moral and legal issues raised will involve sensitivity and tact.

illegitimate forebears

Many family trees include illegitimate children. A number of sources may give clues to their identity, or that of the father:

☞ Parish registers, which began in the 16th century (see page 86), recorded illegitimate births in terms such as base born, bastard or natural child. In most cases the father's name was omitted.

☞ From 1837, when births had to be registered in civil register offices (see page 51), the absence of a father's name from a certificate usually indicated that a child was illegitimate.

☞ Marriage records may reveal the wedding of a mother shortly after a child's birth, but the husband may not be the biological father. Perhaps that child had a different surname at birth.

☞ Court records, including those of quarter sessions and ecclesiastical courts, may include proceedings for a maintenance order against a father. Some parish records include indemnity or bastardy bonds, which committed the father to pay a form of child maintenance. You may also find a father's name in settlement examinations (page 151).

adopted children

Until the Adoption of Children Act 1926, children in England and Wales were often adopted informally without leaving any documentary evidence. These arrangements were closer to what we call fostering or guardianship today, and it was common for children to be raised by grandparents, aunts or uncles. As illegitimacy was sometimes disguised in this way, you might find an adopted child with the surname of a family member, such as a married aunt.

Adoption records The introduction of formal adoption on 1 January 1927 created a mass of documentation. Adoptions in England and Wales since that date are recorded in the Adopted Children Register by the General Register Office. Anyone may see the indexes, which are held at the Family Records Centre. They are arranged in year order by the surname assumed at the time of adoption. See DIRECTORY for addresses.

Copies of adoption certificates can be bought by post, telephone or email from the General Register Office or in person from the Family Records Centre. The certificate includes the child's adoptive, but not previous, name; its date of birth; the name and address of the adoptive parents; the date of the adoption order and name of the court that made it.

For adoptions in Northern Ireland since 1931, contact the General Register Office for Northern Ireland. The public cannot consult adoption records in the Republic of Ireland. For adoptions in Scotland since 1930 contact the National Archives of Scotland; the Scottish Adopted Children Register is held at the General Register Office for Scotland. See DIRECTORY for addresses.

Birth certificates In England, Wales and Northern Ireland, adopted people over 18, and in Scotland over 16, can apply for their original birth certificate. This shows the names and addresses of the biological parents, or of the mother only, and is marked 'Adopted'. In the Republic of Ireland, children at present have no automatic right to see their original birth certificate.

If you were adopted in England or Wales, contact the Adoptions Section of the General Register

Office (see DIRECTORY). If your adoption order was made before 12 November 1975, you must talk with a counsellor before a certificate is issued. If you were adopted after that date, counselling is optional. In Northern Ireland you can apply to the General Register Office for Northern Ireland; you will receive counselling. If you were adopted in Scotland, your birth certificate is available from the General Register Office for Scotland; you will be advised to seek counselling.

Family historians who are not the adopted person would have to apply to the court that made the adoption order for permission to seek information from adoption records. Success is likely to be slim.

Finding and contacting birth parents Even when an adopted person has obtained a copy of his or her birth certificate, there are still practical and emotional issues to tackle before contact can be made with biological parents. The General Register

There are more than half a million adopted people in Britain, many of whom were given up by their birth parents only after much soul-searching. Once a child has been adopted, he or she becomes a permanent member of a new family, sharing a surname and receiving a new birth certificate bearing the adopted name. When adoptees reach their late teens they can, if they wish, try to find their birth parents with the help of agency records and adoption records.

BECOMING PART OF A NEW FAMILY

Unearthing the past
A nurse from a hostel for adoptive babies prepares to hand over an infant to its new parents in 1938 (left). For people adopted before 1927, when formal adoption was introduced, it is difficult to trace their birth parents. Les Davis (below right) was adopted in 1928 and did discover the identity of his. Both parents had died, but family snaps show Les's striking resemblance to his father, Horace.

Horace Moles at the age of 23 in 1920

Les Davis aged 23 in 1950

broken families

Office has maintained a voluntary Adoption Contact Register for England and Wales since May 1991. There are two registers: one listing adoptees, and another containing the names of the adopted person's biological parents, other close blood relatives and the name and address of an adult who has agreed to act as a go-between. Contact is arranged only if everyone agrees to it.

In Scotland an Adoption Contact Register known as Birthlink (see DIRECTORY) was set up in 1984 to provide a confidential point of contact between adoptees and their birth mothers.

The General Register Office for Northern Ireland also keeps an Adoption Contact Register dating from 19 February 1996. In the Republic of Ireland adopted persons wishing to seek their birth mothers should approach the adoption agency that handled their case; for more help, contact the Adoption Board, Shelbourne House, Shelbourne Road, Ballsbridge, Dublin 4.

Advice on tracing members of your biological family is available from the National Organisation for the Counselling of Adoptees and Parents (NORCAP—see DIRECTORY). Social services departments will tell you whether there is a local voluntary help group for those involved in adoption.

Biological parents are not usually told the identity of adoptive parents, or their child's new name. It is not illegal for them to try to trace an adopted child, but there are no public agencies that will help.

children in foster homes

Until the late 19th century, when legislation took children out of workhouses and into homes, fostering was generally an informal arrangement made by verbal agreement. Guardians, tutors and others were sometimes appointed in wills to supervise youngsters in a way we would recognise as fostering.

Today fostering is controlled by local social services departments under the Children Act 1989, and biological parents are usually told where their children are. Records are kept until the fostered child reaches his or her majority (18 years since 1973, 21 years until then) and are retained by the local authority for 75 years. The first point of contact for tracing fostered family members is the local authority social services department. If you are trying to get in touch with a close relative who is fostered, the local authority might agree to forward your letter without revealing the child's whereabouts. Fostering agencies such as Barnardo's (see DIRECTORY) also keep records.

lost and found

The abandonment of children in a place where they could easily be found was widespread by the 18th century. These babies, known as foundlings, were often born to young women, and the practice was usually the result of illegitimacy, poverty or both.

Foundlings were frequently named after the place where they were abandoned. Often this was a church, and the Christian name given might be that of the patron saint, or the clergyman who christened the child. The surname usually identified the locality where the child was found: Porch, Church and Bridge, for instance, were common.

You are unlikely to discover the identities of the biological parents of a foundling. You may, however, find a reference to your ancestor in the following:

☞ records of foundling hospitals, such as Thomas Coram's Hospital, whose records are at the London Metropolitan Archives (see DIRECTORY)

☞ parish registers (see Parish records, pages 86–99)
☞ poor law or workhouse records (see Poor & destitute, pages 150–5)
☞ apprenticeship indentures (see Companies & trades, pages 139–42).

From 1837 until 1977 foundlings were listed without names in birth indexes after the letter 'Z'. Since then they have been recorded by the General Register Office in its Register of Abandoned Children. The child's date and place of discovery, sex and given names are listed.

artificial insemination

About 1500 children a year are born in Britain as a result of artificial insemination by donor (AID). Since 1942, women have not been told the identity of the donor, and the donor has not been informed of any children conceived from his sperm. Since 1991 the Human Fertilisation and Embryology Authority (see DIRECTORY) has maintained a confidential register of donors, recipients and children. If asked, the Authority must tell anyone over the age of 18 whether he or she was born as a result of AID, and over 16s whether they are related to anyone they intend to marry. It is an offence, however, at present to reveal to children the identity of a donor.

The birth certificates of children born by AID may list the mother's partner as the father, so, unless parents want to reveal to a child the role of AID in his or her conception, he or she will have no reason to make any enquiry to the Authority.

The kindly captain

Thomas Coram, an 18th-century sea captain, made a fortune in the colonies. On his return to London, he was shocked at the number of babies abandoned in the city, and used his wealth to set up England's first foundling hospital. Coram's friend George Frideric Handel gave recitals to raise money, and composed a hospital anthem. The Coram girls above, in uniform, are attending a chapel service in 1941. Destitute mothers tied tokens (below) to their children, to identify them if they should ever return.

TAKING IT FURTHER

♦ *Where to Find Adoption Records* (Georgina Stafford, British Association for Adoption and Fostering, 2001).
♦ *Search Guide for Adopted People in Scotland* (Birthlink Adoption Counselling Centre at Family Care, HMSO, 1997).
♦ www.adoptionsearchreunion.org.uk

broken families
searching for lost identity

If you meet a blank wall when looking for members of a broken family, do not despair: there are ways to take your search beyond the available records

You may be unable to find sufficient information to trace an elusive family member in the usual records, such as registrations of birth, marriage and death. Photographs, deeds, wills and stories passed down through generations can offer clues, but it may be worth broadening your view, and perhaps even publicising your search. If you think that the 'missing' person is still alive, you may consider using a specialist search service.

Broadening the search It can be useful to review what you know about your relative. Create a list of questions that might provide additional clues about what or where to research next. For example:

KEY SOURCES OF INFORMATION
♦ Records of educational and professional bodies.
♦ Responses to media publicity.
♦ Specialist search services.
SEE DIRECTORY ➤

☞ Might a child have been brought up by grand-parents, uncles and aunts or an older sibling and, if so, did the child change its surname?
☞ If a woman remarried, what did she give as her previous surname? Was it her maiden name or the name of her divorced husband?

forced child migration

From the late 19th century to 1967, charities such as Barnardo's and the Catholic Child Welfare Council ran migration schemes. Nearly 150,000 youngsters from British children's homes were sent abroad, mainly to Australia, Canada and New Zealand, to populate these countries with 'good British stock'. Many children went without their parents' consent, some while they were in temporary care during a family crisis. Their true identity was concealed and often they did not even know their date of birth. In 1987 the Child Migrants Trust (see DIRECTORY) was set up. It has since counselled and reunited hundreds of families.

A fresh start
With luck a bright future awaited these Barnardo's children, shown here with popular comedian Tommy Trinder on 20 March 1956, as they were about to set sail for a 'better' life in Australia. Some child migrants, however, did not fare well. Schooling was often sparse and many had to work long hours and endure physical abuse. 'We had no shoes. We worked in our bare feet. Every day. Winter and summer,' one man recalls.

☞ Could a change in the spelling of a name, or the Anglicisation of a name, disguise kinship?

☞ Might a birth or wedding have taken place earlier or later than you thought?

☞ Was your ancestor a migrant? (See On the move, pages 236–71.)

PROFESSIONAL AND STUDENT LISTS Many professional bodies, schools and universities have records that could help, such as membership lists, perhaps published as directories, student lists and yearbooks. If information is confidential, some establishments will try to contact members on your behalf, without revealing their whereabouts.

FUNERAL REPORTS Some newspapers publish lists of mourners at funerals. In these you may find family members, who are often identified by their relationship to the deceased.

Announcing your search Some regional and local newspapers, television stations and web sites offer space to publicise your search free of charge.

Family history societies (see DIRECTORY under Federation of Family History Societies) are often generous with practical help and information.

Specialist search services The Salvation Army's Family Tracing Service (see DIRECTORY) may search for close adult relatives, but not divorced partners and anyone separated by illegitimacy or adoption. The service starts more than 4000 enquiries a year

'I've never had a sense of belonging to anyone. Just being able to say "my mother", "my father" or "my sister" once would be terrific.'
Pamela Smedley, a child migrant

and claims an 80 per cent success rate, although you will be put in touch only if the relative agrees to it.

Traceline (see DIRECTORY) helps applicants over 18 to locate lost family and friends, although it will not undertake searches if it thinks contact may be disruptive. If a 'missing' person is found, Traceline asks his or her permission to forward a letter from the applicant. If that person has died in England or Wales, it will advise on death registration details.

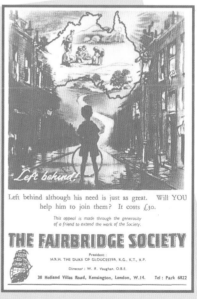

Left behind although his need is just as great. Will YOU help him to join them? It costs £30.

This appeal is made through the generosity of a friend to extend the work of the Society.

THE FAIRBRIDGE SOCIETY

President:
H.R.H. THE DUKE OF GLOUCESTER, K.G., K.T., K.P.

Director: W. R. Vaughan, O.B.E.

38 Holland Villas Road, Kensington, London, W.14. Tel : Park 6822

Tugging at the heartstrings
Generous public donations helped fund charities, such as The Fairbridge Society that shipped off Britain's 'orphans' to train as farmers in the colonies.

blessed rites

Tracing your family beyond the early 19th century in the British Isles will lead you to **parish records** of baptisms, marriages and burials, introduced in 1538 by Henry VIII and still kept today. Forebears who fail to appear in parish registers may have been Nonconformists, Roman Catholics or Jews—**beliefs apart**—who held their own church, chapel or synagogue records. The thrill of discovering an ancestor's grave or tomb may be doubled by an inscription—**in memoriam**—that helps to fill in gaps in a family tree.

A London society wedding in 1958

parish records
starting your search

Old parish records provide vital evidence of your ancestors' baptisms, marriages and burials. Detailed indexes and guides can help you to track them down

Parish registers—the Church's records of baptisms, marriages and burials—date from the 16th century and are key to finding out about your family's past before the introduction of civil records (see page 51). If your ancestors stayed in one place for centuries you may be able to find generations of your family among the records of just one church.

Although many of the records have been put on microfilm or microfiche, occasionally you may experience the thrill of handling an original register that recorded an event in your ancestor's life.

The ancient parishes Since medieval times, the ecclesiastical parish has been an area with a church authorised for baptisms, marriages and burials, and whose residents are under the spiritual care of a clergyman of the established Church.

The area covered by a parish varied widely. In a city it might include only a few streets, but in a rural area it could extend over hundreds of square miles.

Confirming the parish boundaries
The people of St Albans take part in the annual ceremony of 'beating the bounds' in 1913. Walking the boundaries of the parish to confirm their exact position is an old tradition that still continues in some areas. Before maps and when few could read, the march ensured that everyone knew the parish limits.

In 1821, when there were about 11,000 parishes in England and Wales, the city of Norwich had 37 parishes while the county of Lancashire had 66. The number of parishes, and therefore churches, increased rapidly in the 19th century, particularly in the expanding industrial towns.

Maps identifying ancient parishes can help you to decide which registers to search. County and city record offices often have parish maps for their local areas. *The Phillimore Atlas and Index of Parish Registers* (ed. C.R. Humphery-Smith, Phillimore, 3rd ed., 2003) contains a complete set of maps for each pre-1974 county of England and Wales, together with ten maps for the Scottish counties, showing the boundaries of parishes up to about 1832. It also includes the dates of the earliest surviving registers.

how much material survives

Parish records, which are still kept today, first became mandatory in England and Wales in 1538. In that year an injunction was issued requiring every church to keep a book or register to record the date of each wedding, baptism and burial, together with the names of those married, baptised or buried.

Few Welsh but several hundred English registers survive from the 16th century, including a few complete sets of registers from 1538 to the present day.

Older parish registers for England are usually held in county or city record offices—though some remain at the parish church. Welsh registers can be found either in the National Library of Wales or in county record offices (see DIRECTORY). Current and recent registers throughout Britain will, in most cases, still be kept by the parish.

As the registers are scattered, always contact a record office in advance to make sure it holds those you require. In England and Wales, if a register has been lost you may find missing information in copies called bishops' transcripts (see pages 97–99).

Church of Ireland records In Ireland, where the established church was the (Anglican) Church of Ireland until its disestablishment in 1869, registers

were not required until 1634. The earliest, for St John's Church, Dublin, dates from 1619. Elsewhere most registers were kept from the late 18th century.

After 1870, nearly 1000 Irish parish registers were sent to the Public Record Office in Dublin. Luckily not all were deposited and some incumbents had made transcripts, as only four were saved when the record office burned down in 1922.

Most surviving parish records, copies and indexes, are held at the Public Record Office of Northern Ireland, the National Archives of Ireland or the Representative Church Body Library (see DIRECTORY). The library holds the records of more than 650 parishes now in the Irish Republic.

Scotland's parish records Also known as old parish registers or old parochial registers, the earliest date from 1553. Fewer than 20 registers survive from before 1600; some only begin in 1690 when Presbyterians achieved dominance over Episcopalians and became the established Church in Scotland. Many parishes did not have death or burial registers and some had no registers at all. Following

KEY SOURCES OF INFORMATION
- English parish records in county record offices or their metropolitan equivalent.
- Welsh parish records at the National Library of Wales or Welsh county record offices.
- Most Scottish parish records to 1855 at the General Register Office for Scotland.
- Church of Ireland baptismal and burial records to 1870 and marriage records to 1845 in the National Archives, the Representative Church Body Library and the Public Record Office of Northern Ireland. Some originals held locally.
- Bishops' transcripts (copies of parish registers) for English parishes in county or city record offices; those for Wales in the National Library of Wales.
- Throughout Britain, 20th-century records (and occasionally older ones) still at the parish church.

SEE DIRECTORY ➤

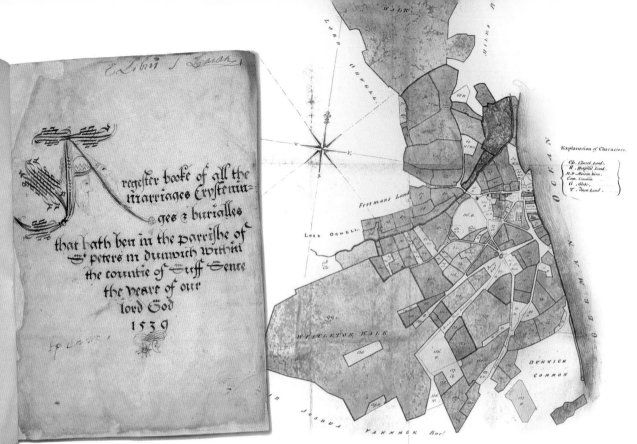

One of Britain's earliest parish registers

From 1538 Dunwich, like other parishes in England and Wales, recorded its baptisms, marriages and burials in a special register (above). The map (above right) shows part of the Suffolk parish in 1801, when the North Sea was known as the German Ocean.

the introduction of civil registration in 1855, the old registers were housed in the General Register Office for Scotland (see DIRECTORY). Some 4000 volumes from 1000 parishes were deposited. For a searchable index of the registers, see the Scots Origins web site www.scotsorigins.com

narrowing down your search

You may have some idea of the parish in which your ancestors are recorded, but to find out where the records are held it is helpful to consult published indexes or other reference works. The best starting points are:

☞ The *National Index of Parish Registers* (NIPR), a continuing county series that

the Society of Genealogists (see DIRECTORY) began publishing in 1966. For the society's own holdings, see the web site www.sog.org.uk/prc

☞ Local record offices for catalogues listing the parish records they hold.

☞ Local family history societies, which may have indexes and will know where copies, originals or transcripts are held.

☞ Family History Centres (see DIRECTORY), which hold copies of the International Genealogical Index (IGI, see pages 100–1), a huge work, containing abbreviated entries of baptisms and marriages for many parishes.

Other important sources The many other indexes and transcripts that can help you to track down entries for your ancestors include:

COUNTY INDEXES Many indexes have been compiled, mostly for marriages, although the area and period they cover varies greatly. A local family history society or record office can tell you which are available for the county and parishes that interest you. Many are listed in the Gibson Guides: *Marriage and Census Indexes for Family Historians* (J. Gibson, FFHS, 2000) and *Specialist Indexes for Family Historians* (J. Gibson, FFHS, 2000).

BOYD'S MARRIAGE INDEX Percival Boyd (1866–1955) compiled a 534 volume index of marriage entries from many English parish registers by county. Marriages are indexed by the bride's and the groom's name. The original volumes are held at the Society of Genealogists. Guildhall Library (see DIRECTORY) has a complete microfiche copy and local record offices often have copies of sections relevant to their area. Boyd's does not cover all counties, or all parishes within a given county.

NATIONAL BURIALS INDEX The Federation of Family History Societies (see DIRECTORY) is compiling a National Burials Index from parish, Nonconformist and cemetery burials registers. The third edition contains more than 18 million records on a single CD. The ultimate aim is to provide a computerised search facility for burials similar to that for baptisms and marriages in the IGI. For a small fee, participating family history societies will usually search their local databases for you.

TRANSCRIPTIONS Many local societies are also transcribing and indexing parish registers, again particularly marriage registers, usually up to 1837 when civil registration began. These can often be bought as booklets or on microfiche and are noted in the current publications of FFHS member societies.

The library of the Irish Genealogical Research Society (see DIRECTORY) holds transcripts of some registers for around ten Irish dioceses, including Cloyne, Cork, Dublin, and Ross and Limerick.

INTERNET AND CD SEARCHES Lists of parishes will be seen on the relevant county pages on GENUKI at www.genuki.org.uk/big.

The Mormon Church's British Isles Vital Records Index supplements the IGI with about 10 million births/baptisms and around 2 million marriages; see www.ancestor-search.info/SRC-IGI.htm.

Exploring the registers For England and Wales, the records are generally better organised and thus easier to use after 1813 (see pages 90–91), when the law decreed that baptisms, marriages and burials should be entered in greater detail in separate registers. Before this, registers often contained a mixture of the three events, although marriages had a separate register from 1754 (see page 94). Parish registers deposited in an English or Welsh record office can usually be examined free of charge. To view the Scottish old parish (or parochial) registers at the General Register Office for Scotland, there is a daily charge (which also covers any searches of Scotland's civil registration records and census returns, which are held in the same building). There is also a charge for using its Scotlands People web site.

> *4 Oct 1823 Mary Swaby dau. Frances Barker, husband transported, parish of Doncaster, married woman, bapt…*
> *13 Oct 1826 Elizabeth Smithson born when her mother was only 13 years old bur. age 1*
> Revd A.C. Verelst, Wadworth, Yorks

Searching in the parish In certain cases you may discover that a parish church retains its old registers or you may wish to investigate a recent event. If you are searching in person, the minister or parochial church council will usually let you see a register but will not necessarily allow you to photograph or photocopy entries. For English and Welsh churches, there is a set scale of fees for searching and you should first make an appointment.

Some parishes appoint a local archivist to handle enquiries about their records or to be present while the researcher is looking at them, again on payment of a fee. If the church authorities carry out research in response to a postal enquiry, they are also entitled to charge for time taken.

Crockford's Clerical Directory, available in most libraries, provides a list of the established Church parishes in all parts of the British Isles, together with the names and addresses of their ministers.

parish records
registers after 1813

Parish registers took their present form from 1813, becoming clearer and easier to use. They are vital to family research before the introduction of civil records

The first parish registers you encounter will probably be from the 19th and 20th centuries. Your search may be prompted by the discovery of family documents such as a baptism certificate that names your ancestor's church or a memorial card that notes the place of burial.

Many people prefer to extract as much detail as they can from civil records (see pages 50–61) before they tackle parish registers. But the two sources can complement each other, helping to confirm your research. A parish register may also record some additional family information. If your ancestors continued to be members of the established Church throughout the 19th century, it may be quicker and cheaper to find members of your family in parish registers rather than consulting civil records and buying copies of birth, marriage or death registration certificates.

registers adopt their present form

In 1813 Rose's Act transformed parish records in England and Wales. The Act required each parish to buy from the 'King's Printer' separate books of paper or parchment for baptisms, marriages and burials—the first time that individual books and printed forms had been required for each event.

The Act also stipulated that these books should be written up and signed at the time of a marriage, and

REGISTERING THE RITES OF PASSAGE

When Baptized.	Child's Christian Name.	Parents Name.		Abode.	Quality, Trade, or Profession.	By whom the Ceremony was performed.		
		Christian.	Surname.					
1829 Feby 15 No. 425.	Edmund son of	James & Leah	Foster.	Abinger	Servant	Fras. Lockey offg Minr		
Decr 14. 1829. No. 426.	Elizabeth daur of	Joseph & Rachel	Stedman	Abinger	Farmer	Wm Margeson offg Minr of Okewood Chapel		
March 1. 1829	William John son of	John & Prescall	Stephens	wootton	Labourer	Fras. Lockey offg Minr		

BAPTISMS solemnized in the Parish of Abinger in the County of Surrey in the Year 1829

Baptism register

A new era for parish registers
The clear format for entries after 1813, as in the 1829 baptism register above, makes it much easier for family historians to identify their ancestors and pick out vital details. A separate marriage register had been required by law since 1754.

Signing the marriage register

within seven days of a baptism or a burial. This ruling introduced the clear, standard format that is still in use today, replacing the confusing inconsistencies in the record-keeping of earlier centuries.

more detail is added

Your several times great-grandmother, living when Queen Victoria came to the throne, would still recognise an Anglican baptism or burial register today, so similar is the present format.

Marriage registers have remained largely unaltered since 1837, when they were changed to bring them into line with marriage certificates, introduced that year with civil registration. Registers dating from 1837 are still in use in a few parishes.

The information (right) was the minimum required by law following Rose's Act, and included greater detail than had been compulsory before.

You may find entries that provide even more detail. Some clergymen included the date of birth or the mother's maiden name at a baptism (common practice in Scotland but not elsewhere), or the date of death or marital status at burial (and, for a woman, the name of her husband). A clergyman might also embellish his entries with comments on the circumstances of an event (see page 89).

WHAT ROSE'S ACT REQUIRED

BAPTISM
♦ date of baptism
♦ child's Christian name
♦ parents' Christian names and surname
♦ abode
♦ quality (social status, such as 'gentleman'), trade or profession of the parents
♦ by whom the ceremony was performed

MARRIAGE
♦ name and parish of residence of groom
♦ name and parish of residence of bride
♦ when and where the couple were married
♦ whether by banns or licence
♦ whether by consent of parents or guardians
♦ by whom married
♦ signatures of the minister, groom, bride and at least two witnesses

BURIAL
♦ name
♦ abode
♦ when buried
♦ age
♦ by whom ceremony was performed

A record of the dead
Burials, recorded in a separate register from 1813, are particularly important in family history because they give the age of the deceased —or an approximation as figures were sometimes rounded up or down. This information can take you back to a probable year of baptism, possibly in the same or a nearby parish.

Page 89.

BURIALS, in the Parish of *St James's Clerkenwell* at *Pentonville Chapel* in the County of *Middlesex* in the Year 1841

Name.	Abode.	When buried.	Age.	By whom the Ceremony was performed.
Elizabeth Howell No. 705. 110	Collier Street	1841 Novr 17	00	D. Ruell
Nathaniel Stock No. 706. 111	Winchester Street	Novr 17	12 yrs	D. Ruell
Margaret Dyke	Saint Mary Islington	Novr 20	74	D. Ruell

A register of burials for 1841

91

parish records
registers before 1813

1791
1743

> The Register of Haworth containing all the christenings Marriages and Burials which have been Solemnized there in the Church in the year of our Lord 1791 as follows
>
> ### Christenings
>
> #### January
>
> 10 Robert Son of William and Mary Shackleton — — — — — Height
> 10 Mary Daug. of Betty Hartley — — — — — — — — Coat
> 10 William Son of John and Ann Shackleton — — — Mushiles
> ... Daug. of Sally Wood — — — — — — — — Hawarth
> ... Neilsen and Betty Drake — — — — — — — B. Sykes
> ... and Betty Gither — — — — — — — — Lees
>
> #### February
>
> ... John and Martha Pighills — — — Stonymile
> ... and Susan Howcroft — — — — Hawarth
> ... and Elizabeth Gither — — — — — Naylease
> ... and Rebecca Holmes — — — — — Starrs
> ... and Mary Jacker — — — — — Ditto
> ... Oakes — — — — Ditto
> — — — — — J. Head
> ... field

Baptism entries in the Brontë parish

The parish register for Haworth (left) dates from 1791, some 30 years before Patrick Brontë, father of novelists Charlotte, Emily and Anne, became curate at the Church of St Michael and All Angels (bottom left) in the West Yorkshire village. The entries are quite legible, in contrast to earlier registers, when baptisms, marriages and burials were often listed together (in Latin) as they occurred.

What you discover in early parish registers can vary greatly from parish to parish and from year to year. Before Rose's Act, enforced in 1813, there was no consistency in the way church records in England and Wales were kept, and the standard of record-keeping varied enormously.

the earliest registers

The injunction issued in 1538 by Thomas Cromwell, vicar general to Henry VIII, that required every church in England and Wales to enter christenings, weddings and burials in a register, gave rise to records that had a legal and social importance. Elaborate instructions were given for the register's safekeeping, in a coffer with two locks. The key for one was to be held by the minister and the key for the other by the churchwardens.

Entries were to be made each Sunday by the minister in the presence of the churchwardens. Then the book was locked away, using both keys, to ensure that no one person had the opportunity to take it and forge or alter entries. Parish registers were then accepted as legal documents, as they were often the only written evidence that could be produced—especially in inheritance cases—to support the existence of a marriage or the legitimacy of a child.

keeping the books

The parish had to provide and pay for its own register book. These were generally of paper, which was cheap but easily damaged or destroyed. Even so, some parishes could not, or would not, pay for the books and did not purchase one immediately, in some cases not until the 17th century.

In 1598 an Act ordered that the registers be copied into parchment books, which were more durable and more expensive. The wording of the Act was unfortunate. Entries from the old registers were to be copied 'but especially since the first year of Her Majesty's reign', providing an excuse to copy only from 1558 when Elizabeth I came to the throne. As a result, many registers begin that year.

In England you should, in theory, be able to locate baptism, marriage and burial entries for most of your ancestors from at least 1600. But from 1643 to 1660, during the Civil War and the Interregnum, registers were often not properly maintained and a gap may occur. Between 1653 and 1660 marriages became a civil matter, so many church registers of this period do not record them.

How registers varied Because it was not stated how entries should be kept, ministers and parish clerks devised their own formats. In some registers, baptisms, marriages and burials appear in separate columns on the same page. In others the events are grouped separately in different parts of the book, often with marriages in the middle. Many run all three events together in a chronological sequence.

You may sometimes find financial accounts in registers, particularly during periods when a tax was levied on baptisms, marriages and burials.

Reading the registers Because of the expense of parchment or vellum, some ministers used tiny writing. Others filled in any small spaces with events occurring perhaps several years later than the main entries on the page.

When you are examining these records, make sure you have seen all the entries. It is easy to overlook a cramped note scribbled at the bottom of a page saying 'for more baptisms turn back 15 pages', where you may find two or three entered in a small space in the middle of the burials.

Many early registers contained the minimum information required by law, but much depended on the person who wrote up the events. For instance, John Aykrigg, vicar at Thornton in Lonsdale on the

3 July baptised Bridget daughter of Robert Bateson of Thusgill begotten upon the body of Elizabeth Wildman in May within Bentham parish and borne at John Sanders house in Thornton

John Aykrigg, vicar at Thornton in Lonsdale, writing in 1698

Yorkshire-Lancashire border between 1663 and 1708, was relatively sparing with comments about those who lived in the parish. But any entries concerning illegitimate children or non-parishioners were written up in detail in case of disputes about who was responsible for paying the bills.

Handwriting and spelling If you notice that certain entries in a register are written in a larger hand—and often more neatly than the rest—you will usually find that they relate to the clergyman's family or to a local landowning family. A prominent, legible entry is often an indication of social status.

Spelling was not a strong point with many clergymen or their parish clerks, and punctuation was often omitted altogether. If you find entries difficult to read it may be helpful to compare different styles of handwriting of the period (see How to read old handwriting, pages 32–33).

From 1733, the use of Latin in English and Welsh parish registers (the only places where it had been widely used) was discontinued, although Latin was still used in Roman Catholic registers.

Ireland and Scotland Parish registers in Ireland and Scotland frequently start at a later date, survive less often, and contain less information, than those elsewhere in Britain. Scotland has few burial registers. Many of the government statutes concerning parish registers, such as Hardwicke's Marriage Act (see below) passed by the British Parliament in 1753, did not apply to, or were never enforced in Ireland and Scotland unless they involved tax levies.

marriages in the 18th century

The majority of 18th-century parish registers in the Anglican Church were maintained in a similar format to that used in the 16th and 17th centuries. But some changes that were introduced can prove useful for family historians.

Until the early 1700s most marriage entries in registers gave only the names of the couple. It was not uncommon to find even less information, such as 'John Brown married his wife'. But between 1700 and 1720, many registers began to record whether the marriage was by banns or licence.

Banns—the public announcement of a marriage in advance of the event—was the cheaper option. Details of banns were rarely retained before 1754, except in Scotland where a few earlier ones survive.

If the couple sought a marriage licence (see page 98), the associated documents often recorded ages, occupations and places of residence as well as the couple's names.

Registers after 1754 Hardwicke's Marriage Act, which came into force on 25 March 1754 in England and Wales, is often seen as a watershed in the history of Anglican registers. It was titled 'An Act for the better preventing of Clandestine Marriages', and its purpose was to tighten up marriage laws because 'great Mischiefs and Inconveniences' had arisen as a result of clergymen performing marriages in places other than a parish church or chapel. Many of these

marriages had taken place without banns having been called or a licence obtained and were often not recorded—though some were, such as Fleet marriages (see page 98).

The Act was read out in all parish churches and public chapels on various Sundays in 1753, 1754 and 1755 for the benefit of those who could not read or write. Its main provisions were that:

☞ All marriages should be preceded by either the publication of banns on three successive Sundays or by the obtaining of a licence.

☞ Parental consent was necessary for those marrying under the age of 21. (Until 1929 the legal age at which a marriage could take place with such consent was 12 for girls and 14 for boys.)

☞ Marriages and banns were to be recorded in 'proper Books of Vellum, or good and durable Paper', with ruled and numbered pages (to avoid fraudulent entries being added later or pages torn out of the register).

☞ The minister, the couple and two witnesses were to sign the register (or make their marks).

☞ Marriage registers were to be based on the 'Form of Register' shown in the Act. There was no mention of entering marital status for either the bride or groom, or of entering the groom's occupation, so legally there was no requirement to do so. There was also no mention on this as to how marriage banns were to be recorded.

A key benefit of the Act for finding ancestors is that all marriage ceremonies (to have legal standing) had to be conducted in a parish church or chapel and recorded in its register. Therefore, the marriages of Nonconformists should be there with all the others, even if they had an antipathy to the teachings and practices of the established Church. Only Quakers and Jews were exempt, being allowed to marry with their own ceremonies in their own places of worship and to keep their own records (see Nonconformists, pages 102–6, and The Jewish Faith, pages 110–11).

Banns books and marriage registers While some parishes recorded the banns as part of the marriage entry, many parishes purchased a separate book. It is always worth asking whether the banns book has survived, as it may include information not given in the marriage register.

If the couple came from different parishes, the banns book may reveal where a marriage was to take place, as banns should have been read in both parishes. But the existence of banns is only evidence of an intention to marry and does not prove that the marriage took place. You still need to trace the marriage entry to confirm the event.

From 1754 almost all parishes kept a separate marriage register, mostly using a book of printed forms. Many parishes then restructured their existing registers; clerks and vicars would often write baptism entries in the front and then turn the registers upside down to enter burials at the back.

registers full of family detail

In the late 18th century many incumbents began to include more information in a register than was legally required. The extra detail might include, for a baptism, the mother's Christian name and father's occupation, for baptisms and burials the place of residence, and for burials the age of the deceased.

A Yorkshire clergyman, William Dade, introduced a scheme to include details of a child's position in the family (such as 'first son and second child') with the names of all four grandparents and where they lived and, for a burial, details of the deceased's parentage, age and cause of death. His ideas were taken up by William Markham, Archbishop of York, who tried to extend the scheme throughout the diocese of York. 'Dade Registers' may be found between 1770 and 1812, mainly in the north of England, although some examples have also been discovered in Devon, Essex, Norfolk, Surrey and Wiltshire.

In practice, the amount of information you will find depended on the individual clergyman or parish

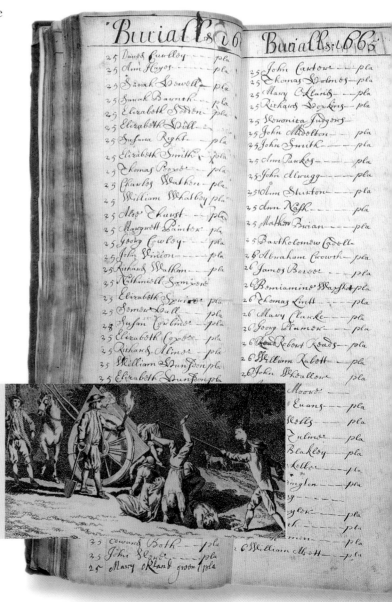

Victims of the Great Plague of 1665
The burial register of St Mary's Church, Whitechapel, records the names of local victims of the Great Plague. In London 100,000 people died and were swiftly buried, an essential measure to prevent further spread of the epidemic. Bodies were despatched with the minimum of ceremony, as depicted in the artist Samuel Wale's grim burial scene at Holywell Lane, Shoreditch.

clerk, and on bishops who sometimes instructed their clergy as to which details they should record.

The effect of taxing entries In 1783 a duty of threepence was put on every baptism, marriage or burial recorded in English, Welsh and Scottish registers. Some people avoided the tax by not having their children baptised. After the Act was repealed in 1794, some families had several children baptised together. If you expected—and failed—to find an earlier baptism, it may be worth looking for an older child being baptised with siblings after this date.

Paupers were exempted from the tax, so do not be surprised if your ancestors, who show no other signs of needing parish relief, suddenly appear to be on the breadline. Many clergymen sympathised with those trying to avoid paying the duty.

Some ministers, particularly in Scotland, helped their parishioners to avoid the tax by performing the ceremony but not entering it in the register so that no tax could be claimed. As a result, you may not discover a written record of your ancestor's baptism.

other information in the records

Parish registers may include additional titbits of information that can provide a colourful background to the regular entries. For instance, John Cock, who succeeded John Aykrigg at Thornton in Lonsdale, recorded the weather on 16 March 1719, noting that it was 'Memorable for a prodigious Quantity of Snow falling'. Some registers also mention 'briefs', appeals that were made through the church to raise money for those in need.

Besides the registers, the parish coffer often held other documents associated with the running of the parish. Some, such as records relating to the local poor (see Poor & destitute, pages 150–6), are particularly relevant to family history. Others include vestry minutes, parish accounts, churchwardens' lists, and lists of confirmations and of pew-owners.

TERMS USED IN THE REGISTERS

Latin and other abbreviations like these are often used in parish registers. The text is usually limited to names, dates and a few common Latin words.

aet. [45]	aged [45]
al[ia]s	also, otherwise known as
c[irca]	about/approximately
conj.	married
de	of
d[itt]o	as previous statement
e[odem] d[ie]	the same day
eius	his
f[ilius]/f[ilia]	son or daughter
gem[elli]	twins
matr.	married
nat[us]	born
nup.[er]	recently
nupt.	married
ob[iit]	died
praedict.	as previously stated
rel[icta]	widow
sep.[ult]	buried
sic	thus (as written)
temp.	in the time of
ux[or]	wife

Christian names are similar in their Latin and English forms. Common examples that might cause confusion are:

Andreas	Andrew
Carolus	Charles
Gulielmus	William
Jacobus	James or Jacob
Johannes	John
Radulphus	Ralph
Xpofer[us]	Christopher

For dates and Roman numerals see page 45.

parish records
matters for the bishop

Records kept by the diocese, and now in various archives, include copies of parish register entries and documents that made a marriage legal rather than 'irregular'

Ecclesiastical powerhouse
For centuries parishes have come under the jurisdiction of archbishops, bishops and archdeacons, based at centres of worship such as Canterbury Cathedral (left). In the past, diocesan registries would have included records relating to parishes, such as marriage documents, parish register copies known as bishops' transcripts, and also wills.

Bishops' transcripts In 1597 English and Welsh parishes began sending copies of their parish registers every year to the bishop of the diocese in which the parish was situated, to be kept in the diocesan registry. The practice continued until the mid 19th century, later in some areas, but marriages were rarely included after 1837. It was never extended to other parts of Britain. The copies are usually called bishops' transcripts or BTs, but may be listed in catalogues as Register Bills, Archdeacons' Transcripts, or Parish Register Transcripts.

Bishops' transcripts provide a second record, which may survive when the parish register does not. Where both records exist, there may be significant differences between them—particularly before 1813, when transcripts became more precise replicas of the registers.

In some cases, bishops' transcripts are in better condition and more legible than the corresponding register. Up to 1733, when parish entries may be in Latin, the transcripts are often in English.

Other useful records related to parishes, such as marriage documents and bishops' transcripts, were not kept in the parish coffer. Most originally came under the bishop's or archdeacon's control and were stored in the diocesan registry; many are now held in county or city record offices. Welsh diocesan papers are all held at the National Library of Wales (see DIRECTORY).

Church of Ireland bishops directed a survey of their parishes in 1766. Surviving returns, listing Protestants and Roman Catholics, are in the National Archives of Ireland (see DIRECTORY).

IRREGULAR AND CLANDESTINE MARRIAGES

From medieval times, the Church required couples to marry in their parish church either by marriage licence or after the reading of banns. Other marriages were deemed 'irregular' or 'clandestine', although, until Hardwicke's Marriage Act of 1753, English law recognised a marriage if a couple who were free to marry (both being old enough and not already married) simply exchanged marriage vows anywhere, without witnesses or even a clergyman.

An irregular or clandestine ceremony appealed to all sorts of people. Most simply wanted to avoid paying for a licence or banns, or for a wedding feast. It was also quick. Some couples needed secrecy, such as apprentices who could not marry without their master's consent. Divorce was not widely available until the 19th century, so many deserted a first spouse and remarried, bigamously, in secret.

Certain churches, such as Holy Trinity Minories in London, became well known for clandestine marriages, and elsewhere some clergymen would also perform them. Fortunately, most of these were recorded in church registers like regular marriages. When the Church threatened errant ministers with

fines or excommunication, most priests began to require marriage banns or a licence. Other irregular and clandestine marriage centres then appeared, including private chapels and prison chapels, which were claimed to be outside the jurisdiction of the Church. In London, the Fleet prison was the most renowned; about 350,000 couples married in or around the Fleet between 1680 and 1754.

Some records of irregular marriages are at the TNA (class RG 7) see DIRECTORY. If you do not find an ancestor's marriage in parish records, the Fleet registers may be the place to look.

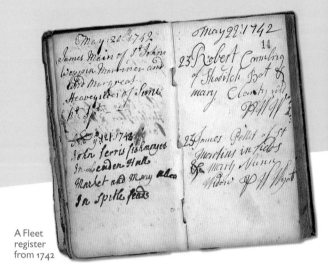

A Fleet register from 1742

Some bishops' transcripts still exist from 1597, but the rate of survival varies dramatically. For a general listing, see *Bishops' Transcripts and Marriage Licences, Bonds and Allegations: a guide to their location and indexes* (J. Gibson, FFHS, 4th ed., 1997). The guide can also help you find records of marriage licences, noting those that have been indexed or published.

marriage licences

If a parish register indicates that your ancestors married by licence (as opposed to banns, the cheaper option), you may be able to find out a great deal about them. Few actual licences survive, but the term 'marriage licence' is effectively shorthand for

the associated paperwork—allegations and bonds—and it is well worth tracking these down. They are usually to be found with other diocesan papers in county or city record offices.

The allegation was a sworn statement that canon law would be observed and also that there was no legal impediment to the proposed marriage. The information recorded varied with the diocese but often included the bride's and groom's marital status, their ages (particularly of minors), occupations, places of residence and the church where the marriage was to take place. If either or both were

A wedding at Gretna Green

A couple marry in haste at Gretna Green on the Scottish border in a scene depicted by the popular historical painter Jerry Barrett (1824–1906). People eloped to Gretna Green because irregular marriages were performed there until 1856, long after the passing of Hardwicke's Marriage Act of 1753.

minors the allegation should also include a statement of consent giving details of the father, mother or the minor's guardian.

The bond, required up to 1823 (up to 1870 in Ireland), was a sworn statement that there was no impediment to the marriage and that, if either of the couple was under 21, parents or guardians had given their consent. One bondsman was usually the groom and the other often a relative of the bride.

Almost all licences were 'common' or 'ordinary' ones, issued by archbishops, bishops or their surrogates, or deputies. A 'special' licence permitting a marriage 'at any convenient time or place' (not necessarily in a church) was very rare and could be granted only by the Archbishop of Canterbury, or, in Ireland, by the Archbishop of Armagh.

The original Church of Ireland marriage licence bonds were destroyed in a fire at the Public Record Office in Dublin in 1922, but some indexes survive for all dioceses except Derry. Some summaries are held in the National Archives (see DIRECTORY).

TAKING IT FURTHER

The many reference works to help you find your way around parish and associated records include:
- *Basic Facts About Using Baptism Records for Family Historians* (P. Litton, FFHS, 1996).
- *Basic Facts About Using Marriage Records for Family Historians* (P. Litton, FFHS, 1996).
- *Basic Facts About Using Death and Burial Records for Family Historians* (L. Gibbens, FFHS, 2nd ed., 1999).
- *Basic Facts About Using Record Offices for Family Historians* (T. Wood, FFHS, 2nd ed., 1999).
- *The Parish Chest: a study of the records of parochial administration in England* (W. Tate, Phillimore, 1983).
- *Clandestine Marriages in the Chapel and Rules of the Fleet Prison 1680–1754* (M. Herber, Francis Boutle, 3 vols, 1998–2000).
- *Irregular Marriage in London before 1754* (T. Benton, Society of Genealogists, 2nd ed., 2000).

the IGI and other Mormon indexes

Stored beneath a granite mountain

Preserved in vaults carved into a granite mountain near Salt Lake City, Utah, in the USA is a vast microfilmed collection of ancestral information. It is maintained by the Genealogical Society of Utah, part of The Church of Jesus Christ of Latter-day Saints. Church members, known as Mormons, collect the records, believing that family ties can be maintained through the posthumous baptism of ancestors. Their web site (right), where records can be accessed, is called FamilySearch.

The Church of Jesus Christ of Latter-day Saints (also known as the Mormon or LDS Church) offers access to vast indexes of parish records. These can prove a boon to family historians trying to find entries for ancestors who moved between parishes.

Since 1938, church members have filmed documents from around the world and indexed their findings by surname and place. The International Genealogical Index (IGI) lists around 600 million entries between 1550 and 1875 from Britain, Ireland, the USA and some 70 other countries. For the British Isles there are about 72 million names.

For England, the records are of baptisms and marriages taken from parish and Nonconformist registers and bishops' transcripts. Less frequently details are taken from other official documents, such as census returns, or from informal sources, including family Bibles and letters. Information from Welsh wills has also been included (with varying accuracy) as the Church in Wales clergy refused to make parish records available to the LDS Church.

VITAL RECORDS INDEX The Mormons also produce the Vital Records Index (VRI). This supplement to the IGI, available on CD, has some 5 million entries for the British Isles, taken from parish registers and other documents (1538–1888).

The VRI can be viewed at Family History Centres (see DIRECTORY) and at many record offices and local study centres.

FINDING THE INDEXES

♦ Much of the IGI can be accessed on the Internet at www.familysearch.org
♦ Family History Centres, the Society of Genealogists, and larger record offices and libraries hold the IGI and the VRI on CD.
♦ The IGI on microfiche can be consulted at the TNA. Family history societies, county and city record offices usually hold copies for their county.

SEE DIRECTORY ➤

Using the index Much of the IGI can be explored on the Internet. The complete index or county sections can also be consulted on microfiche at a variety of places, including national record offices, and the Mormons' own Family History Centres.

The IGI is organised by surname, with variant spellings for similar names grouped together, but is constructed differently for Wales, where surnames were not fully established until the 19th century. See 'The IGI for Wales', chapter 10 in *Welsh Family History: a guide to research* (FFHS, 2nd ed., 1998).

First names may be listed in full or by abbreviations, thus 'William' may appear as Wm, Bill, Billy, Will, Willy or even Gulielmus. Each name is accompanied by the date and place of an event (such as a baptism or marriage), and by a film batch number that identifies the original microfilmed document from which the information was taken.

Avoiding pitfalls The indexes are accessible and a good starting point for locating elusive parish register entries. But to ensure you find a genuine ancestor and not someone who shares the same surname, you should always confirm your findings against original records. Other points to consider when consulting the indexes include:

INEVITABLE ERRORS Some, such as spelling mistakes, incorrect abbreviations and Christian names listed as surnames, could be errors that appeared in the original documents. Other mistakes are the result of faulty transcriptions.

INCOMPLETE COVERAGE The index is not comprehensive: some areas are better recorded than others. If you fail to discover your ancestors in the IGI or the VRI, this does not mean that you will not find them in original parish or other records.

DATE DISCREPANCIES All the dates given in the indexes are based on the Gregorian calendar. This means that dates before 1752, when the Julian calendar was changed to the modern Gregorian style, have been converted (see page 45). As a result, a marriage listed in the IGI as having taken place in January 1735 may be listed under January 1734 in the original source. Dates listed 'about' are guesses.

beliefs apart
Nonconformists

If you cannot find ancestors in parish records, it might be because they were Nonconformists. The first step is working out which of the many denominations they belonged to

During the Middle Ages, the Church in England was devoutly Catholic, although some people criticised the way it was run, complaining of too much secular involvement. When Henry VIII made himself head of the Church in England and put the State directly in charge of Church affairs, those who were already dissatisfied had even greater cause for complaint. To Catholic dissent was added that of new groups influenced by the Protestant movement on the Continent. Apart from the rule of Oliver Cromwell, when radical Protestant groups briefly flourished, the Anglican faith was increasingly

KEY SOURCES OF INFORMATION

♦ Nonconformist registers held at the TNA, city and county record offices, the National Library of Wales, the Public Record Office of Northern Ireland and the National Archives of Scotland.

♦ The International Genealogical Index (see IGI and other Mormon indexes, pages 100–1).

SEE DIRECTORY ➤

THE DISSENTERS AND THEIR BEGINNINGS

1640 Unitarians
They denied the doctrine that God is a trinity, seeing Him as a single entity. They also denied the concept of eternal punishment. Like the Baptists, the sect split into several groups but is now a single body called the General Assembly of Unitarian and Free Churches.

1582 Congregationalists
Congregationalists worshipped in complete equality, as 'the priesthood of all believers' was part of their creed. But they were also governed by elected elders. In 1972 they merged with the Presbyterians into the United Reformed Church.

1532 Anabaptists
Originating in Germany, this sect became established in London. They believed in adult baptism and were forerunners of the later Baptist churches.

1612 Baptists
Believing in adult baptism and universal access to salvation, Baptists spread throughout the British Isles and sank particularly deep roots in Wales. The denomination split into several groups, including the Strict Baptists and New Connexion, but is now reunited as the Baptist Union of Great Britain.

1560 Presbyterians
After the Reformation, Presbyterianism became the official national creed in Scotland, but in England it remained a Nonconformist sect. It believes that a church should be governed by its own elders and not by an imposed hierarchy.

John Bunyan's theological works enhanced the credibility of the Baptists. He wrote most of them, including *The Pilgrim's Progress*, while he was imprisoned for his beliefs.

enforced, particularly after Charles II's restoration. Those who refused to conform to Anglican worship were known as 'Nonconformists' and, like Catholics (see pages 107–9), suffered severe restrictions.

Nonconformist registers

You may suspect that your ancestors were Nonconformists because you cannot find them in parish registers, but determining which denomination they belonged to may not be straightforward. The timeline below gives information about some of the more widely followed Nonconformist groups, but there were numerous other denominations.

Some were breakaway groups from the main body of dissent, others formed when branches merged. Many had their origins on the Continent, such as Arminians, Moravians, Socinians, Calvinists and Walloons, while some began in Scotland and moved south, such as Cameronians, Campbellites, Glassites, Irvingites and Secessionists. The *National Index of Parish Registers, vol. 2* (D. Steel, Society of

Genealogists, 1968, reprinted 1980, revised ed., 2001) is a good starting point when researching the development of the different denominations.

Chapel registers Your Nonconformist ancestors may well have worshipped in a chapel or meeting house, rather than the parish church. Most congregations kept registers of births, marriages and, after 1691, burials. You may also find minutes of meetings and lists of members. Many of these registers are likely to be found at the TNA (classes RG 4–6 and 8).

Followers would be formally admitted to a congregation, and if marriage or work necessitated a move they were 'dismissed' from the congregation. Registers were kept by individual chapels or by ministers on circuit who travelled around to several chapels. Lists of chapels arranged by county are available at the TNA (classes RG 4 and 8). There is also a list that groups chapels by denomination and then by county, which is useful if you cannot find your ancestors in one register and want to see what other chapels or meeting houses were in the vicinity.

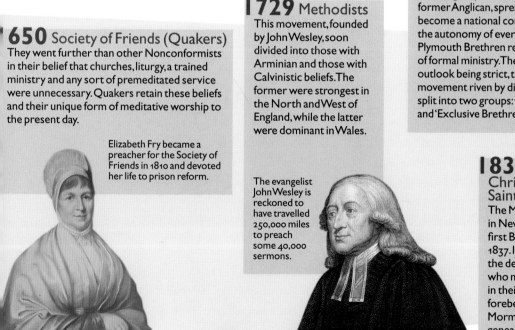

650 Society of Friends (Quakers)
They went further than other Nonconformists in their belief that churches, liturgy, a trained ministry and any sort of premeditated service were unnecessary. Quakers retain these beliefs and their unique form of meditative worship to the present day.

Elizabeth Fry became a preacher for the Society of Friends in 1810 and devoted her life to prison reform.

1729 Methodists
This movement, founded by John Wesley, soon divided into those with Arminian and those with Calvinistic beliefs. The former were strongest in the North and West of England, while the latter were dominant in Wales.

The evangelist John Wesley is reckoned to have travelled 250,000 miles to preach some 40,000 sermons.

1827 Plymouth Brethren
A small group of followers of J. N. Darby, a former Anglican, spread from Plymouth to become a national congregation. Believing in the autonomy of every local church, the Plymouth Brethren rejected the concept of formal ministry. Their social and religious outlook being strict, they quickly found their movement riven by disagreement, and in 1849 split into two groups: the 'Open Brethren' and 'Exclusive Brethren'.

1837 Church of Jesus Christ of Latter-day Saints (Mormons)
The Mormon Church, founded in New York in 1830, opened its first British chapel in Preston in 1837. It believes in the baptism of the dead—salvation for those who made no profession of faith in their lifetimes, and to distant forebears. This is why the Mormon Church has huge genealogical archives (see pages 100–1).

A believer is fully immersed
Charles Haddon Spurgeon baptises a woman into the Baptist Union at his Metropolitan Tabernacle in 1875. At this time he was the most popular preacher in London and his Tabernacle seated 6000 people. He looked on the Gospel as a 'gift of God to the imagination' and published more than 2000 sermons.

Baptismal records Before civil registration began in 1837, people relied on their parish church registers to provide legal proof of baptisms, marriages and burials. Nonconformist registers were not admissible in court, so many Nonconformists had their children baptised in parish churches. Baptists, however, generally did not as they were fundamentally opposed to infant baptism.

From 1742 members of the main Nonconformist denominations in England and Wales—Baptists, Presbyterians, Unitarians and the Independents (known also as Congregationalists)—could register their baptisms in the General Register of Births of Children of Protestant Dissenters at Dr Williams's Library in Red Cross Street in London. Almost 50,000 births were registered there (some retrospectively from 1716) up to 1837. The register is now held at the TNA in RG 4 and RG 5 and microfilm copies can be seen at the FRC (class RG 6).

Marriage records Until 25 March 1754, legally binding marriages could take place in Nonconformist chapels. Afterwards, as a result of the Hardwicke Act designed to eliminate clandestine marriages (see page 98), all marriages had to take place in parish churches, except those of Quakers and Jews (see The Jewish faith, pages 110–11), who were granted exemption.

Burial records The first Nonconformist chapels were usually private buildings put to religious use. They had no burial grounds, so the dead had to be buried in the local parish churchyard. Some Church of England parishes refused to bury Nonconformists because they were considered to be unbaptised. After the Toleration Act of 1691, Nonconformists could set up their own burial grounds (see pages 116–17). You will find burial registers from this time onwards at the TNA (RG 4 and RG 8) or within the appropriate denominational collections.

Quaker registers The records of the Quakers are often more detailed than those in Anglican registers, including information about more family members. Before civil registration in 1837, the Quakers kept their own registers and indexes, which are now held at the library of the Religious Society of Friends in Britain (see DIRECTORY). The registers are also held at the TNA or on microfilm at the FRC (class RG 6).

Wales, Scotland and Ireland

The chances of a Welsh ancestor being Non-conformist are extremely high. By the 19th century, Wales was the most religiously active country in the western world, and in 1851 some 80 per cent of its worshipping population was Nonconformist. Calvinistic Methodists predominated, with the Baptists and Independents active across South Wales and along the Welsh border. Quakers and Unitarians were found only in small numbers.

LOCATING WELSH RECORDS The National Library of Wales (see DIRECTORY) is the main repository, although only the Calvinistic Methodists have deposited records there in any quantity. Quaker records for Wales are held at the Glamorgan Record Office (see DIRECTORY). Most county record offices have some Nonconformist material.

Scottish Nonconformity Scotland was a Roman Catholic country until 1560, when John Knox began to install Presbyterianism as the predominant faith. It was governed by a system of Church councils and the Kirk Session, which administered each congregation. Presbyterianism became the official Church of Scotland in 1690. Following the establishment of Presbyterianism, the largest Nonconformist

denominations were Episcopalians (who believed in rule by bishops), Methodists, Quakers and Congregationalists.

LOCATING SCOTTISH RECORDS Most of the records and registers of Presbyterian churches are held in the National Archives of Scotland (see DIRECTORY). The archives also hold some of the registers of other denominations; further registers can be found at local record offices. Most Methodist records are kept at individual chapels.

Irish Nonconformity Nonconformist denominations soon entered Ireland from mainland Britain and established congregations. As in England, Irish Nonconformists would often marry or be buried at the parish church, so it is important to consult Church of Ireland registers for evidence of Nonconformist ancestors (see page 87). At first, Methodists remained members of the Church of Ireland or the Presbyterian church, in whose registers they will appear.

LOCATING IRISH RECORDS For Presbyterian, Methodist, Baptist, United Brethren and Congregationalist records, you should consult documents held at the Public Record Office of Northern Ireland (see DIRECTORY). Some records may still be in local custody; otherwise try the Presbyterian Historical Society, the Irish Baptist Historical Society and, for Methodist records, the Wesley Historical Society (see DIRECTORY).

The Public Record Office of Northern Ireland also holds copies of the records of Quaker meetings in Ulster; for the rest of Ireland try the Religious Society of Friends' Historical Library in Dublin (see DIRECTORY).

TAKING IT FURTHER

♦ *Sources for the History of English Nonconformity 1660–1830* (M. Mullett, BRA, 1991).
♦ www.nationalarchives.gov.uk/records/research-guides/nonconformists.htm

REAL LIVES
Nonconformists in the family

John and Ann Bellin
Susan knew that Samuel's parents, John (1759–1841) and Ann Bellin (1759–1833), were Nonconformists who moved from the City of London to the hamlet of Chigwell Row in Essex, where they attended an Independent meeting house (below).

It is always worth checking Nonconformist registers in the area where you know your ancestors lived, as they may have attended a chapel or meeting house rather than, or as well as, the local parish church.

For Susan Lumas the search began with family diaries and four early 19th-century family portraits painted or engraved by her great great grandfather, Samuel Bellin. By looking for the relatives' names in a chapel register she was able to find out more about her Nonconformist forebears.

at this meeting Mr. John Bellin, and Ann his Wife, were unanimously receiv'd into Church fellowship, by dismission from the Church at Founders Hall, London under the pastoral care of Rev. In. Thomas

Admission to Chigwell Row chapel, 25 January 1807
When the Bellins arrived in Essex they had to apply for admission to the congregation at Chigwell Row, which was recorded in the chapel's register (above). The entry states that the Bellins received 'dismission' from the church at Founders' Hall in Cloth Fair in the City of London. This simply means that they wanted to move to another congregation.

Samuel Bellin and Susannah Southgate
Samuel (1799–1893) was John and Ann Bellin's seventh son. He married Susannah Southgate (1814–1875), the eldest daughter of a family who had also joined the Chigwell Row congregation when they moved from Walthamstow to Chigwell Grange.

Susannah Southgate, born in 1814
Susannah's birthdate was found by looking in the General Register of Births of Children of Protestant Dissenters at Dr Williams's Library (see page 104), now located at the TNA . Her parents would have been given a copy of the birth certificate (right). Chigwell Row chapel register includes an entry for the birth of Samuel and Susannah's first-born daughter, another Susannah, in 1836.

No.	Names of Children.	Names of Parents.	Witnesses.	Time when born.
1364	Susannah Southgate Forest Hill Par. St Mary, Lewisham County of Kent Regd April 3d 1818		Eliz Mitchell William Forbes Surgeon	30 Dec. 1814

E No 1364

THESE are to certify, That *Susannah Southgate Daughter of James Webb Southgate* and *Susannah* his Wife, who was Daughter of *Thomas Mitchell* was born in *Forest Hill* in the Parish of *St George Lewisham* in the County of *Kent* the *Thirtieth* Day of *December* in the Year *One Thousand Eight Hundred & Fourteen* at whose Birth we were present

Registered at Dr Williams's Library, Redcross-Street, near Cripplegate, London.
April 3d 1818 Thos. Morgan Regist

beliefs apart

From 1559 to 1778 it was illegal to be a Roman Catholic in England and Wales. As a result, tracing ancestors from this period can be a challenge

Roman Catholics

When Elizabeth I came to the throne she decided to remove all influence from the Roman Catholic church to secure her own position. In 1559 the Acts of Supremacy and Uniformity made it illegal to celebrate a Catholic mass in England and Wales. Catholic services continued to be illegal until the Catholic Relief Act of 1778.

Anyone trying to trace Catholic ancestors from this period will find the records incomplete. Though some Catholics were married, buried or baptised in Anglican churches and can be found in parish registers (see pages 86–101), many refused to attend an Anglican church or were not allowed to. Catholic ceremonies did take place in secret, but few registers were kept for fear of them being discovered.

With anti-Catholic legislation repealed, Catholicism experienced a surge in popularity during the 19th century. This was partly due to new converts but mostly to Irish migration (see page 239). Full details of all Catholic baptism, confirmation, marriage and burial registers, and copies that can be consulted, are given in *Catholic Missions and Registers 1700–1880* (M. Gandy, 6 vols, 1993).

Convictions and taxes A good place to look for Catholic forebears is in the records of the local courts—quarter sessions—because Catholics were often prosecuted for not attending their parish

KEY SOURCES OF INFORMATION
♦ Records at the TNA and county record offices.
♦ Extracts from registers and documents published by the Catholic Record Society (CRS).
♦ Printed material from the Catholic Central Library, the Society of Genealogists, the British Library and Catholic schools and religious orders.
SEE DIRECTORY ➤

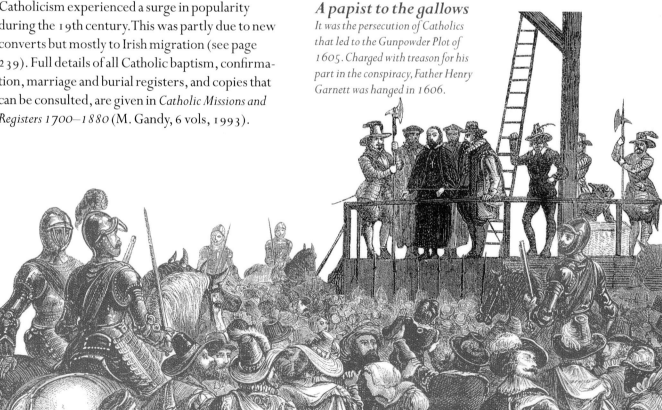

A papist to the gallows
It was the persecution of Catholics that led to the Gunpowder Plot of 1605. Charged with treason for his part in the conspiracy, Father Henry Garnett was hanged in 1606.

church (see Criminal ancestors, pages 159–63). They are usually recorded as 'recusants' and sometimes as 'papists'. Some 16th and 17th-century quarter sessions records are in print and indexed. Anyone refusing to take the Oath of Supremacy should be listed in the 1641 Protestation Return (in the House of Lords Record Office; see DIRECTORY).

The Catholic Record Society (CRS) has published many records: baptism registers, records of convents abroad, recusant rolls and the *Northern Book of Compositions 1629–32*, which shows how Catholics managed to bargain to preserve their estates and religion. Many aristocratic families were Catholic, and all Royalists during the Civil War.

TAXED TO THE HILT Catholics are easy to find in the records of the lay subsidies—taxes levied on movable property—held at the TNA in class E 179, as they were obliged to pay double rates.

under surveillance by the State

Documents from the late 16th and early 17th centuries in the State Papers (at the TNA) show how the government tried to track down Catholic priests. Anglican clergy made lists of Catholics in their parish, and Catholics often appeared before ecclesiastical courts for religious offences such as not bringing their children to baptism. If you fail to find your ancestors here, it does not indicate that they abandoned their faith; many people conformed outwardly to avoid persecution. Every 17th-century list is incomplete for this reason.

TOUGHER STILL After the Jacobite rising of 1715, a new law required Catholic landowners to register details of their property. These registers are in the TNA and also usually in local quarter sessions records. The law operated until 1778, although by then it had largely fallen into abeyance. The wills of

Different from the rest
The national Returns of Papists of 1705 and 1767 (above left) list the Catholics in every diocese. Although Catholics were officially liberated with the 1778 Relief Act, prejudices lingered on, erupting in the bloody Gordon Riots of 1780.

Catholics were proved in the same way as others, but they never refer openly to Catholicism since it was illegal to leave money for 'supertitious uses'. Sums of money for masses or the support of priests were often left to a friend 'for purposes he knows of'.

records of the Catholic church

Many Catholics fled abroad. Priests were trained in colleges on the Continent and entered religious orders there. Young women became nuns in English and Irish convents in northern France and the Spanish-ruled Netherlands. Schools were established by these orders, allowing young English, Welsh and Irish Catholics to be educated in their faith. In the 1790s many of these institutions returned to England and still survive. For example, Stonyhurst College (founded at St Omer, France, in 1593) came to England in 1793. It occupied a large country house in Lancashire and has remained there ever since. Such schools often have superb records, many of which have been published by the CRS or by the religious orders themselves.

Keeping the faith at home For committed Catholics who stayed in Britain, the possibility of practising their faith depended on where they lived. In some parts of England and Wales Catholicism was completely rooted out, but it remained strong in Lancashire and in parts of Durham, North Yorkshire, Northumberland, Staffordshire, Worcestershire and Monmouth. In the south of England many gentry families protected Catholics, their private homes becoming unofficial chapels.

Although Catholic priests seldom kept written records during this time of persecution, some do survive, notably *Bishop Leyburn's Confirmation Registers of 1687* (NW Catholic History Society, 1997; index available from Catholic Family History Society, see DIRECTORY).

In London the embassies of Catholic countries kept large public chapels, which were immune to the anti-Catholic laws. The vast majority of Catholic chapel registers before 1837 are now in county or diocesan record offices. Many have been published and some are included in the International Genealogical Index (IGI—see pages 100–1).

Families in Scotland and Ireland The National Archives of Scotland (see DIRECTORY) has photocopies of Catholic registers of christenings, marriages and deaths, and lists of Easter communicants. Most of the original registers are still held by the individual parishes.

For most of the 18th century, Catholics in Ireland laboured under anti-Catholic laws. Despite this, some city parishes, such as Dublin and Cork, have baptism and marriage records from the mid 18th century onwards; country parishes start from a later date. Catholic burials may be found in Church of Ireland registers. Registers for Catholic parishes are kept locally. Microfilms for most parishes are at the National Library of Ireland (see DIRECTORY).

Other Irish records include the convert rolls, which list Catholics who renounced their faith (or at least pretended to). The Irish Manuscripts Commission (see DIRECTORY) has published these.

TAKING IT FURTHER

♦ *Catholic Family History: a Bibliography of General Sources* (4 vols, M. Gandy, 1996).
♦ *Catholic Family History: a Bibliography for Scotland* (M. Gandy, 1996).
♦ *Irish Records: sources for family and local history* (J. Ryan, Fly-leaf Press, 1997).
♦ 'Catholics in Wales' (J. and S. Rowlands, in *Second Stages in Researching Welsh Ancestry*, FFHS, 1999).

Information on the Internet
♦ www.catholic-history.org.uk/crs
Catholic Record Society's web site.
♦ www.feefhs.org/uk/frg-cfhs.html
Catholic Family History Society's web site.
♦ www.nationalarchives.gov.uk/records/research-guides/catholics.htm

beliefs apart
the Jewish faith

Jews first settled in Britain in 1066 and are now part of the fabric of British life. Records of synagogue congregations reflect how the Jewish faith has been carefully preserved

The first Jewish community in Britain was made up of Norman-French Jews who followed William the Conqueror to England in 1066 and acted as his financiers. But medieval Jewry was brutally curtailed on 1 August 1290 by Edward I's Edict of Expulsion, which decreed that all Jews were to be baptised, banished or put to death. Scarcely any Jews lived in Britain over the ensuing 300 years. In the reign of Elizabeth I (1558–1603), however, a small number, mainly from Portugal, settled in London and formed a clandestine community. Ostensibly Christian, they practised Judaism behind closed doors and survived precariously during the first half of the 17th century. Because of the secretive nature of their existence, there are few records of these early immigrants.

a new age of tolerance

In 1656 Oliver Cromwell ended the enforcement of the Edict of Expulsion, though it was never formally rescinded. In the same year Jewish immigrants from Spain and Portugal founded the Sephardi Jewish Congregation. Their synagogue, Bevis Marks, stands in the City of London; the Congregation, known as the Spanish and Portuguese Jews Congregation (see DIRECTORY), is the oldest in Britain and holds records of the births, marriages and deaths of its members. Eastern European (Ashkenazi) Jews followed as immigrants in the late 17th century; their records can be found at the Archive Office of the Chief Rabbi (see DIRECTORY).

From 1656 until about 1725 Anglo-Jewry was London based. But the guild system of merchants'

A Jewish wedding
The wedding of Jonas Lazarus of Lincolnshire (above) to Rosceia Nathan (top) on 5 August 1810 was reported in great detail in The Gentleman's Magazine, *which often carried colourful vignettes on Jews. Next to the portraits is a Jewish marriage contract, or* ketubah, *dating from a few years later.*

KEY SOURCES OF INFORMATION
◆ Birth, marriage and death registers and census returns at the Family Records Centre.
◆ Membership lists at the Spanish and Portuguese Jews Congregation; the Archive Office of the Chief Rabbi; and the Federation of Synagogues.
SEE DIRECTORY ➤

associations in the City held a near monopoly over many jobs, making it difficult for Jews who would not work on the Sabbath (Saturday) to find employment. Instead, they took up hawking and peddling outside London, and communities began to develop in towns across England and Wales. Over the course of the 18th century the Jewish population in Britain increased tenfold to around 30,000. There was a further large influx at the end of the 19th century as Jews fled persecution in Eastern Europe (see page 265). Many of the migrants settled in Scotland.

researching Jewish records

Start your search for a Jewish ancestor in conventional civil records such as birth, marriage and death registers and census returns, held at the Family Records Centre (see Civil records, pages 50–61, and The census, pages 62–76). Remember that foreign names were often misspelt, and while 'Abrahams' for 'Abraham' is clear, you might overlook a 'Weinstein' spelt as 'Wainstain' (see Regional & foreign names, pages 302–3). Also bear in mind that Jewish marriages often went unrecorded as Jews were exempt from Hardwicke's Marriage Act of 1753, which stated that weddings must take place in the Anglican parish church or chapel. A Jewish marriage ceremony had to be solemnised in the presence of two appropriate Jewish witnesses to be religiously acceptable. And although in 1837 it became a legal requirement to register weddings, many Jews failed to do so. The reasons for this included the expense (registrars had to be paid), the language barrier and ignorance of the law.

Revealing more Once you have exhausted the civil records, try the specific Jewish sources below. (For more details see DIRECTORY.)

☞ The Society of Genealogists holds much of the material that used to be in the Anglo-Jewish Archive in the Mocatta Library, University College, London. This has pedigrees of the Montefiores, Rothschilds and other Jewish families.

TAKING IT FURTHER

♦ *My Ancestors were Jewish* (A. Joseph, Society of Genealogists, 2008).
♦ *The Jews of South Wales: historical studies* (ed. Ursula Henriques, University of Wales Press, 1993).
♦ *The Jews of Ireland from the Earliest Times to the Year 1910* (Louis Hyman, The Jewish Historical Society of England, 1972).
♦ The Scottish Jewish Archives Centre, Glasgow.

Information on the Internet
♦ www.jgsgb.org.uk
Jewish Genealogical Society of Great Britain.
♦ www.jewishgen.org
JewishGen: Jewish genealogical research.
♦ www.nationalarchives.gov.uk/records/ research-guides/anglo-jewish-history-18th-20th.htm

Volume III of the Society's *National Index of Parish Registers* (see pages 88–89) has a section on locating Anglo-Jewish records of births, marriages and deaths.

☞ The *Jewish Chronicle* is a London-based publication that has been printed weekly since 1841. It is partially indexed and included notifications of births, marriages and deaths, and details of wills and obituaries. Back issues can be found at British Library Newspapers.

☞ The *Jewish Year Book* (Vallentine Mitchell, Essex) has been published annually since 1896 and contains a list of all working synagogues with their addresses and founding dates.

☞ The London Metropolitan Archives has records of some Jewish organisations, including the Board of Deputies of British Jews and some schools. These can be consulted only by permission of the organisation that deposited the material.

in memoriam
graves & monuments

Documents are not the only source of clues about past family members. Burial grounds can serve as outdoor archives, where the records are written in stone

Memorials and headstones can offer all kinds of insights into your family history. Sometimes you can discover facts on monuments that together could not be found in any other record. This might include the deceased's date of birth, occupation, place of residence and relationships, along with other personal details.

church burials

The earliest inscribed memorials are those found inside a church, such as effigies, monuments and memorial brasses. A few date from as early as the 12th century, but most commemorate prosperous parishioners from the 16th century onwards. These memorials often give a great deal of biographical information, such as ancestry, birthplace, former parish of residence, marriage, children, husband's or wife's ancestry, children's husbands and wives, and details of relatives buried elsewhere. Bells, pews, communion plate, benefactors' boards, organs, lecterns, vases and stained glass may also have relevant inscriptions, if only a name and a date.

MARKING A GRAVE Until the early 17th century, churchyard graves, especially those of the poor, were unmarked. Even wealthier folk might only have a simple wooden cross or grave board, which would soon rot away. But from then on, the better-off yeomen and craftsmen began to mark their family graves with headstones, which have stood the test of time better. The legibility of the inscription is largely determined by the quality of the carving and by how well the stone has worn.

cemeteries ease overcrowding

By 1800 many churchyards were becoming seriously overcrowded. As more people moved from the countryside into the towns and cities, the demand for burial space became particularly acute in many urban areas. It was resolved over the next few decades by groups of financiers buying up plots of land on which they established large cemeteries in rural surroundings. By the late 1830s, several such cemeteries had been opened, on the outskirts of London, Leeds, Liverpool and Sheffield.

LIVES COMMEMORATED IN THE ART OF THE STONEMASON

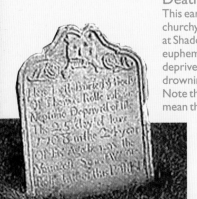

Death by drowning
This early gravestone in the churchyard of St Peter and St Paul at Shadoxhurst, Kent, uses a poetic euphemism—'whome Neptune deprived of life'—to describe the drowning of Thomas Rolfe in 1708. Note that 'in his 24th year' could mean that he was 23 years old.

Tools of the trade
Old gravestones may portray occupations, which were not recorded on a regular basis before the census of 1841. The guns, rods, powder flask, game bird and gun dog on John Murray's 18th-century headstone at Kells in Scotland show that he was a gamekeeper.

In the 1850s a series of Burial Acts authorised local authorities to buy land for non-denominational cemeteries. By 1945 private ownership of burial grounds had proved unprofitable and vandalism had become a problem. Local authorities took them over, but many graves had been damaged or removed before the inscriptions could be recorded.

THE CHOICE OF CREMATION Concern about overcrowded churchyards in the cities led also to the movement in favour of cremation. The first official cremation was that of Mrs Jeanette C. Pickersgill in Woking, Surrey, in 1885. In 1903 the Cremation Act came into force and enabled public burial authorities to provide and maintain crematoriums out of the rates. Today about two-thirds of Britain's dead are cremated.

AN ANCESTOR'S NAME EMERGES

Penny Mortimer's search for the tomb of her great-grandfather, James Grierson, was not as straightforward as she had expected: as general manager of Great Western Railways he had been a famous man in his time. His death in 1887 had been widely reported.

From press cuttings and family memorabilia, Penny learnt that her ancestor was interred in Old Barnes Cemetery in south-west London. But she was not prepared for the overgrown state of the burial ground, where many headstones lay beneath a mass of brambles. It took an hour to locate the tomb, then cut through the undergrowth to confirm his name.

The language of symbolism
From the 18th century, as the art of the stonemason flowered, gravestones were decked with symbolic motifs. The Tree of Life, inscribed here on a Gloucestershire gravestone, was one popular image. Others include the hourglass, which represents time; the globe, symbolising mortality; and the open book, for knowledge.

The family vault
A single burial place can be the source of a wealth of genealogical detail. Eight generations of the Cox family— from 1770 to 1970— are recorded on this elegant 'tea caddy' pedestal tomb in the well-tended graveyard of St Mary's Church at Painswick, Gloucestershire.

in memoriam
what inscriptions reveal

Careful preparation and a methodical approach will help you to glean the most from the mass of genealogical detail to be found on gravestones and memorials

From a single monument you may be able to construct a sizable family tree. To find a mother, father and children buried in the same plot is not rare, and you may discover several generations.

The simplest inscription can fill a gap in your family tree or help to prove relationships. When a married daughter is buried with her parents, her change of name is usually recorded on the memorial. In Scotland and Ireland, a married woman's maiden name will appear on her headstone (see Regional & foreign names, pages 302–3).

If there is a title in the family, a coat of arms on an ancestor's memorial may help to distinguish the family from others of the same name (see Heraldry, pages 288–97).

An inscription can reveal evidence of migration from another area. But burials did not always take place in the parish of death, and the last residence of someone brought 'home' for burial may be given on a memorial.

reading and recording

When you visit a graveyard to record details, follow these simple guidelines:

☞ Draw, photograph or describe the monument and note its position in the graveyard. A sketch plan or a photograph of a general view of the graveyard will help you, and others, find the spot again.

☞ Inscriptions are often much clearer when the sun is low and casting stronger shadows, so time visits to take advantage of morning and evening light. On a dull day or in twilight use a torch held at an angle against the stone to make the inscription appear more clearly.

☞ Copy down everything that can be read in full, from 'Sacred to the memory of' or 'In memory of' at the top of the monument to the religious or other inscription at the end.

In search of family plots

A visit to a graveyard in the area in which your ancestors lived can reveal much information about family connections. Relatives often lie near each other, even if they do not share a surname. Those interred elsewhere may also be listed, along with their place of burial. This can give you some idea of the movements of a family around a county, or even farther afield, perhaps in connection with work.

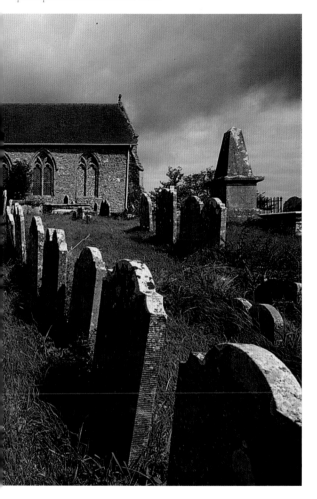

☞ As many of the stones are already in a fragile condition, avoid wire brushes or any other extreme measures to remove lichen. The churchyard ecology should always be treated with respect.

Memorials are owned by the people who erected them or their descendants. Church or local authorities can move them only in the following instances.

IF THE CHURCH IS MADE REDUNDANT
A memorial can be taken away provided that enough information to identify it (with a copy of the inscription), along with the date of removal and the place to which it was transferred (if any), is deposited with the district council and the General Register Office (see DIRECTORY).

IF THE CHURCHYARD IS DISUSED When a church remains in use but the churchyard has become redundant, the parish or district council assumes responsibility for memorials. The council has to record the name and date of any monument it moves, but does not have to copy inscriptions.

Records from the churchyards of more than 200 redundant churches are at the TNA in class RG 37. Most counties hold paper records of inscriptions that have long since vanished; these can be found in local libraries and record offices.

Looking up inscriptions In recent times family history societies have done much to record graveyard inscriptions. In 1978 the Federation of Family History Societies (FFHS—see DIRECTORY) launched a project to transcribe all unrecorded inscriptions in England, Scotland and Wales; this huge task is yet to be completed for the majority of counties. Copies of the various societies' work are often held in local record offices or libraries, and sometimes at a church itself. The Society of Genealogists (see DIRECTORY) also has a huge collection of these transcripts and indexes.

The National Library of Wales has a collection of transcribed Welsh inscriptions, and there is a collection of Scottish inscriptions at the Scottish Genealogy Society (see DIRECTORY).

locating a grave

Basic knowledge of your family's history or a death certificate may lead you to where your ancestor lived; a burial register (see Parish records, pages 86–99), death notice or newspaper obituary should confirm the final resting place. Where the plan of a burial ground survives (usually held at the local record office), it can be invaluable in locating a monument. It may also reveal details of missing stones and inscriptions that are now illegible.

FINDING A GRAVE IN A CEMETERY

The records of most cemeteries are held in the cemetery office or by the local authority or record office. They will help you to locate a grave using plans and the grave register. The register will usually include a grave number and sometimes a 'square' number; you will need to find the square on a general plan and then the grave number within a detailed plan of that square.

Churchyards are usually wider on the south side of the church; the smaller northern part, known as 'the devil's side', was often reserved for criminals, excommunicants, suicides and the unbaptised.

NONCONFORMIST GRAVES

As relatively few Nonconformist groups had their own burial grounds, there are few specifically Nonconformist burial registers (see page 104). The information inscribed on their graves and memorials is therefore often an important way of tracking down Nonconformist relatives and establishing their denomination.

Most members of dissenting chapels were buried in the local parish churchyard. Few parishioners, whatever their beliefs, were refused the dignity of a Christian burial by the local incumbent, although the Nonconformist minister was usually not allowed to be formally

IRISH MEMORIALS Because of the destruction of many parish registers, Irish monumental inscriptions are particularly important. Many have been published, notably in the series *Memorials of the Dead in Ireland* (the journal of The Association for the Preservation of the Memorials of the Dead in Ireland, published from 1888 to 1937). The London library of the Irish Genealogical Research Society (see DIRECTORY) has a collection of tombstone inscriptions. Local history societies have transcribed many inscriptions and published them in journals, including *The Irish Ancestor* and *The Irish Genealogist*.

war memorials

Memorials commemorating local men and women who died in war during the 20th century are to be found the length and breadth of Britain. Schools, town halls, railway stations and larger companies often have created rolls of honour to commemorate employees and former pupils who gave their lives for their country.

The Imperial War Museum and the National Monuments Record Centre (see DIRECTORY) have compiled the UK National Inventory of War Memorials. This remarkable document lists the location and description of all public war memorials as well as those found in hospitals, places of worship and other places. Inscribed names are not recorded but local history societies are transcribing these.

lives lost at sea

The National Maritime Museum (see page 219) has a collection of inscriptions from memorials to British people connected with the sea, including naval men, merchant seamen, shipowners and victims of shipwrecks. There are around 4000 entries, dating mostly from before the First World War and taken from churches, cemeteries and public memorials at seaports and in fishing villages around Britain and abroad. Searches can be made at the museum itself, by post or via the web site at www.nmm.ac.uk/memorials/Index.cfm

involved. In addition, memorials and wall tablets commemorating the dead can be found in some Nonconformist chapels, although not as many as there often are in Anglican churches.

A Nonconformist burial ground was founded at Bunhill Fields on City Road, London, in 1665, and about 123,000 burials took place there up to 1853, including those of writers John Bunyan and Daniel Defoe. Guildhall Library (see DIRECTORY) holds transcriptions of every gravestone inscription at Bunhill Fields that was still legible in 1868.

CREMATION RECORDS

The Cremation Regulations (1930) require the local Cremation Authority to preserve all applications, certificates and other documents that relate to a cremation (originals or photographic copies) for a period of 15 years, after which they can be destroyed. Cremation registers, on the other hand, must be preserved for all time, and if a crematorium closes down, then its registers must be passed to the Home Office. Access to cremation registers is closed to the public, although Home Office staff will carry out free searches for next of kin. The only permanent form of memorial at the crematorium is an entry in a book of remembrance. This is available for inspection and sometimes includes not only the deceased's name and date of death, but also his or her age, date of birth and any official position held.

Memorials to those cremated may be found in the garden of remembrance at the crematorium or in a location nearby. These can take the form of plaques on walls or kerbstones, or dedicated rose bushes, trees, benches and so forth. Ashes may, with permission, be buried in the consecrated ground of a churchyard, a practice first allowed by the Church of England in 1944. In this case there should be an entry in the parish burial register, and there might also be a monumental inscription in the churchyard itself. Where cremated remains are interred in a churchyard, there is no legal requirement for a book of remembrance to be kept by the church, although it is quite usual for this to be done.

Casualties of war

War memorials are a poignant but common sight in Britain's towns and villages, and usually stand near the green or in the churchyard. Most were built shortly after the First World War; more names were added after the Second World War and some list those who died in more recent conflicts. A memorial may reveal links between a particular surname and an area.

TAKING IT FURTHER

◆ *Exploring English Churchyard Memorials* (H. Lees, Tempus, 2002)
◆ *Churchyards of England and Wales* (B. Bailey, Robert Hale, 1987).
◆ *English Churchyard Memorials* (F. Burgess, Lutterworth, 2004).
◆ *Monumental Inscriptions in the Library of the Society of Genealogists; Part I, Southern England* (L. Collins, Society of Genealogists, 1984); *Part II, Northern England, Wales, Scotland, Ireland and overseas* (L. Collins and M. Morton, Society of Genealogists, 1987).
◆ *Monuments and their Inscriptions* (H. L. White, Society of Genealogists, 1987).

their place in society

As you learn more of your ancestors, they become flesh and blood characters who each played a part in society. Their **legacies**, or wills, may include startling bequests, such as a sum of money to a mistress or love child. Academic achievement, sporting prowess and even nicknames might emerge from **education** records kept by schools, colleges and universities, while a forebear's **working life** in the civil service, the Church, a profession such as medicine or law, or a commercial company may be charted. Bad fortune can strike all families, and at some time you may find ancestors **on the fringes** of society as a result of crime, poverty or sickness.

A class divided at the coronation of George V in 1911

legacies
last will and testament

Wills can reveal much about your ancestors' circumstances, telling you where they lived and what they owned. The property of those who did not leave wills may also be recorded

Finding the will of an ancestor, possibly composed when he was on his deathbed with the help of a lawyer or clergyman, can be a dramatic moment. It may describe gifts he had bequeathed to his widow—known as his 'relict'—and his children. He may also have left money for a local school, hospital or charity or finally taken the opportunity to acknowledge an illegitimate child. Perhaps he asked his brother to help his widow by acting as guardian to his infant children.

Do not limit your search to wills of direct ancestors. Those of their brothers or sisters may feature your ancestors as beneficiaries, benefiting under the terms of the will. An ancestor may have acted as an 'executor' (or 'executrix', if female)—someone appointed in a will to carry out the last wishes of the testator (the person who made the will), collect his assets, pay debts and distribute the estate.

A wealth of information An ancestor's 'last will and testament' can be a mine of information about that person's life and family. These documents were prepared with the intention of passing on land, money, jewellery or other property to a spouse, children, other relatives, friends or employees. As

Of sound mind and body…
The reading of a will to assembled relatives is a dramatic device much loved by film-makers. This still is taken from the 1951 comedy classic Laughter in Paradise, *where the beneficiaries learn that they will only inherit if they perform hilarious out-of-character tasks. Were your ancestors as mischievous?*

a result wills are also of importance for confirming the relationship of your ancestor to a number of people. Some were written in simple terms; others include so much information about members of a family that you can construct a family tree from the last wishes of your ancestor and also find out much about his station in life.

You may be lucky enough to find an inventory—a list of his movable goods—associated with your ancestor's will. This can give you a fascinating insight into his standard of living and status (see page 125).

a final judgment

A will records what a person wanted to happen to his or her possessions after death. It was also an opportunity for the testator to set down a final judgment on family and friends. The most common is a tribute to a spouse, such as, 'I leave my gold ring to my dear wife as a sign of my everlasting affection'.

Your ancestor may have taken a different view about various other relatives or friends. One testator, for example, left some money to his friends to 'get drunk one last time at my expense'.

CUT OFF WITH A SHILLING This familiar term refers to the practice of a man leaving just a shilling, or some other token sum, to his eldest son. This was sometimes because much of the man's property—his business, for instance—had already passed to his son during his lifetime. The token sum merely acknowledged that the son had already been provided for. But in some cases a nominal gift indicated a father's displeasure at his son's behaviour. The family would have known what was meant.

a will in the family?

Even if you think your family was too poor to leave any property, it is always worth searching for a will. Although most of the wills dating from a few hundred years ago were left by wealthy men, many farmers, carpenters, blacksmiths and other artisans also made them. By the 18th and 19th centuries, soldiers, sailors, clerks and even labourers were following suit. In the 20th century you will find wills for virtually any class, occupation or income group of the population.

It is worth remembering also that while your immediate ancestors may have been poor, more distant ancestors might have been wealthy.

the law and inheritance

In the Middle Ages land was the main form of wealth. By law it was inherited automatically by the deceased's heir. In most parts of England (but not in Wales) this meant a man's eldest surviving son—the principle of primogeniture. In some areas there were different customs, such as 'borough English', that is inheritance by the youngest son.

A man's property on death, known as his 'estate', usually included personal property such as money, farm stock, tools or furniture. The law stated that a

I give and bequeath to my daughter Amelia one pair of silver spectacles, coal scuttle, tea caddy, best set of china, large blanket… and feather bed.
Last will and testament of Susannah Eagles, 1850

man's widow should automatically receive a third of his personal property—her 'dower'—and his children should share another third. After this, there might be little left for other relatives.

The selection of heirs Some property owners wanted to choose who should inherit. They would attempt to transfer land during their lifetime to the person whom they wished to benefit, or they transferred it to trustees who would hold it on behalf of another. Laws were passed to prevent such transactions. In 1540, however, the Statute of Wills allowed most land to be given to the person of a man's choosing, and not automatically to his heir.

Real property, that is land and buildings, was originally dealt with in a 'will', but a gift of personal property, termed a 'bequest', was contained in a document that was known as a 'testament'. By the

121

16th century, a will and testament were usually contained in the same document, thus explaining the opening words of so many wills. In the remainder of this section (up to page 131), these will be considered together as a 'will'.

who could make wills

The Statute of Wills of 1540 allowed males from the age of 14 and females from 12 to make wills, but the minimum age is currently 18. A will was invalid if made by a lunatic, traitor, prisoner, heretic or slave.

A married woman could make a valid will only with the consent of her husband. Ownership of her property, even if acquired before she was married, was transferred to her husband and became part of his estate. In law, a woman had no property to leave in a will unless her husband had agreed to it. This remained the position until 1883. As a result you are unlikely to find a will for a married woman before that date.

intestacy and administration

Some men died suddenly; others simply neglected to 'settle their affairs' before death. Dying 'intestate' (leaving no will) caused problems. The property deeds would be in the deceased's name, so the transfer of land, the distribution of goods and who should administer the estate would all be in question.

Legal procedures have developed to deal with intestacy, so even if your ancestor did not make a will there may be a legal record of what happened to his property on his death.

the ancient language of wills

Although the language of wills has varied over time and between different areas of Britain, the basic terminology and sequence of information has remained remarkably consistent for centuries. Wills generally opened with the familiar wording 'This is the last will and testament of me (name) of (address)…' and continued by stating the occupation of the testator and naming his executors. The opening statement often included strong religious overtones, particularly before the 19th century.

As they often give details of the executors' and beneficiaries' occupations, towns of residence and, if relevant, relationship to the testator, wills can be a mine of biographical information for several individuals.

WHAT A WILL MIGHT TELL YOU

The name, occupation and place of residence of the testator.

The name or names of the executor(s).

Arrangements for the payment of debts and funeral expenses.

Arrangements for payment of sums of money to family members, other relatives or friends, or gifts to them of items of personal property, such as jewellery or furniture.

A gift of the main assets of the estate, perhaps the testator's property or business, usually to the wife or eldest son.

The names of trustees, if appointed.

The disposal of the rest of the estate to one or more people (such as wife and son jointly) or to trustees to hold for the benefit of family members (for example, children or grand-children who would receive shares on reaching maturity).

Assets, but no will Intestacy was dealt with by a legal process known as 'administration'. A court issued 'letters of administration', known also as 'admons', giving legal authority to one or more 'administrators' to gather the deceased's assets, pay his debts, administer the estate and distribute it in accordance with the law. The administrator was usually the deceased's eldest son, brother or widow. But creditors of the deceased—keen to obtain payment of a debt—could also apply.

The law also specified who should receive the deceased's assets. Under current law, the composition of the deceased's remaining family decides how the estate is transferred. For example, if the intestate has left no issue, parent or sibling, the whole estate goes to the spouse, but if there is a surviving parent, sibling or issue of a sibling the spouse receives the 'personal chattels' (movable property, such as pictures and furniture), a fixed sum (currently £200,000), and half of the remainder of the estate.

Administration was necessary only if property had to be transferred out of the deceased's name. If he had just a few possessions, it was usual for them to be kept by the widow, or for the family to agree how they should be divided, so records may not exist.

Role of the courts The courts have dealt with thousands of applications for administration each year since the 16th century. The process has become even more important during the 20th century as British people have become wealthier—although even today, only a little over 30 per cent of people leave a will—and more property is registered in people's names at death, such as land, shares, bank accounts and insurance policies.

These assets must be transferred to the beneficiaries, usually by a legally authorised representative of the estate, the executor or administrator. If your ancestor did not leave a will, there may still be court records of his intestacy. The letters of administration

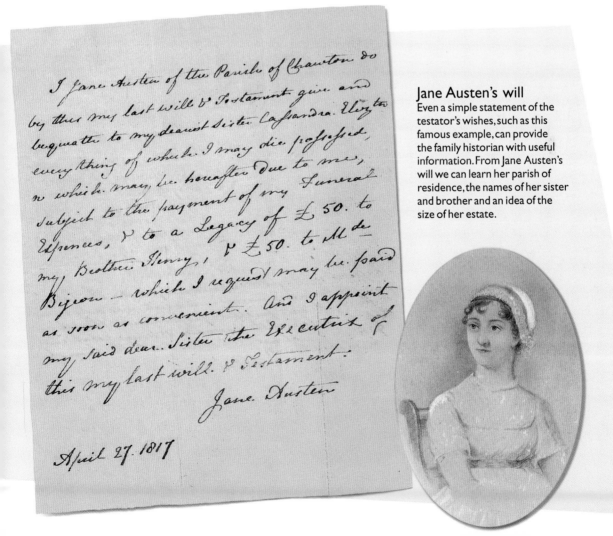

Jane Austen's will
Even a simple statement of the testator's wishes, such as this famous example, can provide the family historian with useful information. From Jane Austen's will we can learn her parish of residence, the names of her sister and brother and an idea of the size of her estate.

123

do not list property or name beneficiaries, but will state who acted as administrator and, in recent times, the value of the estate.

A WILL BUT NO EXECUTORS You may also find 'letters of administration with will annexed'. These are papers issued to a relative or creditor to carry out the testator's wishes because the deceased had failed to appoint executors, or because the appointed executors had died before the testator had moved abroad or were too ill to act. The will would remain valid and the estate was distributed in accordance with it.

the role of the lawyers

A lawyer might draft a man's will and advise him on distributing his property (and, today, on the tax consequences). If a man's circumstances changed, he might be advised to execute a new will, or amend his earlier will—by a document known as a codicil.

Granting probate The law also had a role after death of a testator. Executors had to apply to court for the will to be validated—a process known as probate. If satisfied that the will was valid, the court granted probate to the executors, authorising them to act. Grants of probate can be found with the will.

Spoken wills The law recognised oral declarations by a dying man who had not made a will. Those who heard the declaration could be called upon to give sworn evidence of his wishes to a court. The court then decided whether the deceased had made such a declaration, and, if satisfied, recorded the words and granted probate, authorising the administrators to distribute the deceased's estate according to his wishes.

These 'nuncupative' wills often resulted in family arguments and litigation before the courts. The Wills Act of 1837 made such wills invalid except for members of the armed forces who died in action.

TRUSTS AND TRUSTEES

Property could be transferred into a trust; that is be held by someone (a trustee) on behalf of other persons (the beneficiaries). Trusts could be established by a deed or in a testator's will and exist for many years. If his children had not reached maturity, for instance, a testator might leave much of his property in trust for them. The trustees could manage it until the children reached adulthood and could look after it themselves.

Convict Magwitch placed money in trust for young Pip in Dickens' novel *Great Expectations*.

actual distribution of property

Estates were not always distributed as set out in a will. If the testator's financial position deteriorated between the making of a will and his death, and the estate could no longer cover the gifts specified, some beneficiaries may have received smaller sums. A named beneficiary received nothing if a specific gift of property, perhaps a horse or a painting, was no longer in the testator's possession on death.

Until the law was changed in 1969, illegitimate children were not entitled to benefit from their father's estate unless he had specifically named them as beneficiaries in his will.

their goods and chattels

An inventory of an ancestor's movable belongings complete with valuations can give you a vivid sense of how he lived, his status and taste. From 1530 to 1750 many probate courts required inventories; later they were made only at the relatives' request to avoid disputes.

The lists were drawn up by two, three or four 'appraisors', often family or friends, whose names, addresses and occupations are noted. Belongings were catalogued room by room, with an additional listing of livestock and tools.

Inventories are usually with other probate records at the TNA, county or city record offices (see DIRECTORY).

What was left

On 1 September 1724 this inventory was made by Robert and Edward Hillor. It records the belongings of John Rawlins of Southwark, who had lived in comfort rather than luxury—he ate off pewter and slept on a 'sacking bottom' bed. The list includes a copper porridge pot, three brass candlesticks and some old books in the kitchen, various tables and 'looking glasses' (mirrors).

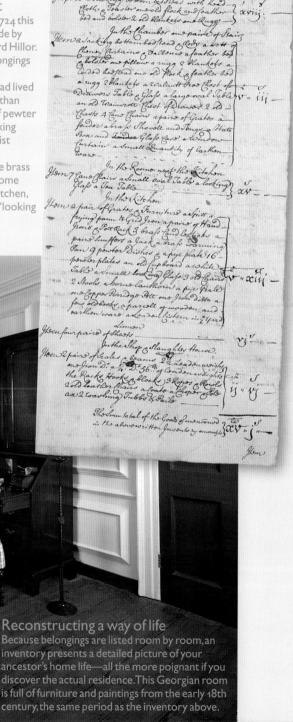

Reconstructing a way of life

Because belongings are listed room by room, an inventory presents a detailed picture of your ancestor's home life—all the more poignant if you discover the actual residence. This Georgian room is full of furniture and paintings from the early 18th century, the same period as the inventory above.

legacies

You will find it very easy to trace English and Welsh wills and administrations made since January 1858; the Principal Registry in London holds records since that date

tracing wills after 1858

Over the years, most copies of wills held by families, executors or administrators have been lost. However, the originals are preserved in official court records. The Probate Act of 1857 required that all applications for probate or administration be made to the newly established civil Court of Probate with Probate Registries across England and Wales. The Principal Registry in London (see below and DIRECTORY) holds copies of all the wills proved, or administrations granted, in these registries. It also has calendars (alphabetical lists of wills proved and

KEY SOURCES OF INFORMATION

♦ English and Welsh wills and administrations at the Principal Registry (now part of the Family Division of the High Court of Justice).

♦ Welsh wills at the National Library of Wales.

♦ Irish wills and indexes at the National Archives and Public Record Office of Northern Ireland.

♦ Scottish wills at the National Archives.

SEE DIRECTORY ➤

research in the Principal Registry

Finding the entry

At the Principal Registry you can consult yearly calendars, or alphabetical lists, of all people for whom grants of probate or letters of administration have been made since 1858, as well as copies of the documentation. It could take months or even a year or two to grant probate or letters of administration and names appear in the calendar for the year in which the grant was made rather than the year of death. So, if your ancestor died in 1880, search the 1880 and 1881 calendars. The registry searchroom is open from 10am to 4.30pm, Monday to Friday.

What's in a calendar

A calendar entry can provide you with much information, including the deceased's full name, occupation, address and date of death, the gross value of the estate, the names of the executors or administrators, and sometimes their occupations, addresses and their relationship (if any) to the deceased.

You should always copy out the full entry in the calendar, since all the information may turn out to be important.

administrations granted) since 1858. Microfilms of the calendars for 1858–1935 can be seen at the Society of Genealogists and other major archives. Copies of Welsh wills (except Montgomeryshire) are also held at the National Library of Wales.

Searching closer to home If you cannot get to London, check if your local family history society or archive holds calendars. There are also District Probate Registries, where some calendars can be inspected and copies of wills and probate grants ordered. Check with a registry first to find what is available (see DIRECTORY under probate offices).

Irish probate records

Probate in Ireland was similar to England. Since 1858, wills and administrations have been dealt with in the Probate Court, consisting of a Principal Registry in Dublin plus 11 District Registries. These regional registries kept copies while the originals were sent to Dublin. Although most of the post-1858 Principal Registry will and grant books and original wills and grants of the Principal and District Registries were destroyed by fire in 1922, copies survived in the regional registries and many lost records have also been replaced by copies from solicitors, family papers and property records. Others are represented by transcripts or abstracts made before the fire. These collections are held in the National Archives in Dublin. Post-1922 probate records for Northern Ireland are held at the Public Record Office of Northern Ireland.

Scottish probate records

Until 1868 real property (land and buildings) in Scotland descended automatically to the eldest son (or to the daughters equally if there were no sons). Only personal property could be left in a 'testamentary disposition'. Probate records consist of a person's testament and a 'grant of confirmation',

Seeing documents

You can ask to view a copy of a will, grant of probate or letters of administration up to 3pm. You need to fill in a form and pay £5. Extra copies of the same document cost £1 each. The records are ready to be collected in about an hour, and you can make notes or take the copies away with you.

You may be able to obtain a literary research pass, allowing you to look at documents over 100 years old without paying the £5 fee. For details, contact the Principal Registry.

Copies by post

You can ask for copies of wills, grants of probate or letters of administration to be sent to you after you have made your search. The fee is £5 per estate. If you cannot get to London, a search can be done and copies of documents sent to you. Write, enclosing a cheque for £5 payable to HM Paymaster General, to:

The Postal Searches & Copies Department
York Probate Sub-Registry
Duncombe Place
York YO1 7EA

which is a court order confirming the appointment of executors or administrators.

Sheriff Courts, with a jurisdiction approximating to the Scottish counties, have dealt with probate in Scotland since 1824. Their older records are in the National Archives of Scotland (see DIRECTORY), but the most recent records are held by the individual courts. The National Archives holds various indexes to Sheriff Court probate records for 1824–75 and annual volumes, listing alphabetically by name of the deceased all confirmations for 1876–1959.

Scottish and Irish held property When Scottish and Irish people died holding property in England or Wales, the executors or administrators would bring the probate papers to London. The English registry would 'reseal' the original papers, that is stamp them as 'approved' in this jurisdiction, then enter them in the national English and Welsh indexes. Scottish and Irish executors or administrators could then deal with property in London.

probate in other jurisdictions

ISLE OF MAN Church courts dealt with Manx probates before 1884; the Manx High Court of Justice took the task over after 1884. Records up to 1910 with indexes are in the Manx National Heritage Library (see DIRECTORY). More recent probate records are in the Probate Offices in Douglas (see DIRECTORY). After 1858 some wills were proved in the Principal Registry in London, or before this in the Prerogative Courts of York or Canterbury (see page 130).

GUERNSEY Wills and administrations are proved and held by the Ecclesiastical Court in St Peter Port; wills since 1841 dealing with real property are held by the Greffe of the Royal Court of Guernsey. See DIRECTORY for addresses.

JERSEY Land in Jersey descended automatically until 1851. Wills dealing with real property made

since that date are held at the Public Registry in St Helier, while those dealing with personal property and administrations are held by the Judicial Greffe. See DIRECTORY for addresses.

death duty records

Death duty registers at the TNA can be useful. To assess tax (levied on a deceased's estate since 1796) the authorities copied information on the value and recipients of the property from English and Welsh administrations and wills. The registers for 1796 to 1903 are in class IR 26 with indexes in IR 27. They give details on the deceased, executors, administrators and beneficiaries and their relationships to the deceased, as well as the property they received. This can be important as letters of administration do not record the names of beneficiaries. Even a will may omit their names—for example, if property was 'to be divided between my four children equally'.

Death duty registers for Scotland are held at the National Archives of Scotland and date from 1804.

TAKING IT FURTHER

♦ *Wills and Other Probate Records* (K. Grannum and N. Taylor, TNA, 2004).
♦ *Ancestral Trails* (M. Herber, Sutton, 2000).
♦ *Tracing Your Ancestors in the National Archives* (A. Bevan, National Archives, 7th revised ed., 2006).
♦ *Probate Jurisdictions: Where to Look for Wills* (J. Gibson and B. Langston, FFHS, 5th ed., 2002).
♦ *Tracing your Irish ancestors* (J. Grenham, Gill & Macmillan, 1992).
♦ www.nationalarchives.gov.uk/records/research-guides/wills-and-probate-records.htm
♦ www.nationalarchives.gov.uk/documents online/death-duty.asp
♦ www.ancestor-search.info/NAT-Probate.htm

legacies

tracing wills before 1858

The thread of life
The frontispiece of a finely illuminated book of wills from 1562 produced by the Prerogative Court of Canterbury shows the three Fates: Clotho, Atropos and Lachesis. In Greek mythology these ancient spinsters governed human destiny, spinning threads representing each mortal life.

B. Langston, FFHS, 5th ed., 2002). The book is arranged by English and Welsh county names, making it easier to determine which courts might have dealt with your ancestor's will.

the jurisdiction of the courts

The location of your ancestor's property would have determined to which court or courts an application for probate was made. Personal possessions would usually be in the deceased's house, but a man could own land in a number of places.

Archdeacons' courts These had jurisdiction over a group of parishes, which might vary greatly in extent, some covering most of a county. Maps in Gibson's work (see above) show these jurisdictions. If a man's property lay within one archdeaconry, application for probate should have been made to that court.

Superior courts If a person owned property of £5 or more (known as *bona notabilia*) in more than one archdeaconry, application for probate should have been made to a superior court—that of a bishop or an archbishop. If

Earlier wills and letters of administration are similar in form to later documents, but as you step back in time the language becomes more archaic and religious. They are handwritten documents, sometimes in Latin, which may be difficult to decipher. Locating pre-1858 wills is also a more complex process. Until that year ecclesiastical courts in England and Wales dealt with probate. An excellent guide to the Church courts, the places within their jurisdiction, the location of their records and the existence of indexes is provided by *Probate Jurisdictions: where to look for wills* (J. Gibson and

the property was in one diocese, application could be made to the bishop's Consistory Court.

Some archdeacons did not exercise their jurisdiction, and wills and administrations in these areas also had to be dealt with by a bishop's court (known as a Commissary Court under these circumstances).

Courts of Canterbury and York If the property lay in different dioceses, but the same archbishop's province, application was made to the Prerogative Court of Canterbury (PCC), or to one of the courts of the Archbishop of York. The jurisdiction of the York courts varied, so you should search the records of the Consistory Court of York, the Prerogative Court of York and the Exchequer Court. If a man's property lay in the provinces of both Canterbury and York, the application should have been made to the PCC, as it was the higher court. The PCC also dealt with probate for people dying outside England and Wales but owning property there.

Applications were sometimes made to a higher court than was necessary. The PCC had offices in London and the provinces and was the busiest and most prestigious probate court. Many used it for that reason alone. Ideally, therefore, you should always search the PCC records.

'Peculiar' parishes Some parishes, known as 'peculiars', were in one archdeaconry or diocese but came under another jurisdiction—usually that of other church officials and their courts. Some peculiars had their own probate courts. The peculiars in each county are noted by Gibson, together with the names of the courts that had jurisdiction.

Closure of the church courts Between 1653 and 1660 the church courts were closed, and almost every will or administration in England and Wales was dealt with by a civil 'Court of Probate of wills and granting administrations'. Its records can be found within the PCC wills at the TNA.

KEY SOURCES OF INFORMATION
♦ Most church court records in local record offices.
♦ Prerogative Court of Canterbury records at the TNA.
♦ Archbishop of York's court records at the Borthwick Institute for Archives.
♦ Welsh courts' records of wills at the National Library of Wales.
♦ Irish records and indexes of wills in the Registry of Deeds and the National Archives of Ireland.
♦ Most pre-1824 Scottish wills at the National Archives of Scotland.

SEE DIRECTORY ➤

Other probate courts A few other courts had jurisdiction over probate matters. This usually occurred in large towns and cities such as the City of London, where the Court of Hustings proved wills until the 17th century.

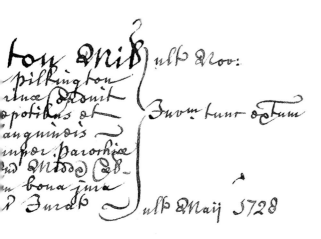

Finding the records Most church court records
are in county record offices, as listed by Gibson
and Langston. So probate records for most
Bedfordshire inhabitants are at Bedford Record
Office. Records of other courts are generally in the
city or borough record office where the court
had jurisdiction.

PCC RECORDS These are at the TNA. Many PCC
indexes have been published. Copies are available at
the TNA, Society of Genealogists and county record
offices. An index of PCC wills is available online at
www.documentsonline.nationalarchives.gov.uk.

THE YORK COURTS Probate records for
the York province are held at the Borthwick
Institute of Historical Research (see DIRECTORY),
which has indexes for 1688–1858. See *A Guide to
Genealogical Sources in the Borthwick Institute of
Historical Research* (C. C. Webb, York University,
4th ed., 2002).

WELSH COURTS Consistory and archdeacons'
court records are in the National Library of Wales
(see DIRECTORY). The courts (and indexes to the
records) are listed in Gibson and Langston. Some
Welsh indexes are by given name, reflecting the
existence of the patronymic naming system (see
pages 302–3).

Other collections of wills Property deeds held
in county record offices sometimes include wills of
the property owners used by executors to distribute
the estate. Copy wills can also survive in family
papers and solicitors' records deposited in archives,
and they may be indexed.

Some published and typescript copies of wills
exist in record offices and at the Society of
Genealogists. If your ancestor's original will has
been lost, these may be the only remaining evidence
of its existence. Published volumes often index the
names of everyone referred to in the wills they
contain. Such indexes offer an easy way to find your
ancestor if he was a beneficiary or executor.

Irish probate records pre-1858

Finding a will in Ireland can be difficult. Before 1858
applications for probate, as in England, had to be
made to church courts, and most of these records
were destroyed by fire in 1922. *Tracing Your Irish
Ancestors* (J. Grenham, Gill & Macmillan, 3rd revised
ed., 2006) lists the surviving records and indexes,
and collections of will transcripts.

Published and indexed abstracts of more than
2000 wills from 1708 to 1832 can be found in the
Registry of Deeds in Dublin and about 10,000
indexed wills in family estate papers are held in the
National Archives of Ireland (see DIRECTORY).

Scottish probate records pre-1824

The church courts of Scotland dealt with probate
until about 1560, when jurisdiction was transferred to secular courts known as commissariots.
The highest of these courts was the Principal
Commissariot Court in Edinburgh, which also had
jurisdiction over the property of Scots dying abroad.

Maps of the commissariot jurisdictions are avail-
able from the Institute of Heraldic and Genealogical
Studies. The National Archives of Scotland holds
most pre-1824 wills. Indexes are at the National
Archives, the Society of Genealogists and Family
History Centres. See DIRECTORY for addresses.

education
finding school records

How did your ancestor perform at school? You may find clues in original school records or printed registers. Many survive from the 19th century and some date back to medieval times

Records of your ancestors' schooldays can provide a rare glimpse of their childhood. A school report, a leather-bound book prize or family papers may reveal what school they attended.

Schools and their head teachers can often be tracked down in commercial directories. In the 19th century, a boarding school and its staff would be listed in census returns. Local newspapers may name pupils who won prizes or did well at games.

English and Welsh schools of the past Most of the records date from the late 19th century onwards as education became more widespread, but some material, particularly from public schools, survives from much earlier times.

In the Middle Ages, the Church, monasteries, guilds and private benefactors established schools. Some still exist, such as Winchester College, founded in 1382, whose records date back to 1394. By the 16th century, there were several hundred grammar schools. In the 17th and 18th centuries hundreds of Nonconformist and charity schools were founded.

Social change Reforms in the late 18th and 19th centuries brought education to the masses. Sunday schools were started by Robert Raikes in Gloucester in 1785 and by 1851 they had nearly 2.5 million pupils. In the early years of the 19th century Nonconformist chapels provided 'British and Foreign Schools' and the Church of England

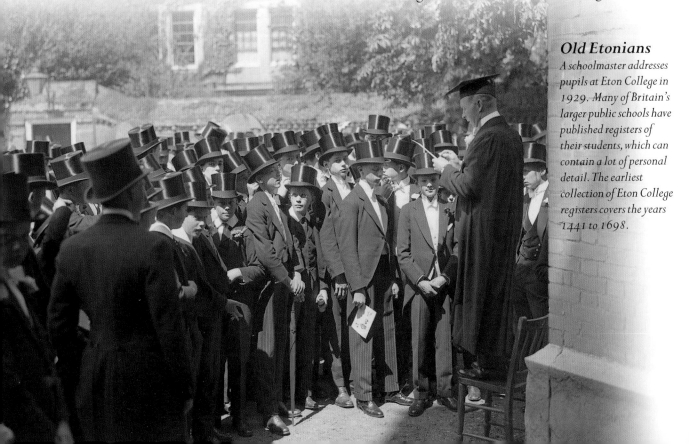

Old Etonians
A schoolmaster addresses pupils at Eton College in 1929. Many of Britain's larger public schools have published registers of their students, which can contain a lot of personal detail. The earliest collection of Eton College registers covers the years 1441 to 1698.

founded 'National Schools'. Between them, they had 1.5 million pupils on roll in nearly 7,000 schools by the 1860s.

But half the nation's children did not attend day school. The Education Act (1870) provided for the election of school boards with powers to raise local rates to build 'Board Schools', many of which are still in use. These were subject to government inspection. In 1880 all children were compelled to attend day school up to the age of 10. This was raised to 11 in 1893 and to 12 in 1899.

In 1902 responsibility for elementary, secondary and technical education was transferred to 330 local education authorities (LEAs) under a central Board of Education. The 'Board Schools' now became 'Council Schools'. The school-leaving age was raised to 14 in 1918, to 15 in 1944, and to 16 in 1972.

Documents you may find

Some original school records have survived. They fall into several different categories:

ADMISSIONS REGISTERS Mostly kept after 1870, these can contain a wealth of detail. Some tell you which schools pupils came from and which they went on to attend. In one Lincolnshire register various pupils had 'left the village', 'gone to a home' or 'gone to blind school', and some died.

SCHOOL LOGBOOKS Written up in great detail by head teachers, these books recorded visitors to the school, inspections, examination and other successes, changes of staff, holidays, school treats, the impact of harvest time on school attendance or events of local significance such as an epidemic of whooping cough.

ATTENDANCE REGISTERS These records, together with class lists, punishment books, honours books and accident books, reveal further details of an ancestor's school life. Letters to and from parents may be found in correspondence files.

SCHOOL MAGAZINES Names and fascinating biographical snippets can be found in newsletters, magazines or alumni association publications.

Where the records are held Some schools have retained their older records, but the survival rate is sporadic. Church and State school records may be held in local record offices, libraries or museums.

In county record offices you may find Church of England school records among other parish papers, while workhouse school records will be held with those of poor law unions (see pages 153–5). The records of Nonconformist schools can often be found in the archives of that denomination (see pages 102–5). A collection of records from the British and Foreign School Society, which founded nondenominational schools and colleges in Britain and abroad, can be searched at its Archives Centre,

December 3, 1875: Punished James Garlick for impudence ... Jas. Garlick wanted to fetch his father—would not allow him
From the logbook for Farmor's School, Fairford, Gloucestershire

Brunel University, Lancaster House, Borough Road, Isleworth, Middlesex TW7 5DU. The records date from the early 19th century.

Records relating to the administration of education in England and Wales, which can be useful for background information, are held at the TNA.

What you find in a register Printed registers often include photographs of individuals, groups, teams and buildings, together with single-page or folding maps. Probably the grandest of all such publications is *Alumni Carthusiani*: a record of the foundation scholars of Charterhouse School, Surrey, 1614 to 1872, privately printed in 1913 for F.A. Crisp on handmade paper.

Teaching poor children in Edinburgh

In the mid 19th century the Revd Thomas Guthrie ran a ragged school in a church in Princes Street, Edinburgh. Girls were taught how to sew, knit and cook, while boys were trained as tailors, cobblers, boxmakers and carpenters.

Others are much more modest, with typescript text or even produced on an ink duplicator and stapled into card covers. The quality of entries could also vary, where these depended on information supplied by ex-pupils. The best entries list the pupil's scholastic and sporting achievements, and provide details of higher education and subsequent career. Most are less substantial and may not give parents' names or may carry in-depth biographies of only the school's more notable pupils.

Public schools such as Harrow, Malvern and Tonbridge School update their registers every few years. But each edition must be studied carefully as the registers may, for instance, only feature the ex-pupils from earlier editions who are still alive.

Useful school histories A history of a school may also contain interesting material as some mention many names and have substantial indexes. *The History of the Grammar School of Charles King of England in Kidderminster* (1903), for instance, has lists of pupils' names and dates, and some fathers' names, while *The History of Wisbech Grammar School* (1939) has a short list of distinguished old boys.

Education in Wales 'Circulating schools' were founded in Wales by the Revd Griffith Jones in the early 1730s, with itinerant teachers to cater for the scattered population. For 50 years their success resulted in a high national level of literacy.

Many boys from wealthier families attended English schools and appear in their registers. Among the few printed school registers for Wales is that for the Methodist Rydal School in Colwyn Bay.

Irish schools Royal schools and grammar schools were founded in Ireland in the 17th century, though few records exist from that time. A few early registers exist for the charity schools that opened in the early 18th century, which together with residential 'charter' schools set up by royal charter provided only a Protestant education.

Catholics often attended so-called 'hedge' schools set up in parents' homes and recorded in personal diaries and letters; no registers were kept.

The National School System was established in 1831 to provide nondenominational education. Its records are incomplete but they include pupil applications, registers and rolls, housed at the Public Record Office of Northern Ireland, the National Archives of Ireland, the National Library of Ireland (see DIRECTORY) and in local libraries.

Scotland's schools As early as the 16th century most Scottish towns had a grammar school. In the 17th century, Acts of Parliament established primary schools in every parish. State school records, including logbooks, can be found among church and town council records. Inspectors' reports on schools from 1872 are held in the National Archives of Scotland (see DIRECTORY), which also has a collection of school logbooks. Private schools flourished from the 18th century such as those founded by the Society in Scotland for Propagating Christian Knowledge, whose records are in the National Archives (reference GD 95).

Many prominent Scottish schools have published registers. Among the more substantial are those for the Edinburgh Academy, the Edinburgh Institution, Aberdeen Grammar School, Loretto, Fettes, Merchiston Castle and Glenalmond.

A register to make the old boys squirm
You never quite know what you will find in a published school register. The history of Whitgift School in Croydon, Surrey, with a register of all Whitgiftians from 1871 to 1892, published in 1892, adopts the wonderful ploy of giving the school nicknames of many of the boys. Long after 'Apple Dumpling' Hickman, 'Bird' alias 'Ladybird' alias 'Bagpipes' Mackenzie or 'Lucy' Morland have left school, their embarrassing names live on.

TAKING IT FURTHER
♦ www.nationalarchives.gov.uk/records/ research-guides/education.htm and other guides under the heading 'Education'.
♦ *The Oxford Companion to Family and Local History* (D. Hey, Oxford University Press, 2nd ed., 2010).
♦ *Record Sources for Local History* (P. Riden, Batsford, 1987).
♦ *The Growth of British Education and Its Records* (C. R. Chapman, Lochin Publishing, 2nd ed., 1992).
♦ *School, University and College Registers and Histories in the Library of the Society of Genealogists* (Society of Genealogists, 2nd ed., 1996).

THE REGISTER.

820. GRANVILLE, G. W.; son of W. T. Granville, 1 Souldern [...] Green, Lond.; V.B–V.A; L., 80_3; addss., as above.

821. HARROD, J. T. (Bird, MacOiseau); son of J. Harrod; I. [...]

822. HICKMAN, R. N. (Apple Dumpling); son of Rev. W. R. [...] St. James' Vicarage, Tavistock Rd., Croydon; V.A; L., 80_1; [...] as above.

823. KNIGHT, J. C.; son of C. Knight; I.A–II.; L., 81_2.

824. LANE, E.; son of H. Lane, Addiscombe House, Hav[...] Croydon; I.B–III.B; fifteen, 83–4; L., 84_1; Veterans, 88; pte. above; in business, Old Shot Tower, Commercial Rd., Lambeth, [...]

825. LANGLANDS, R.; son of J. Langlands, Kent House Fa[...] S.E.; I.B; L., 79_3; pte. and business addss., as above.

826. MACKENZIE, R. D. (Bird, Ladybird, Bagpipes); son [...] kenzie, M.A., Dingwall Lodge, Dingwall Rd., Croydon; II.–VI.; [...] and 6, took 126 wkts., aver. 8.8, in 86; fifteen, 83–4 to 5–6; G[...] 85_3–6_2; Gymn. Com., 85_3–6_2, and hon. sec., 86_1–6_2; Chess Com[...] winner of Chess Tournament, 87_1; Chess Team, 85–6, 86–7, [...] L., 86_2; Gymn. Com., 86_3–8_3; pte. addss., as above; in busines[...] and Sons, 2 Suffolk Lane, Cannon St., Lond.

827. MORLAND, H. J. (Lucy); son of C. C. Morland, Ras[...] Morland Rd., Croydon; III.B–V.A; Heath and Clarke Exhib[...] Stephenson Clarke Exhibitioner, 86; L., 82_3; re-entered, 86_3; V[...] son Clarke Exhibitioner, 87; L., 87_1; Lond. matric., 86; B.A[...] pte. addss., as above; at Cambridge.

Many of Britain's universities and colleges have kept a record of past alumni. The most detailed tell you much about a student's academic and sporting achievements and subsequent career

education
colleges & universities

If your ancestor went to university in England before the 19th century he could only have gone to Oxford or Cambridge, both established in the 13th century. St Andrews, founded in 1411, is Scotland's oldest university. Ireland's oldest is Trinity College, Dublin, which was established in 1591 but did not admit non-Anglicans until 1793.

Other British universities were not founded until the 19th century, such as London in 1826 and Durham in 1831. Queen's College, Belfast, now Queen's University, opened in 1849, and the University College of Wales, Aberystwyth, in 1872.

Where original records of university and college students have survived, you will generally discover them stored away in an archive within the institution itself, or at a local studies library or record office.

Anglicans at Oxbridge

Anyone with Anglican clerics as ancestors should study the biographical registers of Oxford and Cambridge universities. For centuries they were Anglican male preserves and theology was the central discipline. Dissenters were excluded before

1871, and women were not admitted until the late 19th century. The principal published registers are:

☞ *Alumni Oxonienses 1500–1886* (J. Foster, James Parker & Co., 1887). Reprinted in 1968 by Kraus Reprint, it lists Oxford students (and often their fathers' names) and also includes details of their subsequent careers.

☞ *A Biographical Register of the University of Oxford to* AD *1500* (A.B. Emden, Oxford University Press, 1989), which has biographical notes on earlier Oxford students. Emden also compiled a more detailed volume for 1501 to 1540 (Oxford University Press, 1974).

☞ *Alumni Cantabrigienses* (J. Venn and J.A. Venn). This is a ten-volume work that appeared between 1922 and 1954 and was reprinted by Kraus Reprint in the 1970s. It lists all known students, graduates and holders of office at Cambridge University from the 13th century to 1900. Some entries carry considerable detail, including parentage, career and even place of burial.

☞ *A Biographical Register of Cambridge to 1500* (A.B. Emden, Cambridge University Press, 1963) contains further information about Cambridge students in the Middle Ages.

Other registers and records Many Oxford and Cambridge colleges have produced their own registers and may hold other documents, including team photographs. The records of Jesus College, Oxford, reveal a large number of Welsh students because of its traditionally strong links with Wales. Elsewhere in England and Wales, the number of detailed works on alumni is very limited; printed calendars—the universities' own annual surveys—often give little more than the names of graduates past and present. The records are usually held in university archives or at local studies libraries.

Irish and Scottish universities

The most substantial Irish work is *Alumni Dublinenses 1593–1860* (G.D. Burtchaell and T.U. Sadleir, Thom & Co., 1935), with more than 35,000 entries. It has considerable detail on past students of Trinity College, Dublin, and lists professors and provosts as well. Most Trinity students were Protestant, and

He was sent, as usual, to a public school, where a little learning was painfully beaten into him, and from thence to the university, where it was carefully taken out of him.
Nightmare Abbey (1818) Thomas Love Peacock

boys from a number of English schools studied at the university from the 17th century onwards.

Several Irish universities, including the 'Queen's Colleges' established from 1845 in Belfast, Cork and Galway, have published lists of honours graduates. Some detailed student records from the 19th century are still held in the archives of universities such as University College, Dublin—founded as the Catholic University of Ireland in 1854.

Calendars and more detailed works exist for Scottish universities, including Aberdeen and Glasgow, both founded in the 15th century. Their intake included many English and Irish students.

KEY SOURCES OF INFORMATION
♦ Calendars in university or college archives.
♦ Collections of university and college registers at the Society of Genealogists and at the Institute of Heraldic and Genealogical Studies.
♦ Some registers in local and national libraries.
SEE DIRECTORY ➤

Records of other colleges You may be able to
find calendars or registers for other colleges of
higher education, including:

VOCATIONAL ESTABLISHMENTS These
would include institutions such as the Royal
Agricultural College at Cirencester.

DENOMINATIONAL COLLEGES These offered
general education or training for teachers
or missionaries. They include Cuddesdon College,
near Oxford, for Anglicans; Bristol Baptist College;
and the Congregationalist Brecon Memorial
College. Nonconformist colleges date from the
17th century; some students are listed in a series
of articles in the *Transactions of the Congregational
Historical Society*, vols 3–10 (1907/8–1927/9),
which can be consulted at Dr Williams's Library
(see DIRECTORY) and some reference libraries.

OVERSEAS STUDY Your ancestor may have
completed his education abroad. Roman Catholics,
whose educational opportunities in Britain and
Ireland were severely limited until the 19th century,
flocked to colleges in France, Italy, Portugal and
Spain (see Roman Catholics, pages 107–9). The
Catholic Record Society (see DIRECTORY) has
published some relevant records.

A march of history
*Students and staff of Scotland's oldest university, St Andrews,
take part in a grand procession in 1911 to celebrate the
fifth centenary of the foundation in 1411. The high quality
of Scottish education attracted many students from England
and elsewhere.*

working life
companies & trades

Documents relating to your ancestors' work may indicate a family trade, or a talent that you and other descendants share. They can also give you vivid glimpses of the way people lived at that time

Builders of the past
Old brickmakers at Millbrook Kiln, Bedfordshire, in 1867 had lived to see the industry flourish in the Victorian building boom. The photograph was used in 1910 by the Ampthill News *and later turned up in a family album.*

Some ancestors' working lives are likely to be well documented, especially in jobs such as apprenticed trades. But you may find scant evidence if they were servants or farm labourers. Occupations are often noted on birth, marriage and death certificates, census returns and in parish registers.

For occupational sources, see *Trades and Professions: The Family Historian's Guide* (S.A. Raymond, Family History Partnership, 2011).

company and industry records

Businesses and industries in the 19th and 20th centuries have generated more employment records than in previous eras and many of their documents survive.

Some businesses have deposited their archives at county record offices and may be listed in the record office's holdings. The National Register of Archives, which is now part of the National Archives, (see DIRECTORY), lists the location of records for around 25,000 companies, some dating back to the 17th century. The indexes can be accessed online at www.nationalarchives.gov.uk

The Business Archives Council (see DIRECTORY) has encouraged firms to preserve their records and identified important collections in sectors such as banking, brewing and shipbuilding. It has listed the archives of the 1000 oldest registered British companies. Its library is open by appointment.

Finding registered companies By law since 1844 all limited companies (not sole traders or partnerships) in England and Wales have had to register their details. You can study the register at Companies House in Cardiff and London for a small fee, and consult a computer database for existing companies and those dissolved in the past 20 years (see DIRECTORY under 'Company registries').

Company records for Scotland and Northern Ireland, which have separate registration systems, can similarly be examined (see DIRECTORY under 'Company registries'). Details of Scottish business records may also be found in the Index to the National Register of Archives at the National Archives of Scotland (see DIRECTORY).

The railway companies Around 1000 railway companies were registered between the early 19th century and 1923. Although some were small and short-lived, others such as the Great Western Railway kept vast files on employees.

Many records are kept at the TNA in class RAIL and others can be found in county record offices. *Railway Ancestors* (D. Hawkings, The History Press, revised ed., 2008) is a guide to the staff records of railway companies in England and Wales 1822–1947.

At the National Archives of Scotland (see DIRECTORY), British Rail records (reference BR) also include documents and details of some of the earlier private Scottish companies.

finding an ancestor by trade

If your ancestors belonged to a trade union, they may be mentioned in national trade union records. A large collection is held at the Modern Records Centre, University of Warwick (see DIRECTORY).

The records date back to 1825, when unions gained legal recognition, and include registers of members listing their ages, occupations, addresses and dependants. *Nineteenth Century Trade Union Records* (H. Southall, D. Gilbert and C. Bryce, Historical Geography Research Series, 1994) describes the collection and other major archives.

Trade directories If you know your ancestor's trade and where he worked, you may find him listed in a local directory. Trade directories for many areas of Britain were published from the early 1800s and

Moving with the times
Pickfords, the removal company, is one of many businesses that has preserved its old records. Some documents in its archive in Enfield, Middlesex, date back to 1776. If a company holds indexed records they may help you to track down an employee, and discover his or her position in the company and level of pay.

often showed the names of firms' proprietors (see Town & county directories, pages 174–5).

Telephone directories may also help you to track down a business or trade. The British Telecom Archives (see DIRECTORY), which can be visited by appointment, has an almost complete set of British telephone books from 1880 to the present day.

Trades licensed by the magistrate Some trades can be traced through quarter session records in county or city record offices because the type of work required a local magistrate's licence. The licences were generally issued for a year.

Typical licensed positions included innkeeper, canal boatman, printer or gamekeeper. The records list the applicant's name and usually the period and location for which the licence was valid.

KEY SOURCES OF INFORMATION
♦ The National Archives has research guides on its website www.nationalarchives.gov.uk/records/research-guides/. See those that continue: /business-history.htm; /railway-staff.htm; and /apprenticeship-records.htm.
♦ Companies House (London, Cardiff and Edinburgh) and the Registry of Companies and Friendly Societies in Northern Ireland.
♦ Railway records at the TNA, county record offices and National Archives of Scotland.
♦ Guild records at Guildhall Library and county and city record offices. SEE DIRECTORY ➤

guilds and apprenticeships

Many craftsmen belonged to a trade association or guild, which promoted skills and standards. The first guilds were established in the 12th century and became the exclusive regulators of their particular trade or craft, imposing mandatory training on new entrants or apprentices (usually for seven years).

The London guilds became known as livery companies because of their distinctive dress or livery. The City of London had 48 companies in 1515; at present they have 108. The leading companies are known as The Great Twelve.

Though present-day members rarely practise the trade, some of the companies still exist in the City of London and hold archives, which can be consulted by permission from the clerk to the company. Most of their records are held at Guildhall Library (see DIRECTORY) and are of more than local interest as apprentices came from all parts of Britain.

The surviving records of guilds in other towns and cities, with a similar listing of masters and apprentices, are held in local record offices.

If you come across an obsolete trade that you do not recognise, you can find out more about it in *A Dictionary of Old Trades, Titles and Occupations* (C. Waters, Countryside Books, revised ed., 2002) or the web site www.gendocs.demon.co.uk/trades.html.

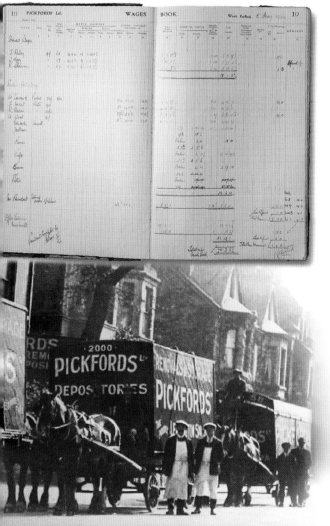

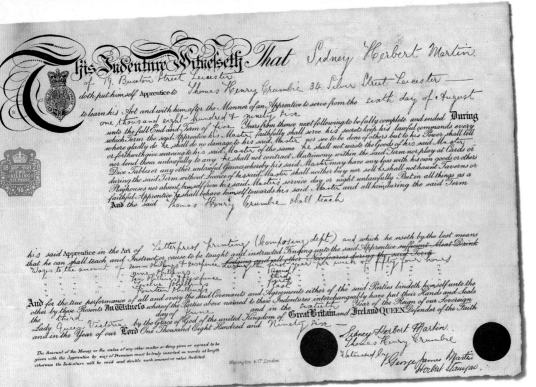

Apprentices From the 14th century, many boys and some girls underwent a formal apprenticeship in order to practise a craft or trade. In return for a fixed sum, they were indentured to a master or mistress under strict conditions. From 1601, the poorest children were also sent as apprentices by their parish to avoid the expense of their upkeep.

Surviving apprenticeship records can help your research a lot, as indenture papers required the signature of the master and a parent or guardian. The papers name the trade to be practised and may include both the father's name and his occupation and address. The apprentice's birth date and birthplace may also be noted.

Where records are held The only central register of apprenticeships in England and Wales is the collection of Apprenticeship Books (class IR 1) held at the TNA (see DIRECTORY).

The books cover the period 1710 to 1811 and record the tax imposed on the sums that masters received for taking on apprentices. They give the masters' names, addresses and trades, the names of their apprentices and the dates of their indentures. Indexes covering 1710–74 are held at the TNA,

Guildhall Library and the Society of Genealogists (see DIRECTORY), which has also published 31 volumes of indexes to livery company apprentices.

The names of thousands more apprentices can be found listed in guild and livery company records and among parish records in county record offices. See www.origins.net for London apprentices.

Apprentices in Ireland and Scotland
In Ireland, the completion of an apprenticeship was a qualification for becoming a freeman. As a result, many craftsmen and tradesmen are named in records such as the listing of free citizens of Dublin from 1225 to 1918, held in the Dublin City Archives (see DIRECTORY). Craftsmen and tradesmen are also listed in city and provincial directories (see Town & county directories, pages 174–5).

Similarly in Scotland, serving an apprenticeship qualified a man to become a burgess, which gave him voting rights in chartered towns and cities. Records of burgesses are held at the National Archives of Scotland (in Burgh records, reference B), and many registers of burgesses have been published by the Scottish Record Society (see DIRECTORY).

REAL LIVES
living above the shop

In 1995, shortly before he died, retired retailer Raymond Andrews wrote 'History of a Family Business', the story of Andrews' Stores, the family firm started by his father, William. Combined with photographs, directory entries, newspaper cuttings and advertisements, this precious family archive charts the firm's trials and triumphs.

A business is born

The history begins: 'After three horrific years as a sapper in the Royal Engineers in France during the Great War, William Andrews returned home in poor health, to his wife, Mildred. They opened their first shop in High Street, Shoeburyness in 1919.'

...good news for **MEN!**

the second stage of Andrews great expansion programme is complete . . . following the wonderful Fashion Floor comes the completion of splendid department specially for men.

It's Magnificent!

Designed for men, planned for men, this very modern MAN'S SHOP is far better than anything seen in Dagenham before. (Some say equal to any man's shop anywhere).

Come and judge for yourself!

You'll find VALUE, to MONEY, and the BEST that's made for men, for example :—

Real Brook, "Banner," and "Mentor" Shirts, Wolsey and Sparwick Underwear and Socks "Swallow" and Drwav Rainwear

ANDREWS
MAN'S SHOP
Corners at BECONTREE AVE and VALENCE AVE.
ANDREWS

Fresh opportunities

William (right) sold up to his father-in-law (above) and, after running a variety of shops, including four in Colchester, moved in 1927 to Becontree Estate, a huge housing project built on Essex farmland at Dagenham. He saw the trading potential of this 'new town' and opened for business on Becontree Avenue selling fish. Mildred disliked living above a fish shop and persuaded William in 1928 to take a lease on the corner shop, which became Andrews' Stores, Men's Outfitters and General Merchants.

Hard times

William died in 1936, leaving Mildred—in her early 40s with two young sons, Norman and Raymond—to run the firm. They, and the business, survived the Second World War, but only just, as 'a large shell, fired from the gun battery in Barking Park, landed on the shop forecourt, but miraculously failed to explode'.

Looking up

A scarcity of supplies made life hard after the war, but by the time a new store (left) opened in 1958, Andrews', with Raymond and Norman in charge and nearly 50 staff, 'was recognised as the best departmental store in Dagenham'.

End of the road

The 1960s and 70s were good times for Andrews'. Then customers began to desert local stores for shopping centres. In 1993 Raymond's sons, Richard and Peter, decided to sell up and create a new business elsewhere. The end of 'Andrews Corner', known to all Dagenham people, brought to a close one chapter in a family's history.

143

working life
for Crown & Church

Both Crown and Church have long maintained efficient and extensive archiving systems. Their records may reveal your ancestor's full name and date of birth, and chart that person's career path

Penny-farthing post
Postmen have been delivering letters since the Post Office was established under Charles I in 1635. By the end of the 19th century, the Post Office employed 170,000 people. Records of appointments and pensions may reveal a person's birth date, wages and cause of retirement.

If you have an ancestor who worked for the Crown you will find the relevant records at the TNA, usually under the particular government department, such as the Treasury or Home Office. Note that Customs and Excise were separate departments until 1909. Brief details of people in key positions have been published in works such as the 11 volume series *Office Holders in Modern Britain* (J.C. Sainty, Athlone Press and University of

London, 1972-2006), from 1660, and directories such as the *British Imperial Calendar* (from 1809) and *The Civil Service Year Book* (from mid 19th century).

RECORDS FOR SCOTLAND From the start of the 19th century, lists of Scottish civil servants occasionally occur in parliamentary papers held at the National Archives of Scotland (see DIRECTORY). These give the surname, forename, occupation, salary, age, cause of retirement and pension. Note that while most ministries' records are at the TNA, those for Scottish offices, such as the Scottish Board of Excise, General Register Office and Post Office will be at the National Archives.

Police force records There are no central records since most police forces were created locally by boroughs and counties between 1835 and 1860. Many forces have deposited their records at county record offices. You can find records of London's Metropolitan Police at the TNA in group MEPO. Indexes to the records are held at the force's archives (see DIRECTORY). Details of the City of London Police since 1832 are held at that force's record office (see DIRECTORY). Records of the Irish Constabulary (1816–1922) are held at the TNA.

Postal employees The Post Office's archives are open to the public at its Mount Pleasant complex in London (see DIRECTORY). Its records include Irish appointments up to 1922.

A licence to teach Until the late 18th century, schoolteachers had to obtain a licence from the Church authorities. Licences were recorded in bishops' registers, now held in county record offices (in Wales they are held at the National Library—see DIRECTORY). Teachers also appear in education records, such as school logbooks (see page 132).

KEY SOURCES OF INFORMATION
♦ Government employee records at the TNA and National Archives of Scotland.
♦ Records of police, teachers, clergy, parish and local government officials at county record offices.
♦ Postal worker records at the Post Office archives.
♦ Occupational directories at the Society of Genealogists and major reference libraries.
SEE DIRECTORY ➤

Clerical Directory (from 1858) and *Fasti Ecclesiae Anglicanae* (1066–1857).

IRISH AND SCOTTISH RECORDS For Church of Ireland appointments (especially in the 17th century) see the *Leslie Biographical Index* at the Representative Church Body (see DIRECTORY). *Fasti Ecclesiae Scoticanae* (H. Scot, Oliver and Boyd, 1915) lists the succession of ministers in the Church of Scotland from the 16th-century Reformation onwards. It is available at the National Library of Scotland (see DIRECTORY).

Nonconformist records The names of Nonconformist ministers may be found in quarter sessions records as Nonconformist chapels and ministers required licences. Many Nonconformist

members of the clergy

Clergy are ordained and allocated to a parish by a bishop. The appointments are recorded in bishops' registers. Published lists of Anglican appointments include the *Clergy List* (from 1841), *Crockford's*

Many paths to enlightenment

If you know a vicar's surname you can look him up in Crockford's Clerical Directory. You will be given brief biographical details and his address at the time. In this example, the 1865 entry for Caddell Holder ties him to St Juliot's in Camelford. Alternatively, you can use an alphabetical listing of churches and benefices to find out the name of the incumbent.

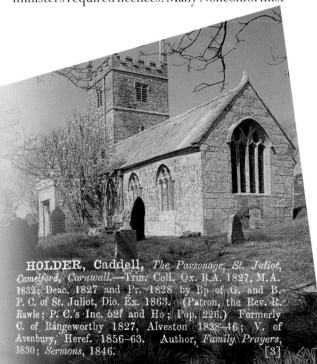

HOLDER, Caddell, *The Parsonage, St. Juliot, Camelford, Cornwall.*—Trin. Coll. Ox. B.A. 1827, M.A. 1832; Deac. 1827 and Pr. 1828 by Bp of G. and B. P. C. of St. Juliot, Dio. Ex. 1863. (Patron, the Rev. R. Rawle; P. C.'s Inc. 52*l* and Ho; Pop. 226.) Formerly C. of Rangeworthy 1827, Alveston 1828–46; V. of Avenbury, Heref. 1856–63. Author, *Family Prayers*, 1830; *Sermons*, 1846. [3]

Balancing the books
The constables' accounts of 1825 for Northallerton parish would have been scrutinised at the annual vestry meeting. Like surveyors, churchwardens and other local officials, constables had to justify their spending to the local parishioners.

denominations also published lists of their leaders. Examples are the *Baptist Bibliography 1526–1776, 1777–1837*; the *Congregational Year Book*, published yearly from 1846; and *Hall's Circuits and Ministers*, listing Methodists from 1765 to 1969.

IRELAND Irish Presbyterian ministers are listed in *Fasti of the Irish Presbyterian Church, 1613–1840* (J. & S. McConnell, 1951) and *Fasti of the General Assembly of the Presbyterian Church in Ireland, 1840–1910* (J.M. Barkley, 1986–7).

Roman Catholic records In four volumes, *The Seminary Priests* (Anstruther, 1966–76) gives information about Roman Catholic clergy from 1558 to 1800. Names of clergy, churches, schools and charities can also be found in the *Catholic Directory*, which has been published yearly since 1837. The annual *Irish Catholic Directory, Almanac and Registry*, published since 1836, is available from the Catholic Central Library (see DIRECTORY) and the National Library of Ireland (see DIRECTORY).

local parish officials

Anglican parish clerks, appointed for life by the vicar or rector, are recorded in the bishops' registers and often in parish records too. These are available from county archives.

The office of churchwarden began in medieval times. Nominated by the clergy, the churchwarden would be ratified by the parishioners at an annual vestry meeting. Parish constables (who maintained law and order), hedgewardens (responsible for trimming hedges) and waywardens or surveyors (responsible for road maintenance) were elected at vestry meetings. Minutes of the meetings are now held with the parish registers; in Wales many are at the National Library. Similar information is held in the Kirk Session records at the National Archives of Scotland (see DIRECTORY).

Local government employees By the 19th century, vestries were becoming less important, with many of their duties transferred to new civil local authorities (county councils were created in 1888). Papers relating to local government officials are usually found in county record offices.

The *Municipal Corporations Companion, Directory and Year Book of Statistics* (yearly from 1877), and the *County Companion, Diary Statistical Chronicle and Magisterial and Official Directory* (yearly from 1879, and combined with the former from 1889), hold the details of county and borough officials for England and Wales. For Scottish officials, see *Central and Local Government in Scotland Since 1707* (G.S. Pryde, 1960).

working life
in the professions

Our ancestors' professions may have changed or even no longer exist. Yet there are plenty of records available that can help with family history research

Until the mid 18th century, the relatively few men who were educated at university, or one of the Inns of Court, either returned to their fathers' country seats to help to manage the family estates, or embarked on a career as a clergyman, lawyer or physician. Professions such as architect, engineer and scientist did not emerge as separate career paths until the 19th century.

Well-educated professionals of this era had the time and money to indulge their interests, however bizarre. If you know your ancestor's pet subject, you may find his name in a specialised biographical directory. These books, listing hymn writers, book collectors, entomologists, ornithologists and so on, can be found in most reference libraries.

medical practitioners

Up to the 19th century, the medical profession was divided into physicians, surgeons and apothecaries. Physicians diagnosed and treated ailments and were the most highly educated (a university qualification was mandatory from 1522). Surgeons performed operations, and apothecaries were skilled herbalists who prepared the medicines.

From 1511 until the late 18th century, all three were regulated by the Church, with licences issued by the diocesan bishop and, from 1580 to 1775, also by the Archbishop of Canterbury. The issue of each licence was recorded in bishops' registers, generally held at county record offices.

The *Medical Register*, which lists qualified medical practitioners, was first published by the General Medical Council in 1859, while the *Medical Directory*

A little bit off the ears?
Surgeons were closely linked to barbers in medieval times, and from 1540 to 1745 formed the Worshipful Company of Barber-Surgeons. Some records are held by the Barbers' Company, but the most useful registers can be found at Guildhall Library in London.

for Ireland was first published in 1852. *The Roll of the Royal College of Physicians of London, 1518 to 1825*, compiled in 1878 by William Munk, and continued until 1983, is available in some reference libraries. Records of members are also held in the Royal College library (see DIRECTORY).

Apothecaries belonged to the Grocers' Company in medieval times, but formed their own Society of Apothecaries in 1617. Records for both professions are at Guildhall Library (see DIRECTORY).

Teeth were originally pulled by barbers, but pioneer dentists set up on their own and began registration in 1878 and are listed in the *Dentists' Register*.

Midwives Until the mid 18th century midwives had to obtain a licence from the bishop. From 1825 to 1965 the Royal College of Surgeons published an annual *List of the Members, Fellows and Licentiates in Midwifery of the Royal College of Surgeons*.

the legal profession

Advocates, attorneys, barristers, coroners, judges, magistrates, notaries, sheriffs and solicitors generally underwent specialised training. Details of lawyers in England and Wales have appeared in *The*

Did your ancestors take to the stage?
Entertainers are difficult to research since there were no formal training records. Who's Who in the Theatre, published since 1912, contains biographies of actors and theatre personnel. The Theatre Museum (see DIRECTORY) holds over a million playbills (like the one above), but they are not indexed. You may find information in trade magazines such as the Theatrical Journal (1839–73) and The Stage (since 1881). Copies are held at British Library Newspapers (see DIRECTORY).

SPORT AND LEISURE

The introductory pages of any county directory (see pages 174–5) will give you an idea of local leisure facilities, such as cricket, bowls, swimming, rowing, tennis, fencing and rifle clubs. If the organisation ran a private bar, a licence would have been granted by the local magistrates, a note of which will be in quarter sessions records, held at county record offices. If the club is still running, the local library should hold its contact address, and the club secretary can direct you to any surviving records.

An ancestor who excelled at a particular sport may be listed in a directory of sportspeople and sporting organisations. *John Wisden's Cricketers' Almanack*, published annually from 1864, is the cricketing bible, while top rugby players between 1871 and 1987 are identified in the *Complete Who's Who of International Rugby* (T. Godwin, Blandford Press, 1987). Many reference libraries stock a collection of handbooks for a selection of sports.

Law List, published regularly since 1798; this and other biographical dictionaries of judges and those who studied law at the Inns of Court and Inns of Chancery are available in large reference libraries.

IRELAND All law students admitted to the King's Inns in Dublin are listed in *King's Inns Admission Papers 1607–1867* (Irish Manuscripts Commission, 1982), available from most major reference libraries in Ireland. Aspiring Irish barristers also had to attend one of the English Inns of Court and will therefore be listed in the English records, as mentioned above.

SCOTLAND For Scottish advocates consult *The Faculty of Advocates 1532–1943* at the National Archives of Scotland (see DIRECTORY). Scottish solicitors were formerly known as writers and are listed in the *Register of the Society of Writers to Her Majesty's Signet*, held in the Signet Library (see DIRECTORY). The *Scottish Law List* (formerly *Index Juridicus*) has been published since 1848 and is available from major reference libraries.

TAKING IT FURTHER

♦ *Records of the Medical Profession* (S. Bourne and A.H. Chicken, Bourne & Chicken, 1994).
♦ *Eighteenth Century Medics* (P.J. and R.V. Wallis, Project for Historical Bibliography, Newcastle upon Tyne Polytechnic Products Ltd, 2nd ed., 1988).
♦ *A Biographical Dictionary of the Judges of England, 1066–1870* (E. Foss, John Murray, 1870).
♦ *Brief Lives of Irish Doctors, 1600–1965* (J.B. Lyons, Blackwater, 1978).
♦ *The Judges in Ireland, 1221–1921* (F.E. Ball, Dutton, New York, 1927).

The activities of local Scout and Girl Guide troops from 1908 may be followed in their own district and county newsletters and magazines—for details contact the Scout Information Centre (see DIRECTORY). The National Federation of Women's Institutes (formed in 1917) has details at its headquarters (see DIRECTORY) of many local activities. Extra snippets of information may even be gleaned from local newspaper reports of club activities.

Looking for team players

If you know that your ancestor was a keen cricketer it is worth checking the local club's archives. Team pictures, such as the one shown of Oxshott Village Cricket Club's first XI in about 1913, often list the players' names on the back. Scorebooks, such as Byfleet v Woking on 6 June 1914 (above), may also contain the name of your ancestor and will reveal just how good he was.

on the fringes
poor & destitute

Poverty-stricken forebears may have been driven to seek poor relief. Were they helped from parish rates, or forced to endure the shame of the workhouse?

The poor are always with us
You will find beggars in poor law and workhouse records. Since the late 14th century the authorities have tried to control them. An edict at the end of the 16th century provided for 'rogues, vagabonds and sturdy beggars' over the age of seven to be arrested and, after a whipping, sent back to their place of birth or wherever they had lived for a year or more.

Did your ancestors fall on hard times?

There is a mass of records about those who, through poverty or illness, could not fend for themselves. The shadow of the workhouse, immortalised in Charles Dickens's novel *Oliver Twist*, stalked our 19th-century and early 20th-century forebears, fearful of its cruel regime. Only in 1929 were workhouses abolished, close enough to be part of living memory.

The system of poor relief that prevailed until the 20th century stemmed from the Dissolution of the Monasteries in the 1530s. Until then, charity and care for the poor and sick were dispensed largely by the monks and nuns of religious houses. Henry VIII then placed this role in the hands of individual parishes. The mass of legislation relating to the poor that was enacted over the following 400 years applied equally to England and Wales, although the laws were administered with varying degrees of severity from county to county, and parish to parish.

the poor law and its overseers

At the end of the 16th century all parishes were ordered to levy a poor rate to fund relief, in the form of money, food or firewood, to poor parishioners, and apprenticeships for pauper children. This system, with overseers collecting locally levied rates to be distributed to the poor, was then formalised by the Poor Law Act of 1601. It became the basis of poor law administration for more than 200 years.

Under the Act, two overseers of the poor in every parish were appointed annually. They raised rates from the owners of property within their parish and provided for the parish poor. At the end of each year, they set down all their transactions in an account book. By 1690 they also had to include a list of those parishioners being relieved.

Who were the poor? Those who depended on poor relief included the old, the sick and mentally ill, orphans, illegitimate children, unmarried mothers, widows, deserted wives and children, and the able-bodied unemployed. Even tradesmen and the gentry might fall on hard times and find their way into the records. Whatever the person's circumstances, relief, such as rent, sickness payments and work tools, only just sustained life.

Rattle his bones over the stones;
He's only a pauper, whom
nobody owns!
Thomas Noel 1799–1861

GOING TO A NEW WORLD Sometimes, parish officers encouraged pauper families to emigrate to the colonies. The officers paid their passage and provided basic necessities, removing from the parish rates the cost of maintaining them. Some charitable trusts also paid for passage for families. These records are held in vestry minutes and in the accounts of the overseers of the poor.

What the account books reveal Some of your forebears might have been maintained by poor relief from the cradle to the grave or been temporarily 'on the poor'. Others would have been on the other side of the fence, paying parish rates, or acting as parish officials or overseers. The accounts, therefore, of payments to poor parishioners, the removal of destitute incomers to their settlement parishes, pauper apprenticeships and bastardy maintenance payments are a vital source of information, whether your ancestors were receivers or givers of relief.

The accounts are held in parish chest collections at county or local record offices. If you cannot find them there, they may still be held within the parish.

Tracing errant fathers An illegitimate child could be a burden on the parish if the father was estranged from the mother, so the parish overseers

would want to make the father liable for supporting mother and child. Justices of the peace could investigate an illegitimate birth and issue a bastardy bond, ordering a father to pay maintenance—examples of this are rare before the 18th century. Women were not exempt from punishment, and from 1609 a mother of a bastard child likely to require parish relief could be sent to a house of correction for a year. A mother often refused to name a father, so in 1732 an Act forced unmarried women to declare a pregnancy and to reveal the father's identity.

BASTARDY RECORDS Bastardy bonds and maintenance orders are held in county and other record offices. They can help you to find the name of a father who is not recorded in a parish register.

moving a person on—settlement certificates and examinations

A flaw in the poor relief system was that parish populations were not static. A person who moved to a new parish to find work, lived there and became impoverished was a burden on that parish. This problem was particularly acute after the Civil War (1642–51), when many former soldiers roamed England often far from their home parish.

The examination The Settlement Acts of 1662, 1691 and 1697 empowered two justices of the peace to examine incomers and order the removal of those who seemed likely to seek poor relief in that parish. Some parishes insisted also on a 'bond to save the parish harmless' from newcomers. This required anyone entering a parish to pay a sum of money, or have two persons stand as bondsmen so that if the person ever needed relief the bond would be forfeit.

A person was settled in the parish in which he or she was born to settled parents, or to a settled mother in the case of an illegitimate child. You could also qualify by:

☞ Apprenticeship to a master settled in the parish where the full-term apprenticeship was served, often far from the place of birth.
☞ Owning or renting property worth £10.
☞ Paying rates or taxes in a parish.
☞ Being hired and paid for a full year.
☞ Serving as a parish officer.
☞ Taking a husband's parish of settlement on marriage.

It was the latest qualifying act that determined the place of settlement.

The Old way of bestowing Charity.

THE VAGRANT MILITARY WIFE

Judith Anneson was the wife of a soldier who probably served overseas, leaving her to find her own way home, begging along the way. She underwent an examination as a vagrant (below left) on 27 July 1756.

The report states that she was formerly Judith Pilcher of Dover, Kent, and was arrested in Marlborough, Wiltshire. Nine months before, she had married James Anneson of the King's Own Regiment of Foot. James's settlement was in Norfolk at 'Flagborough'. Judith had no means of support and sought relief. She was 'troubled with falling fits and not able to walk at any rate'. A removal order was made and a pass to her husband's parish granted.

Left in the lurch
Wives of soldiers fighting overseas, and women abandoned by husbands, were often arrested as vagrants. It was only in 1792 that women could no longer be whipped for vagrancy.

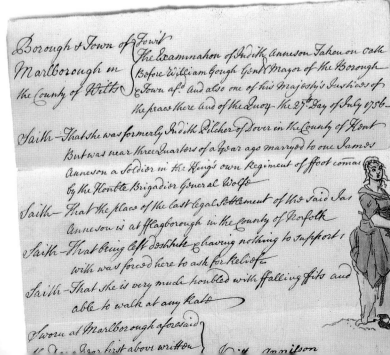

The speech bubble text in the cartoon reads:

"There's a Halspenny for you! and if you are found begging again I shall send you to the Treadmill for 2 Months."

The New way of bestowing Charity!!

The before and after face of poor relief

A cartoon of the 1830s chillingly depicts a radical change in attitude towards poverty and its victims. On the left a well-to-do man of the 18th century performs his duty as a good parishioner by giving generously to a beggar and promising future support. On the right a contemporary man dismisses a destitute mother and her children with a derisory sum, threatening them with the physical grind that became a feature of workhouse life.

An early work permit By the end of the 17th century individual parishioners and their families were allowed to live and work outside their own parish, provided that they had a settlement certificate stating they would be taken back if they needed poor relief. A person asking for poor relief would be brought immediately before the magistrates by the overseers of the poor and examined to establish his or her last place of legal settlement. A person the magistrates decided was settled in another parish would be sent back there by a removal order. Settlement certificates, examinations and removal orders can be found in county and other local record offices among the parish chest collection records.

End of the settlement system By the time the Settlement Acts were abolished in 1948 they had fallen into disuse. Some 20th-century settlement papers may be found in local poor law union records, either as separate settlement examinations and removals or inscribed in the minute books of a poor law guardian (see below).

the dreaded union workhouse

An increase in urban and rural poverty in the early 19th century led to a search for new ways of coping with the growing numbers of paupers. It culminated in the Poor Law Amendment Act of 1834, which brought parishes together into unions, each with a Board of Guardians to administer poor relief. The old, the sick and widows with dependent children could sometimes receive 'outdoor' relief at home, but the able-bodied poor now had to find work and support themselves or enter the workhouse. Your destitute or sick ancestor may appear in the records of the workhouse guardians and officers.

The last resort A few parish poor houses, or workhouses, had existed since the late 17th century as the end of the line for paupers, though conditions were often better than they could expect outside the workhouse. The 1834 Act unveiled the purpose-built union workhouse recommended by the Poor Law Commission as 'a place of hardship, of coarse fare, of degradation and humility... it should be as repulsive as is consistent with humanity'. The new workhouse enforced a much harsher way of life on its inmates, who might include the elderly, babies, children, and the mentally sick and physically handicapped.

Benjamin Disraeli, the future prime minister, condemned the 1834 Poor Law Amendment Act saying, 'It announced to the world that in England, poverty is a crime'.

Workhouses admitted the poor until 1929. Vagrants or 'tramps' continued to pass through the temporary, or 'casual', wards, known as 'the spike', until the poor law was abolished in 1948.

Union records Records that survive include the guardians' minute books, birth and death registers,

BEGGING LETTER FROM AFAR

By the early 19th century some parish overseers were organising reciprocal poor relief. Paupers living and working away from home would be told to send letters to the overseers of their parishes of legal settlement requesting relief. These letters can provide evidence of the movement of missing forebears.

In the overseers' papers for Longbridge Deverell in Wiltshire there are several letters requesting relief. A small bundle dating from 1818 to 1820, including the example on the left, were written by the settled parishioner John Grant, an out-of-work shearman living in Leeds, with no money and eight mouths to feed.

In his final letter Grant states that if the Longbridge Deverell overseers will send him £10 he can gain his settlement in Leeds and will never have to bother them again. As Grant then disappears from the overseers' records it would seem that his request was granted.

and creed registers, stating an inmate's religion. *Poor Law Union Records* (J. Gibson and others, FFHS, 4 vols, 1993–7) has precise information on the poor law unions of England and Wales and their records. The first three volumes list records after 1834 by county, then by union, including their dates and the record office in which they are held. The fourth volume is a gazetteer of the places in each union.

For names and descriptions of wanted absconders and deserters of families, see the *Poor Law Union Gazette* (April 1857 to April 1903) at the British Library Newspaper Library (see DIRECTORY).

the poor and destitute in Ireland

Poor law unions were formed in Ireland in 1838. Before that, the Irish poor relied mostly on private and religious charities for relief. Details of charitable donations may occasionally be found in city or church records, or in landlords' estate papers (see Property records, Using Irish archives, pages 184–5), but most went unrecorded. Some towns had almshouses, and records of these may be found in the town records.

Irish itinerant or seasonal workers who went to England often applied to their new parishes for relief and so appear in English poor law records. Especially useful are settlement examinations and vagrants' passes, which record the Irish parish of origin of the pauper.

After 1838 When poor law unions were established in Ireland, at first only indoor relief, meaning detention in a workhouse, was granted. The huge increase in those seeking assistance caused by the Irish Famine of 1845–51 (see page 239) meant that outdoor relief was granted if the workhouse was full; soup kitchens were also established.

Union records At first there were 130 poor law unions, based on market towns, and as the 19th century progressed the number grew. Each union kept minute books and 'Registers of Admission and Discharge, Out-Relief and Accounts'. Surviving records can be found at various locations, including:

☞ county libraries
☞ National Archives of Ireland
☞ Public Record Office of Northern Ireland.

See DIRECTORY for contact details.

A new life overseas Some unions organised emigration to America, Australia, Canada and South Africa for their workhouse inmates. Details of who was sent, their names, ages, where they came from, who they went with and where they were going can be found among poor law records.

the poor and destitute in Scotland

The Poor Law (Scotland) Act 1579 meant that the Scots stole a march on the English in recognising the need for organised care for the poor. Records of poor relief in Scotland are, however, sparse. Until 1845 the care of the poor, if they were old, infirm, orphans or destitute—but not if they were able-bodied—was the responsibility of the individual parish, using money raised from the principal local landowners, who were known as 'heritors'. Rates and payments were noted in the minutes, accounts and heritors' records of the Kirk Session, a court or council. These records are held in the National Archives of Scotland (see DIRECTORY).

After 1845 The Poor Law Amendment (Scotland) Act 1845 transferred the burden of relief from the parish to the government. Parochial boards were set up to administer poor relief and poor houses, and to give financial aid to hospitals. Names of the poor receiving relief appear on Poor Rolls, which record amounts paid and paupers' disabilities. The records of parochial boards are in regional record offices or the National Archives of Scotland (see DIRECTORY).

TAKING IT FURTHER

♦ *The Workhouse: A Social History* (N. Longmate, Pimlico, 2003).
♦ *The English Poor Law 1531-1782* (P. Slack, MacMillan, 1990).
♦ *The Oxford Companion to Family and Local History* (D. Hey, ed., Oxford University Press, 2010).
♦ *Sources for Local Historians* (P. Carter and K. Thompson, Phillimore, 2005).
♦ *The Relief of Poverty 1834–1914* (M.E. Rose, Macmillian, 2nd ed., 1986).
♦ 'Parochial Records' (ch. 15, *Welsh Family History: a guide to research*, J. Rowlands, 2nd ed., FFHS, 1998).
♦ *Records of the Irish Famine: a guide to local archives 1840–55* (ed. D. Lindsay and D. Fitzpatrick, Trinity College, Dublin, 1993).
♦ *Poor Relief in Scotland* (Scottish Record Office, 1995).

Some family history societies publish summaries of poor law documents. The FFHS has details of local societies (see DIRECTORY). The Poor Law Union workhouse at Southwell, Notts., has been restored and opened to the public by the National Trust.

Information on the Internet
♦ www.workhouses.org.uk Information on poor laws and workhouses, plus documents, background on union workhouses and links to related web sites.
♦ www.nationalarchives.gov.uk/records/research-guides/poor-law-records.htm.
♦ www.nationalarchives.gov.uk/documentsonline/workhouse.asp.
♦ www.genuki.org.uk/big/eng/Paupers/ A 10 per cent sample of adult paupers in English and Welsh workhouses in 1861.
♦ www.gendocs.demon.co.uk/institute.html Lists of public institutions in Victorian London, including workhouses, lunatic asylums and hospitals.

Not much to smile about

Workhouses were not renowned for their leisure facilities, although at Crumpsall, Manchester, children were given a seesaw. The boys in heavy boots and shapeless garments had their hair cropped on entry. Heavily regulated visiting days allowed fleeting contact with the outside world.

life in the workhouse

Workhouses of the mid to late 19th century were grim institutions. The buildings were stark with iron railings, high walls and small barred windows. Rules were strict and had to be obeyed implicitly, while everyone, including the elderly and infirm, had to work for many hours a day.

On entry, paupers had a medical examination, which classified them as able-bodied or infirm, and they were segregated into wards for males, females, boys and girls. The able-bodied were made to break stones, pick hemp, grind corn, crush bones and make firewood. Elderly or infirm women were often put to sewing or looking after children; elderly men laboured in the kitchen gardens. Some of the inmates rebelled against the harsh regime and their names can be seen in punishment books.

In defence of the workhouse system, it did at least offer access to medical care, food (if meagre and monotonous) and shelter.

Name and Age.	Where Resident.	Weekly Relief.	Cause of Requiring Relief.	Amount given to Pauper during half	
				In Money.	In
		s. d.		£ s. d.	£ s
YSTRADGUNLAIS LOWER.					
Aubrey, William, 77	Oddfelws. r.	4 0	old age	5 4 0	0 7
Aubrey, Elizabeth, 12	Ynis	2 6	infancy	0 5 0	
Alexander, M. 35, D. 12, R. 8, J. 5, M. 3, W. 1	Cwmygiedd	7 6	for children	9 0 0	
Basset, Alice, 12	College row	2 0	infancy	2 12 0	
Bevan, Margaret, 66	Ddoyrgaled	4 0	sore legs	5 4 0	
Beynon, Jane, 70	Cwmtwrch	5/7/62	old age	4 0 0	0 12
Bowen, J. 57, Wm. 15	ditto	3/6 4/6	bedridden	5 7 0	
Charles, J. 72, wf. S. 68	ditto	6 0	blind	7 16 0	0 10
Charles, Richard, 39	Gurnos	5/ 7/6	idiot	6 15 0	
Chalk, Henry, 47	Dunfant	5/ 5/6	blind	7 2 0	
Corbett, Mary, 70	Ystrad vill.	3 0	old age	3 18 0	
Davey, Richard, 86	College row	2 6	ditto	0 10 0	
Davies, D. 48, David 15, Jno. 11, Thos. 6, J. 4	Cwmtwrch	10 0	blind	13 0 0	
Davies, J. 68, w. Ef. 75	ditto	7/ 9/8/	paralysis	11 2 0	
Davies, M. 23, John 4	ditto	2/6 1/6	husband deserted	3 3 0	
Davies, Mary, 73	Ystrad vill.	3 0	old age	3 18 0	
Davies, Margaret, 76	ditto	4 0	ditto	5 4 0	
Davies, Elizabeth, 11	ditto	2 0	infancy	2 12 0	
Davies, E. 35, Mary 3	ditto	1 6	for child	1 19 0	
Davies, M. 42, Wm. 16, S. 12, Ann 8, N. 7	Pelican st.	4 0	for children	5 4 0	
Davies, M. 28, M. A. 3	Cwmygiedd	1 6	husband deserted	1 1 0	
Davies, T. 51, w. S. 49, Margaret 15	ditto	7 0	fractured leg	9 2 0	
Davies, William, 72	Ynis	3 0	old age	1 16 0	2 3
Davies, M. 38, John 12, Arthur 9, Mary 6	College row	3 0	for children	3 18 0	

A catalogue of distress

An extract from a list of paupers receiving outdoor relief from the Pontardawe Poor Law Union in Wales illustrates the diversity of paths that often led people to the workhouse. Causes of need included physical and mental illness, old age and the desertion of husbands. Mothers of illegitimate children often entered workhouses purely to give birth and their children were baptised in workhouse chapels.

Hospital and asylum records include those unlucky enough to fall ill in the days before the NHS. Some were cured, others never again saw the light of day

on the fringes
sick & mentally ill

Ailing ancestors whose family could not tend to them would have been forced into the care of a workhouse, hospital or asylum. Many of their records are in county record offices, but generally you will have to look back more than a century as patient records are kept confidential for 100 years.

Throughout the Middle Ages the sick were cared for in hospitals by monks and nuns. The Dissolution of the Monasteries put an end to this and few records of medieval hospitals and asylums survive.

In the 17th and 18th centuries, people with mental and physical disabilities were either accommodated in a parish poor house or cared for by their family. They were included in censuses, but the large

KEY SOURCES OF INFORMATION
♦ Hospital and asylum records, and collections of county clerks of the peace, at county record offices, individual hospitals and health authorities.
♦ Ministry of Health (class MH 12) correspondence at the TNA.
♦ Irish hospital and asylum records at the National Archives of Ireland, the Public Record Office of Northern Ireland and individual hospitals.
♦ Scottish health board archives. Hospital and asylum records at the National Archives of Scotland.
SEE DIRECTORY ➤

numbers looked after at home were revealed only when 'imbecile or idiot' and 'lunatic' were added as categories on the 1871 census.

From the late 18th century, large towns began to build infirmaries and dispensaries, often funded by public subscription. Records of these may be held either at the hospital concerned, if it still exists, or in the local county record office.

private and county asylums

People categorised as 'dangerous' were often sent by parish authorities to private asylums. Acts of Parliament in 1774 and 1828 required private asylums to be licensed by county justices, with local justices of the peace appointed as visitors to ensure that patients were well treated. Records are kept in the collection of the county clerk of the peace in county record offices. They may include lists of patients, reports of visitors, reports of inspections by justices of the peace, case records, and registers of admissions, removals, discharges, deaths and abscondments. Returns covering pauper and criminal lunatics are also in county clerk of the peace collections in county record offices.

An Act of 1845 ordered the building of county asylums for the poor insane, despite opposition from landowners and other ratepayers who feared that they would be an unnecessary burden on county rates. Many were not built for another 20 or 30 years, and private asylums continued to house paupers and the mentally ill.

hospitals and asylums in Ireland

The sick and mentally ill in Ireland were usually cared for at home. Hospitals, funded by charitable donations, began to appear in the 18th century. But until 1821, when 23 asylums were built, there was little organised provision for the care of lunatics. Surviving records may still be held at the hospital; otherwise, they are in the National Archives of Ireland or the Public Record Office of Northern Ireland (see DIRECTORY).

hospitals and asylums in Scotland

Before the 16th-century Reformation in Scotland, hospitals were usually attached to monasteries. Once the established church became Presbyterian in 1560, heritors (property owners liable to pay parish rates) and Kirk Sessions (church councils or courts) funded and provided medical care. Hospital records are held in the archives of health boards or in the National Archives of Scotland (reference HH).

Some large towns set up charitable institutions for the care and education of orphans and poor children; their records are at the National Archives of Scotland (references GD and HD)—see DIRECTORY.

Records of the mentally ill Few records exist of pre-1857 asylums. Records after 1857, including a register of all 'lunatics' in asylums, are held in the National Archives of Scotland (reference MC). You cannot view anything less than 75 years old.

Workplace dangers
The Great Western Railway workers of Swindon were lucky enough to have their own hospital. A doctor's report (right) lists the unfortunates who had to be admitted in the six months up to June 1883.

NAME.	AGE.	OCCUPATION.	RESIDENCE.	INJURIES.	DAYS IN HOSPITAL	REMARKS.
John Grant	17	S Shop	Old Swindon	Punctured wound of left leg with artery divided	111	Discharged convalescent
Edward Akers	24	Mason	Purton	Severe injury of left arm with fracture into elbow-joint	38	Discharged convalescent
William Stephens	26	Guard	Gorse Hill	Caught between truck and platform and badly contused	37	Discharged convalescent
Henry Woolford	39	R Mills	New Swindon	Crushed toes	38	Made an out-patient
Joseph Gravell	70	B Shed	Even Swindon	Fractured skull	15	Discharged convalescent
Joseph Jefferies	30	R Mills	Purton	Scalp wound	15	Discharged convalescent
William Eyres	54	Carriage Shop	New Swindon	Lacerated wound of hand	2	Made an out patient
John Ovens	30	Packer	New Swindon	Knocked down by engine, hip contused, and generally shaken	7	Discharged convalescent
Henry Morton	35	Permanent Way		Contracted knee-joint, necessitating operation	41	Very much improved
Thomas Cook	16	Steam Hammer	Old Swindon	Ulcerated leg	11	Discharged convalescent
George Manton	29	B Shop	Old Swindon	Sprained ankle	19	Discharged convalescent
William Turtle	42	Masons	Haydon	Knocked down by heavy fall of clay, and severely contused on thigh, and generally much shaken	17	Discharged convalescent
William Auger	21	Masons	New Swindon	Severe scald of left leg and foot	29	Discharged convalescent
William Kirby	46	Grinder L 2	New Swindon	Severe scalp wound, middle finger fractured, two front teeth and part of lower jaw knocked out, and generally	66	Discharged convalescent

on the fringes
criminal ancestors

A criminal in the family can be good news for the family historian. Crime and punishment generated records that do not exist for more law-abiding folk

Historical criminal records encompass a huge range of crimes. Poor people were driven to crime in order to survive and many were tried for nothing more than stealing bread. Poaching too was common. But it is not just the poor who appear: people from all levels of society committed offences and documents refer also to judges, policemen, parish constables, witnesses, jurors and innocent victims, so all family historians will probably find something of interest. The search is not always easy but can be well worth the effort.

How do you find out if your ancestor was a criminal? A range of sources can help:

☞ A relative may remember that someone was in prison.

☞ A few census returns for prisons list the prisoners by name.

☞ Parish records such as constables' accounts may uncover criminal activity.

☞ Local newspapers may report your ancestor being charged with an offence.

☞ Name indexes to criminal records may include your ancestor or a member of his family.

More often, you will simply notice that he, or she, disappears from the family home and does not

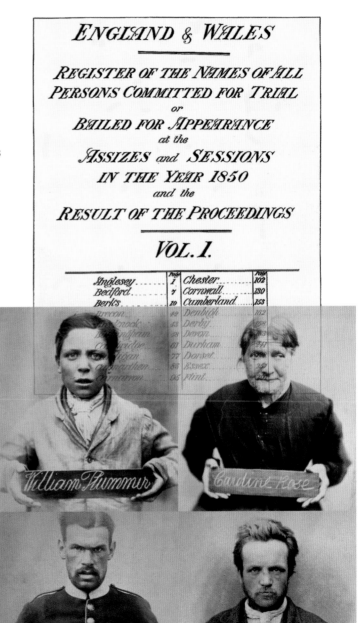

Mugshots Victorian style
Photographs in criminal records may bring you face to face with an ancestor: here, clockwise, are an errand boy, a dust-woman, a labourer and a soldier in the 6th Dragoon Guards. All of them were imprisoned in Cambridge in 1875–6 for larceny. You can also check in criminal registers at the TNA.

ENGLAND & WALES

REGISTER OF THE NAMES OF ALL PERSONS COMMITTED FOR TRIAL

or

BAILED FOR APPEARANCE

at the

ASSIZES and SESSIONS

IN THE YEAR 1850

and the

RESULT OF THE PROCEEDINGS

VOL. I.

	Page		Page
Anglesey	1	Chester	102
Bedford	7	Cornwall	130
Berks	19	Cumberland	153
Brecon	32	Denbigh	162
Buckingham	33	Derby	168
Cambridge	58	Devon	
Cardigan	67	Durham	247
Glamorgan	77	Dorset	
Carmarthen	88	Essex	
Carnarvon	95	Flint	

William Plummer
Caroline Rose
Alexander Pratt
William Lee

appear in the census or parish records for a period. Your ancestor might have joined the armed forces or gone to sea (see Joining up, pages 204–35), but prison is a possibility you should consider.

Starting the search To pick up and follow the trail successfully, you will find it essential to understand the court system (see What sort of court?, below). Which records you should check will depend on the period, circumstances and place where your ancestor was last heard of. The best places to begin searching are:

☞ Published or indexed quarter sessions or other justices' records at county record offices.

☞ Criminal registers from 1805 (1791 for London) at the TNA.

☞ Calendars of prisoners and prison registers at county and city record offices and the TNA.

consulting court records

Records of actual court proceedings are harder to locate and not always very informative. But you can occasionally strike a vein of fascinating information.

QUARTER, BOROUGH OR PETTY SESSIONS Records of the justices of the peace who presided over these cases are in local record offices. Few records survive before 1600. *Quarter Sessions Records for Family Historians* (see Taking it further, page 163)

what sort of court?

Records of criminal court proceedings go back to the 17th century for most of England and Wales, and even farther in some places. Modern police forces were founded in the 19th century. Before this, suspects were apprehended by the parish constable, local people or the sheriff (an officer of the Crown). In medieval times, some criminals were tried in the Court Leet—a court of the lord of the manor—or by the king's justices, who moved around the country 'on circuit'. Few records of these trials and criminals survive, although the TNA does hold some in Latin. By the mid 16th century, lords of the manor no longer had jurisdiction over criminal law. The king appointed justices of the peace to administer it in each county.

QUARTER SESSIONS
Offenders were taken before the justices of the peace, sitting at quarter sessions, held every three months (quarter year), in all counties of England and Wales. A wide range of crimes was tried at quarter sessions, including petty theft, burglary, assault and arson. Serious offences such as treason, murder and manslaughter could not be tried at these sessions but offenders were sometimes brought there for preliminary hearings.

BOROUGH SESSIONS
In many towns and cities, justices of the peace sat at borough sessions, which were similar to county quarter sessions and were usually held every quarter year.

PETTY SESSIONS
These developed in the 18th century. Justices of the peace met, between quarter sessions, to deal with minor crimes and juvenile offenders.

ASSIZES
In the 16th century a new system of itinerant judges travelling from Westminster was created, known as the assizes. The judges travelled in 'circuits', which covered a number of counties. Cases were heard by a judge and 12 jurors, and it was only here that crimes such as murder could be tried.

If a serious crime was presented at quarter sessions it was then referred to assizes and the alleged offender would have to be held in custody until a judge arrived for the next assize sessions.

describes the surviving records and where they are held for English and Welsh counties.

For most counties there is a series of sessions (or 'process') books, rolls and minutes noting brief facts of the cases heard by the justices, whether a prisoner was convicted and the sentence, if any. You may also find lists of jurors, depositions of witnesses and records of prisoners (see page 162). Some of these have been published by county record societies.

ASSIZES You can see assize records at the TNA, in classes ASSI 1 to ASSI 77, arranged by the circuit a county was included in. Surrey, for example, was in the 'Home Circuit'. *Criminal Ancestors* (see Taking it further, page 163) contains lists of assize records and how to use them.

Arrested for campaigning
A suffragette is arrested after chaining herself to the railings of Buckingham Palace in 1913 to bring attention to the cause of votes for women. You may find ancestors whose 'crimes' were politically motivated.

PALATINATE COURTS

The counties of Cheshire, Durham and Lancashire were known as 'Palatinates' and governed differently from other English counties. Each had its own courts, including a court that heard similar criminal cases as those tried at assizes. The Palatinate court of Chester was abolished in 1830, and Cheshire was included in a new assize circuit with Wales. Those of Durham and Lancashire were abolished in 1876, and County Durham and Lancashire were in turn included in assize circuits.

OLD BAILEY SESSIONS

London and Middlesex were not included in the assize system either. However, the Lord Mayor and aldermen of the City of London sat as justices of the peace at Guildhall and Mansion House, and the King's Judges sat in a Sessions House in Old Bailey. These judges heard cases similar to those at assizes, as well as cases of national importance. The Old Bailey Sessions House became the most important criminal court in England and was known as the Central Criminal Court from 1834.

COURTS OF LAW IN WALES

Until 1543 Wales was subject to its own laws, together with Marcher Law (which governed the region that bordered England, historically an area of unrest). From 1543 Wales was subject to English law, which was administered until 1830 through the Courts of Great Sessions. These dealt with civil and criminal cases. There were four circuits for the Welsh counties but Monmouthshire was attached to the Oxford circuit of the English assizes. The records for the Great Sessions are at the National Library of Wales (see DIRECTORY). Although largely unindexed, they contain much family history information. The English assize system was extended to Wales to replace the Courts of Great Sessions in 1830.

Very few records survive from before 1559, or even later in the case of some counties. They include 'calendars' (or lists) of prisoners, minute books and indictments with some personal details of the accused, the crime and the victim, usually noting the verdict and any sentence. Some 16th and 17th-century indictments for south-east England have been published by HMSO.

PALATINATE COURT RECORDS Similar to assize records, these are also held at the TNA in classes CHES 17 to CHES 24, DURH 15 to DURH 19 and PL 25 to PL 28.

OLD BAILEY SESSIONS RECORDS The TNA, Guildhall Library and the Corporation of London Records Office (see DIRECTORY) hold these, which are more detailed and complete than assize records. There are also many published reports of these cases, some of which are almost transcripts of a trial.

The 'Old Proceedings' at the Old Bailey are available on the web site www.oldbaileyonline.org TNA Records of the Central Criminal Court are held at the TNA, in classes CRIM 1 to CRIM 5.

records of criminals

From 1805 the Home Office kept records of everyone charged with a criminal offence. These were written into annual volumes, each covering several counties. Names were entered by date and place of court hearing. They are not indexed by name. The offence is given, with the outcome of the trial and, if guilty, the sentence. Many people sentenced to death were reprieved later, and this is usually noted.

Where to find registers The registers are held at the TNA in class HO 27. Registers for a number of

courts in Ireland and Scotland

Like England, Ireland had county assizes, and quarter and petty sessions, but with some courts of its own. In Scotland, the system was different in many ways. In most cases, Scottish court records give more information than the English equivalent.

IRISH COURTS

County assizes were held twice a year in cities and large towns. Quarter sessions heard cases of larceny and all misdemeanours except forgery and perjury. Petty sessions were presided over by justices of the peace. Trials and cases in all courts were recorded in local newspapers, particularly 19th-century ones (see page 171). Grand Jury Presentment sessions carried out some court functions, which included listening to applications for compensation from people whose property had been damaged and establishing infirmaries, asylums and hospitals. Rebellions and insurrections were dealt with by special courts such as the Courts Martial set up after the 1798 Rebellion. All records are in the National Archives (see DIRECTORY), which also holds the General Prison Board Collection 1836–1928, including registers of convicts and prisoners discharged.

SCOTTISH COURTS

Sheriff courts dealt with minor offences, assault and theft. Their records usually give the full name of the accused, the crime and the sentence. They survive from the late 18th century (reference SC at the National Archives of Scotland, see DIRECTORY). Justices of the peace also tried minor offences. Their records include criminal trials, juvenile court cases, small debt, drunkenness and petty offences and are also at the National Archives, reference JP. The High Court of Justiciary, the highest criminal court in Scotland, sat in Edinburgh and on circuit. Some of its records (National Archives, reference JC) are indexed and published (see Taking it further, opposite). The Lord Advocate decided whether alleged crimes should be prosecuted; statements presented to him ('precognitions') include descriptions of the accused (National Archives, reference AD).

counties have been indexed up to 1828 by S. Tamblin (see Taking it further, right). For the period not covered by these indexes you must read through the county registers to find a particular person.

NEWGATE GAOL AND OLD BAILEY A further series of criminal registers was compiled for people held at Newgate Gaol in London and tried at the Old Bailey. They date from 1791 and continue to 1849. (From 1850 the Old Bailey trials are included in the county series under Middlesex.) In addition to the information in the county series, they record the accused's age, height, place of birth, and sometimes his or her trade, colour of hair and eyes, and complexion. The TNA class reference is HO 26.

calendars of prisoners

Lists of people to be tried, with their age and details of the offence, were prepared before trials. Many of these calendars survive from the 17th century, handwritten into the court sessions book or minute book. From about 1800 they were printed.

From the mid 19th century calendars were printed again after the trial (known as 'post-trial' calendars), and included the outcome of the trial and usually details of the accused's previous crimes.

Consulting calendars of prisoners Those calendars which survive are in county record offices and the TNA. A complete series of post-trial calendars from 1868 for the whole of England and Wales (and the Channel Islands) is also held at the TNA in class HO 140.

TAKING IT FURTHER

♦ *Quarter Sessions Records for Family Historians* (J. Gibson, FFHS, 4th ed., 1995).
♦ *Criminal Ancestors* (D. T. Hawkings, Sutton, 1992, repr. 1996).
♦ *Tracing Your Ancestors in The National Archives* (A. Bevan, The National Archives, 7th ed., 2006).
♦ *A Guide to the Records of the Great Sessions in Wales* (G. Parry, National Library of Wales, 1995).
SCOTLAND
♦ *Ancient Criminal Trials in Scotland 1498–1624* (Bannatyne Club, 3 vols, 1833).
♦ *The Records of the Proceedings of the Justiciary Court, Edinburgh 1661–78* (Scottish History Society, 1st series, 2 vols, 1948 and 1949).
IRELAND
♦ *Memoires of the Irish Rebellion of 1798* (Sir R. Musgrave, Round Tower Books, 1801, repr. 1995).

Information on the Internet
♦ www.nationalarchives.gov.uk/records/research-guides/criminals-18th-20th-centuries.htm
♦ www.oldbaileyonline.org The Proceedings of the Old Bailey, 1674-1913, a searchable edition of nearly 200,000 criminal trials held at London's central criminal court.

Up before the court in Buckinghamshire

Registers of criminals include few personal details, although you can still see whether your ancestor was flogged or fined in addition to being imprisoned or transported.

48

County of Buckingham
RETURN of all persons Committed, or Bailed to appear for Trial, or Indicted at the General Quarter Session of the Peace held at Aylesbury on the 31st day of December 1849, shewing the nature of their Offences, and the result of the Proceedings.

No.	NAMES	Offences of which those tried were Convicted or Acquitted, and of which those Discharged without Trial were charged on Indictment or Commitment.	Convicted and Sentenced				Acquitted and Discharged
			Death	Transportation	Imprisonment: (state if also Whipped or Fined)	Whipped, Fined, or Discharged on Sureties	
1	Hannah Hill	Larceny – before Convicted of Felony			1 week		
2	Richard Bovingdon	Larceny			2 Months		
3	Humphrey Short	Larceny			2 Months		
4	John Williams	Larceny			1 Month		
5	Joseph Harman	Larceny – before Convicted of Felony			3 Months		
6	William Harman	Larceny			1 Month		Not Guilty

BIRMINGHAM BOROUGH PRISON,
COUNTY OF WARWICK.

28th October 1871

PARTICULARS of a Person convicted of an offence specified in the First Schedule of Habitual Criminals Act, 1869, and who will be liberated from this Gaol within seven days from the date hereof, either on expiration of sentence, or Licence from Secretary of State.

Name and Aliases	*1665 John Fagan*
Age (on discharge)	*16 Years*
Height	*5 0¾*
Hair	*Brown*
Eyes	*Grey*
Complexion	*Fresh*
Where Born	*Scotland*
Married or Single	*Single*
Trade or Occupation	*Tinner*
Any other distinguishing mark	*Scar left cheek*
Address at time of apprehension	*47 Allison St Birmingham*
Whether summarily disposed of or tried by Jury	*Tried by Jury*
Place and date of conviction	*Borough Sessions 3 July 1871*
Offence for which convicted	*Simple Larceny*
Sentence	*4 Calendar Months HL*

PHOTOGRAPH OF PRISONER.

If subject to supervision of Police, when liberated, and for what period	*Nil*
If liberated on Licence, date when sentence will expire	
Date when liberated	*3rd November 1871*
Intended residence after liberation	*47 Allison St Birmingham*
Summary convictions, dates, nature of offences, and places where convicted	*None*
Trials by Jury, dates, nature of offences, and places where convicted	*None*
Names of Police Officers or others who can identify and prove convictions	*P Warder S Jeffries*
Any other particulars as to antecedents, associates, &c.	

Previous Convictions.

Once criminals were sentenced they were either transported, imprisoned or executed. Each outcome is usually recorded in criminal registers

on the fringes
punishment records

Until the 19th century few criminals were held for long periods in gaol. Those convicted of serious offences were generally either executed or transported. Houses of correction were used to secure vagrants and vagabonds and put them to productive work. Offenders were kept in county gaols before trial with petty criminals, who received short sentences, usually with hard labour. In 1823, houses of correction and county gaols were amalgamated and called prisons, regulated by justices of the peace at quarter sessions. County and city record offices hold surviving records of these institutions.

KEY SOURCES OF INFORMATION
♦ Archives for houses of correction and county gaols at county and city record offices.
♦ Records of government prisons before 1877, and all prisons afterwards, at the TNA.
♦ Records of prison hulks and transportation at the TNA and the National Library of Wales.
♦ Records of prisoners in Scotland at the National Archives of Scotland.
SEE DIRECTORY ➢

In the 19th century various 'government prisons' were established to house serious offenders. Records of government prisons are held at the TNA (see DIRECTORY). In 1877 all prisons were put under the control of the government and managed by the Prison Commission.

SENTENCED TO TRANSPORTATION The practice of sending convicts to the colonies began in about 1620. Many offenders who would otherwise have been executed were sent to America or the West Indies and sold to landowners as 'bond servants'. Transportees were attached to a landowner for the period of their sentence, and worked either on the land or as house servants. At the end of the sentence, a convict was free to return home but most remained in their new country as 'free' labourers or servants. Transportation was recorded as the sentence of the court, although little more is likely to be found in British court records. For the main sources see pages 248–53.

After American independence in 1776, convicts were transported to New South Wales in Australia, a practice that continued until 1868.

gaol records

Prison registers These registers record dates of entry and removal or transfer of criminals. An individual can easily be identified because the date and place of conviction are always given. Sometimes a criminal's physical description is recorded, and from 1869 registers often include photographs of inmates. Some registers describe the prisoners' clothing and effects on arrival at the prison.

English and Welsh prison records are closed for 100 years. In Scotland, where records are held in the National Archives (see DIRECTORY) under reference

PRISON HULKS

Although America stopped being a destination for transported convicts in 1776, many people continued to be sentenced to transportation. They were held in gaols, which soon became overcrowded, provoking a public outcry. As a 'temporary expedient', disused ships, including some warships, were moored in the Thames estuary and at ports along the south coast. The convicts lived on these hulks and worked on building projects, such as the Royal Arsenal at Woolwich, if they were healthy; if not, they stayed on hospital ships.

Transportation was re-introduced in 1787 (this time to Australia), but the hulks continued to house convicts until 1873, many held there temporarily before transportation. The only hulk that housed women was the *Dunkirk* at Plymouth, which appears to have been abandoned by 1792. Records at the TNA list the convicts with their ages, type of crime and term of transportation. There are often lists of articles issued, such as breeches and blankets, and sometimes references to time spent in the sickbay.

Prison hulk *York* in Portsmouth harbour, 1828

HH, closure is for 75 years. Scottish admission and discharge books may give a prisoner's place of birth.

Governors' journals Prison governors kept day-to-day accounts of prison life, including details of unusual events. Fights among the prisoners and swearing will be found alongside more serious events such as escapes and suicides. The governor also kept a record of punishments to offenders.

Medical journals Some medical officers kept detailed records of sick inmates and their treatment.

home ground

To build up a picture of what life was like for your ancestors, it is essential to know something of where and how they lived. Looking through old newspapers or town and country directories that describe communities and their inhabitants, you may find their **names in print**. Generations of landowners, and even tenants, can be uncovered in the deeds and other documents that make up **property records**. You can also have fun finding out more of the **local history** of your ancestors' communities, through recordings of older inhabitants, diaries, photographs and maps.

An Oxford newsagent delivers his papers from an old Bath chair in 1932

names in print
people in newspapers

Most of us appear in print at some time in our lives, at least in the births, marriages or deaths section of a local paper. But did your forebears figure in the press?

If your ancestors were abnormally tall or speedy, criminal or scandalous, they may feature in a newspaper before 1800. But you are more likely to find them if they were among the gentry, professionals or tradesmen who would have read papers. It is easier to find names in the Victorian age, when more people could read and wanted the latest news.

the beginnings of the press

News-sheets appeared in the 1640s, taking sides in the Civil War. In the early 18th century the merchant and political classes demanded more news, which led to a proliferation of mostly short-lived local newspapers. By 1785 eight morning papers were being published in London, including *The Daily Universal Register*, renamed *The Times* in 1788.

Local papers Most papers read outside London in the 18th and the early 19th centuries were weekly 'provincials' such as the *Norwich Post*, first published in 1701, containing national and some local news. Most counties were covered by 1750, although not every region, so you may have to search the papers of a number of towns to find your ancestors.

what you get from an early paper

Looking at a provincial paper such as *The Lincoln, Rutland, and Stamford Mercury* from before the mid 19th century can help to fill in the social background of a community. Floods, protracted cold weather, cholera or smallpox epidemics, bankruptcies and court cases all affected your ancestors, ruining crops, damaging homes, and putting people out of work or into prison.

The Lincoln, Rutl
FRIDAY, May 7, 1819.]
PRINTED a

Who's been up in court?
Court cases were reported in detail, often on the third page, sometimes with quotations from the evidence. News of the quarter sessions held after Easter 1819 in the Lincolnshire town of Louth (right) lists the justices of the peace presiding and provides the names of those convicted, mostly for stealing, and sent to hard labour or transported.

LINDSEY SESSIONS.

LOUTH.—At the general quarter sessions of the peace holden at Louth, in the first week after Easter, (before William Chaplin, Clerk, chairman ; Richard Elmhirst and Robert Cracroft, Esqs ; Edward Brackenbury, Marmaduke Alington, John Fretwell, Thomas Roe, John Mounsey, and William Dodson, Clerks, Justices, &c.)

Samuel Selby, late of Toynton All Saints, laborer, convicted of stealing a pair of leather quarter jack boots from George Enderby, of Spilsby, cordwainer, and *David Palmer*, late of Coningsby, laborer, convicted of stealing four pecks of oats from Thomas Sellers, of the same place, farmer, were severally sentenced to be transported for seven years.

Thomas Abbot, late of Fulletby, laborer, convicted of stealing a peck of oats and a peck of beans from Richard Elmhirst, Esq. was committed to Kirton Bridewell to hard labour for six months, and the last month solitary.

Robert Alliwell, late of Revesby, laborer, convicted of stealing six hempen sacks and one peck-measure from John Wright, of New Bolingbroke, farmer, and *Thomas Farnsworth* and *William Farnsworth*, of Mareham le Fen, laborers, convicted of stealing a fowl from Christopher Sleight, of the same place, were committed to the

The need for news Readers relied on their local paper to keep up with events in London, with warnings of new laws and taxes likely to affect them. Reports of cases in the local quarter sessions always appeared and were avidly read.

the Victorian news boom

The rapid growth of the railway network in the mid 19th century made the quick distribution of newspapers throughout Britain possible, opening up access to mass readerships and allowing local papers to incorporate pages of national news. The repeal of the stamp duty (the charge for the official badge stamped on each sheet, without which it was illegal to sell news) on newspapers in 1855, created a cheaper press. This contributed to the success of new national papers such as *The Daily Telegraph*, founded in 1855.

More local news for your money Cheaper newspapers meant more provincial titles, including many in the London suburbs. From the 1860s most areas had at least two papers, often of opposing political views. With the great events of the day

---

Bankrupts.
(From Saturday's Gazette—May 1.)

PETER STATHAM and JONATHAN STATHAM, of Ardwick, co. Lancaster, dyers, d. c. & cops.—May 14, 15, June 12. Walker, Manchester.

EDWARD ROSSITER, of Warminster, co. Wilts, clothier, d. & c.—May 8, 20, June 12. Rotton, Frome.

JOHN GORTON, HENRY GORTON, JOSEPH GORTON, & WILLIAM ROBERTS, of Torrington, co. Lancaster, cotton-spinners, d. c. and cops.—May 13, 15, June 12. Cunliffe, Manchester.

Old debts and new life
Shopkeepers and tradesmen needed to know when suppliers had gone out of business. News of bankrupts (left) would be quoted from a London paper, often on the back page, joined perhaps by details of sailings to the New World (right).

AMERICA.
Last Ship this Spring for QUEBEC,
WITH GOODS AND PASSENGERS.

THE very fine new Ship ARETHUSA, WILLIAM WHARTON, Master, burthen 350 tons. Has every possible accommodation for Cabin and Steerage Passengers, and will sail on the 25th of MAY.—For particulars apply to the Master on board ; or to

Widow HOLLINGWORTH and HOLDERNESS, Hull, April 30, 1819. Exchange-Buildings.
☞ Goods forwarded to Montreal at ship's expense, but shipper's risk.

L. 88.—No. 459

and Stamford Mercury.

D, by and for R. NEWCOMB and SON.

Stamp Duty......4d.⟩
Paper & Print....3d.⟨ Price 7d.; or 8s. per Quarter.

Well worthy the Attention of Parents.
Interesting abstract of a Letter lately received by Mr. Lignum, from Mr. Wallwork, of Bolton.

MR. W. writes, that his daughter Ann, a girl of about five years of age, was in her second year attacked with a scorbutic eruption, which continued to increase till her whole body was covered with eruptions, and she became quite blind. She remained in this distressing situation for nearly three years; finding nothing to relieve her, though the most eminent medical men were employed. Mr. W. was induced to try Mr. LIGNUM's ANTISCORBUTIC DROPS, one bottle of which completely restored her to health.

Sold by Mr. Lignum, Manchester; Drury, bookseller, Stamford; Drury, Lincoln ; Squire, Grimsby ; Ridge, Newark ; and one or more principal medicine venders in every market town in the united kingdom. Price 2s. 9d., 4s. 6d., and 11s.

Just Published by Mr. Lignum, a practical TREATISE on the VENEREAL DISEASE, price 2s. 6d., and sold by all booksellers.

To FAMILIES and SCHOOLS.
IT is a fact verified by daily experience, that the ut-

Cures and commerce
Advertisements crammed the front and back pages, placed mostly by tradesmen promoting their wares. Patent medicines (left) were popular, with claims for pills and potions to cure all ills. Mr Clarke, 'mercer, tailor and habit-maker' of Stamford (right), touts his services and is hot on the heels of a wayward apprentice.

CLARKE, MAN'S MERCER, TAILOR, & HABIT-MAKER, *Saint Mary's Hill*, STAMFORD, begs with gratitude to return thanks to his friends for their liberal support, and humbly solicits a continuance. He takes this method of informing them, he has received the best instructions in the new and improved method of Cutting, on the principle of Geometry ; and flatters himself he will be enabled to please all who may honor him with their commands.
Stamford, 4th May, 1819.

ABSCONDED from T. C., his Apprentice WILLIAM GUNNISS, aged 20, about 5 feet 5 inches high, much marked with the small pox. Any person employ-

SHREWSBURY OFFICER KILLED.—Sec.
Lieut. Wilfred E. S. Owen, eldest son of
Mr. and Mrs. T. Owen, Mahim, Monkmoor
Road, attached to 2nd Batt. Manchester
Regt., was killed in action on November
4th in France.

The Mayor of Shrewsbury (Ald. S. M.

The First World War (1914–18) touched all British families, and newspapers recorded many of the local men involved in the conflict. The death of a soldier, sailor or airman might merit a simple notice or perhaps a description of his service, heroism and death, with a list of his siblings still in uniform, often accompanied by photographs. When conscription was introduced in 1916, applications for exemption from service were often reported. In the Second World War (1939–45) reporting was constrained more by paper shortages and security considerations, but after the war local papers often printed obituaries of former servicemen.

Death of a Shropshire lad

On 4 November 1918, one week before the end of the First World War, the poet Wilfred Owen was killed in action on the banks of a French canal. The Owen family's local paper, the *Shrewsbury Chronicle*, carried the news of Wilfred's death in the matter-of-fact way that was used to record the loss of so many sons.

covered in national papers, the amount of local news increased, including reports of sudden deaths, with inquest details, funeral reports and obituaries for more ordinary folk such as farmers and tradesmen.

EVERYDAY STORIES By the late 19th century, papers were increasingly covering the trivia of everyday life, such as flower shows and sports events, and the arrivals and departures of clergy and doctors. If your ancestor had a hobby, look for the newsletter of its society in local libraries.

Faces in the news There were very few illustrations in local papers before about 1860, mostly woodcuts of battles or major national events such as a coronation with the occasional line drawing of a notable local figure. In contrast, London-based papers such as *The Illustrated London News* were full of engravings of newsworthy people, with criminals

and deserters featured in *The Police Gazette* (later *Hue and Cry*). Posed photographs first appeared in the 1890s, but the high pictorial content of the modern press was largely absent until after the First World War. Magazines and single cartoons attacking political targets were sold. There were often good drawn likenesses of criminals included with law reports.

Births, marriages and deaths In 18th and early 19th-century papers the births, marriages and deaths section will help only if your ancestor could pay for inclusion. There may be entries for marriages and deaths among the middle classes, but most local people were not mentioned unless they were more than 90, servants of the gentry or left large numbers of orphans to the parish. Some causes of sudden death were mentioned. From around 1880, far more families began to pay for announcements.

how to find old newspapers

The largest collection is at British Library Newspapers (see page 172). Local studies sections of reference libraries and county record offices also hold newspapers. The British Library has London newspapers from 1603 to 1800, mostly on microfilm, and news-sheets from 1641 to 1660. It also holds the widest collection of Irish newspapers, particularly post-1826. The Bodleian Library (see DIRECTORY) has many early papers.

The National Library of Ireland has a large collection. The main collection of Scottish newspapers is held at the National Library of Scotland; the collection at the National Library of Wales is extensive, and is enhanced by a range of Welsh-language papers. See DIRECTORY for addresses.

Finding the right paper *The Times* is the only national paper that has been indexed from its early days. *Palmer's Index* covers 1790–1908 and can be viewed on CD at British Library Newspapers, Guildhall Library, the Society of Genealogists and some local reference libraries. Most entries concern the gentry, naval and military personnel, bankrupts, criminals and other subjects of interest to the ruling classes. The other general index is the *Official Index to The Times*, 1785–90 and 1906 to date, which can be viewed on CD at British Library Newspapers. The Society of Genealogists and Guildhall Library have microfilm of *The Times*' birth, marriage and death notices, with surname indexes. See DIRECTORY for addresses.

Few local newspapers are indexed. You need to find the county or market town nearest to your ancestors' home and discover which papers were published during your ancestors' lifetimes. If the first search fails, focus on the next nearest centre.

LOOKING UP THE PAPERS The following aids will help in your search:

☞ *Local Newspapers (England and Wales, Channel Islands, Isle of Man) 1750–1920* (J. Gibson, B. Langston and B. W. Smith, Baltimore Genealogical Pulishing Company 2002) is a list of which local papers are available and where they are held.

☞ *The Tercentenary Handlist of England and Welsh Newspapers, Magazines and Reviews, 1620–1919* (The Times Publishing Co. Ltd, 1920) lists and dates English and Welsh provincial papers and local papers in and around London.

☞ *Catalogue of the Newspaper Library Colindale* (P. E. Allen, 8 vols, British Library, 1975) covers, by location and title, most newspapers and journals published in the British Isles. It can be seen at the Society of Genealogists and large reference libraries.

☞ www.earl.org.uk on the Internet shows you where and how to find magazines, journals and newspapers in British public libraries.

☞ For links to newspaper collections, see www.nationalarchives.gov.uk/records/research-guides/newspapers/htm.

☞ For Scottish newspapers see the NEWSPLAN project at www.nli.ie/en/newspapers-newsplan-project.aspx.

☞ For Irish newspapers see the NEWSPLAN project at www.nli.ie/en/newspapers-newsplan-project.aspx.

BRITISH LIBRARY NEWSPAPERS

The collection of newspapers found in this outpost of the British Library, opposite Colindale Tube station in north London, is the largest in the British Isles. It includes more than 650,000 volumes and 320,000 reels of microfilm. The library is open Monday to Saturday, 10am to 5pm, except on public holidays. To obtain a day pass you need to show identification such as a driving licence. Copies of newspaper pages can be printed from microfilm, or if you have a precise date and reference, the staff may be able to supply photocopies by post. If you know which papers you want to consult beforehand, you should reserve them in advance.

Colindale Avenue, London NW9 5HE
Tel. 020 7412 7353
www.bl.uk/aboutus/quickinfo/loc/colindale/index.html

your ancestor's vote

If your 18th or 19th-century ancestor could vote in an election you may find him named in poll books and electoral registers. Until suffrage was extended in 1918 to women aged over 30, the right to vote was far from automatic, and up to the end of the 19th century depended largely on the ownership of property. Parliamentary constituencies were first drawn up in the Middle Ages, and from 1429 men in rural areas had to own land of a certain value to qualify for a vote; in urban areas the qualification varied—sometimes all householders had the vote, sometimes only freeholders.

Poll books In England and Wales poll books recorded the names and parish of electors. Who they voted for was also noted as this was open knowledge until the introduction of the secret ballot in the 1874 election. Poll books were not kept from this date.

FINDING POLL BOOKS Surviving poll books date from 1700 to 1872 and are held in various archives, including county record offices, major reference libraries and the Society of Genealogists. Consult the following aids and archives to help you to track down poll books:

☞ *Poll Books c. 1696–1872: a directory to holdings in Great Britain* (J. Gibson and C. Rogers, FFHS, 1992).

☞ The National Archives of Scotland (reference E 70) and the National Library of Scotland for Scottish poll books.

☞ In Ireland, the National Library, the National Archives and the Genealogical Office (see DIRECTORY) have some lists of voters. The Public Record Office of Northern Ireland (see DIRECTORY)

keeping it official in the journals

If your 18th or 19th-century ancestor moved in court or government circles, worked for the military or the Church, went bankrupt or was executed, there is a chance that he might appear in *The London Gazette* or *The Gentleman's Magazine*. These two national journals are full of detail on the privileged or notorious. The TNA, British Library, Society of Genealogists and many reference libraries have good runs of *The Gentleman's Magazine*. The British Library and Society of Genealogists also hold some surname and subject indexes, including marriage and obituary notices. The Internet Library of Early Journals at http://www.bodley.ox.ac.uk/ilej/ has a digital library of 18th and 19th-century journals, including the first 20 years of *The Gentleman's Magazine*.

holds voter lists for the province. Surviving poll books are listed in 'Irish Election Poll Books 1832–1872' (B.M. Walker and K.T. Hoppen in *Irish Booklore* vol. 3, no. 1, and vol. 4, no. 2, 1976–7).

electoral registers

The most interesting electoral registers, compiled annually for national elections since 1832, are those up to 1918 as these list electors by name, address and the basis of their eligibility to vote. Early in the 19th century the electorate was listed by place and then alphabetically, but as numbers grew names were grouped by electoral wards. The names were not indexed so it can be difficult to find ancestors in a large town or city unless you know their address.

After 1891, the year of the latest census available for public viewing, you can use electoral registers to find out if and when your ancestors moved house. A county-by-county listing of archives that hold the registers can be found in *Electoral Registers Since 1832 and Burgess Rolls* (J. Gibson and C. Rogers, FFHS, 1990). A large collection of electoral registers is held at the British Library.

FINDING SCOTTISH REGISTERS Registers are held at the National Archives of Scotland (references B and SC), the National Library of Scotland and Edinburgh Public Library (see DIRECTORY). Some registers are also held in regional record offices.

The London Gazette
This journal was first published in 1665 as the *Oxford Gazette*, changing its name in February 1666. Originally a bi-weekly publication, now appearing every weekday, it included Church and military appointments, grants of peerages, medal awards, bankruptcies, liquidations, naturalisations and changes of name. The *Gazette* has been indexed since 1787 by subject matter and surname. Complete sets are held at the TNA (in class ZJ 1), Guildhall Library and the British Library. The National Library of Wales has a complete run from 1910, and more limited coverage before that date.

The Gentleman's Magazine
Published monthly from 1731 to 1907, this contains similar information to that in *The London Gazette*, with the addition of notices of births, marriages and deaths. Many of the people mentioned are from the upper classes, although tradesmen, clergymen and military officers appear, along with others, including criminals executed at Tyburn.

A LIST *of* DEATHS *in the Year* 1740
Oct. 21. *John Essington*, Esq; Clerk to the Mercers Company, suddenly, after eating Grapes.
Oct. 24. Mr *Clutterbuck*, an eminent Confectioner in St *Paul's* Church-yard.

names in print

Before phone books and the *Yellow Pages* there were town and county directories. Our forebears turned to them for names, addresses and local information

town & county directories

Devonshire. **EXMOUTH.** **Pigot & Co's**

CARRIERS.
EXETER. Joseph Hayne, every day, (Thursday excepted)
EXETER. George Potter, every Mon Wed Fri & Sat
EXETER. S. Wilson, every Thurs

SIDMOUTH. J. Carter, every Mon
COACHES.
FROM THE GLOBE.
EXETER. Every morning, (Sundays

excepted,) at eight, and returns the same evening
FROM THE LONDON HOTEL.
EXETER. Every morning, (Sunday excepted,) at eight, and returns the same evening

HATHERLEIGH,

AN ancient and incorporated town, situated on a branch of the river Torridge, near its confluence with the Oke. The town, (in which there is a small woollen manufactory,) has but a mean appearance, the houses being in general built of what is called cobb-walling. The church is an ancient building situated on an eminence, and the prospect of the country round from the church-yard is very picturesque. The fairs are held on the third Friday in March, May 21st, June 22d, September 4th, and November 8th. The market day is Tuesday. The population according to the returns, in 1821, was 1,499 inhabitants.

POST OFFICE, John Turner, *Post Master.* The post leaves every afternoon at five, and arrives every morning at half-past five.

PROFESSIONAL PERSONS, &c.
Betty John, surgeon
Day James, surgeon
Fisher John, surgeon
Roberts Thomas, academy
Wivell Nathaniel, attorney
SHOPKEEPERS, &c.
Badeford Wm. hatter
Balkwell Elizabeth, corn miller
Brannd John, watch, &c. maker
Chasty Robt. watch, &c. maker

Chudleigh Thos. joiner, &c.
Chudley John, grocer, draper, &c.
Ford Emanuel, cooper
Gaffill Jane, linen draper
Martin John, saddler
Palmer Christopher, tailor& draper
Pearse Geo. woollen manufacturer
Short John Smale, druggist & draper, and agent to the West of England fire office
Smale George, cooper
Turner John, spirit dealer

White Wm. saddler, &c.
TAVERNS AND PUBLIC HOUSES.
George, Richard King
London Inn, Vincent Bird
New Inn, Wm. Kemp
CARRIERS
FROM THE LONDON INN.
BIDEFORD. Wm. Fursdon, Friday.
CREDITON. Thos. Durant, Wednesday
EXETER. Thos. Durant, Friday.
PLYMOUTH. Wm. Fursdon, Monday

HOLSWORTHY,

A SMALL market town, 214 miles from London, 19 from Bideford, 15 from Torrington, 42from Exeter, 24 from Tavistock, 38 from Plymouth, 15 from Hartland, and 20 from Okehampton. The country around Holsworthy is very dreary and destitute of wood. Market day Wednesday. Fairs 27th April, 9th, 10th, and 11th of July, and 2d of October, except they chance to fall on Saturday or Monday. The parish contained, in 1821, 1,440 inhabitants.

POST OFFICE, at the White Hart Inn, Lucy Perers, *Post-mistress.* A horse post to Stratton and Exeter, Monday, Wednesday, Thursday, and Saturday afternoons at two, and arrives the same mornings at eight.

PROFESSIONAL PERSONS.
Cann Hugh, attorney
Cock Richard, attorney
Cohan Arthur, surgeon
Cory Samuel, surgeon
Kelly Benedictus Marwood, attrny
Kingdon Rev. Roger, rector
SHOPKEEPERS, &c.
Bassett ---, draper & agent to the Phoenix fire office
Bennett Joseph, butcher
Bennett Wm. architect
Blake Wm. maltster
Bickle Tristram, druggist
Bussell Edmund, saddler
Chiug James, maltster
Cory Thomas, saddler
Coumbe John, draper
Downe Geo. ironmonger, &c.
Dunn Robt. corn miller

Ellis John, joiner
Friend Arthur, schoolmaster
Friend Walter, clock & watch makr
Fry Samuel, draper, &c. spirit dealer, & agent to the West of England fire office
Higgs Horatio, draper, &c.
Honey John, cabinet maker
Hoskin Arthur, boot & shoe maker
Hoskin John, tanner
Hoskin Josias, wheelwright
Johns Thomas, maltster
Johns Thomas, maltster
May John, dealer & chapman
Robins John, earthenware dealer
Shepherd Wm. maltster
Slee John, hat manufacturer
Taylor Thos. fellmonger
Thorne Francis, iron

ber, &c. and agent to the Nor...
wich...
Tosse... grocer
Woo... plumber&brazier
Y... & watch maker

D PUBLIC
Cro...
Glo...
Ki...

HON...

A LARGE and respectable market town, is most... side of the river Otter, distant 156 miles west by s... ancient place ; before the Conquest it belonged to... brother, the Earl of Mortaigne. In the reign of... vers, from whom it descended to the Courtnays, town at present principally consists of one street, mostly built since the fire in 1747, which consumed... and has recently been much improved ; there remai... (which is contemplated) to make it one of the neatest tow... trance into this place from London is Honiton Hill, which commands the kingdom ; from it may be seen Dumdon, a lofty insulated hill, n... a British intrenchment are still visible, supposed to have been erecte...

the south ... This is an ... to his half ...rd de Ri... ...ute. The ...od houses, ...d lighted, ...l shambles ...re the en...rospects in ...remains of ...island.

226

Commercial travellers of the late 18th and 19th centuries relied on directories for information on people, trades and facilities in the towns on their patch. The few directories published before 1750 were mostly lists of London merchants. A county directory for Hampshire appeared in 1784, and within 20 years many cities and industrial towns were covered.

The first national series of county directories was published in 1814 by Pigot & Co., whose rival, Kelly & Co., launched the Post Office Directories of provincial towns and counties in 1843. Kelly took over Pigot in 1853, by which time directories included most counties and urban centres.

Getting a feel for the place The first directories include descriptions of towns and villages, their transport links, banks and businesses, public houses and lists of wealthy residents (the 'Court' section) and tradesmen ('commercials'). The early trade addresses are likely to be where the tradesman and his family lived. By around 1875,

Pulling no punches

A page from the Devon section of Pigot's Directory *of 1830 is less than flattering about the pleasures of Hatherleigh, 'an inconsiderable market-town' with a parish church that has 'nothing to attract particular notice'. Details of local industries, the town big-wigs and traders, and the existence of a manorial court, all provide clues for the family historian.*

the more affluent shopkeepers started moving their families out, leaving a manager in charge, who lived 'above the shop', sharing with the unmarried staff. Where a tradesman has moved away from his work premises, a 'Court' address may be given for him as well. Directories do not record labourers and other employees, although village entries include the names of farmers and craftsmen.

Wider coverage

By 1900 many town directories listed heads of households with their addresses, usually in a 'street' or 'residential' section. Married women were mentioned only if they ran a business. There are often gaps in listings in poor areas. Not until the 1920s did street directories become a more or less complete record.

TAKING NAMES FURTHER A directory may prompt a search for a person in census or civil registration records. For example, if a pub landlord in an 1856 directory looks like a possible ancestor, the 1851 or 1861 census returns for that town may fill in more family detail for him. Remember that by the time a directory was published the information was often a year or more out of date.

where to find a directory

Apart from the main collections listed in Key sources, above, local libraries hold directories for their own area. Old directories are expensive and in demand so collections may be incomplete.

HELP WITH THE SEARCH To find out which directories are available, you should consult the following lists and indexes:

☞ *A Guide to the national and provincial directories of England and Wales, excluding London, pub. before 1856* (J.E. Norton, Royal Historical Society, 1984).

☞ *British Directories: a bibliography and guide to directories published in England and Wales, 1850–1950, and Scotland, 1773–1950* (G. Shaw and A.Tipper, Leicester University Press, 1988).

☞ Irish directories are listed in *Irish Genealogy: a record finder* (ed. D. Begley, Heraldic Artists, 1981) and *Irish Records: sources for family and local history* (J.G. Ryan, Flyleaf Press, revised ed., 1997).

☞ *The Directories of London 1677–1977* (P. J. Atkins, Mansell, 1990).

☞ www.genuki.org.uk
This web site has county pages with on-line indexes to county directories.

INFORMATION AT HOME Many directories are being published by S&N Genealogy Supplies, which can be found on:

☞ www.genealogysupplies.com
☞ www.nof-digitise.org
This is a web site about a national project to digitise a wide range of directories.

Telephone directories

The telephone caught on quickly in the commercial world, so you may find the business address of an ancestor in a Post Office directory of the early 20th century. If you have an unusual surname, searching for it in telephone directories may uncover forgotten family.

LOCATING PHONE DIRECTORIES The British Telecom Archives (see DIRECTORY) holds the majority of London and provincial directories from 1880 to 1984. Guildhall Library (see DIRECTORY) holds some London directories from 1881 to 1918 and most from 1920 onwards. Local libraries and county record offices also keep directories for their particular area.

property records in England and Wales

Property records can tell you where your family lived and how much money they had. They also give details of family relationships

More than a social gathering

In September 1913, the tenants of an estate in Llandrindod Wells, Wales, met, as they did every year, at the Rock Park Hotel to pay their rents to their landlord and enjoy a Michaelmas dinner at his expense. But such popular traditions do not necessarily go on for ever—even as this photograph was taken the landlord and tenant system of farming was in decline. Against a background of agricultural crisis dating from the 1870s, the 1894 budget of Sir William Harcourt, the Liberal Chancellor of the Exchequer, had placed the huge new burden of death duties upon the great landed estates. The consequent sale of land allowed many tenant farmers to become owners of the fields they worked.

Nowadays, almost 70 per cent of us own the house or flat in which we live. But until the early years of the 20th century, owner-occupiers were in the minority. The usual way to put a roof over your head was to rent.

A small number of great landed proprietors owned large estates, which could include whole towns and villages. Some of their tenants had long leases, but many simply paid a weekly or monthly rent with no written documentation and little security. In England and Wales the chances of finding your ancestors in property records are probably best

KEY SOURCES OF INFORMATION

KEY SOURCES OF INFORMATION
♦ Title deeds, manorial court rolls, leases and
estate papers at county record offices and the
National Library of Wales.
♦ Collections of old deeds at the TNA and Oxford
and Cambridge college archives.
♦ The return of owners of land and valuation
survey field books at the TNA.
♦ Fire insurance records at Guildhall Library.
♦ The National Register of Archives at the TNA.
SEE DIRECTORY ➤

if they either owned, or were tenants of, a big estate.
An estate's archives may include a range of different
records, such as freehold deeds for the estate's land
(often acquired from several families); court rolls of
manors; counterparts (the landlord's copies) of
leases granted to tenants; surveys, rentals and maps;
correspondence with tenants; personal papers; and
account books.

An estate's accounts and papers have always been
private property and you will usually only be able to
view them if they have been deposited at a county
record office.

finding modern records

In England and Wales there are two ways to own
land: freehold and leasehold. Freehold land is yours
for ever; leasehold land is yours for a specified time,
perhaps 99 years, and you pay rent to a landlord who
owns either the freehold or a longer leasehold
(which he in turn rents from a freeholder). At the
end of the lease, the land returns to the freeholder.

From the Middle Ages (see Early records, pages
274–87) property ownership was proved through
documents called title deeds. In 1862 the principle
was established of proving the title to property in
England and Wales simply through an entry in a
central register, held at HM Land Registry (see
DIRECTORY). Hardly any land was registered before
1899, and very little outside the Home Counties
before the 1960s. Since 1998 all land in England and
Wales has had to be registered if it changes hands.

As as result, the amount of registered land varies
from place to place. Most land in London is registered, but less than half in some rural areas. HM
Land Registry will tell you if a property in England
or Wales is registered. If it is, the register includes a
map of the property, and the name and address of its
present owner. It does not include all previous
owners of the property, but it will mention owners
since the date of the first registration. To find out
about more ancient landowners you will need old

Dec. 9th Fanny Crawley.

Burials in 1775.

Feb: 12th Ann Hanks.
17th Betty Maul.
march 1st Elizh. Baily

Nov 15th Benjami...

HAVE YOU FOUND THE RIGHT ONE?

Manorial court rolls contain extra details about family relationships that can help you to identify a person. Compare the information given about the death of Ann Hanks in a burial register (above) and a manorial court roll (right). The burial register of St Mary's Westport, Malmesbury, Wiltshire, 12 February 1775 states: 'Buried Ann Hanks'. Which Ann Hanks in particular is not clear.

In the manor of Malmesbury a court was held about every six months. The first court after Ann's death was on 4 May 1775 and its proceedings were written in the court roll. This tells you that Ann Hanks was a widow whose maiden name was Tanner. It also tells you where she lived and that she had a daughter called Sarah, now Sarah Hillier. From this you can decide if you have found the Ann Hanks you are seeking. Sometimes a death was not reported until a later court.

title deeds, many of which have been destroyed. Those that have been saved are often in county record offices, or perhaps with families who own or once owned the property.

going back to earlier records

Manorial court rolls and copyholders For many of our ancestors in England, and parts of Wales, the manor was a dominant feature in their lives from the Middle Ages until well into the 19th century. Until 1926 there was a form of property ownership, called copyhold, whereby land was held from a lord of a manor. The steward of the manor held a regular court on behalf of its lord. The court made regulations, for example, about pasturing animals on the common, and could fine tenants who broke these rules. Some manors could try petty criminals or act as a small claims court. Records of these activities can be found in a manorial court's rolls (see Reflecting local life, pages 286–7).

COPYHOLDERS The most important task of the manorial court was to record the ownership of copyhold land. This property could be bought, sold, inherited or mortgaged, but each new owner had to be admitted as a tenant in the manorial court. A copyholder sold land by surrendering it to the lord of the manor, on condition that the lord admitted the buyer as the new tenant. The 'surrender' and 'admittance' were noted in the court roll of the manor, and the new tenant was given a copy of the entry, so becoming the copyholder.

When a tenant died, the death would be reported at the next sitting of the court, and the heir would apply to be admitted as the new tenant. Thus, the court rolls are a valuable source of information about the tenants of the manor, and you can often trace several generations of a family in them. Before 1732 they are usually written in Latin, although some have been translated and published, such as those for Hornsey in Middlesex, Wimbledon and Wakefield. They can be seen at local record offices.

Leases for lives Until the mid 19th century, especially in Wales and south-west England, leases were often granted, not for a period of years, as they are now, but for three lives. The lease lasted until all three people named as lives had died. They did not necessarily inherit it in turn—they were just named to determine the length of the lease. Often, when one 'life' died, the tenant would renew the lease (for a fee), naming a new life (such as a younger family member) and so prolonging the tenancy. Some manorial courts granted copyholds in the same way.

USING LIVES TO MAKE A TREE The 'lives' were often those of tenants and their children, and the lease usually states their ages. This can be used to construct a family tree, especially when there are no baptismal records, as in the following example. Thomas Lewis, who died in 1784, was a Baptist. In his will he mentions his sons, James, Thomas and George, and his house at the Posterngate in Malmesbury, 'held for lives'.

Because the boys were Baptists, their baptisms are not recorded in the parish register (see Nonconformists, pages 102–6), and the 18th-century registers of Abbey Row Chapel are lost. However, two leases of Thomas Lewis's house survive in Wiltshire County Record Office. The first, dated 15 April 1762, is for the lives of his daughter Sarah, aged 10, and his sons James, aged four, and Thomas, aged two. The second, dated 24 April 1777, is for the lives of his sons James, aged 19,

Thomas, aged 17, and George, aged 15. It also says that Sarah has died.

RENTALS AND SURVEYS Landowners have always needed to keep track of their tenants, so it was common practice during the 16th to 19th centuries for manors and estates to make 'rentals' or 'surveys'. These are lists of individual properties, their tenants, and the amount of rent due each year.

INHERITING LAND

A landowner's will (see Last will and testament, pages 120–4) or a settlement (see below) governed who should inherit. Otherwise, under common law, freehold land was inherited, before 1926, by the eldest son as 'heir at law'. If he was dead, his eldest son took it instead. If there were no sons, any daughters shared it equally. If there were no children, the property generally went to the father of the owner, or, if he was dead, to the eldest brother, and so on. A widow had a right (called 'dower') to a third of her husband's land until she died or remarried, after which it went to the heir. A widower had a right to all his wife's land until he died, provided there were children of the marriage. It then went to the heir.

Copyhold land was inherited according to the local custom of the manor. This might be the same as the common law, but often was not. In some manors, especially in Kent, all the sons inherited the land equally; in others, the youngest son inherited. Under Welsh law, which applied to most of medieval Wales, land was inherited equally by all the sons and sometimes other male relatives. After 1536, Wales had the same law as England, but the old practice continued in some areas for much longer.

Settlements Settlement deeds were generally used in two cases: by the aristocracy to keep their estates in the family; and by middle and upper classes as marriage agreements to protect a wife's property. They can provide useful evidence about the marriage and the parents of the spouses.

If properties were held for three lives, the list usually includes the names and ages of those nominated as lives. The estate records may even be accompanied by a map, which could help you to identify your ancestor's house (see pages 201–2).

Freeholds—lease and release Various types of deeds have been used to transfer the ownership of freeholds. You may come across 'conveyances', 'deeds of bargain and sale', or 'deeds of feoffment'. The most common deed, and also the most confusing, is the 'lease and release', which, despite its name, was the standard way of conveying freehold land in England and Wales from about 1614 to 1841.

The seller gave the buyer a lease for a year, enabling him to take possession of the land, and the next day 'released' the freehold to him. You should read the lease, although all the most important information, including details of any third parties involved in the property, is in the release.

Abstracts of title An 'abstract' is a summary of the title deeds prepared at the time of a sale. It is easier to read than the original deeds and may contain details that are lost. The abstract for land that was inherited will give details of the family tree to prove the inheritance, occasionally supported by birth, baptism, marriage or death certificates.

finding deeds and manorial rolls

Most county record offices have better indexes of places than of people. Use them to discover what they have for your ancestor's parish. Then find what lists they have of depositors. Investigate anything deposited by local landowners or solicitors from

how to read a deed

A common form of deed is an indenture. Indentures were originally a medieval anti-forgery device. Two copies of a deed were written on a single sheet of parchment, which was then cut apart with a jagged ('indented') line. Each party kept one half. To check that a copy was genuine, the edges were matched to see if they fitted. Later, any deed involving more than one party might be called an indenture, even if there was no second copy. Some of the terms found in deeds in bold, enlarged type are explained on the right.

The indenture on the right was made out in 1890 for the sale at auction of a lot comprising land and property as coloured pink in the map that accompanies it.

THIS INDENTURE The date follows.

BETWEEN Here you will find the names and whereabouts of the parties involved. In this case, the first party (Phillips Cosby Lovett) is selling to the third party (William Edwins).

WHEREAS This introduces the 'recitals', which give details of previous dealings with the property and often family history information. Always read them.

WITNESSETH This introduces the main part of the deed. It is followed by the price paid for the property, and formal words transferring ownership.

ALL THOSE A description of the property follows, often naming the occupiers of it and adjacent properties.

TO HOLD This says who gets the property and on what basis. In this case it says, 'unto and to the use of the purchaser in fee simple'. This means that William Edwins ('the purchaser') is getting the freehold. A more common wording would be, 'unto and to the use of the said William Edwins and his heirs'. A lease might say, 'for the term of 99 years from the date hereof YIELDING AND PAYING during the said term the yearly rent of one pound.'

There will then be several 'covenants' (promises), which sometimes stipulate how the land should be used.

SIGNED SEALED AND DELIVERED Signatures and seals of the parties. Signatures of witnesses.

nearby towns. Some collections will have detailed catalogues on open shelves. Deeds were also copied or 'enrolled' in the records of various courts, but a lack of indexes makes most of them difficult to find.

Deeds in archives are only a fraction of what once existed. Many remain in private hands, with the owners of the properties concerned, or with their mortgage lenders. If you know the present address of your ancestor's property, you could try asking the current owners if they have the old deeds.

Registries of deeds In the 18th century, registries of deeds were set up in Middlesex and Yorkshire. They do not contain the original deeds but 'memorials', that is copy extracts that noted the parties and the main contents of the deeds. The registry for Middlesex covers 1709–1938 and is held at the London Metropolitan Archives. The registry for Yorkshire is divided into three areas:

Soulbury—past and present

The photograph, above, shows the Buckinghamshire village of Soulbury as it appears today. The postcard, below, is the same site as it would have looked at the time the indenture, bottom, was drawn up, on 31 December 1890. The land concerned in the deed is behind the white thatched cottage on the right of the postcard. The building on the left, which was once a school, is still standing.

West Riding (1704–1970) at West Yorkshire
Archive Service; East Riding (1708–1974) at East
Riding of Yorkshire Archives; and North Riding
(1736–1970) at North Yorkshire County Record
Office. See DIRECTORY for addresses. For details of
the Irish registry, see page 184.

The cities of London and York were not included
in these registries, but in York many deeds were
enrolled in the city archives (1719–1866). There
was a similar registry in the Bedford Levels area of
the Fens (1663–1920) and the deeds are held at
Cambridgeshire County Record Office (see
DIRECTORY).

further useful lists

The land tax This was a tax on the value of land in
England and Wales levied from 1692 to 1963. The
annual assessments usually list both owners and
occupiers of property. Local copies covering many
years survive in county record offices, but most
often for 1780–1832, when they were used to prove
the entitlement to vote. There is an almost complete
set of assessments for England and Wales for 1798 at
the TNA in class IR 23.

The return of owners of land This return,
known as the 'Modern Domesday', was made in or
around 1873. It covers all counties in Britain and
Ireland, listing all owners of more than one acre of
land. The return can be seen at the TNA and many
reference libraries. It is also available on CD and
commercial websites.

Valuation surveys The Valuation Office carried
out extensive surveys of properties in Britain from
1910 to 1913. The information, including names of
owners and tenants, and descriptions of properties,
was recorded in field books, available at the TNA.
See www.nationalarchives.gov.uk/records/
research-guides/vaulation-office-records.htm.

Fire insurance companies Guildhall Library
(see DIRECTORY) has a large collection of records of
British fire insurance companies, including lists of
policyholders, starting around 1700. Some county
record offices have records for other companies.

Look farther afield If your ancestors arrived in a
country parish apparently out of the blue, it may be
worth looking to see if there was a landowner in the
village who also had land somewhere else. Did he
move workers from one estate to another? If so, start
looking at the estate records for the landowner's
other properties—you may find more ancestors.

TAKING IT FURTHER

♦ *Old Title Deeds* (N. W. Alcock, Phillimore, 2nd
ed., 2001).
♦ *Land and Window Tax Assessments* (J. Gibson,
M. Medlycott and D. Mills, FFHS, 2nd ed., 1998).
♦ *My Ancestors Were Manorial Tenants* (P.B. Park,
Society of Genealogists, 2nd ed., 1994).
♦ 'Leases for Lives' (H. Peskett, in *Genealogists'
Magazine*, June 1973).
♦ 'The Deeds Registries of Middlesex and
Yorkshire' (F. Sheppard and V. Belcher, *Journal of the
Society of Archivists*, vol. 6, pages 274–86).
♦ *Manorial Records: an introduction to their transcription and translation* (D. Stuart, Phillimore, 1992).
♦ *Welsh Manors and Their Records* (H. Watt, National
Library of Wales, 2000).

Information on the Internet
♦ www.landreg.gov.uk
HM Land Registry's web site.
♦ www.ultranet.com/~deeds/legal
Explanation of legal terms in land records.
♦ www.nationalarchives.gov.uk/nra

A PHILOSOPHER'S FAMILY FROM ONE DEED

Between the lines

Property deeds can reveal a wealth of information about a family. Using just three property deeds, Chris Pitt Lewis was able to construct a family tree for Thomas Hobbes, the philosopher. The information in the green boxes was obtained entirely from the deeds. If you hit a wall with parish records and wills, try using property records as a second line of attack.

Thomas Hobbes
b. 1588, Malmesbury.
d. 1679, Hardwick House, Derbyshire. Philosopher.

Edmund Hobbes

Francis Hobbs
d. 1668. Skinner, of Westport. m. Sarah (who later m. Thomas Eastmead, mason, of Westport).

Thomas Hobbs
Will dated 28-8-1727. Tanner, of Westport.

Edward Hobbs

William Hobbs
Will dated 27-2-1693. m. Sarah, d. before 1719.

Sarah Hobbs

Thomas Hobbs
Will dated 1-1-1746. Currier, of Westport.

Edward Hobbs
d. between 1755 and 1780. Yeoman, of Westport.

William Hobbs
Leather dresser, of Bristol in 1719.

Thomas Hobbs
d. before 1780. Currier, of Bristol, m. soon after 3-6-1752 Mary Bosville, later widow of Llanellen, Monmouthshire in 1782.

Thomas Hobbs
Doctor in Physick; of Abergavenny, Monmouthshire in 1780.

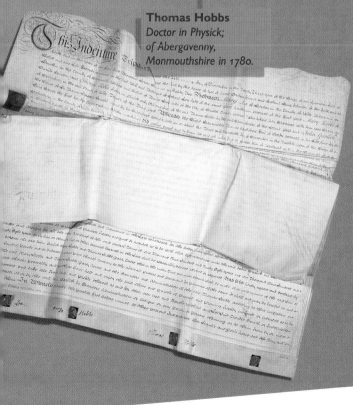

When Chris Pitt Lewis discovered that his 5 x great grandfather, Joseph Lewis, married an Anne Hobbes in Malmesbury in 1740 he was intrigued. He wondered whether she could be related to Thomas Hobbes, the philosopher and author of *Leviathan*, who was also from Malmesbury.

Anne Hobbes' parentage drew a blank and her baptism was not in local parish registers or Nonconformist records. So Chris decided to look at the archives at Wiltshire County Record Office.

Using the surname index, Chris found several entries for Hobbes, or Hobbs, reflecting the careless spelling of the times. In deposit 62 was a bundle of deeds relating to land belonging to the family of Thomas Hobbes. One deed (left) contained names and information about family relationships spanning 150 years—a lucky find. Chris could not prove a connection to his Anne Hobbes, but an Anne appeared in the will of Thomas Hobbs of Westport, so the possibility remains.

183

property records using Irish archives

To understand Irish property records you need to untangle a web of Church of Ireland, Roman Catholic and civil boundaries

Living off the land
A peat cutter stands outside his cottage in the early 20th century. At this time Ireland was still predominantly agrarian and less developed than the rest of the British Isles.

Although you will find freeholders, lease-holders, indentures, leases for lives, and so on, as in England and Wales (see pages 176–83), the form of property records in Ireland is not the same. Finding your way round them can be complicated. This is because of the way the land was apportioned. Each county is divided into civil parishes, baronies and townlands. The latter do not necessarily contain towns and vary from one acre to thousands of acres.

The civil parish is usually, but not always, the same as the Church of Ireland parish and must not be confused with the Roman Catholic parish. Sometimes you need to be aware of all three kinds of parish (which may or may not cover the same geographical area and usually have different names). Church of Ireland and Roman Catholic parishes are both grouped into dioceses, again not necessarily covering the same area. To add to the confusion,

many places in Ireland have the same name. A good starting point for those trying to unravel the Irish land system is the Townland Index, which is available at many archives.

early Irish records

The Tudor Fiants 1521–1603 These concerned matters such as appointments, pardons, leases and grants of land. The originals were destroyed in 1922, but they had been listed in the 19th-century *Reports of the Deputy Keeper of the Public Records in Ireland* and have been reissued in *The Irish Fiants of the Tudor Sovereigns* (É. de Burca, Dublin, 4 vols, 1994).

184

The Civil Survey 1654–6 This survey listed new landlords of each townland, as well as pre-1641 landowners whose property had been confiscated. All that has survived is published by the Irish Manuscripts Commission (see DIRECTORY) and is available in major Irish libraries.

The Census of Ireland 1659 This has been published (edited by Seamus Pender, Dublin Stationery Office, 1939). It lists those with title to land and the total numbers of residents in each townland.

the Registry of Deeds

Voluntary registration of deeds was established in 1708, mainly to prevent land from reverting to Catholic hands, although acknowledged Catholics began to register land transactions in the late 18th century. Copies of deeds were lodged at the registry and transcribed into registers. As well as land transfers, you will find deeds relating to mortgages, marriage settlements and wills.

further sources of information

Estate papers Documents relating to leases and tenancies may still be in family hands or deposited in a local record office. Many have been lodged in the National Archives of Ireland (see DIRECTORY) and the Public Record Office of Northern Ireland (PRONI—see DIRECTORY). *Manuscript Sources for*

the History of Irish Civilisation (R.J. Hayes, G.K.& Co., 1965) lists the locations of some estate papers.

Some Irish estate records were transferred to England and their location is listed in the National Register of Archives (see DIRECTORY). A number of estate records have been published by the Irish Manuscripts Commission. The National Archives, National Library and PRONI hold catalogues listing tenants on bankrupted estates from 1849.

Tithe applotment books These books list, by parish and townland, the occupiers (tenant farmers) of agricultural land in Ireland between 1823 and 1838. The originals are held in the National Archives; microfilm copies can be viewed at PRONI and in Family History Centres (see DIRECTORY).

Griffith's Valuation This took place from 1848 to 1864 and lists occupiers and their immediate landlords. Griffith's is important because it includes poor tenant farmers and forms the nearest thing to a census for the period. It is available on microfiche and (as an index) on CD-ROM in large libraries such as the Society of Genealogists (see DIRECTORY).

The valuation office Valuations of properties have been continuously updated since the mid 19th century as the landlord, tenant or property changed. These 'cancelled' books can be seen at the Valuation Office (see DIRECTORY). PRONI has the records for the six counties of Northern Ireland.

property records
using Scottish archives

Scotland has long had a system for keeping property records. You are more likely to find a deed there than anywhere else in Britain

In Scotland there are two ways to own land. You may have a heritable estate (similar to a freehold) or a lease for a number of years. Until recent times, Scotland relied on the recording of deeds as proof of land transactions. In 1981 a new system of land registration, the Land Register (see DIRECTORY), was introduced, with the intention of covering all of Scotland by 2003. For a fee you may view registered titles and take away a copy of the 'title sheet', which gives the current owner of a property, its location and a description.

the Register of Sasines

From the Middle Ages onwards, transfers and mortgages of heritable land were carried out by a deed called an Instrument of Sasine. Since the early 17th century, copies of these deeds have been recorded in a central Register of Sasines, which is made up of several different registers:

THE GENERAL REGISTER This dates from 1617 and was divided by county from 1868.

THE SECRETARY'S REGISTER This is a predecessor of the General Register, running from 1599 to 1609.

PARTICULAR REGISTERS Each one covers a single county, or a group of counties, beginning at various dates from 1599 to 1620, and up to 1868.

BURGH REGISTERS The earliest of the 67 Royal Burghs' registers starts in 1602. They were discontinued between 1927 and 1963. The areas of the Royal Burghs were usually much smaller than the modern towns of which they form part.

Who owned what?

The Register of Sasines is held at the National Archives of Scotland, which is housed in the General Register House in Edinburgh (right). The trawl through the Register becomes less onerous after 1781 due to the volumes of abridgements (far right), which contain summaries of the documents recorded. The summaries are listed chronologically and by county, but you can easily find what you are after by using the indexes of persons and (except 1831–71) places.

(824)   Jan. 3. 1812.
JOSEPH COOK, Shoemaker, College of Elgin, *Seised*, Dec. 31. 1811,—in lands called SPYNIE MANSE in the COLLEGE OF ELGIN;—on Disp. by John Harral, Gardener, College of Elgin, to Isobel Adam, his spouse, in liferent, and Margaret, Katharine, Janet, Christian, and Isobel Mathew, daughters of Alexander Mathew in Cloves, in fee, Jun. 27. 1786; and Disp. & Assig. by them, Dec. 26. 27. 1811.
                                                    P. R. 10. 49.

(825)   Jan. 13. 1812.
JOHN COULL, Gardener, Elgin, & Ann Stewart, his spouse,—and James Coull, their son, *Seised*, in liferent & fee respectively, Jan. 13. 1812,—in part of the south end of that Habitation Manse or Messuage commonly called the MANSE OF KINNORE with the Houses thereon, on the south side of the Cathedral Church of Moray and on the west of the Vennel called Niddry's wynd within the COLLEGE OF ELGIN;—on Disp. by Alexander Shiach, Cartwright, Elgin, Nov. 21. 1811.
                                                    P. R. 10. 53.

(826)   Jan. 13. 1812.
JANET WILLIAMSON, relict of James Lillie, Butcher, Forres, *Seised*, Dec. 31. 1811,—in 2 Ridges of land consisting of 1 Acre in the middle of the MUIRYSHADE; & 9 Ridges of land on the west side of the said Muiryshade consisting of 3 Acres & 1 rood, all in the neighbourhood of FORRES;—in security of a liferent annuity of £10;—on Bond by John Lillie, Merchant, Forres, Jul. 10. 1810.   P. R. 10. 57.

(827)   Jan. 28. 1812.
WILLIAM TOD, Factor for the Duke of Gordon at Fochabers, *gets Ren.* Oct. 17. 1808,—Dec. 2. 1811, by Jean Grant, relict of Alexander Smith, Vintner, Fochabers, Edward Smith at Slave Lake, North America, George Smith at Pictou, Province of Nova Scotia, & Isobel Smith, & William Reid, Merchant, Mill of Fochabers, her husband,—of 2 Tenements of ground with the Houses thereon on the south side of the principal Street called Gordon's Street of FOCHABERS, par. Bellie;—and of £200, in Disp. by the said Jean Grant, May 18. 1793.   P. R. 10. 62.

(828)   Feb. 15. 1812.
JOHN FORBES, Advocate, *Seised*, Feb. 15. 1812,—in SCOTSTOWNHILL, par. St. Andrews;—on Ch. Resig.
G. S. Feb. 3. 1812.   P. R. 10. 76.

(829)   Feb. 15. 1812.
JOHN FORBES, Advocate, *Seised*, Feb. 15. 1812,—in

The registers are held at the National Archives of Scotland (see DIRECTORY) except the Burgh Registers for Glasgow and (before 1809) Aberdeen and Dundee, which can be found in the respective city archives. The National Archives is the key source for all Scottish property records.

Searching the Register of Sasines From 1781 onwards there are printed 'abridgements' of the General and Particular Registers, arranged by county and year. These have indexes of persons and (except for 1831–71) places. There are copies in the National Archives, the Society of Genealogists (see DIRECTORY) and some libraries. The abridgements are relatively easy to search, especially if you know the county and approximate date. The Burgh Registers are not included in the abridgements. Only some have indexes.

EARLY SASINES Before 1781 the search is more difficult. There are published indexes to some of the Particular Registers, and unpublished indexes in the National Archives to a few more. Otherwise, you have to use contemporary 'minute books', if they exist, or simply wade through an unindexed register. The General Register is indexed from 1617 to 1720, and has minute books up to 1780.

RECENT OWNERS If you know the property concerned, and are looking for a recent owner, you can use the 'search sheet'. This contains a brief entry for every piece of heritable property in Scotland. It is divided into six districts—Central, Edinburgh, North, South, East and West—and includes every reference to the property in the General Register since 1871. Enquiries should be made to the Registers of Scotland (see DIRECTORY).

other Scottish registers

There are a few other resources that may be worth searching, all at the National Archives.

The Register of Deeds This dates from 1554. Any deed could be voluntarily registered here—not only deeds concerning land, but also commercial

and private contracts, such as marriage settlements, and even apprenticeships. Published indexes cover 1661–95, and the National Archives has indexes from 1770 and for some earlier periods. Some local courts kept similar registers, indexes for which you will find in libraries and the Society of Genealogists.

Retours or services of heirs When a tenant of the Crown in Scotland died, his heir had to prove his right to the land by an inquest and 'retour' (return). Records go back to 1530. They are indexed by the name of the heir, and not the deceased. Indexes are held in libraries and the Society of Genealogists.

Valuation rolls These records, kept annually since 1855, list proprietors, tenants and occupiers. Some earlier valuations also exist.

leases or tacks

Before the 20th century, most people in Scotland were not landowners. If they had property at all, they were leasehold tenants, as in the rest of the British Isles. In Scotland, leases are sometimes called 'tacks'. These documents occasionally survive with estate records, which you may find at the National Archives and in local archives. As in England, estate records include copies of 'rentals' or lists of tenants. Some tacks were recorded in the Register of Deeds, and, after 1857, in the Register of Sasines.

TAKING IT FURTHER

♦ *Tracing Your Scottish Ancestors* (C. Sinclair, HMSO, 1997).
♦ *Scottish Local History* (D. Moody, Genealogical Publishing Co. Inc. US, revised ed., 2010).
♦ *Tracing Scottish Local History* (C. Sinclair, HMSO, 1994).

Information on the Internet
♦ www.ros.gov.uk The Registers of Scotland.

local history
looking into the past

Putting names and dates on a family tree is only the first step for a family historian. You will soon want to find out as much as you can about your ancestors' day-to-day lives

A bit of hokey-pokey
Ice cream was as popular among children at the turn of the 20th century as it is today. It was known as hokey-pokey and sold from barrows in the street. The hokey-pokey man was generally of Italian origin and the ice cream was often fruit-flavoured water ice.

Once you have traced relatives who lived in past times you will start to wonder what their homes were like, what jobs they did, and what sort of towns or villages they inhabited. Finding out the answers to these questions puts your ancestors' lives into context and you may even pick up a lead for further research. Many of the records you need are the same as those used to build a family tree; they are kept in the same record offices and reference libraries. But rather than looking for information about individuals, you are now trying to get a sense of past communities. In the 19th century these communities were often surprisingly diverse. If you manage to trace all 16 great-great-grandparents you may well find that they came from many different backgrounds and parts of Britain, with quite different experiences of life.

filling in the gaps with oral history

Many important details about your ancestors and how and where they lived will not have been written down, and can only be learnt from talking to your relatives (see Tackling the home front, pages 14–15). This is especially relevant when researching the lives of female ancestors (see below). Elderly relatives are storehouses of family history, so make sure you record their memories.

It is worth enquiring at local libraries and museums to see whether tapes and edited collections of oral history projects have been deposited by adult education groups or local societies. The journal *Oral History*, which can be seen at public reference libraries, has up-to-date information on oral history projects and resources.

KEY SOURCES OF INFORMATION
♦ Oral history collections, photographs, postcards and newspapers at local libraries and museums.
♦ Diaries at county record offices.
♦ Directories, gazetteers, local history books and published census returns at local and larger reference libraries.
♦ Public Health reports at county record offices.
SEE DIRECTORY ➤

Preparing the ground It is essential to prepare for interviews with relatives or others. Make sure you have a list of topics in mind, and ask specific questions (see page 15), such as 'How did you get to work?', 'Who else lived in the same street?' or 'Can you name any of the people in this photograph?' Practical guidance on interview techniques and the transcription and analysis of tapes can be found in *Oral History and the Local Historian* (S. Caunce, Longman, 1994). Another useful source of information is *Researching Local History: the human journey*

WOMEN'S HISTORY

The past concerns and activities of women are rarely noted in documents such as census returns. Much of a married woman's work, such as taking in washing or plaiting straw bonnets, was done at home on a casual or part-time basis and not recorded. The lives of such women are best discovered through tape-recordings of recollections or from books, such as *A Woman's Place: an oral history of working class women, 1890–1940* (E. Roberts, Basil Blackwell, 1984), that combine oral evidence with other historical sources. The Fawcett Library (see DIRECTORY) houses collections of papers relating to women's groups.

Washing for a living

Mrs Stott, born in 1896, recalled how her mother took in washing: 'She used to wash Saturday, Monday, Tuesday and Wednesday and the other two days she'd be ironing. She used to wash for all these important people, these gentry . . . but she wouldn't do anything on a Sunday. She wouldn't even let you put a button on on a Sunday.'

Picture postcards with views of streets and rural scenes became popular in the late 19th century and are usually authentic representations. The Revd Francis Kilvert noted in his diary for 4 October 1870: 'Today I sent my first post cards... they are capital things, simple, useful and handy. A happy invention.'

(M. A. Williams, Longman, 1996), which shows you how to combine family and local history, using oral and documentary methods, and concentrates on the 19th and 20th centuries.

photographs and prints

Before the late 19th century almost all family photographs were taken by professional photographers at special occasions or in their studios (see What old photographs can tell you, pages 18–19). Local libraries often have family albums (or copies) or, more importantly, collections of photographs of local scenes, groups and events, which provide vivid images of past communities from the earliest years of photography, especially after 1860.

When viewing early photographs, keep in mind that photographers were attracted by the quaint and unusual or by things going out of fashion, such as styles of dress or late survivals of hand crafts. Scenes like this should not be regarded as typical of the period in which they were taken.

Most towns and villages appear in books of old photographs, often comparing past scenes with the same view now. Sutton Publishing (see DIRECTORY) produces a series of titles on towns seen through old photographs. Check also local libraries for similar publications by small local publishers.

Picture postcards Local libraries and museums may hold collections of old postcards showing local scenes. It has been estimated that by about 1910 an average of 860 million picture postcards were sent each year. Subject matter varied widely: some depict a single street, or important landmark, while others are of landscapes and may include people, showing how they dressed at the time.

An earlier view Before photography, prints and paintings of local views were popular. Most towns have collections dating back to the 18th century in their libraries and museums. The buildings and natural features shown in the earliest can often be compared against town maps and plans and give a sense of the growth of a town from the late 18th century onwards.

diaries and autobiographies

William Holland, the parson of Over Stowey in Somerset, noted in his diary for 13 July 1800: 'Not many at Church this morning tho' all the better sort were, but most of the lower were, I suppose, in parties gathering hurtle-berries on Quantock.' Day-to-day observations noted down in diaries can provide glimpses of former customs and attitudes that are not recorded elsewhere.

At first, diaries were written by gentlemen and clergymen only, but in the 19th and 20th centuries people further down the social scale, mostly skilled workers, began to record their memories. Such diaries are usually found in local libraries and county record offices, although they are sometimes kept as heirlooms within a family (see A man with a taste for adventure, pages 212–13). They record local events and are rich in details about family, work and leisure. *British Manuscript Diaries of the 19th Century: an annotated listing* (J.S. Batts, Centaur Press, 1976)

I know men servants do kiss the mistress in preference to the maid but this only happens sometimes…
From the diary of William Tayler, a 19th-century servant

catalogues more than 3000 manuscript diaries, indexed by author, subject and region or place.
A Sketch of the Life of George Marsh, a Yorkshire Collier, published at Barnsley in 1912, is a typical worker's memoir in the detail it provides. Although it is now

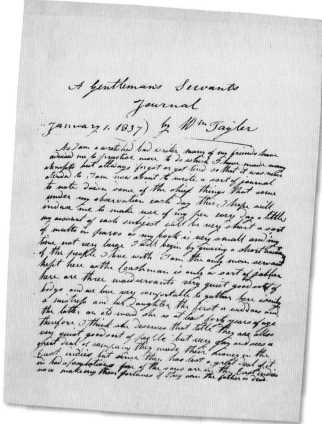

A year in the life…
William Tayler, a gentleman's servant, kept a diary with the intention of improving his writing, as his first entry explains. The diary is notable for its lack of punctuation and poor spelling, but the content makes up for that, telling the details of a working day that usually began at 7.30am and finished at 11pm.

out of print, a typescript copy is held at Barnsley Library. George Marsh's life story is a reminder that the occupation recorded on a census return might give only a partial indication of how someone earned a living and how that might change over time. George Marsh was born in 1834 and was about four years old when his father died. As a child he worked at a coal pit, pulling loaded trucks with 'belt and chain from daylight to dark'.

He gained a basic education at Sunday school. On getting married he did joinery work in the evenings after a day at the pit. 'My spare time afterwards was taken up going about killing pigs, killing as many as three or four in a night and cutting them up next day.' Eventually, he ran a market and carrying business. When he wrote his autobiography at the age of 77 he claimed to be 'in the very best of health' and able 'to ride a horse today with my boots on, better than I could ride the mule when I was barefoot at seven years of age'.

local newspapers and directories

Much information about Victorian and Edwardian communities and their members can be found in local newspapers, especially after 1855, when the repeal of stamp duty on papers led to an increase in their numbers (see People in newspapers, pages 168–73). Few newspapers are indexed, so it can be time-consuming to trawl through columns of small print for reports of local events, although you may also find obituaries of ancestors. Look at the

advertisements as well as the stories, for they give a flavour of the times, while sales of property may list the 'stock in trade' of local businesses.

Directories Trade and commercial directories are usually found in reference libraries and county record offices (see also Town & county directories, pages 174–5). Directories are good indicators of the commercial life of a town, listing the various professions and trades of its inhabitants. They may also help to date old photographs (see pages 18–19), for many photographers did not stay in business long and are listed in only one or two directories.

National gazetteers Between 1831 and 1849, Samuel Lewis published *A Topographical Dictionary of England* in four volumes, with an atlas. He also

A picture of Paignton

By 1896 Paignton in Devon (below) had developed from a small village into a bustling resort. Both old photographs and contemporary trade and commercial directories (left) often paint a detailed picture of past times in Britain's towns and villages.

produced similar volumes for Wales, Scotland and Ireland. The books contain descriptions of places, with information on local institutions and markets. The six volumes of J. M. Wilson's *The Imperial Gazetteer of England and Wales* (1870) and *Imperial Gazetteer of Scotland* (1882) contain similar information about places both large and small. These books are available in large reference libraries.

The Victoria History of the Counties of England provides accurate and detailed information on the history of English parishes, including population figures and local amenities. However, even though work started on it in 1899, only a few counties are complete and some have not even been started. Your local public reference library should be able to tell you whether your district has been covered.

Local histories There are thousands of published histories on counties, cities, towns and villages. It is worth seeking them out in local libraries, as they provide background information and will give you an insight into the development of communities. They may even include references to your ancestors.

making use of census returns

Nineteenth-century census returns (see The census, pages 62–75) are useful for studying the local communities to which our ancestors belonged. Look at other houses in the street where your ancestors lived—from this information you can gain an idea of what the community was like, learning about the size of households, the range of occupations and where everyone had come from.

Every ten years from 1801 the returns note the total population of each location. These figures are usually available at local reference libraries, either in large volumes published by the Office of Population Censuses and Surveys or in one of the early volumes of *The Victoria History of the Counties of England*. They show how some places grew rapidly while others declined. The population of England and Wales was recorded in 1801 as 8.9 million and in 1911 as 36.1 million. In 1801 London was the only place with

more than 100,000 inhabitants (in fact 865,000); by 1901 nearly 40 towns had grown to that size and London had 4.5 million inhabitants. At the same time the population of some agricultural counties declined; Somerset had about 444,000 inhabitants in 1851, dropping to 433,000 in 1901.

To measure the growth of towns in Scotland, compare the population figures given in the three Statistical Accounts (1791–9, 1845 and 1951–66). These documents, which detail the economic and social development

'You shared a toilet with about five different houses and you shared the wash-house too.'
Woman who grew up in Golgotha in Lancaster at the turn of the 20th century

of parishes, are available at the National Library of Scotland and the British Library (see DIRECTORY).

Work and home From the occupations recorded in census returns, you can get a feel for the character of a place. For example, East Midlands villages such as Thurmaston, where in 1851 more than half of the inhabitants were framework-knitters, or the metal-working settlements of the Black Country, where families made specialist products such as nails, locks and chains, were a world apart from quiet farming communities. Estate villages, dominated by the local squire, were often characterised by neat houses built using the same materials and in a similar style, a pub named after the local gentry family and a restored medieval church. Many other villages, with no squire, were sprawling and populous, with several pubs and chapels. Their inhabitants often worked in cottage industries or at a local mine, quarry or mill.

OLD WAYS OF WORK The occupational structure of a Victorian town or village was very different from that of the same place today, with a surprisingly wide range of activities (see Working life, pages 139–49). Some occupations recorded by the census enumerators have since disappeared, including old hand crafts such as file-cutting or the making of straw bonnets.

Many Victorian tradesmen and women were producers as well as sellers of goods; they lived and worked behind and above the shop front. You should bear in mind that the job description in a census return is brief and takes no account of people carrying on more than one occupation, which leads to inconsistencies of occupational descriptions from one census to another.

AGRICULTURAL WORKERS A large proportion of rural workers were described in censuses as 'Ag. lab.' or 'Farm labourer'. The distinction between a labourer and a 'farm servant' was that a servant was hired on a yearly basis from about the age of 14 and lived on the farm, whereas a labourer was usually a married man, employed on either a regular or a casual basis, who lived elsewhere, sometimes in a tied cottage. The great increase in the national population from the mid 18th century onwards meant that more and more families had to seek employment as wage labourers. Earnings were higher in the north of England, where there was greater competition from industries. The worst-paid men in England were farm labourers in south-western counties such as Somerset.

A church-going public? On Sunday 30 March 1851, a census of religious worship was taken in England, Wales and Scotland. Every parish submitted information on the places of worship of each denomination, including the attendance figures at morning, afternoon and evening services, and the number of children at Sunday school. The returns show that well over half of the population did not attend any form of religious service and that in some cities the proportion was as low as one in ten.

About half of those who did attend were Nonconformists (see pages 102–6). The patterns varied greatly from one region to another. Some chapels attracted particular groups of people—farm labourers, for instance, were the mainstay of the Primitive Methodists. Employees in rural areas often attended the place of worship of their employer, irrespective of their personal beliefs. The

records are held at the TNA (see DIRECTORY) in class HO 129, although some record societies have published the returns for their areas. All the returns for Wales are published in *The Religious Census of 1851: a calendar of the returns relating to Wales. Volume 1, South Wales* (I.G. Jones and D. Williams, 1976) and *Volume 2, North Wales* (I.G. Jones, 1981).

housing and public health

The rapid growth of Victorian towns in the 19th century created huge problems of sanitation and public health. At the beginning of the century responsibility for these matters had been divided between local authorities, such as vestries, manorial courts, boroughs and improvement commissioners. Three Public Health Acts (1848, 1872 and 1875) slowly transformed the situation. The extensive records generated by the boards and bodies set up under each Act can be consulted at county record

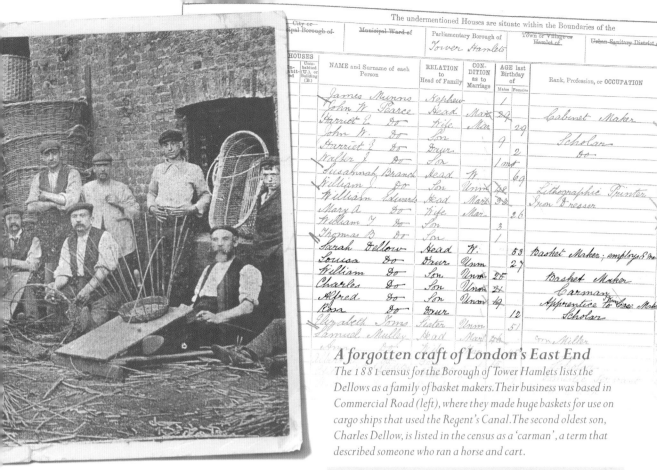

A forgotten craft of London's East End

The 1881 census for the Borough of Tower Hamlets lists the Dellows as a family of basket makers. Their business was based in Commercial Road (left), where they made huge baskets for use on cargo ships that used the Regent's Canal. The second oldest son, Charles Dellow, is listed in the census as a 'carman', a term that described someone who ran a horse and cart.

offices. In them you may find details of public health improvements that relate to the area of the town where your ancestors lived. There may be information on sewage disposal, drainage schemes, the removal of privy middens, closure of churchyards and the creation of general cemeteries.

Graphic, detailed descriptions of local conditions are available in the published reports of government inspectors; some 300 public health districts were investigated between 1848 and 1857.

In Scotland, under the Local Government Act 1889, counties were divided into districts that were responsible for public health, housing, water, roads and bridges. The National Archives of Scotland (see DIRECTORY) holds these records (reference DC1). At this time of industrial development, overcrowding was of particular concern. You can ascertain which were the worst-affected areas from the files of the Congested District Board 1897–1912, which are also held at the National Archives (reference AF).

TAKING IT FURTHER

- *Oral History and the Local Historian* (S. Caunce, Longman, 1994).
- *Sources for Local Historians* (P. Carter and K. Thompson, Phillimore, 2005).
- *Spoken History* (G.E. Evans, Faber, 1987).
- *The Oxford Companion to Family and Local History* (D. Hey, Oxford University Press, 2nd ed., 2010).

Information on the Internet

- www.bl.uk/collections/sound-archive/tipsoral.html Oral history collection at the British Library.
- www.local-history.co.uk Advice on starting research and a list of local history groups.
- www.balh.co.uk The web site of the British Association for Local History.
- www.englandpast.net Web site of the Victoria County History; offers advice for beginners.

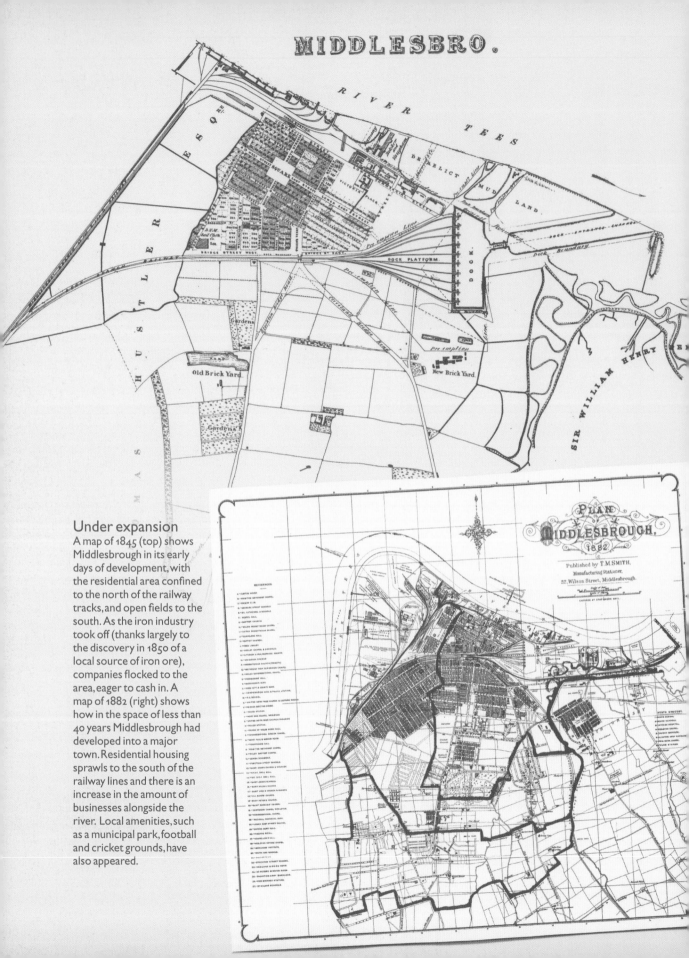

MIDDLESBRO.

Under expansion

A map of 1845 (top) shows Middlesbrough in its early days of development, with the residential area confined to the north of the railway tracks, and open fields to the south. As the iron industry took off (thanks largely to the discovery in 1850 of a local source of iron ore), companies flocked to the area, eager to cash in. A map of 1882 (right) shows how in the space of less than 40 years Middlesbrough had developed into a major town. Residential housing sprawls to the south of the railway lines and there is an increase in the amount of businesses alongside the river. Local amenities, such as a municipal park, football and cricket grounds, have also appeared.

Middlesbrough: from open fields to the age of iron

The Industrial Revolution transformed many rural communities in Britain into thriving towns. The rise of Middlesbrough, as shown in census records, was as spectacular as any: in 1801 the population was 25 and by 1891 this had risen to 75,532. The expansion began after the Stockton and Darlington Railway was extended to the coal dock at Middlesbrough in 1830, but the town's fortunes rocketed in the second half of the 19th century with the growth and development of the iron industry.

In connection with the 1848 Public Health Act, William Ranger carried out an inspection of the town. His report of 1854 gives an insight into living conditions at the time:

'These places vary little from one another. In each there were houses on three or more sides and a dead wall or the backs of houses or an adjoining court on the remaining side. The entrance is through a covered passage and the places of accommodation [toilets] are placed in the centre of the court or on the side of the occupied dwellings. Middlesbrough is an instance of a town springing into existence in the course of a few years, and increasing in population and commercial importance with almost unexampled rapidity; consequently building sites have become scarce, and the value of land proportionately increased. Naturally, under such circumstances each house builder has made it his chief care to put together as many houses as possible on the smallest place.'

An article in the *Middlesbrough Weekly News and Cleveland Advertiser* on 8 January 1859 describes the interiors of the houses and the way people were living:

'Very often you will find, as a substitute for a bedstead, four bars of wood, placed length-ways and crossways, with a couple of bricks under each corner, the woodwork being lashed together with cords to hold it firm.'

But not all was hardship. The burgeoning town soon developed amenities, which by 1882 included banks, schools, churches and Nonconformist chapels. There was even a music hall and a skating rink, showing Middlesbrough to be a modern town of its day.

Waiting in line for a drop of water
The industrialisation of Middlesbrough was so rapid that the town's services failed to cope with the increase in population. Overcrowding, and the health problems that went with it, was an ever-mounting problem. The women and children of 1910, below, had to queue for the use of a single shared tap.

local history

Where your ancestors lived can tell you a great deal about their lives. Maps convey the character of a place, from its landscape to its density of population

mapping out the land

Of a time and place

Yates's map of Staffordshire (1775) is a good example of a county map. Like other maps of the period, it records the names of settlements and rivers, and shows roads, lanes, woods, parks and commons. The Industrial Revolution was beginning to sweep across and transform the landscape, and maps of the time note the position of mills, coal pits (as portrayed in the 18th-century engraving below) and other industrial sites.

You can save research legwork by using a map that is contemporary with your ancestors. You will be able to see their home in relationship to the surrounding area, and identify likely influences on their lives. Maps, particularly the Ordnance Survey (OS) maps of the Victorian and Edwardian eras, also enable you to locate public buildings such as town halls, railway stations or churches, and places of entertainment such as pubs, music halls and football grounds, which may alert you to possible fields of enquiry into your ancestors' lifestyles.

The reference libraries of large towns usually have a series of maps that show how new streets were laid out as the place expanded. They often mark houses and streets that have since been demolished, including those named in census returns.

he earliest maps

The first county maps of England and Wales were those made by Christopher Saxton in the 1570s. They are quaint but of little use since they are rarely to scale and do not show roads. John Speed's maps of 1605–10, which include Ireland and Scotland, are a little better, but are not large enough to show any great detail. Their most useful feature are small plans of county towns.

In the second half of the 18th century county maps of England and Wales were made on a one inch to one mile scale, under the sponsorship of the Royal Society of Arts. Libraries and county record offices have copies of these maps, which show how counties looked before the great expansion of population and settlements in the 19th century.

pportioning the land

From 1750 to 1830 nearly 7 million acres of open fields, commons and wastes were enclosed into smaller, rectangular fields by hundreds of Acts of Parliament, known as the Enclosure Acts. Under each Act commissioners were appointed to draw up an 'award', outlining their decisions on how the land should be redistributed. The various parcels of land

KEY SOURCES OF INFORMATION
♦ County maps, estate maps, enclosure maps and OS maps at county record offices and libraries.
♦ Tithe awards and maps at county and diocesan record offices and the TNA.
♦ The largest collection of OS maps in Britain is available at the British Library's Map Library.
SEE DIRECTORY ➤

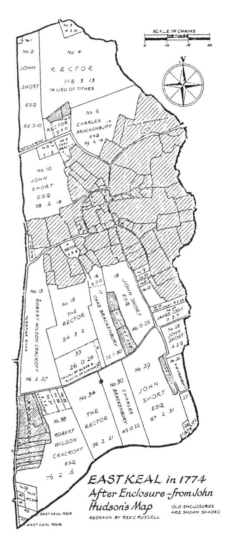

Named and numbered

An enclosure map of East Keal in Lincolnshire shows how the surveyor, John Hudson, intended to divide the land. Each numbered plot notes who it belonged to and its area in acres, roods (four to an acre) and perches (40 to a rood).

would be hedged or walled. In total, 5341 awards were made for England and 229 for Wales, and they and their accompanying maps can be consulted at county record offices.

tithe awards and maps

The ancient system by which each parishioner contributed a tithe (one-tenth of his or her income) to the Church was changed to a money payment by the Tithe Commutation Act of 1836. Between 1836 and 1852, about 86 per cent of England and Wales was surveyed so that tithe awards could be drawn up. The award maps are of great use in identifying individual properties and are the principal source for the study of land ownership and field names. The awards and maps are kept at county and diocesan record offices, and at the TNA (see DIRECTORY). The National Library of Wales (see DIRECTORY) has an outstanding collection of tithe and other types of maps.

Ordnance Survey maps

The Ordnance Survey (OS), Britain's national mapping agency, began making maps, at the scale of one inch to the mile, in 1805 and completed its first national survey in 1873. (The date of publication is the date by which a map is known.)

tracing cottagers in the New Forest

Maps and other local history sources can be used together with civil records to build up a fuller picture of how our ancestors lived. A search of census returns, civil registration records and the International Genealogical Index (IGI—see pages 100–1) for families bearing the surname Sandy in west Hampshire shows the various branches centred around North Gorley and its neighbouring villages.

By using census information and maps (see right) it is possible to pinpoint the cottage where a particular family lived. Newspapers, photographs and other information from local archives reveal that the Sandys were cottagers, originally squatting on the edge of the New Forest. Their main income was from labouring on nearby farms. Local industry in Fordingbridge to the north and Ringwood to the south offered employment for some, but by the end of the 19th century most members of the Sandy family had moved south to better-paid jobs in Poole and Bournemouth.

Charles Sandy was born a New Forest boy in 1841. But he was among the first generation of Sandys to move to Poole.

Using various maps of an area, it is possible to pinpoint where your ancestors lived. This example shows the Sandy family in Gorley Hill.

Current OS map
Having determined the region where the Sandys settled (Gorley Hill), the area was located on a current 2½ inch OS map. This shows the village's relationship to the various towns and settlements that are named in census returns and civil registration records. It is a good idea to walk around a district to get a sense of its geography, and this detailed map is an essential guide on a visit to the area.

The larger-scale OS maps are detailed and accurate, and the rural maps are a rich source of minor place names. The maps can be used to identify properties named in census returns, and are of particular value where houses have since been demolished. You can locate streets named in census returns and civil registration records on maps of the same period and then compare them with modern maps to see if the streets survive and the houses can be identified.

Local libraries and record offices have good collections of 19th and 20th-century OS maps, covering virtually the whole of the British Isles. Some old OS maps have been reprinted.

Inland Revenue field books After the Finance Act of 1910, the Inland Revenue began to value land in Britain in readiness for a tax (which was never actually introduced). The inspectors' field books are arranged by counties, with each unit of property numbered on an Ordnance Survey map of 25 inches to one mile. Information includes a description of the property, rent paid, length of tenancy, name of the owner and tenant. For England and Wales the records are available at the TNA (class IR 58). Scottish records are held at the National Archives of Scotland (reference IRS 51–88).

estate maps and plans

Some 16th and 17th-century estate maps are held in county record offices. These can show the complete layout of a village and its surrounding fields and commons, the names of tenants and the size of their properties. Maps that survive among 18th

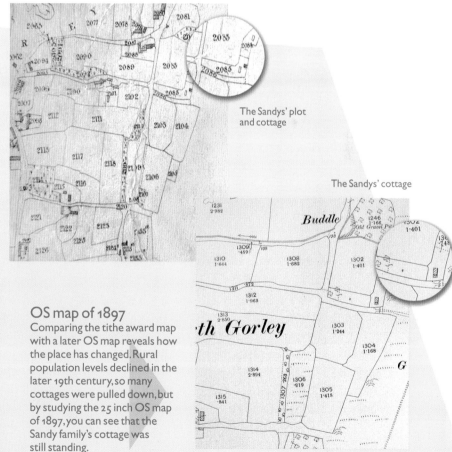

Tithe map and schedule
The 1841 census showed the Sandys as living in Fordingbridge parish. Using the 1841 tithe award map you can see their plot of land. The schedule lists the landowners and tenants, their property and their fields. Plot 2085 is listed under the name of Stephen Sandy.

The Sandys' plot and cottage

The Sandys' cottage

OS map of 1897
Comparing the tithe award map with a later OS map reveals how the place has changed. Rural population levels declined in the later 19th century, so many cottages were pulled down, but by studying the 25 inch OS map of 1897, you can see that the Sandy family's cottage was still standing.

Gorley Hill

and 19th-century estate papers (also in county record offices) often accompany a written survey. They locate properties and their boundaries, measure the size of buildings, gardens, fields and woods, indicate how buildings were used, what crops were grown and what industries were pursued. The best ones provide a detailed inventory of the local landscape, although these are rare finds.

SCOTTISH ESTATES The National Monuments Record of Scotland (see DIRECTORY) has collections of estate plans that have been used in connection with surveys of sites and buildings. The National Archives of Scotland (see DIRECTORY) has a large collection of plans of towns, railways, public services, buildings and government departments.

another use for fire insurance plans

From the late 18th century onwards fire insurance companies had town plans made so that they could assess potential liabilities. These can be used to trace the development of British towns, cities and industrial districts, particularly the plans produced by the London-based firm Charles E. Goad Ltd from about 1885. The Map Library at the British Library (see DIRECTORY) has a large collection, including the first series of 73 volumes, covering London and nearly 40 other cities and towns.

The National Library of Wales holds many of Goad's plans for Newport, Cardiff and Swansea. Sun Alliance insurance records are at the National Archives of Scotland (reference GD 354).

searching for Irish maps

English cartographers were map-making in 16th-century Ireland and some early maps record the owners of the land. Sir William Petty conducted a civil survey in 1654–6, producing a collection of maps in an atlas, *Hiberniae Delineatio*, in 1685. Bernard Scale and John Rocque drew maps of

Ireland in the 18th century, including estate maps. Rocque compiled an *Exact Survey* of Dublin in 1756.

Irish maps can be seen at major archives, such as the TNA, the British Library Map Library, the National Library of Ireland and the Public Record Office of Northern Ireland (see DIRECTORY).

searching for Scottish maps

Joannis Blaeu produced the earliest county map of Scotland in 1654. The *Town Atlas* produced by James Wood in 1828 is useful because the owners of properties are sometimes shown. You will find Scottish maps in the National Library of Scotland and the National Archives (see DIRECTORY).

TAKING IT FURTHER

♦ *Maps for Family and Local History* (G. Beech and R. Mitchell, TNA, 2004).
♦ *Enclosure Records for Historians* (S. Hollowell, Phillimore, 2000).
♦ *The Early Maps of Scotland to 1850* (Royal Geographical Society, vol. 1, 1973; vol. 2, 1983).

Information on the Internet
♦ www.bl.uk/collections/maps.html The British Library's map collection.
♦ www.nls.uk/maps The National Library of Scotland's map collection.
♦ www.ordnancesurvey.co.uk/oswebsite/get amap Has the large scale OS 1:50,000 and 1:250,000 series of maps.
♦ www.old-maps.co.uk Web site for six inch OS maps, 1846-99.
♦ www.nationalarchives.gov.uk/records/ research-guides/. There are individual sections on: maps-for-research.htm; tithe-records.htm; enclosure.htm; and ordnance-survey.htm.

The Booth notebooks:
a vivid portrait of London

At the end of the 19th century, Charles Booth, a wealthy Victorian businessman with an interest in social policy, made a set of maps that plotted London's social structure. His researchers walked through the city making notes and colour-coding each street according to its social class and character. The categories are shown in the chart on the right.

The Booth maps and notebooks bring late Victorian London to life. Among the detail about streets and houses, there is often mention of employers, charities, public houses and entertainment halls.

Booth's *Life and Labour of the People of London* is held in many reference libraries and is available as the Charles Booth Online Archive at booth.lse.ac.uk.

COLOUR-CODED CLASS DIVISIONS
- 'Upper-middle and Upper classes. Wealthy.'
- 'Middle class. Well-to-do.'
- 'Fairly comfortable. Good ordinary earnings.'
- 'Mixed. Some comfortable, others poor.'
- 'Poor. 18s to 21s a week for a moderate family.'
- 'Very poor, casual. Chronic want.'
- 'Lowest class. Vicious, semi-criminal.'

Street of ill repute

Charles Booth (right) described the Southwark thoroughfare of Tabard Street (running parallel to Great Dover Street on the map and inset above) as follows: 'The black-barred line consists mainly of houses owned by a widow living somewhere in the neighbourhood. They are let out in rooms for single nights and short periods and are much used by prostitutes and shady people generally....'

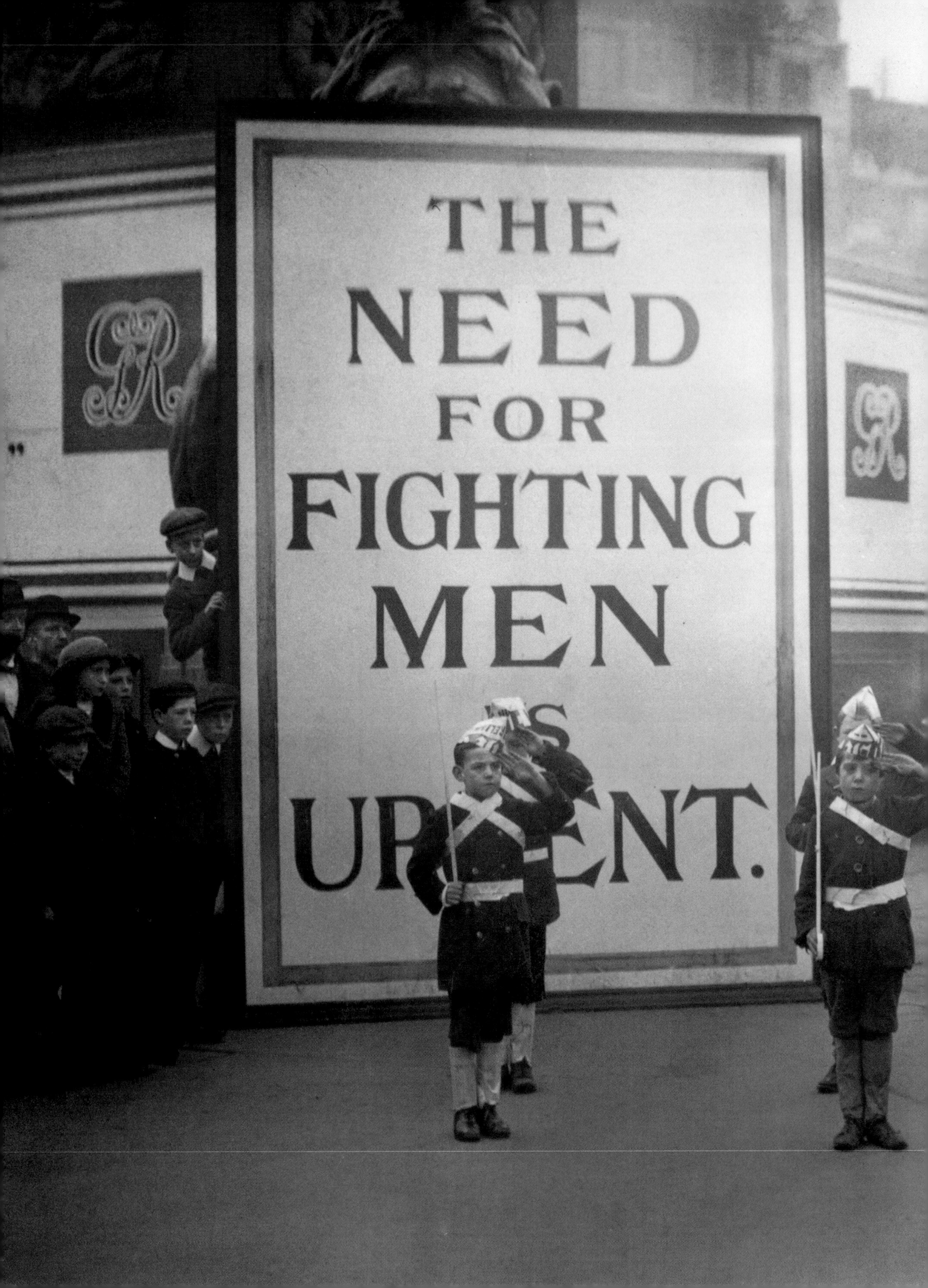
THE
NEED
FOR
FIGHTING
MEN

joining up

Do you have a battered medal, faded photographs. of men in uniform, or other memorabilia of ancestors who served in Britain's **armed forces?** They and something of the military life they led may come to light in the many records that survive of the army, Royal Navy and Royal Air Force. As important to Britain's welfare for hundreds of years has been its **merchant navy**—a source of both employment and adventure, perhaps to a seafaring ancestor, who may emerge from merchant marine records of ships and crew members.

Boys play soldiers in Trafalgar Square in November 1914

armed forces
how the army evolved

Nearly everyone has an ancestor who served in the military, and his career will almost certainly be recorded. But it is easier to explore the records if you understand the army's history

Who's who on parade
Lord Lennox inspects the 25th Regiment of Foot (originally The Earl of Leven's Regiment of Foot, later The King's Own Scottish Borderers) in 1805, while subalterns check names in the muster book. You may find one of your ancestors in such a volume.

Before the outbreak of the Civil War in 1642, regiments of armed men were raised only for specific purposes. The first full-time trained force in England and Wales dates from the restoration of the monarchy in 1660. It comprised two regiments of Horse Guards, later called the Life Guards and the Royal Horse Guards (or the Blues) and known collectively as the Household Cavalry, and two regiments of Foot Guards, later called the Grenadier Guards and the Coldstream Guards. The Guards regiments were responsible for the safety of the sovereign.

Scotland had its own army up until the early 18th century, but with the Act of Union of 1707 uniting the crowns of Scotland and England, the British army was formed. The broad term 'militia' covered all sorts of part-time units and dated back to the Middle Ages, with men who were 'volunteers' and 'yeomanry' or, more recently, members of the Territorial Army and Home Guard.

regiments and their names

Regiments are the basic unit of the army, consisting of several hundred men. From 1660, regiments were known by the names of their colonels, such as Prince George of Denmark's Regiment of Foot. A numbering or ranking system was introduced in 1694, so Prince George's was also the 3rd Regiment of Foot. A Royal Warrant of 1751 decreed that regiments should no longer be known by their colonels' names, but that they could be given titles, so the 3rd Regiment of Foot was called 'The Buffs' and the 4th 'The King's Own'. In 1782 some infantry regiments took territorial titles. This led to the 3rd Regiment of Foot becoming known as the 3rd (East Kent) Regiment of Foot (The Buffs).

In 1881, numbers were abolished, many regiments were amalgamated and county names were adopted—for example, The Buffs (East Kent Regiment). Unofficially, regiments retained the old tradition; members of the Cheshire Regiment, for example, referred to themselves as 'the 22nd (Cheshire) Regiment of Foot'.

the many kinds of troops

This variety of titles means you may find a confusing range of names for your ancestor's regiment. You may also encounter more general descriptions of regiments, as the British army uses particular words for different types of troops, such as cavalry, infantry, artillery and Foot Guards.

CAVALRY These mounted regiments included the Household Cavalry and other mounted troops such as the Dragoon Guards, Hussars and Lancers.

INFANTRY The foot soldiers of the army, who served in the line. They comprised as many as 109 regiments at the time of the Revolutionary and Napoleonic wars (1793–1815).

ARTILLERY These are the various regiments that specialised in the use of large mounted guns.

FOOT GUARDS The regiments of Grenadier, Coldstream, Scots, Irish and Welsh Guards were initially involved in the protection of the monarch.

India The East India Company's army, broadly covering the three company Presidencies (administrative districts), Bengal, Bombay and Madras (see Servants of the Empire, pages 254–5), became the Indian Army in 1861. Both armies' records are in the Oriental and India Office Collections at the British Library (see DIRECTORY). British regiments also served in India, so check also the regular army documents (see pages 208–11).

Corps These are specialist army units. They include the Royal Engineers, as well as signals, transport, medical, ordnance (weapons and ammunition), police, pay, veterinary, military provost (prison), military chaplains, educational and physical training as well as nursing personnel.

Scottish and Irish soldiers

After the union of Scotland with England in 1707, Scots soldiers served alongside Englishmen in the British army, although you are more likely to find them in Scottish regiments. Irishmen were in the army in great numbers during the 19th century, both in Irish and other regiments. Many Irish regiments, such as the Connaught Rangers, were disbanded in 1922 when the Irish Free State was created, but a few were renamed.

TAKING IT FURTHER

♦ *Army Records for Family Historians* (S. Fowler and W. Spencer, Public Record Office, 2nd ed., 1998).
♦ *Records of the Militia and Volunteer Forces 1757–1945* (W. Spencer, Public Record Office, 1997).
♦ *Tracing Your Ancestors at the National Archives* (A. Bevan, National Archives, 7th ed., 2006).

Information on the Internet
♦ www.genuki.org.uk/big/MilitaryRecords.html
♦ www.army.mod.uk/unitsandorgs A list of present-day regiments, with brief histories, and a list of museums.
♦ www.nationalarchives.gov.uk/records/research-guides/armed-forces.htm

armed forces

Individual army records contain a lot of personal detail. They can also reveal your ancestor's travels, his disciplinary record and even his life after leaving the military

using army records

To find an army ancestor you need to know his approximate dates of service, if possible his regiment and whether he was an officer (general, brigadier, colonel, major, captain or lieutenant) or 'other rank' (a private soldier or non-commissioned officer—sergeant major, sergeant, lance corporal or corporal).

personnel records of 'other ranks'

Before 1883 the records of the lower ranks can be traced only when the regiment is known, as most records were kept by the regiment and are archived in regimental sequence. However, there is a key set of documents that should make your search easier.

When a soldier was recruited he signed an 'attestation' form, and he received discharge papers when he left. These records, known as Soldiers' Documents, are held at the TNA (see DIRECTORY) in class WO 97; they are rich in detail, giving the serviceman's place of birth, age on enlistment, previous occupation, details of appearance and a career summary. Next of kin are also included.

Up to 1883 the documents cover only those who collected pensions on discharge, but from 1883 they include those who had died in service, bought their way out, or completed short-service

The Woolwich Arsenal
Gunners from the Royal Artillery pose with their weaponry at a major armament base on the south bank of the Thames, in London.

commissions. Various indexes make the records easy to search. If you still cannot find your ancestor's regiment try the options shown on pages 210–11.

The Soldiers' Documents themselves are arranged by discharge date:

- ☞ 1756–1872: by regiment
- ☞ 1873–82: alphabetically by name within groups for the cavalry, artillery, infantry and corps
- ☞ 1883–1913: alphabetically by name for the whole army.

Pension records From the 17th century soldiers who had completed their agreed term of service and those who were wounded were entitled to pensions. They were known as Chelsea Pensioners after the Royal Hospital at Chelsea, which opened in 1692, although most of them were 'out-pensioners' who lived at home. Entries in the pension records are by order of precedence of regiment or corps in the British army (see page 206) and then chronological, so you need to know roughly the date of discharge in order to consult them. At the TNA the soldiers' pension records are held in four series:

- ☞ WO 116, 1715–1913: medical
- ☞ WO 117, 1823–1913: long service
- ☞ WO 120, 1715–1857: registers of pensioners
- ☞ WO 121, 1782–1887: certificates of pensioners' service

There are also registers for soldiers discharged to Kilmainham, near Dublin. These are held in WO 118 and WO 119. An index of Chelsea Pensioners for 1806–38 (see Taking it further, page 211) is available on microfiche from the Manchester and Lancashire Family History Society.

Muster rolls and regimental pay lists These lists record who was present at regimental musters (inspections), their careers, absences and date of enlistment and/or departure. They also show the

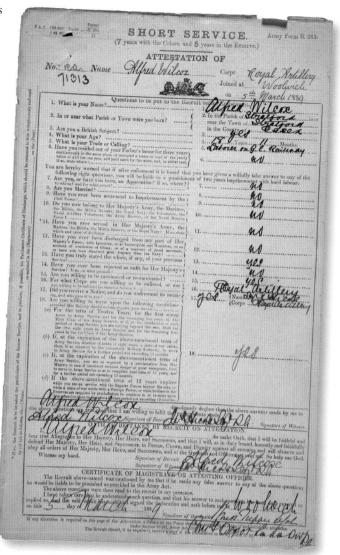

You're in the army now
The attestation of Alfred Wilcox (above) records his oath of loyalty to Queen Victoria and obedience to his officers. He bought his way out just 45 days later for £10.

place and date of the muster, so you can use them to trace an ancestor's career in detail. They are in TNA classes WO 12 (1732–1878) and WO 16 (1878–98), but you must know the soldier's regiment. Musters for the artillery are in WO 10, engineers in WO 11, and militia and volunteers in WO 13.

Further information at theTNA

ARTILLERY Service records are in class WO 69, with description books and pensions in WO 54.

ENGINEERS Like the artillery, they came under the Ordnance Office; their records are in WO 54.

MILITIA AND VOLUNTEERS Their records are in WO 13, WO 68 and WO 127–129, with militia attestation papers in WO 96.

finding officers in the records

This should be fairly straightforward, even if you do not know much to start with. If you have a name and an approximate date, the official Army Lists should confirm the officer's service, his regiment and any previous regiments in which he served. You can then follow him by comparing the information you have found with that in later volumes. The annual lists start from about 1754 and are available at the TNA and most reference libraries; there are a few earlier manuscript lists in class WO 64. Early lists of officers are included in *English Army Lists and Commission Registers 1661–1714* (C. Dalton, 6 vols, 1892–1904, reprinted Francis Edwards, 1960).

Another very useful series of lists, known as *Hart's New Army List*, ran from 1839 to 1915. These give much more information about an officer's service, with details of campaigns and postings. They were published by Lt. Gen. H. G. Hart (1808–78).

There are also published lists for medical officers and artillery officers: see Taking it further, opposite.

OtherTNA records You can find more about an officer's career in the following documents:

RETURNS OF SERVICE These are the official War Office compilations of the service of many 19th-century officers. Often the forms were completed by the officers themselves. Early ones give service details only, but later ones have information on families, with dates of marriage and children's

find the regiment for 'other ranks'

If the TNA indexes to Soldiers' Documents in class WO 97 do not reveal your ancestor's regiment, try the sources right. If you know the location and date of his service, *In Search of the 'Forlorn Hope'* (John M. Kitzmuller II, Manuscript Publishing Foundation, Salt Lake City, 1988) should also help. This guide covers British regiments and records from 1640 to the First World War.

A Chelsea Pensioner with his Royal Hospital cap

FAMILY LORE, MEDALS, BATTLES OR CAMPAIGNS
It may be family legend that an ancestor served in a particular historic campaign. Links between soldiers and battles, campaigns and medals are provided by *Battle Honours of the British Army 1662–1901* (C.B. Norman, Murray, 1911, reprinted David & Charles, 1971).

You should also look at the information on medals on pages 222–3.

REGIMENTAL REGISTERS AND CHAPLAINS' RETURNS
There are incomplete indexes to birth registers 1761–1924, giving regiment and place of birth of children born to wives of serving soldiers at large libraries or record offices. Indexes of regimental marriages and burial registers are also held at these centres, with chaplains' returns for the army's foreign stations 1796–1880. These may supply only the name, place and year for the event, but copy certificates can yield your ancestor's unit.

births. They are 'snapshots' of officers' histories at particular dates, and there are five useful series:

☞ WO 25/744–748: returns of officers' services, 1809–10

☞ WO 25/749–779: services of retired officers on full and half pay, 1828

☞ WO 25/780–805: services of officers on full pay, 1829

☞ WO 25/808–823: services of retired officers, 1847

☞ WO 25/824–870: officers' services, 1870–2.

COMMANDER-IN-CHIEF'S MEMORANDA
Concerned with applications for commissions, promotions and resignations of officers, these papers are by date and by regiment, 1793–1870, in WO 31.

HALF PAY LEDGERS AND LISTS Until 1871 retiring officers either sold their commissions or went on to half pay. The Paymaster General's records show where officers drew their half pay and can help you to trace ancestors after their army service.

TAKING IT FURTHER

♦ *Army Records: A Guide for Family Historians* (W. Spencer, The National Archives, 2007).
♦ *Medals: The Researcher's Guide* (W. Spencer, The National Archives, 2007).
♦ *Guide to Military History on the Internet* (S. Fowler, Pen & Sword, 2007).
♦ *My Ancestor was in the British Army* (M. J. and C. T. Watts, Society of Genealogists, 2nd ed., 2009).
♦ *Militia Lists and Musters, 1757–1876* (J. Gibson and M. Medlycott, FFHS, 2004).

Information on the Internet
♦ www.nationalarchives.gov.uk/records/research-guides/armed-forces.htm
Military records at the TNA.

PENSION PAYMENTS

Between 1842 and 1862 in England and Scotland, or 1842–82 for Ireland and abroad, the pension payment records (mainly in TNA class WO 22) are organised by district pay offices and note men's regiments. *British Army Pensioners Abroad, 1772–1899* (N. K. Crowder, Baltimore, 1995) is an index of 9000 pensioners who drew their payments in India, Canada and South Africa.

CENSUS RETURNS

If you find an ancestor in a census surname index and discover the barracks where he was recorded, or you know where he was in a census year, his regiment will be noted. You may also find him at a home address described as, for example, 'pensioner —40th Regiment of Foot', though the return may say only 'army pensioner'. Listed children's ages and birthplaces will help you to find birth certificates that may state the father's regiment. The 1881 census has been indexed: see Counting people, pages 62–64.

An army groom's regiment may appear in a civil marriage register

CIVIL REGISTRATION

You may find reference to a soldier's regiment in the civil registers of births, marriages and deaths (for more information, see Civil records, pages 50–61).

For example, when James Sells died at Britten Street, Chelsea, in June 1843, aged 48, his death certificate described him as a 'Beer retailer, Pensioner of Chelsea Hospital, 7th Regiment of Foot'.

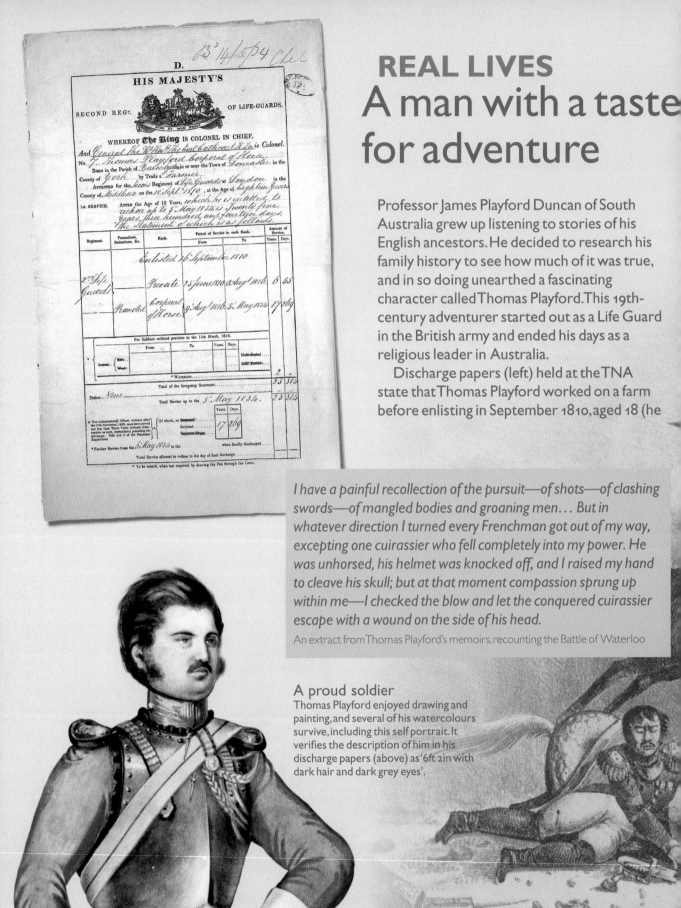

REAL LIVES
A man with a taste for adventure

Professor James Playford Duncan of South Australia grew up listening to stories of his English ancestors. He decided to research his family history to see how much of it was true, and in so doing unearthed a fascinating character called Thomas Playford. This 19th-century adventurer started out as a Life Guard in the British army and ended his days as a religious leader in Australia.

Discharge papers (left) held at the TNA state that Thomas Playford worked on a farm before enlisting in September 1810, aged 18 (he

I have a painful recollection of the pursuit—of shots—of clashing swords—of mangled bodies and groaning men… But in whatever direction I turned every Frenchman got out of my way, excepting one cuirassier who fell completely into my power. He was unhorsed, his helmet was knocked off, and I raised my hand to cleave his skull; but at that moment compassion sprung up within me—I checked the blow and let the conquered cuirassier escape with a wound on the side of his head.

An extract from Thomas Playford's memoirs, recounting the Battle of Waterloo

A proud soldier
Thomas Playford enjoyed drawing and painting, and several of his watercolours survive, including this self portrait. It verifies the description of him in his discharge papers (above) as '6ft 2in with dark hair and dark grey eyes'.

was really 15). He served with the Second Regiment of Life Guards as a private for six years, then as a corporal of horse for 17 years. He went to the Peninsular Wars from 1812 to 1814, including the battle of Vittoria on 21 June 1813, and on 18 June 1815 fought at the Battle of Waterloo. He was discharged in 1834.

Armed with the outline of Playford's military career, Professor Duncan wanted to know more. When a set of memoirs came into his possession upon the death of an elderly aunt he was able to fill in some of the details. The memoirs were written by Thomas Playford and his son and cover the period 1759–1900. Like any personal account, the memoirs offer an insight into the character of the person who wrote them. Most fascinating are the passages that relate to Playford's experiences at the Battle of Waterloo.

On his retirement from the army, Thomas Playford was given 200 acres of land in Ontario, Canada. He went in search of this land only to find that no treaty had been signed with the native Huron inhabitants and the area was wild, thickly wooded and 'full of wolves and bears'. His return journey to England was equally cursed: he lost his young son to illness, was nearly shipwrecked off Ramsgate and his wife died shortly after arrival.

Yet Playford's spirit was undiminished and in 1844 he set sail for Australia with his second wife and family. There he founded an independent church, called 'The Christian Church', where he ministered until his death in 1873.

A charismatic preacher
After establishing his church, Pastor Thomas Playford preached regularly. His son, also named Thomas ('Honest Tom'), became premier of South Australia and in 1901 was one of the six 'founding fathers' of Australia.

armed forces

What our ancestors did in the world wars is often a starting point in the hunt for our families' histories. Your family may have medals or papers that help you to begin

world war army records

To trace a soldier ancestor who served in a world war, you need to find his rank, regiment and number, as you would for an earlier soldier. Medals, discharge papers, army pension books and other mementos of 20th-century army service, will either reveal these details or help you to find them.

soldiers of the Great War

If the soldier fought in the First World War, you can begin a search in the campaign medal rolls (as most British and Empire soldiers received at least one medal). These will tell you his unit, service number, where he served and medals awarded. The rolls are at the TNA (see DIRECTORY) in class WO 329, with an index in WO 372. (See Taking it further, page 217, and Memories of service and valour, pages 222–3.)

Army service records Two-thirds of the service records of the 'other ranks' who served in the First World War were destroyed by bombs in 1940 and many of the rest were badly damaged. These 'burnt' records are now available on microfilm in class WO 363 at TNA and at the various Mormon Family History Centres. Individual records for 2.8 million

KEY SOURCES OF INFORMATION
♦ Army records at the TNA.
♦ Indexes of war deaths since the Boer Wars at the TNA.
♦ Details of 1.75 million world war military dead from the Commonwealth War Graves Commission.
SEE DIRECTORY ➤

Going over the top

Extremes of bravery were required of soldiers climbing out of their trenches to attack the enemy through barbed wire and machine-gun fire. The trenches were not much safer: gas or grenade killed there too. Official war diaries (see page 216) evoke the drama and the courage but not the discomfort or the boredom, the rats or the stench.

soldiers who completed their service between 1914 and 1920 range from a single sheet to over 60 pages. They may note a soldier's age and physical appearance, his place of birth, occupation, and any former service.

The 'unburnt' records in WO 364 at the TNA are from government departments, especially the Ministry of Pensions. They provide detailed medical histories of men who were discharged from the Army because of sickness or wounds. See also class PIN 26. However, these records comprise only about 8 per cent of Soldiers' Documents from the First World War, so the chance of finding an ancestor mentioned is fairly small.

OTHER REFERENCES For further details consult *Army Service Records of the First World War* (W. Spencer, Public Record Office, 3rd expanded edition, 2003).

Indexes to war dead

The National Archives (see DIRECTORY) hold indexes dating from the Boer Wars onwards; microfiche copies can be seen at the TNA, large libraries and some record offices.

For the First World War, you can also consult *Soldiers Died in the Great War*, available on microfilm

or on CD at the TNA. First published by HMSO in 81 volumes (1919–21), the work lists all officers and men who died between 1914 and 1919.

tracing a First World War officer

If you know that your ancestor was an officer, there are two main series of service records to explore at the TNA. For Territorial Army officers or those on a temporary commission, around 78,000 records survive, held in class WO 374 and arranged alphabetically. For regular officers, records covering about 140,000 men are held in class WO 338. The content of these records varies because they are supplementary to the files destroyed in 1940. Some

Lt Col. Holberton behaved in a very gallant and courageous manner, going to and fro amongst the men in the open and encouraging them to spare their amm[unition] and only to fire when they had a certain target. He was killed whilst doing this … by a stray machine-gun bullet.
War diary, 26 March 1918

records contain a wealth of detail while others may simply be a note of death.

Regular army officers If the officer's service ended before 1922 and he was either a pre-war regular army officer, or commissioned into the

WAR GRAVES AND MEMORIALS AT HOME AND ABROAD

Because some 750,000 British soldiers died in the First World War and 305,000 in the Second World War, there were very few families who were not affected by loss. As a result war graves and memorials can be a valuable source of information for your family's history.

If you are trying to locate a grave or a particular war memorial, the Commonwealth War Graves Commission, which maintains the records of war dead of 1914–18, 1939–45 and the Korean War, as well as the cemeteries and memorials themselves, is the best source.

You need to provide basic information, such as a person's rank, unit/service, home town and place and date of death. The commission will help you free of charge if you are searching for a relative; others must pay a small fee. Contact the head office (see DIRECTORY) for details.

You can search the commission's index on-line at www.cwgc.org/cwgcinternet/search.aspx The site provides full details and a memorial certificate, for example: 'P. J. Watts, private 6071, 8th Bn.,

Queen's Own (Royal West Kent Regiment) died on Friday 5 November 1915—Remembered with honour at Elzenwalle Brasserie Cemetery, Voormezeele, near Ypres, West Flanders'.

The Royal British Legion leads pilgrimages to Commonwealth war cemeteries and memorials, and to campaign areas around the world. For information contact the Pilgrimage Department (see DIRECTORY, under Royal British Legion). Or visit the web site www.britishlegion.org.uk for more information on organised pilgrimages to war graves and battlefields.

War memorials in cities, towns and villages often list service people's names as well as their regiments, corps, ships or squadrons (see What inscriptions reveal, page 116). They usually commemorate local residents, but some are national. The Imperial War Museum (see DIRECTORY) and English Heritage (see DIRECTORY) are compiling an inventory with photographs of the estimated 54,000 memorials situated throughout the British Isles.

special reserve of officers, you will find the records of his service in class WO 339. Also included are records of those who were given an emergency wartime commission in the regular army—the medical or technical experts, such as tunnellers who worked far below the trenches.

HOW TO SEARCH The collection is arranged by the officer's 'long number' (the official number he received with his commission). To find this number, consult the index in class WO 338, organised by surname, which also names the regiment in which your soldier served. If his name is common, his regiment's name will confirm identification.

You will find further information in *World War I Ancestry* (N. Holding, FFHS, 3rd ed., 1997) and *More Sources of World War I Army Ancestry* (N. Holding, FFHS, 3rd ed., 1998). For on-line details and an

overview of other First World War documents in the TNA archives see www.nationalarchives.gov.uk/records/research-guides/looking-for-person

War diaries From 1907 active service units had to keep a daily diary of events, known as a war diary or an intelligence summary. Most for 1914–22 are in TNA class WO 95. A few, initially retained by the Ministry of Defence because they contained secret or confidential information, are now in WO 154.

The amount of detail recorded can vary greatly depending on the unit's activities and who compiled the entries. The diaries rarely give names of ordinary soldiers but sometimes officers are mentioned. They can be useful for discovering more about specific campaigns and battles. Some are also descriptive and contain personal notes or the writer's observations.

…we will remember them

The Menin Gate memorial in Belgium was opened in 1927. It commemorates the 54,896 members of the Commonwealth forces with no known grave who died between the outbreak of the First World War and 15 August 1917 in the Ypres area. The local fire brigade still undertakes an act of remembrance there daily.

Second World War archives

No Second World War service records have yet been released to the TNA. However, *The Second World War: a guide to documents in the TNA* (J.D. Cantwell, Public Record Office, 3rd ed., 1998) will give you a good idea of other relevant material at the TNA. There are indexes to all Second World War service deaths at the Family Records Centre, so you can obtain a death certificate from there.

The dead of other wars You should ask the Ministry of Defence directly for service records for soldiers who died in conflicts after 1918. The address is: Ministry of Defence, Bourne Avenue, Hayes, Middlesex UB3 1RF. Only next of kin are permitted access to these records, and the Ministry charges a fee of £25 for this service.

TAKING IT FURTHER

♦ *Soldiers Died in The Great War 1914–1918* (HMSO, 81 vols, 1919–21) Also available on CD—on-line details at www.great-war-casualties.com —which can be ordered from bookshops (quote ISBN 1 897632940).
♦ www.nationalarchives.gov.uk/records/research-guides/british-army-soldiers-1914-1918.htm
♦ www.nationalarchives.gov.uk/records/research-guides/war-dead-first-second-world-wars.htm
and other such guides under the general heading of the 'British Army'
♦ www.genuki.org.uk/big/MilitaryHistory.html
Links to world war web sites.
♦ www.CyndisList.com/milres.htm
Links to military web sites worldwide.

IMPERIAL WAR MUSEUM

Britain's largest military museum (see background picture) covers the history of world conflict from 1914 to the present. It holds no personal service records but has seven reference departments, of which Printed Books holds most material of interest to the family historian. The museum's collection includes service lists, rolls of honour, war grave registers, personal papers, gallantry awards and campaign medals. It also has regimental histories and journals that may give details of postings, promotions, marriages and sports events in which a forebear is mentioned. The Imperial War Museum North, Trafford, near Manchester is an interactive centre complementing and reflecting the London collection.

The Imperial War Museum has published a series of guides—*Tracing Your Family History*—to researching soldiers, sailors and airmen. The three volumes—*Army*, *Royal Air Force* and *Royal Navy*—are available from the museum or from genealogical bookshops. The museum's outpost at Duxford, Cambridgeshire (see DIRECTORY), houses a collection of hundreds of military aircraft, tanks and artillery pieces.

Lambeth Road, London SE1 6HZ TEL. 020 7416 5000
www.iwm.org.uk

At the RAF Museum you may see the type of plane, such as this Sopwith Camel, flown by your pilot ancestor in the First World War. In the archives you may even find his photograph.

ROYAL AIR FORCE MUSEUM

The records at the museum date from well before the establishment of the RAF on 1 April 1918. There is material relating to the earliest military aeronautical ventures by the Royal Engineers, as well as to the Royal Flying Corps and Royal Naval Air Service, which merged to form the RAF (see pages 220–1). For the two world wars, only personnel who were casualties are recorded. For the First World War the records are indexed alphabetically by name. For the Second World War they are in chronological order, classified by date and aircraft number. The museum also holds squadron histories, logbooks and photograph albums covering all RAF activities.

Grahame Park Way, Hendon, London NW9 5LL
TEL. 020 8200 1763
www.rafmuseum.org.uk

NATIONAL ARMY MUSEUM

The National Army Museum traces the history of the British army from 1485 to the present, including the Indian Army and other colonial units. It has a reading room and its holdings include 45,000 books, a range of Army Lists (from 1754 onwards—see page 210) as well as a few regimental diaries, some muster rolls, campaign histories and sets of standing orders. The museum also has more than 100,000 photographs.

Royal Hospital Road, London SW3 4HT TEL. 020 7730 0717
www.national-army-museum.ac.uk

National museums for the armed forces and the merchant navy

Military museums flesh out an ancestor's service career. You might find the kind of uniform he wore, see the type of plane he flew or learn of the battle in which he died. By thumbing through regimental histories and journals, you may even discover clues to his character, such as a record of him winning a sports event.

The five main museums of interest to the family historian are outlined here. You should write or telephone in advance to make an appointment if you wish to use their reference facilities.

Some specialist branches of the forces have their own museums, such as the Royal Marines Museum, the Fleet Air Arm Museum and the Airborne Forces Museum (see DIRECTORY), and most British regiments and corps have museums, with regimental records, uniforms, photographs and other memorabilia. For information about these museums, including addresses, opening times and what collections they hold, consult *A Guide to Military Museums and Other Places of Military Interest* (T. and S. Wise, T. Wise, 9th ed., 1999).

NATIONAL MARITIME MUSEUM

The museum library has information on all types of British maritime vessel, both Royal Navy and merchant navy. There is a complete set of Navy Lists (from 1797), giving the names of naval officers (see page 228). For the merchant navy there are masters', mates' and engineers' successful applications for certificates of service and of competency, both from 1845 onwards (see pages 233–4). There is also a large collection of *Lloyd's Lists*, with information on every British vessel.

Park Row, Greenwich, London SE10 9NF TEL. 020 8858 4422
www.nmm.ac.uk

ROYAL NAVAL MUSEUM

In 1990 the Royal Naval Museum Library merged with that of the Admiralty (which dates from 1808). Most of the library's records cover the 19th and 20th centuries and are more useful for finding ancestors who were officers rather than ratings, whose details are easier to find at the PRO. The records include a complete set of Navy Lists (from 1797) and of Sea Officers' Lists (1807–46)—see pages 228–9.

Buildings 1–7, College Road, HM Naval Base, Portsmouth, Hampshire PO1 3LJ TEL. 023 9283 9766
www.royalnavalmuseum.org

armed forces
the Royal Air Force

In the 20th century an adventurous few were drawn to the drama of war in the air. Military records give vivid insights into the lives of those in the RAF

Military aviation began in 1911 with the creation of the air battalion of the Royal Engineers, who used balloons, kites towed from warships, and planes for observation. In the same year, the Royal Navy established an aeroplane base at Eastchurch, on the Isle of Sheppey, Kent. In 1912 the Royal Flying Corps (RFC) was formed to coordinate Britain's airborne services. The corps was made up of military and naval wings, and totalled 141 officers and 63 planes.

In July 1914 the naval group split off and became the Royal Naval Air Service (RNAS). This resulted in confusion and inefficiency, and on 1 April 1918 the RFC and RNAS were reunited, creating the Royal Air Force (RAF).

finding an officer

Officers and men are listed separately in air force records. Remember that although today all pilots are officers, this was not always the case, and the last sergeant pilot did not retire until the 1950s. To check whether the person you are looking for was an officer, consult the *Air Force List*, a yearbook of officers dating back to March 1919, from which basic career details can be ascertained. It can be found in major reference libraries and in the TNA reference room (see DIRECTORY), and is indexed. A second, confidential version of the list was produced between September 1939 and December 1954, giving the names and addresses of all RAF stations; copies are held at the TNA in class AIR 10.

The service records of officers in the RFC and RNAS from 1912 until 1 April 1918, or the RAF from its foundation until the early 1920s, are held in TNA class AIR 76, in approximate alphabetical order. Records of RFC officers may also be found among the army officers' service records in TNA classes WO 339 and WO 374. For previous RNAS service you should also look in class ADM 273.

Records of those who served after the early 1920s are still held by the RAF. For details write to Personnel Management Agency, (sec) 1b, Room 5, Building 248a, RAF Innsworth, Gloucester GL3 1EZ.

Reaching for the skies
During the First World War, when flying was still in its infancy, aircraft replaced cavalry and fast ships for reconnaissance. Planes were also armed with guns for aerial dog fights. These Bristol Fighters are setting off for enemy lines in 1918.

Normally it will only disclose information to the individual concerned or, if that person is deceased, to the next of kin or a very close relative.

searching for lower ranks

Noncommissioned officers (NCOs) and ground crew provided vital support to the men in the air. Some of these recruits took to the skies themselves, as gunners, observers and even as pilots.

The RFC before 1918 Those who served in the RFC between 1912 and August 1914 are listed in the biographical dictionary *A Contemptible Little Flying Corps* (J. V. Webb and I. McInnes, London Stamp Exchange, 1991).

Men who were discharged from the RFC before 1 April 1918 may appear in army records at the TNA in classes WO 363 or WO 364 (see Using army records, pages 208–11). Occasionally, records of men who served in the RFC and then the RAF may be found in these classes, although most have been transferred to class AIR 79.

The RNAS before 1918 To find other ranks of the RNAS, whether or not they later transferred to the RAF, you need to search Royal Navy records at the TNA in class ADM 188 (see The Royal Navy, pages 224–30). Records of service in the RNAS were not transferred into the RAF series (as was the case with RFC personnel) because the early Royal Navy records were kept in registers and not as individual sheets.

The RAF after 1918 The sole complete RAF muster (the roll call of men in a unit) was the one taken when the service was first formed in 1918; copies are held at the TNA in classes AIR 1/819 and AIR 10/232–37.

To find a record of service in the RAF after 1918, look in the index (TNA class AIR 78) for a service number, then use this number to locate the record in AIR 79. These records supply considerable detail, including date and place of birth, date of joining,

physical description, religion, next of kin, spouse and children, medals and date of discharge.

For airmen with service numbers greater than 329,000, and for all those who subsequently saw service in the Second World War, the records are held by the RAF. For details write to the address given on page 220 for officers.

women join the force

The Women's Royal Air Force (WRAF) was created alongside the RAF in 1918. Women were recruited into the air service as clerks, cooks, storekeepers and drivers, and by the end of the First World War there were more than 25,000 women serving. The WRAF was disbanded in 1920. Records of these early airwomen are arranged alphabetically in TNA class AIR 80, but the records of service of WRAF officers have not survived.

In June 1939 the Women's Auxiliary Air Force (WAAF) was formed. In 1949 it was renamed the Women's Royal Air Force (WRAF). Records of those who served are held by the RAF (see address on page 220). Since 1994, when the WRAF was disbanded, women have served in the RAF.

TAKING IT FURTHER

♦ *Air Force Records for Family Historians* (W. Spencer, PRO, 2000).
♦ *The Records of the Royal Air Force: how to find The Few* (E. Wilson, FFHS, 1991).

Information on the Internet
♦ www.nationalarchives.gov.uk/records/research-guides/raf-service-1939-1945.htm and similar guides under 'Royal Air Force'.
♦ www.raf.mod.uk
Ministry of Defence service records for the RAF.
♦ www.rafmuseum.org.uk Web site for the RAF Museum at Hendon (see pages 218–19).

Waterloo Medal
1815

Crimea Medal
1854–6

Victoria Cross
1856–

Distinguished Service
Order 1886–

Volunteer Long Service
Medal 1894–1908

Campaign Service Medal
1962–

United Nations Medal for
Korea 1950–4

George Cross
1940–

memories of service and valour

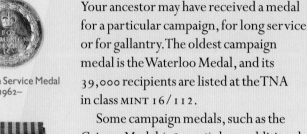

Your ancestor may have received a medal for a particular campaign, for long service or for gallantry. The oldest campaign medal is the Waterloo Medal, and its 39,000 recipients are listed at the TNA in class MINT 16/112.

Some campaign medals, such as the Crimea Medal (1854–6), have additional clasps for single battles. TNA class WO 100 lists awards of the Crimea Medal and other campaign medals up to 1912.

WORLD WARS Millions of First and Second World War medals were awarded. Those who served in France or Belgium in 1914 received the 1914 Star. Further awards for service overseas included the 1914–15 Star, the British War Medal and the Victory Medal, a trio known as 'Pip, Squeak and Wilfred' after three cartoon characters in the *Daily Mirror*.

Those who served 28 days or more in the Second World War earned the War Medal, plus the 1939–45 Star for at least six months' service. Single campaign medals included the Africa Star.

First World War medal rolls are held at the TNA in WO 372 (index), WO 329 and ADM 171. For records of awards since 1919 contact the Ministry of Defence (see DIRECTORY). Citations for awards for the Second World War and after are in WO 373.

ACTS OF BRAVERY Medals for gallantry were first issued in the Crimean War. The Distinguished Conduct Medal (DCM), introduced in 1854, was awarded to NCOs and privates. The Victoria Cross (VC), which dates from 1856, remains the highest military award for all ranks. The Distinguished Service Order (DSO) was instituted in 1886 for junior officers in all services and extended in 1914 to merchant navy and later Home Guard officers. The Military Cross (MC) was awarded to junior army officers and warrant officers.

Records of gallantry medals are in TNA class WO 98 for the VC; WO 32 for the DSO and MC; and WO 146 for the DCM. Awards, including the George Cross (GC), instituted in 1940 largely for

Canada Volunteer Service
Medal 1939–45

New Zealand War Service
Medal 1939–45

Australia Service Medal
1939–45

Defence medal
1939–45

1939–45 Star

Queen's South Africa Medal
1899–1902

Africa General Service
Medal 1902–56

1914–15 Star

Victory Medal
1914–19

British War Medal
1914–20

For king and country

George VI confers the British Empire Medal (BEM) on Flight Sergeant B.H. Hornden in 1941.

Military Cross
1914–

Croix de Guerre
1915–18

Next of Kin Memorial
Plaque 1914–20
Sent to the named next of
kin of members of HM
Forces who were killed in
the First World War.

329 (medal rolls) for those in the Royal Flying Corps (RFC), or class ADM 171 for those in the Royal Navy Air Service (RNAS). Gallantry medals for airmen were the same as those awarded to army and navy personnel. From 1918, when the RFC and RNAS merged to form the RAF, there were four gallantry awards specifically for aviators: the Distinguished Flying Cross (DFC), the Air Force Cross (AFC), the Distinguished Flying Medal (DFM) and the Air Force Medal (AFM).

Recommendations for RFC or RAF awards are in class AIR 1. For RNAS award recommendations, see ADM 1, ADM 116 and ADM 137, or *The London Gazette*.

Records of Royal Navy personnel who received campaign and gallantry medals, including First World War awards, can be found in TNA class ADM 171.

IDENTIFYING MEDALS You may find your medal in *British Battles and Medals* (E.C. Joslin, A.R. Litherland and B.T. Simpkin, Spink & Son, 6th ed., 1988). See also *Medals: the Researcher's Guide* (W. Spencer, National Archives, 7th ed., 2006). Local military museums may also be able to help.

civilian gallantry, were listed also in *The London Gazette* (see page 173).

FOREIGN MEDALS France and other Allied countries issued medals to British servicemen in the world wars. Records of foreign awards are at the TNA in classes FO 83 (pre 1906) and FO 372. See also 'Warrant Books: Licences to accept and wear foreign orders', in class HO 38.

RAF AND NAVY MEDALS For First World War campaign medals up to 1918, look in TNA classes WO 372 (index) and

War Medal
1939–45

India General Service
Medal 1936–9

British Empire Medal
1917–

Distinguished Flying Cross
1918–

Naval General Service
Medal 1915–64

armed forces
the Royal Navy

As an island nation, Britain for centuries had a large navy to guarantee her security, so there is a good chance that someone in your family served his country on the high seas

Britain's first naval force was created in the 9th century by King Alfred, but the modern Navy dates back to Henry VIII. By the time of Nelson's victory at Trafalgar in 1805, its size and influence was at its height, and for nearly a century Britain truly 'ruled the waves', the Navy playing a central role in building and maintaining the Empire. The force has shrunk considerably since then, now numbering some 68,000 uniformed and civilian personnel, but remains crucial to national security.

World war service For many people the most immediate link with the Navy is a family member who was killed on active service in one of the world wars. Registers of naval war deaths for the periods 1914–19 and 1939–48 are held at the TNA in class ADM 104. A register entry will simply state the cause of death as 'On War Service', but will include details of date and place of birth.

Life below decks
Sailors relax on a minesweeper in 1943 (right). Conditions for ordinary seamen were crowded and often uncomfortable with poor food. Hammocks remained in use until the 1960s.

KEY SOURCES OF INFORMATION
♦ *Tracing Your Naval Ancestors* (B. Pappalardo, Public Record Office, 2003).
♦ *Tracing Your Ancestors in the National Archives* (A. Bevan, National Archives, 7th ed., 2006).
♦ www.royal-navy.mod.uk/static/pages/168
♦ www.nationalarchives.gov.uk/records/research-guides/royal-navy-offices-services.htm

It is always helpful when searching any naval records to know the ship or ships on which your ancestor served (see page 227) and his rank, as ratings and officers are often listed separately.

ecords for naval ratings

Naval ranks Today there are three levels of naval appointment: junior ratings (junior, ordinary and able seamen, and leading hands), senior ratings or warrant officers (petty officers and chief petty officers), and officers (midshipmen, lieutenants and more senior officers such as captains and admirals). But in the 19th century and earlier, ranks were less distinct. For a detailed analysis see *Naval Records for Genealogists* (N. Rodger, Public Record Office, 1998).

Before 1853 naval ratings were recruited to a particular ship for a single commission, not to the service as a whole. It is therefore difficult to trace your sailor unless you know any of the ships on which he served. Men either volunteered or were taken by the press gangs, particularly during the Revolutionary and Napoleonic Wars (1793–1815) when the Navy grew from 45,000 to 145,000 men. When the ships returned to port, sailors were signed off and could then re-enlist on the same ship or an alternative, either Royal Naval or merchant, frequently taking little or no shore leave in between.

Musters and pay books The main records of ordinary ratings are the musters (lists of ships' companies) and pay books (records of pay owed) kept by individual ships. Samuel Pepys, more famous for his diaries, introduced systematic musters, the earliest dating from 1667. Their purpose was to record all seamen and others on board (such as senior officers of the fleet, specialists or passengers) and also what charges should be made against sailors' wages for items such as tobacco, trusses (braces for sailors who had ruptured themselves heaving sails aloft), venereals (charges made by the surgeon for 'cures'

Following in father's footsteps

The navy was often a family calling, sometimes with several generations serving on the same ship. The 1795 muster of HMS Lion (below right) gives Samuel Grandy as boatswain, and its list of 'Volunteer Boys 1st Class' (below left) includes two of his sons: Samuel junior and Richard, then aged only 11 and 12.

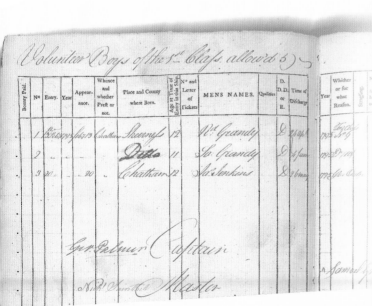

REAL LIVES
sacrifice at sea

'We had tea & settled ourselves on the chesterfield. E found a book & remarked "at last I can settle down to a good read—it seems years—" I listened to the news on the wireless—at last the announcer came to "the Admiralty regret to announce"…at the name "Hecla" E gave one awful cry and rushed to the phone.…'

So Charles and Emily Blake learnt that their eldest son, Charles John Edward, had died for his country. He is commemorated on the Chatham Naval Memorial in Kent.

A record of his death certificate is held at the General Register Office (see DIRECTORY) as an entry in Naval War Records of Death 1939–1948. As was usual for someone killed in action, the cause of death is simply stated as 'On War Service', although, unlike on most death certificates, a place of birth is given—in this case, Putney in south-west London.

A lost son

The photograph of the 7-year-old Charles John Edward (Eddy) Blake (right) takes on a prophetic quality when placed next to one of him in uniform taken shortly before his death on active naval service in the Second World War (far right). His ship, HMS *Hecla* (below), was torpedoed by a U-boat in the Atlantic on 11 November 1942. He left behind three young children, so his family line did not die with him.

venereals (charges made by the surgeon for 'cures' for venereal disease, supposed to deter the activities that caused it) and various pension funds. Until well into the 19th century, these musters followed much the same form: pages were divided into columns giving details of the officer or rating. Until 1764, a man's age and place of birth were not recorded, and even after that all the information is often not filled in, especially in the case of officers. The musters are only occasionally indexed.

There were two types of muster: the Monthly Muster and the General Muster or Open List, covering periods of two months and twelve months respectively. Both often survive and are frequently bound together. From about 1800, Description Books are occasionally preserved with the musters. These may record details such as age, complexion, height, scars or tattoos.

At the TNA, musters are kept in classes ADM 36–39, 41, 115 and 119. Where a ship's muster is missing, its pay books, held in ADM 31–35 and 117, may survive and offer similar information.

Eddy
1940

Certificates that were used for admission to the Greenwich Hospital School are with the school's records in class ADM 73, as the offspring of seamen who had died in service had a special claim to entry. Other school records, dating from 1728 to 1930, in ADM 73 and 161 can yield a wealth of information about scholars, including details of a father's career.

Continuous service engagement books A committee appointed in 1852 to consider the 'hire and discharge' system of entry into the Navy described it as 'highly detrimental to efficiency'. Advances in technology meant that part-time service was no longer feasible on board a man-of-war. A full-time trained force was required. As a result the Admiralty introduced continuous service. Every new entrant had to sign on initially for ten years and was issued with a CS (Continuous Service) number. The first series of continuous service records (class ADM 139 at the TNA) covers the

TRACING YOUR ANCESTOR'S SHIP

If your ancestor served in the Royal Navy in the latter half of the 19th century, but you have no idea on which ship, you may find it mentioned on his marriage or death certificate. A more fruitful place, however, to search for this information could be in the records of census returns (see pages 62–75).

Attempts made to count naval personnel in the 1841 and 1851 returns were not very systematic and no records survive, though from 1861 onwards, special schedules were issued to naval vessels. The Genealogical Society of Utah has produced a name index for the census return of 1861, which can be seen at Family History Centres (see DIRECTORY) and at the Family Records Centre. The 1881 census returns have also been indexed by surname and can be viewed on CD or microfiche at the aforementioned places, and at the Society of Genealogists and many local record offices.

Certificates of service For the period 1802 to 1894, the Navy Pay Office used ships' pay books to compile Certificates of Service for individual naval personnel. These were used to grant medals, administer naval pensions and decide on the admission of seamen's children to Greenwich Hospital's Lower School, also known as the Royal Naval Asylum. They cover the service of junior ratings and warrant officers (the middle ranks between junior ratings and commissioned officers: boatswains, cooks, carpenters, gunners and others) and give a brief record of ships and dates, and the total wages paid. You will find a collection of them at the TNA, held in class ADM 29. They are well indexed.

Navy during that period, with his date and place of birth and physical description. They are arranged by CS number, but indexes link numbers with names.

In addition, you may find re-engagement forms attached, occasionally with other documents that can add more detail. These may include forms and letters giving parental consent and proof of age, for boys enlisting under the age of 18.

Registers of seamen's services For 1873–1923 the TNA holds registers of seamen's services in class ADM 188. They are arranged by service number, with a name index. Entries give a date of birth, ship or shore establishment and an account of service.

To view records dating from 1924, only the rating or next of kin can apply. For service until 1938 the address is Ministry of Defence, Navy Search, Bourne Avenue, Hayes, Middlesex UB3 1RF; after 1938 it is Ministry of Defence, Post Service Enquiries, Room 1045, Centurion Building, Grange Road, Gosport, Hampshire PO13 9XA. Research into Royal Naval officers is much easier

finding an officer

than for ratings. Records go back to 1660, but snags may arise with those held at the TNA because they are spread over numerous class numbers rather than arranged in a single series. There are also many indexes and printed biographies. Two invaluable sources of information, found in many reference libraries, are: *The Commissioned Sea Officers of the Royal Navy, 1660–1815* (ed. D. Syrett, Navy Records Society, 1994), an alphabetical listing of officers with dates of promotion; and *A Naval Biographical Dictionary* (W.R. O'Byrne, John Murray, 1849), covering all commissioned officers alive in 1846.

Navy Lists These provide the dates of commissions and other promotions that will then help you to research the many other official records. *Steel's Navy*

List, published intermittently from 1782 to 1817, was superseded by the official *Navy List*, published quarterly from 1814, which lists officers and ships and notes the stations (command posts, usually overseas) and ports where they served. Copies of both are held at the National Maritime Museum (see page 219) and the TNA. See also http://yourarchives.nationalarchives.gov.uk/index.php?title=Navy_List.

Officers' service registers The service registers note the ships on which an officer served and often record entire careers from enlistment to retirement or death. They date from 1756 to 1920 and are held at the TNA in class ADM 196. The later registers, especially from the second half of the 19th century, give dates of birth, marriage and death, names of next of kin, and pay and pension details.

Records relating to officers who served after 1920 up until the early 1970s are held by the Ministry of Defence, Bourne Avenue, Hayes, Middlesex UB3 1RF.

Surveys of officers' service Between 1817 and

THE SIGNING UP OF JAMES BINGHAM

James Bingham, from Belfast, joined HMS *Vanguard* as a Boy 2nd class on 23 October 1872 when he was just 16. Recruits under the age of 18 needed parental consent to serve in the Navy, and in James' continuous service record at the TNA (in class ADM 139) is an official parental consent form, which confirms his date of birth as '11th August 1856', and a touching letter from his father, John: 'Since it is becume the will of my son…to joine him selfe on board of his Royal Majestys Navy I give him my free consent…I hope and trust in God to be his gide & protection may God bliss him & be with him where ever he goes…'

1859, the Navy shrank from 145,000 to 19,000 men, and the Admiralty discovered that it lacked sufficient information to select the best officers from the large pool on half-pay (not on active service). It therefore organised a number of surveys of officers' services, in 1817 and 1846, in a bid to improve its personnel records. These records are held in classes ADM 6, 9 and 11 at the TNA, with indexes in classes ADM 10/1–7 and ADM 11. They are far from comprehensive, as many officers did not receive or complete the forms.

Passing certificates These certificates, issued when a man qualified as an officer, summarise his career and training. There are many series, dating from 1660 to the early 20th century. The most complete set is of lieutenants' passing certificates, held in three overlapping series at the TNA—in classes ADM 107 (1691–1832), ADM 6 (1744–1819) and ADM 13 (1854–66 and 1868–1902).

Passing certificates for other officers at the TNA include: engineers, 1863–1902, in class ADM 13; masters, 1660–1830, in ADM 106, and 1857–99 in ADM 13; cadets who qualified as midshipmen,

1857–99, in ADM 13; surgeons, around 1700–1800, in ADM 106; gunners, 1731–1812, in ADM 6; and pursers, 1851–89, in ADM 13.

Commission and warrant books The term 'warrant officer' covered different ranks and jobs at different times. Generally it would have included armourers, boatswains, carpenters, cooks, masters and sailmakers (before 1808), and pursers and surgeons (before 1843).

Records for warrant officers include the Commission and Warrant Books, 1695–1849, held in class ADM 6 at the TNA. There is a typescript index covering the period 1695–1742, and a card index for 1742–5 and 1779–89.

Another good source of information on warrant officers is the Succession Books, 1695–1849, held in classes ADM 6, 11, 29 and 104. The books list officers who served successively on individual ships during the period covered by each volume, along with the date an officer joined the ship and names of his previous ships. They are indexed by both ships' and officers' names.

Until the introduction of continuous service in

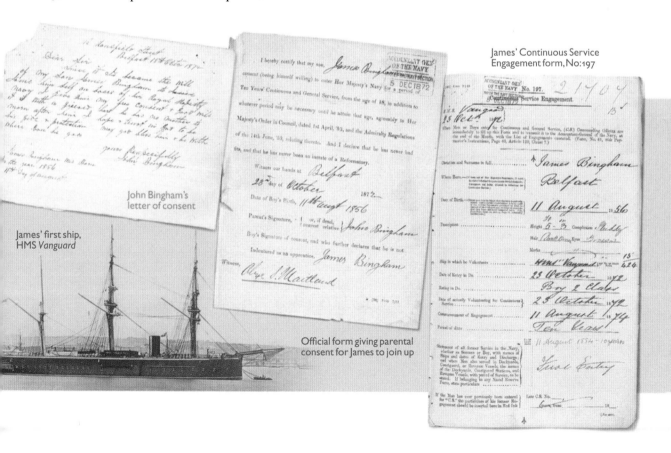

John Bingham's letter of consent

James' first ship, HMS Vanguard

Official form giving parental consent for James to join up

James' Continuous Service Engagement form, No: 197

naval pension records

Until the introduction of continuous service in 1853, Navy personnel were generally not entitled to a pension for long service. Pensions were available only for the injured or the dependants of those who had died in service. Surviving papers are full of personal details because, in most cases, a great deal of information had to be supplied before the pension would be granted. Four main bodies handled naval pensions from the 17th to the 19th century—the Navy Pay Office, the Chatham Chest, Greenwich Hospital, and the Charity for the Payment of Pensions to the Widows of Sea Officers.

Details of the pensions paid from the late 17th century until well into the 20th century are in the TNA's Military Records Information leaflets, at www.nationalarchives.gov.uk/records/research-guides/royal-navy-officer-pension.htm and royal-navy-rating-pension.htm.

Chatham Chest and Greenwich Hospital

The earliest naval charitable foundation was the Chatham Chest, dating from around 1581. It was funded by a charge of 6d a month on the wages of every man in the Navy. Pension payments from the Chatham Chest were made to those wounded in naval service, and widows of sailors and dockyard employees. There are records for 1653 to 1837 in classes ADM 22 and 82 at the TNA. The fund was closed in 1814, following its transfer to the management of Greenwich Hospital in 1803.

Greenwich Hospital was another charitable foundation supported by 6d a month from seamen's wages, as well as other contributions. The TNA has records of 'in-pensioners' from 1704 in classes ADM 6, 23, 65, 73 and 80, and of 'out-pensioners' from 1781 in classes ADM 2, 6, 22, 71 and 73. These are packed with information, including copies of birth, marriage and death certificates, details of service and evidence of need and entitlement.

Officers' pensions Like ratings, officers received no automatic superannuation payments until well into the 19th century. For commissioned officers not on the active list, and later some warrant officers, half-pay was the general alternative. The Charity for the Payment of Pensions to the Widows of Sea Officers was established in 1732, funded by parliamentary grants and 3d in the pound from all naval officers' wages. Surviving records are held at the TNA in class ADM 6.

Royal Bounty From 1675 to 1822, some widows and other dependents of officers and ratings killed in action were entitled to a lump sum payment known as the Royal Bounty. Applications for the Bounty, held at the TNA in classes ADM 16 and 106, give the name and address of the relation to whom the money was paid. Baptism and marriage certificates to prove a relationship are often included.

tracking down a will

Men on active service in the Navy often made a will and you may uncover useful information by tracking one down. A set of wills, mainly made by ratings and dating from 1786 to 1822, were deposited in the Navy Pay Office and are now held at the TNA in class ADM 48. It is also worth looking through the registers of seamen's wills held in ADM 142.

Most wills made by seamen before 1858 were proved (granted probate) in the Prerogative Court of Canterbury, although some were proved in the Commissary Court of London (London Division) or the Archdeaconry Court of London (see pages 129–31). For information on wills made after 1858 see pages 126–8.

Copies of original wills made by officers and ratings are also often found attached to applications made by their next of kin for their back pay or a pension (see above) or for the admission of a child to the Greenwich Hospital School (see page 227).

merchant navy
merchant marine records

Throughout history the British have traded, fished and carried passengers on the high seas. Many families will find that they have some nautical connections

Britain has always relied on her shipping for trade and communication with the rest of the world. Whether through financial necessity or the perceived romance of life at sea, generations of men, and later women, have taken to the waves.

tracing an ordinary seaman

Tracing the careers of men who went to sea before the 19th century can be difficult. Records before 1747 simply name the owner and master of the vessel, not the crew; these are held at the TNA, mostly in classes E 190 and E 122. Many records of maritime disputes survive from this time. These name the owners, masters and sometimes crew of

Full steam ahead for a shipping line
The P & O steamship company was formed in 1837, when it began carrying mail to Gibraltar. Many men went to sea on ships like P & O's Benares (above, photographed in 1862 with her officers and some of the crew). P & O vessels also carried tourists and servants of the Empire to India and the Far East, where local men were recruited to work on board.

KEY SOURCES OF INFORMATION
♦ Crew lists, seamen's registers and officers' certificates of competency and service at the TNA.
♦ Lloyd's captains' registers at Guildhall Library.
♦ Central Index Register at the TNA.
SEE DIRECTORY ➤

the ships involved, and are held at the TNA in HCA and DEL classes. Finding an ancestor in these records is a matter of luck, as there are no name indexes.

From 1747 onwards, ships' masters had to keep crew lists, but few from earlier than 1835 have survived, and those that have are unindexed.

registering seafarers

Seafaring became more regulated in the 19th century, and the chance of discovering your ancestor in the records improves significantly from then on. In 1835 the Merchant Shipping Act required masters to file crew lists centrally; from these seamen's registers were compiled, with the aim of creating a reserve for manning the Royal Navy in times of war. Crew lists from 1835 to 1861 are held at the TNA, but they only hold a 10 per cent sample of lists from that date until 1989. The rest have been distributed among various archives worldwide (see TNA leaflet 'Merchant Shipping: Crew Lists and Agreements after 1861' for further information).

Seamen's registers There are four series of seamen's registers, spanning the period from 1835 to 1857, when the system was abandoned. They are held at the TNA.

REGISTERS OF SEAMEN SERIES I (1835–6) This series (class BT 120) is arranged alphabetically by surname. Records include age at date of voyage, place of birth, position held (known as 'quality') and ship's name. There should be an entry for each voyage your ancestor undertook.

REGISTERS OF SEAMEN SERIES II (1835–44) This series (class BT 112) consists of two separate sets of registers which, while still in use, were unbound and reassembled in an attempt to produce a single alphabetical set.

Part 1 covers the period from early 1835 to February 1840, and is indexed in class BT 119. From this index you can obtain a reference number, which can be used to locate an entry in BT 112, consisting of the seaman's name, age, place of birth and the ship or ships he served on.

Part 2 covers the period from December 1841 to late 1844. Entries are arranged roughly alphabetically by name, and give the seaman's age and place of birth, along with the names of the ships on which he sailed, date of filing of crew lists and types of voyage.

REGISTERS OF SEAMEN'S TICKETS (1844–53) Before 1844 registers were simply compiled from crew lists. But from 1844 to 1853 every British seaman (including, for part of the period, coastguards and Royal Navy sailors) was issued with a register ticket. The majority of the original parchment tickets have disappeared, as seamen had to carry them at all times, but the registers recording their issue have survived.

TAMING THE CRUEL SEA

The Corporation of Trinity House is a charitable foundation for the safety, welfare and training of mariners. It was constituted under a royal charter granted by Henry VIII in 1514, and today has three main functions: it is the lighthouse authority for England, Wales, the Channel Islands and Gibraltar, providing lighthouses, light vessels, buoys, beacons and radio navigation systems; it is the licensing authority for deep-sea pilots; and it provides financial assistance to impoverished mariners and their dependants.

You will find petitions for aid from seamen and their families from 1787 to 1854 in Trinity House records at Guildhall Library (see DIRECTORY). The records also include information on almspeople and pensioners, and registers of pilots' licences. For more details ask at the manuscripts enquiry desk or see the library's web site at www.history.ac.uk/gh/thouse2.htm

To access the registers:

☞ First use the indexes (class BT 114), which record the seaman's name, place of birth and ticket number.

☞ Using the ticket number, consult class BT 113; note that no tickets survive after number 546,000, and that those marked with a letter are in the supplementary volumes.

☞ The entry in class BT 113 will provide more personal details about your ancestor, including date of birth, capacity (for example, apprentice or mate), physical description, whether he had previously served in the Royal Navy, town of residence when unemployed, date and place of issue of ticket, age when ticketed, literacy and reported voyages (given in encoded form, and not always recorded).

REGISTERS OF SEAMEN SERIES III

(1853–7) The register ticket system was abandoned in October 1853, and a system similar to those used earlier was re-introduced. This series (class BT 116) is arranged alphabetically by name of seaman, and records age at date of voyage, his place of birth, voyage details (the date and port of departure) and register ticket number, if the seaman previously held one.

This system was discontinued in 1857 and nothing replaced it until the Central Index Register (see page 234) was introduced in 1913.

tracing an officer

From 1845 onwards, officers' details were also recorded. You should consult the certificate registers (see page 234) if your ancestor served as a master, mate or engineer. He may also be recorded in the alphabetical registers of masters (1845–54), which are similar to the seamen's registers (see opposite). The entries are arranged alphabetically by name, giving age, place of birth and voyage details. They are held at the TNA in class BT 115.

Certificates of competency and service

A system of voluntary examinations for certificates of competency was introduced in 1845 for masters and mates. Registers of those who gained one of these certificates are held at the TNA in class BT 143/1. They are indexed and include the date and place of examination and the ship on which the candidate was serving at the time.

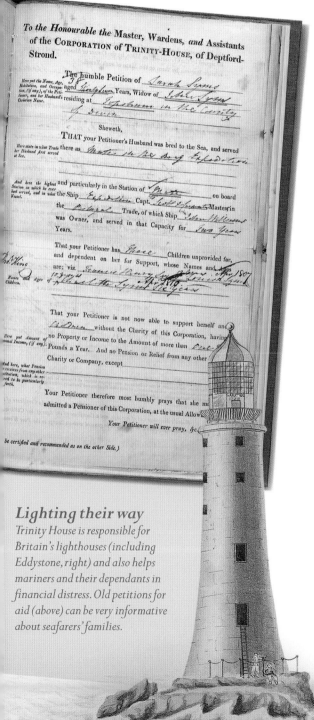

Lighting their way

Trinity House is responsible for Britain's lighthouses (including Eddystone, right) and also helps mariners and their dependants in financial distress. Old petitions for aid (above) can be very informative about seafarers' families.

ALL AT SEA?

If you fail to find a seafaring ancestor, it may be for one of these reasons:

♦ He may not have served in the merchant navy. If he was said to have been a sailor he was probably in the Royal Navy; men who served on merchant vessels were usually known as mariners or seamen. If he was said to have been a captain, he might have been in the Royal Navy, the army or Royal Marines.
♦ He may not have been the master or mate, as he claimed. Men sometimes aggrandised their status, and ship owners often employed unqualified men in order to save money.
♦ The vessel on which he sailed may have been too small to be covered by the regulations.
♦ He may have owned the vessel of which he was master.

On the cards

In 1913 the Central Index Register came into being to keep records of seamen. The register is made up of a series of cards carrying mariners' details. The cards vary in the amount of information they give, but usually include rating and place and date of birth. Sometimes they also give nationality and a physical description of the cardholder or carry a photograph. The register remained in use until 1942.

Compulsory examinations came in from 1850, although certificates of service were still granted to masters and mates whose experience made them exempt. There are 11 series of certificate registers, all held at the TNA. Masters and mates are in classes BT 122 to BT 126 and BT 128; engineers are in BT 139, 140 and 142; and skippers and mates of fishing vessels are in BT 129 and 130. The indexes (BT 127, 138 and 141) give a name, place and year of birth, and certificate number. This number shows which certificate register series to look at to discover your officer ancestor's qualifications and subsequent voyages up to 1888. The certificate numbers are also needed to locate candidates' applications for certificates, which often give details of voyages made before a certificate was granted. They are kept at the National Maritime Museum (see DIRECTORY).

Lloyd's captains' registers Lloyd's investigated the competence of captains who might command ships that it insured, and its findings were recorded along with details of a captain's earlier voyages as either a master or a mate. These records cover the period 1869–1948 and are at Guildhall Library (see DIRECTORY). Each volume covers a number of years and is arranged alphabetically.

Central Index Register (1913–41) A new system for registering merchant seamen was introduced in 1913, but the main series of records before 1921 has not survived. The Central Index Register consists of a series of cards with information about each seafarer, and covers both ordinary seamen and officers. Until the beginning of the 20th century seafaring was an exclusively male activity, and this is the first register to contain records of seafaring women, mostly stewardesses on passenger liners. The register is held at the TNA.

To find a seafarer:

☞ First consult the Alphabetical Series (CR 1 cards, 1921–41, in class BT 349). The CR 1 cards are arranged alphabetically by surname, and include a seafarer's date and place of birth, discharge number, rating and description. Some have a photograph.

☞ Using the discharge number from the CR 1 cards, consult the Numerical Series (CR 2 cards, 1921–41, in class BT 348), which includes a brief record of the ships on which the seafarer served, usually by ship's number, and the dates of signing on.

☞ For service between 1918 and 1921, you should also consult the Special Index, Alphabetical Series (CR 10 cards, 1918–21, in class BT 350). This records the issue of seamen's identity certificates during the First World War and gives similar information to CR 1 cards, but has a photograph of the bearer.

For the Central Register of Seamen, 1941 to 1972, see www.barnettmaritime.co.uk/crs.htm. For the current Registry of Shipping and Seamen from 1973 see www.lr.org/documents/173507-registry-of-shipping-and-seamen.aspx.

the ships on which they sailed

The following sources give useful information about ships and their voyages:

LOGBOOKS These were officially required from 1852, but generally only those that record a birth or death at sea have been kept. These are mostly held with the crew lists (see page 232).

LLOYD'S REGISTER OF SHIPPING This has been published annually since 1764. It gives details of ships insured by Lloyd's: date and place of build, ownership, master's name and intended trips for that year. Most reference libraries hold copies.

THE MERCANTILE NAVY LIST Published annually since 1857, this also gives basic ships' details and can be found in major reference libraries.

LLOYD'S LIST This newspaper for seafarers includes ships' movements worldwide. Copies from 1741 are in Guildhall Library.

TAKING IT FURTHER

♦ *Records of Merchant Shipping and Seamen* (K. Smith, C.T. Watts and M.J. Watts, Public Record Office, 2001).
♦ *My Ancestor Was a Merchant Seaman. How can I find out more about him?* (C.T. Watts and M.J. Watts, Society of Genealogists, 2nd ed., 2002).
♦ *Tracing Your Ancestors in the National Archives* (A. Bevan, National Archives, 2006).
♦ *A Guide to the Lloyd's Marine Collection at Guildhall Library* (D.T. Barriskill, Guildhall Library, 1994).

Information on the Internet
♦ www.nationalarchives.gov.uk/records/research-guides/merchant-seamen-sea-service-1913-1972.htm and other merchant seamen information guides
♦ www.genuki.org.uk/big/MerchantMarine.html Genuki's merchant marine sites.
♦ www.angelfire.com/de/BobSanders/Site.html Has links to maritime genealogy research sites.
♦ www.port.nmm.ac.uk The National Maritime Museum's site 'Port' is a catalogue of nautical sites on the web.

SEE DIRECTORY ➤

on the move

Few families have stayed in the same place for many generations. Britain was always a **restless nation**, so it may take a little detective work to trace ancestors who moved around these islands to escape war, plague and famine, or to find work. The British were also great explorers and exploiters of foreign lands, and documents from the late 16th century onwards record the millions who became **Britons abroad**, planting roots in America, Australia and throughout the Empire. In turn, Britain's peace, prosperity and tolerance attracted millions of immigrants—the **new Britons**, from 16th-century Huguenots to post-war West Indians and Asians.

Wartime evacuees leave for the safety of Canada in 1941

restless nation
migration within Britain

People moved home more frequently in the past than we sometimes assume. Ancestors may turn up in unexpected places, and lateral thinking may be needed to find them

If you manage to trace your ancestors through the registers of a single parish for hundreds of years, you should consider yourself lucky. Even in medieval times, people had many good reasons to move around: to escape poverty, to find work, to take up an apprenticeship or to better themselves. Sometimes events, such as the 1845–51 Irish Famine or the Highland Clearances in the 18th and 19th centuries, enforced relocation upon whole communities. Others left home to escape religious or political persecution.

All this movement can be challenging for the family historian. For example, an ancestor may be mentioned in a will, but you may have no idea of where he or she originally came from. Where you look next will, in part, depend on when your ancestor lived.

Try to imagine how the person may have been affected by historical events (see the timeline below for examples) and keep in mind that as transport networks improved during the 18th and 19th centuries people could move farther afield, so you may have to consider widening your search.

HISTORY ON THE MOVE WITHIN THE BRITISH ISLES

In 1348 the Black Death hit England's south coast and soon swept through the country, killing about a third of the population. Thousands of villages were deserted and surviving farm workers could demand high wages.

During the 15th century the growing English textile industry began to move from towns to the countryside, where labour was cheaper and less regulated. Textile workers and their families then followed the work from town to country.

Royalist and Parliamentarian armies moved around Britain in the Civil Wars (1642–51), followed by women, children and traders. When the armies disbanded, many soldiers and hangers-on found themselves stranded far from home.

Large numbers of people moved to urban areas for work during the Industrial Revolution, starting in the 18th century and greatly increasing in the first half of the 19th century. Movement within Britain became easier as road and canal networks grew.

FAMINE AND FLIGHT

In 1841 the population of Ireland was more than 8 million; it had halved by the end of the century. The catastrophic potato blight of 1845 reduced vital potato crops to stinking, rotten pulp for the next six years.

Starving families, unable to pay rent, were evicted by landlords. There was little option but to cram into boats—themselves hotbeds of typhus and dysentery—and head across the Irish Sea in the hope of some kind of welfare or work.

Waves of immigrants entered British ports, especially Glasgow, Swansea, Newport and Cardiff. But most ships docked at Liverpool, and in 1847 alone some 296,000 Irish temporarily doubled the city's population.

Irish people had been coming to Liverpool since the 17th century, often for work or to escape from sectarian violence. The 1841 census records around 50,000 Irish living there. That figure had risen to 84,000 by 1851—by which time most of the 'famine immigrants' had moved on and settled in other British towns and cities. Others were itinerant labourers, going wherever work took them, whether digging canals, building railways or helping on farms. And thousands had taken assisted passage to the New World (see Britons abroad, pages 248–53).

Many Irish immigrants can be traced in workhouse registers and burial books in city archives and record offices.

Irish immigrants landing in Liverpool were often confused and disorientated. Those seeking lodgings were at the mercy of swindlers and robbers—some of whom were children.

In 1863 the Metropolitan line in London was the first of a network of railways that set the scene for middle-class commuter-land. By 1923 there were 123 railway companies and a web of lines nationwide. A semi-rural home life with work in the 'smoke' became commonplace.

239

Migration for work One of the most likely reasons to move home was for work, a point clearly illustrated by the 1851 census returns for Kent. Boilermakers originally from Lancashire and Cheshire were found living in Ashford, especially near the new railway station; miners and their families from Nottinghamshire now lived in the small Kentish mining village of Tilmanstone; and fishermen from Brixham in Devon had moved hundreds of miles to fish from the port of Thanet.

Enforced migration In the Scottish Highlands and Islands, generations had lived off the land under the ancient clan system. Each clan had a chief who ensured that all clan members had equal access to land for farming and grazing. But from the mid 18th century through to the 1850s, many chiefs turned to lucrative sheep farming and forcibly evicted their tenants in what became known as the Highland Clearances. The Highlanders were moved to lowland coastal areas or emigrated to America, Australia and England.

the lure of town and city

Even before the Industrial Revolution, towns and cities were a magnet to country people looking for work, a spouse or a good time—and sometimes hiding from the law. You might find an ancestor's baptism record in one town, but no record of his or

trailing ancestors on the move

Tracing mobile ancestors is easier after 1851, as this is when census records began to include a person's exact age and place of birth. The 1841 census gives ages by year up to 15, and in five-year bands thereafter, while official census data before 1841 is just a head count (see Counting people, pages 62–64). Here are some suggestions as to where you might look if you have no idea of where someone came from, or where they went after a particular date.

DEVELOP A SENSE OF PLACE
You can narrow your search of the archives with informed speculation. If you know where an ancestor lived at a particular time, see if you can find a contemporary map of the area (see Mapping out the land, pages 198–202). Does the geography suggest a direction for migration? For example, would a migrant have been more likely to take a turnpike road going west than to negotiate tracks across steep hills or a desolate moor to the east? Where was the nearest local market town or port? Was there an accessible city that may have attracted your ancestor with the prospect of a better working and social life? Was there anything on the way to the city—a monastery, mill or farm, perhaps—that might have been a magnet to your ancestor, possibly because of work opportunities?

WHAT'S IN A NAME?
Some surnames indicate an association with certain areas, Penhaligon and Cornwall, for example (see Putting a place to a name, pages 304–5). Many generations of the family may have lived there, or their name may have originated there.

CHECK THE INDEXES
Instead of searching all the records where your ancestor might be found, save time and improve your chances by using indexes that include records for a number of parishes. Various indexes and their scope and function are described in Following a paper chase, pages 242–5.

her parents' marriage. It is worth checking the records of nearby rural parishes, while reading local histories may offer clues as to why an ancestor moved (see Local history, pages 188–203).

Trade apprenticeships As early as the Middle Ages, many young men moved to cities to take up apprenticeships. A newly qualified craftsman might then leave his master's employ to become a journey-man or day labourer before setting up in business for himself. A journeyman did not necessarily travel and the term should not be confused with 'sojourner', used in parish registers for a temporary resident.

Apprenticeships were regulated by town guilds of self-employed artisans or merchants. Apprentices could become freemen of the guild and then of the town, gaining the right to vote (see pages 172–3) and to conduct a trade. Registers of apprentices and lists of freemen (see page 141) may be held with other guild and borough records, usually at public libraries. A number of indexes to the London guilds' records of apprentices have been published by the Society of Genealogists. The Registers of Edinburgh Apprentices 1583–1800 have been indexed by the Scottish Record Society. The indexes are available at the Society of Genealogists and large libraries.

Skills in demand
A specialist could always find work if he was prepared to move to a centre noted for his trade. A cutler might be lured to Sheffield, for example, or an explosives expert to a gunpowder factory such as this one in Woolwich, south-east London.

ON THE TRADE TRAIL
If you know the trade of an ancestor who has 'disappeared' from the records of one area, try looking in the town or city where he might have trained or worked. Certain areas had reputations as centres of excellence for particular trades, and attracted workers from other districts. Birmingham and London, for example, had thriving gun-making industries from the 17th century onwards. Northamptonshire was famous for its shoe-making and Nottingham renowned for lace. From the 18th century to the early 19th century the woollen industry employed thousands of framework knitters in Nottinghamshire and Leicestershire.

Web sites that provide alphabetical lists of archaic and obsolete occupations include www.cpcug.org/user/jlacombe/terms.htm and www.gendocs.demon.co.uk/trades.

html Indexes covering trades such as gunsmiths, brush makers, comb makers, brass workers or coastguards can be found in *Specialist Indexes for Family Historians* (J. Gibson and E. Hampson, FFHS, 1998).

If your ancestor was a craftsman making items such as clocks, watches or silverware, which are now prized as antiques, a bio-graphical trade directory may help you. An example is *Watchmakers and clockmakers of the world* (G.H. Baillie, NAG Press, 3rd ed., 1976). The Society of Genealogists (see

DIRECTORY) has a large collection of biographical directories, and they are also held by trade associations, museums and reference libraries. (See Working life, pages 139–49.)

Local trade directories (see Town & county directories, pages 174–5) contain alphabetical lists of local traders, as do most county Post Office directories (largely dating from the mid 19th century). Guildhall Library (see DIRECTORY) and the Society of Genealogists hold collections.

restless nation
following a paper chase

When an ancestor's trail goes cold, you need to turn detective. Hunting for a 'missing' relative may seem daunting at first, but there are several ways to shorten your search

You will probably need to consult more records for migrant ancestors than for those who remained in the same district. But do not despair: there are many records available that can help to narrow your search.

The most important source of information about migrants before the 1851 census is the poor law records (see Poor & destitute, pages 150–6). The poor law system, devised to prevent paupers becoming a burden on parish coffers, tied individuals to a particular place. Poor law records, such as settlement certificates, examinations and removal orders, give information about relationships, ages, places of residence, job history and other details. The documents can be particularly useful in tracing migrant or seasonal Irish workers in England.

a list of the main indexes

Using an index can save a lot of time, but it is important that you have details of its coverage and contents. Ask yourself the following questions: Does the index cover all the records of the area or just some for a few years? Was it compiled from the original records or from copies? How much margin for human error is there?

Index of strays People who came to one place from another (usually outside the county) are known by family historians as strays. There are large numbers of strays in urban areas such as London and Birmingham. Family history researchers have made indexes of them, which could prove useful if your ancestor fails to show up in the records of likely

Moving with the tide
Anyone who fished from British ports or worked on the waterways —bargemen and canal boatmen—had plenty of opportunity to move around the country, perhaps marrying and settling far from their place of birth. The fishing port of Wells-next-the-Sea in north Norfolk (above) was famous for its mussels and whelks.

geographical areas. The Federation of Family History Societies (see DIRECTORY) publishes the National Index of Strays on microfiche, available at the Society of Genealogists (see DIRECTORY).

Parish register indexes One of the most useful developments for family history research has been the indexing of parish registers (see pages 88–89). The International Genealogical Index (IGI) is the

242

largest index of births, baptisms and marriages (see pages 100–1). The CD and Internet editions allow countrywide searches, although the amount of information available varies region by region.

There are also county indexes available, compiled by local family history societies or dedicated enthusiasts. Some are listed in *Marriage and Census Indexes for Family Historians* (J. Gibson and E. Hampson, FFHS, 2000). The Society of Genealogists holds copies of many of the indexes.

Marriage indexes If an ancestor's marriage did not take place where you might have expected it to, perhaps because of parental disapproval, an index may help you to locate the couple's chosen parish.

BOYD'S MARRIAGE INDEX Of the many marriage indexes, each covering a wide area, the first and largest is Boyd's, compiled in the 1920s from English parish registers by a renowned genealogist called Percival Boyd. Seven million names are recorded, representing around 12 per cent of all marriages in England between 1538, when registers began, and 1837, when civil registration was introduced. The original is at the Society of Genealogists, which has published a list of all the parishes it covers. Guildhall Library (see DIRECTORY) has a microfiche copy and local record offices and Family History Centres may have copies of relevant sections.

THE PALLOT INDEX Marriages account for the majority of this index, which covers some parishes in the City of London, and what we now recognise as Greater London, from 1780 to 1837. It is held by Achievements Ltd for the Institute of Heraldic and Genealogical Studies (see DIRECTORY), who will make a search on your behalf for a fee.

TRACING A SHOEMAKER'S ROOTS Marriage indexes can be used to find places where there are clusters of a family name, which is especially useful if there is no baptism index for the area. For example, one family historian had a copy of the 1861 marriage certificate of Francis Fewell, a 24-year-old bachelor and shoemaker of Hope Place, Great Cambridge Street, London, but his origins were obscure. The 1861 census confirmed Fewell's

KEY SOURCES OF INFORMATION

♦ Numerous indexes at the Society of Genealogists and libraries of local family history societies.

♦ Boyd's marriage index.

♦ The International Genealogical Index (IGI) at Family History Centres, major record offices and libraries, or online at www.familysearch.org.

♦ Parish register indexes from local family history societies.

♦ Occupational licences in quarter sessions records at county record offices.

♦ Index to obituaries from national newspapers, and a Catholic marriage index at the Institute of Heraldic and Genealogical Studies.

♦ Records of apprenticeship taxes at the TNA (indexes are at the Society of Genealogists).

SEE DIRECTORY ➤

address, but his birthplace was given only as Essex. As Francis Fewell must have been born around 1836–7, just before the introduction of civil registration, his baptism had to be sought in parish records. There are more than 280 parishes in Essex, so a search of every parish register for a record of this baptism could have taken months.

Using Boyd's marriage index, the detective family historian was able to compile a list of men with the name Fewell (including variant spellings). He then cut the list to men who had married in the county between 1776 and 1837, presuming that Francis's father must have married during that period. All these marriages were plotted on a map to reveal significant local clusters of the name. This narrowed the field of parish records needing checking and, working through the clusters, the family historian found the baptism of the infant Francis in the parish register of Great Canfield.

Tracing an ancestor in this way is exciting, but you should exercise caution—treat any such identification as preliminary until you can corroborate it.

Apprenticeship indexes In 1710 a stamp duty was levied on some apprenticeships (see Companies & trades, page 142). Records of the tax, which give the apprentice's name, master, trade, length of service, tax levied and, before 1762, parents' names, are held at the TNA in class IR 1. The Society of Genealogists has completed an index to these records, from 1710 to 1774, and microfiche copies can be viewed in some large reference libraries, such as Guildhall Library (see DIRECTORY).

Will and burial indexes The will of a migrant ancestor may provide clues to his or her movements or place of origin. The bequest of money to the poor of a particular parish, or the ownership of property there, probably indicates a close connection with that parish, while friends or relatives who are beneficiaries of the will may have lived in your ancestor's parish of birth (see Legacies, pages 120–31).

THE BRITISH RECORD SOCIETY (www.britishrecordsociety.org) has published numerous indexes of wills in various holdings, such as *Wills in the Consistory Court of Lichfield, 1650-1700* (vol. 125, ed., C. Webb, 2010).

BOYD'S LONDON BURIALS This index is a collection of adult (over the age of 12) male burials in London City churches and cemeteries from 1538 to 1853. It is held by the Society of Genealogists.

NATIONAL BURIALS INDEX A new index of national burials is being coordinated by the Federation of Family History Societies. The second edition contains 13.2 million records on a set of four CDs. Compiled from parish registers, it includes a person's name, age, residence and date of burial, and should help to narrow the search for an ancestor's burial place (see In memoriam, pages 112–17).

Obituaries and notices The death of a migrant ancestor may be recorded in an obituary published in the local press, and this may reveal his or her place of birth. Surviving relatives also sometimes announced the death of a loved one in the home town (see People in newspapers, pages 168–73). The Andrews Index at the Institute of Heraldic and Genealogical Studies (see DIRECTORY) lists entries from several national newspapers (from around 1903 to 1966), including *The Daily Telegraph*, the *News of the World* and *The Times*, recording attempts made by solicitors to contact next of kin.

Occupational licences Some migratory and partly migratory workers, including publicans, badgers (pedlars of food or corn dealers), higglers (pedlars with a horse and cart), drovers, hawkers,

A mobile profession

A medieval doctor tends to a mother, and a midwife holds the newborn, after a difficult birth. Midwives often ended up living far from the parishes where they were born and grew up. Like other professional people, such as surgeons and schoolteachers, midwives were prepared to move some distance for a permanent home and settled occupation—not unlike today.

physician and schoolmaster, often attracted people from outside a parish. Records of their licences, issued by a bishop, can be found among the records of church courts (see For Crown & Church, pages 144–6) although these were phased out during the 18th and 19th centuries.

The London mercantile class London was highly regulated during the medieval period, particularly by the guilds and City livery companies (see pages 141–2). A fascinating source of information about families from this period and up to the 17th century is Boyd's *Inhabitants of London*. The collection holds information on approximately 60,000 families, particularly relating to members of guilds and City livery companies, sometimes in astonishing detail. It can be seen at the Society of Genealogists. There are also freemen records for many cities, some of which—Canterbury, York and Bristol, for example—have been published.

TAKING IT FURTHER

♦ *Migration and Mobility in Britain since the 18th Century* (C. G. Pooley and J. Turnbull, UCL Press, 1998).
♦ *My Ancestors Moved in England and Wales: how can I trace where they came from?* (A. J. Camp, SoG, 1994).
♦ *Occupational Sources for Genealogists: a bibliography* (S. A. Raymond, FFHS, 2nd ed., 1996).
♦ *Lists of Londoners* (J. Gibson and H. Creaton, FFHS, 2nd ed., 1997).
♦ *My Ancestors Were Londoners: how can I find out more about them?* (C. Webb, SoG, 4th ed., 2002).

Information on the Internet
♦ www.genuki.org.uk Lists on-line indexes of parish registers and strays.
♦ website.lineone.net/~rtfhs Romany and Traveller Family History Society web site.

barge and wherry owners, were licensed by quarter sessions from the late 17th century into the 19th century. The records are held at county record offices. A sailor or soldier might also have lived temporarily, or settled, in an area other than his birthplace. You might be able to trace his places of residence through regimental and service records (see Joining up, pages 204–35). More settled occupations, including those of parish clerk,

When a sepia print of her great-grandmother Pamela inspired Sharon Floate to hunt down her Gypsy forebears, she began searching out official records, and had some success. From the 1860 marriage certificate of Pamela's parents, Lamentina Smith and Tom Mullenger, Sharon learnt that Lamentina's father, William, was a horsedealer, but her new husband was a hairdresser—not a traditional Gypsy trade. It seems that a non-Gypsy had, unusually, been allowed to marry 'in'. But by the time baby Pamela was born, Tom had joined the family business: on Pamela's birth certificate, Tom is described as a horsedealer.

As luck had it, the couple were living in a house on census night, 1861, but even armed with Lamentina's place and year of birth (c.1841), the trail now grew cold.

Sharon needed a new approach. Delving into Romany culture, she discovered the Gypsy Lore Society and its *Journal*. Then, to her surprise and delight, in a 1910 issue, she found a Smith family tree—which included 'Lementeni'—and also discovered that hers was the family featured in George Borrow's novels *Lavengro* (1851) and *Romany Rye* (1857).

Family historians can consult issues of the Gypsy Lore Society's *Journal* in the Sydney Jones Library (see DIRECTORY) at the University

REAL LIVES
my great-grandma was a Gypsy…

It all began with an old photograph
Sharon Floate's exploration of her family's connections began with a photograph of a young woman in Victorian dress standing outside a tent (far left). 'This is your great-grandmother, Pamela Mullenger,' a great-aunt told her. 'And she was a Gypsy.' Another striking photograph portrays Pamela around 1910 (above), while her 1861 birth certificate reinforces the link: Pamela was born in Norfolk, a long way from Blackpool where she lived and died; her mother, Lamentina Smith, had a Gypsy surname and suitably exotic forename; and her father, Tom, was described as a horse-dealer—the trade of many Gypsies. Sharon (left) began a search that culminated in a book: *My Ancestors Were Gypsies* (S. Floate, Society of Genealogists, 2nd ed., 2010).

The route to Blackpool beach

Sharon traced her Gypsy ancestry as far as she could through official documents, such as birth and marriage certificates (right and below). It then took a measure of lateral thinking to take the trail further: in a 1910 issue of the *Journal of the Gypsy Lore Society* (below right), Sharon discovered a Gypsy family tree and instantly progressed two generations. She also learnt of dozens of relatives. This in turn helped her research, leading to the discovery that 'Lementeni' and her daughter Pamela were fortunetellers who lived in a tent similar to the one pictured (bottom) in an encampment on the beach at Blackpool.

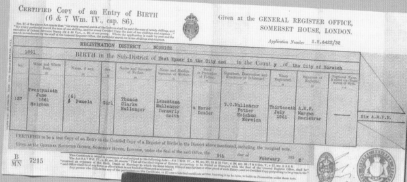

of Liverpool and several other libraries. The society's huge archive, largely based on Gypsy oral history, is extremely precious, as other documentation is so limited. Gypsies rarely registered births, for example, or married in church, and they almost never appear in the 1841 or 1851 censuses because, until 1861, information was collected only from people who lived in houses.

Gypsies tended to marry within their own people and travelled in family groups, so there is a good chance of meeting 'cousins' through organisations like the Romany and Traveller Family History Society (see DIRECTORY).

Sharon's trail led her from Blackpool via East Anglia, Oxfordshire and the West Country to Arthur Smith, her seven-times great-grandfather, born c.1699. A spell in Oxford Gaol in 1744 earned Arthur a mention in a rare early newspaper, *The Reading Mercury*, as 'Prince of the Gypsies'.... The tale behind the nickname has yet to be uncovered.

Fortune Telling at Blackpool.

Britons abroad

a roaming nation

Most people can find relatives who in the past were forced or chose to go overseas. A wealth of material in British and foreign archives can help you to track them down

At some stage you will probably discover family members who emigrated from the British Isles, for reasons ranging from religious persecution to transportation or just the search for a better life.

Hundreds of thousands of people left for the Americas in the 17th and 18th centuries. Around 10 million Britons emigrated in the 19th century, to the United States and all parts of the British Empire.

Searching for overseas links with your past is exciting. But it is crucial to do your homework before undertaking research abroad.

Start by investigating published guides to records for the country of emigration and take a look at the records held in British and Irish archives (see below). Join a family history society associated with the country. Some can be contacted through the Federation of Family History Societies or have links with the Society of Genealogists (see DIRECTORY).

Having done the groundwork and acquired new leads, you will know which overseas records are likely to help and where to find them. As a result, research abroad is much more likely to be a success.

British emigration records at a glance

The TNA (see DIRECTORY) has Colonial Office, Board of Trade, Treasury and Home Office records relating to emigration as well as passenger lists, indentures (of assisted emigrants) and some overseas civil records (in group RG). Passports were not required before 1914, but some registers of passports from 1795 are in class FO 610. Records of an earlier document, the 'Licence to Pass beyond the Seas', are in classes E 157 and CO 1.

Records of Irish transportees are at the National Archives of Ireland. The Centre for Migration Studies has an emigration database. The Royal Irish Academy has a list of emigrants from Co. Londonderry and Co. Antrim; a copy is held at the Public Record Office of Northern Ireland, whose other records include passenger lists (1847–71) for the J. & J. Cooke and the McCorkill shipping lines from Londonderry. See DIRECTORY for addresses.

Farewell to the Highlands and Islands

A crowd of Hebrideans gathers at the quayside to wave goodbye to fellow countrymen emigrating to Canada in 1923 on board the Matagama. By the early part of the 20th century, many thousands of men and women had sailed west, lured by the prospect of new land to farm and the challenge of Canadian outback life. Most are unrecorded in Scotland but you may find their names in passenger lists at the TNA or in the National Archives of Canada (see DIRECTORY). You can also consult immigration records in Canada up to 1920—and later if you have the permission of the immigrants or proof of their death.

The National Archives of Scotland (see DIRECTORY) holds records of Scottish emigration, including some for criminal transportation. Records of the Highland and Island Emigration Society (reference HD 4) list assisted emigrants who went to Australia from 1852 to 1857. Scots who applied to emigrate from 1886 to 1889 are listed in AF 51. Some details of emigrants in Manitoba, Canada, after 1889 can be found in AF 51/188–211.

Specialist archives, such as that of the Society of Genealogists (see DIRECTORY), have vast collections of material from all over the world, particularly the Americas and Australia, as well as bibliographies and other reference books.

Write to or email foreign archives (see DIRECTORY). Use web sites such as www.familysearch.org to explore surname links in the country to which your ancestors emigrated.

Britons abroad
planting roots in America

If your ancestors sailed to the New World to seek a fortune or pursue their religion, or were transported convicts, a range of documents can help you to trace them

In search of fortune and freedom

The English artist John White accompanied Sir Walter Raleigh on his expeditions to the east coast of North America in the late 16th century. Among the sketches and watercolours he produced is the map of 'Raleigh's Virginia' (above), stretching from south of modern Cape Lookout to the north side of the entrance to Chesapeake Bay. Virginia soon attracted thousands of settlers seeking fortunes on its tobacco plantations. Later, between 1892 and 1954, 12 million people, fleeing poverty and oppressive regimes, emigrated to America via the port of New York and were processed at Ellis Island. Thousands of the immigrants' names are recorded on the island's 'Wall of Honor' (below).

Emigration from Britain to the Americas began as early as 1585, when Sir Walter Raleigh founded a settlement on Roanoke Island, off the coast of what is now North Carolina. This failed, as did several others. It was not until 1607 that the first successful British settlement was established at Jamestown, which soon became the centre of the thriving colony of Virginia. In 1620 another major settlement sprang up in New England, when the *Mayflower* arrived from Plymouth. Among the new immigrants she carried were 36 Puritan refugees, the first of many religious dissenters to settle there.

Building the great plantations Virginia attracted large numbers of workers for its tobacco plantations. Thousands of them arrived under an arrangement known as the 'headright' system, whereby 50 acres of land were granted to whoever paid an emigrant's fare to the colony.

Some settlers paid their own fares and farmed their 50 acres, but many more fares were paid by plantation owners who would then claim a new arrival's land and secure his services for up to seven years. The names of such indentured servants appear in official lists of headrights, held at the TNA (see DIRECTORY) in classes CO 1 and CO 5.

Tied by indenture As the colonies grew, and new ones sprang up, the practice of indenture became more widespread. Before the Act of Union in 1707 Scots were not allowed to be employed in the colonies as indentured workers, but from 1710 they too crossed the Atlantic in large numbers. Many indenture records are held at the TNA and Guildhall Library (see DIRECTORY).

Puritan founders of New England The dissenters of New England were driven by the desire to practise their religion in freedom. If your relatives were among them, find out which church they belonged to, and where it was based in Britain (see Nonconformists, pages 102–6). Records of the church may help you to find their place of origin.

Early settlers are also listed in detailed biographical registers such as the *Directory of Scottish Settlers in North America, 1625–1825* (D. Dobson, GPC, Baltimore, 6 vols, 1984–6) or *The Complete Book of Emigrants* (P.W. Coldham, GPC, Baltimore, 4 vols, 1987–93), also on CD.

sentenced to transportation

From about 1617 until the outbreak of the American War of Independence in 1775, the law courts of England and Wales, and also Scotland, provided another major group of emigrants to the Americas. These were men, women and children who fell foul of the law and received a sentence of transportation, usually for either 7 or 14 years. Some were vagrants, while others were criminals (both serious and petty), rebels or even prisoners of war.

People were also transported from Ireland to the American colonies in the 17th and 18th centuries. See *Emigrants from Ireland to America 1735–43* (ed. F. McDonnell, GPC, Baltimore, 1992).

Where to find transportation records A good place to start is *The Complete Book of Emigrants in Bondage, 1614–1775* (P.W. Coldham, GPC, Baltimore, 1988), which lists convicts and tells you where they were tried. *Bonded Passengers to America* (P.W. Coldham, GPC, Baltimore, 1983) includes an overview of other published information.

If the transportee was convicted in a court of assizes, the records may survive at the TNA or, for Welsh transportees, the National Library of Wales (see DIRECTORY). Contracts to transport convicts may be among quarter sessions records at county record offices. See Criminal ancestors, pages 159–63 for more information.

As the cost of their passage was funded by the State, convicts to be transported are also listed in Treasury records at the TNA (class T 1); some are indexed. They include the name of the ship, its master and its destination in North America or the West Indies.

later waves of emigration

Large-scale emigration to America from Britain and Ireland continued well into the 20th century. Between 1837 and 1920 it is estimated that some 6.5 million people made the journey. Passenger lists from 1890 to 1960 are at the TNA (class BT 27) but you need to know the ship, its port of departure or date of sailing. These lists of more than 24 million passengers are now available on the commercial on-line site www.findmypast.co.uk. See also www.nationalarchives.gov.uk/records/research-guides/passenger-lists.htm.

Many Irish people emigrated via Liverpool, but passenger lists were deposited at the port of arrival and are not archived in Ireland. The National Archives in Washington (see DIRECTORY, under USA) holds customs passenger lists from 1820 and immigration passenger lists from 1883, which are also available on microfilm at Family History Centres (see DIRECTORY).

KEY SOURCES OF INFORMATION
♦ Lists of 'headrights' for plantation workers, and indenture and transportation records at the TNA.
♦ Indenture records at Guildhall Library.
♦ Passenger lists at the National Archives, Washington, USA.
♦ *Passenger and Immigration Lists Index* (P.W. Filby and M.K. Meyer, Gale, 1981) A guide to arrival records for North America.
♦ *Americans from Wales* (E.G. Hartmann, Octagon Books, New York, 1983).
♦ *The Famine Immigrants* (GPC, Baltimore, 1983) Lists of Irish arriving at New York 1846–51.
SEE DIRECTORY ➤

Britons abroad
setting sail for Australia

Many records exist for the founding fathers of Australia, whether they were convicts, assisted immigrants or free settlers who went in search of gold

A new life down under

Free settlers sailed to Australia in search of land and work, formed small communities and built their own homes (such as the one in Sydney, above, housing 72 people). For them it was a country of hope and promise. For convicts (such as the man and woman, right, who were transported in 1793) the immediate prospect was near-slave labour. The weakest did not survive the long voyage from Britain——26 per cent of those on the second fleet to sail to Australia died at sea; another 14 per cent died within eight months of landing. But the hardiest, who lived to complete their sentence, were finally able to start a new life with a grant of free land.

In 1783, after eight years of war, Britain was forced to reliquish control over 13 rich colonies that became the newly independent United States of America. An immediate consequence was a sudden increase in Britain's convict population.

Thousands of prisoners who would have been transported to America had to live on prison ships, called hulks, which were moored in Britain's rivers and coastal waters (see page 165). A solution was needed. In 1787 a fleet of 11 ships set off to establish a new penal colony at Botany Bay on the east coast of Australia. A second fleet followed in 1790 and a third left in 1791. In all more than 160,000 people were transported—to New South Wales until 1840 and to other parts of Australia until 1868.

tracing a transported ancestor

Extensive records of transportees exist at the TNA (see DIRECTORY) and in state archives in Australia. Details of convicts who sailed on the early fleets appear in books such as *The Founders of Australia: a biographical dictionary of the first fleet* (M. Gillen, Library of Australian History, 1989), *The Second Fleet: Britain's grim convict armada of 1790* (M. Flynn, Library of Australian History, 1993) and *The Third Fleet Convicts* (R. J. Ryan, Horwitz Grahame, 1983).

For later transportees, records are in the TNA (see TNA leaflet 'Transportation to Australia') or in Australia. As there is no single list of names, it helps to know the year of transportation.

Narrowing down your search One place to start is the census records, or musters, of early Australian settlers conducted in Australia. Some are in the TNA; several have been published. They often state the place of conviction and the ship's name and date of arrival in Australia. This helps you to consult the 21 volumes of transportation registers in the TNA (class HO 11), which are arranged according to the names of ships, and when they sailed.

Trial records may briefly mention a transported ancestor's background and conviction (see Criminal ancestors, pages 159–63). A better source of information are petitions for clemency in the TNA (classes HO 17 and 18), with an index (class HO 19).

CONVICTS' FAMILIES A petition for a family reunion can be very useful. Wives often asked to join convict husbands, and male convicts who had served four years of their sentence could ask for wives and children to be given free passage to Australia.

The petitions and accompanying papers are full of family details. They are in the TNA (classes PC 1 and HO 12) and in the National Archives of Ireland (see DIRECTORY) under *Free Settlers Papers 1828–1852*.

KEY SOURCES OF INFORMATION
♦ Transportation records and passenger lists at the TNA.
♦ Irish transportee records in the National Archives of Ireland.
♦ *Bound for Australia* (D. Hawkings, Phillimore, 1987).
♦ *Australians from Wales* (L. Lloyd, Gwynedd Archives and Museums Service, 1988).
♦ *Bound for Botany Bay: British Convict Voyages to Australia* (A. Brooke and D. Brandon, National Archives, revised ed., 2007).

Transportation from Ireland Convicts were transported from Ireland from 1791 to 1853, and in 1868 the practice was restored in order to send 63 Irish nationalists to Western Australia. Many records of these forced emigrants are in the National Archives of Ireland, including *Transportation Registers 1836–57* and *Prisoners' Petitions and Cases 1788–1836*. They can be accessed at www.national archives.ie/topics/transportation/search01.html

those who chose to go: free settlers

Australia also attracted free settlers, such as traders and farmers, whose numbers soared after the discovery of gold in the 1850s. They may be listed in the many published 19th-century musters or censuses. The 1828 census for New South Wales, with details of more than 35,000 people, is at the TNA (class HO 10).

Passenger lists may also help. Those for ships leaving British ports from 1890, arranged by port and date of sailing, are held at the TNA (class BT 27).

Earlier lists are noted in *National Register of Shipping Arrivals, Australia and New Zealand* (A.G. Peake, Australian Federation of Family History Organisations, 3rd ed., 1992). On-line try www.searchforancestors/locality/australia/passenger.html. For other key records, consult the National Archives of Australia (see DIRECTORY) or web site www.cohsoft.com.au/afhc.

Britons abroad
servants of the Empire

At the height of Britain's imperial power, thousands emigrated to work in far-flung colonies and may be recorded in a variety of official or commercial documents

The expansion of the Empire in the 18th and 19th centuries opened up possibilities across the globe for Britons eager for adventure, trade or a new life abroad. Between them, military and commercial enterprises, and missions to teach, preach and care for the sick, drew millions to regions as far afield as India, South Africa, Canada and New Zealand.

India—'the jewel in the Crown' India did not attract emigrants in search of a new life. Most went on temporary assignments as merchants, or as civil or military officials. Nevertheless, around 4 million Britons were born or married in India, or died there. There are two phases of British activity: from 1600 to 1858, when the East India Company controlled the region, and from 1858 to 1947, when India was ruled by the British government through the India Office.

families in India

A Royal Charter granted by Elizabeth I in 1600 gave a group of London merchants exclusive rights to trade in the East Indies. As a steady flow of traders and mariners headed east hoping to make their fortunes, the East India Company, as it was later known, grew in wealth and influence. By the mid 18th century it was, in effect, running India.

The company compiled and kept a huge amount of information about its activities and staff, including early records of appointments of traders, merchants and mariners. When the Crown took over the governing of India in 1858, its India Office continued to record the lives of emigrant Britons in the days of the Raj.

Landing at the port of Madras Founded as Fort St George in 1639, Madras was the East India Company's first real foothold on the subcontinent. It was not an ideal port as ships had to anchor out at sea and passengers were rowed by native outriggers through rolling waves to the shingle shore. Later Madras became the capital of a presidency that took its name; the other two presidencies, Bengal and Bombay, had similar trading and political structures.

Records of colonial life in India The Oriental and India Office Collections at the British Library (see DIRECTORY) contain extensive records of both periods, including an expanding biographical card index with details of some 295,000 civil and military personnel, their families and others.

The collections also contain copy registers of births, marriages and burials, records of wills and pension funds, information on railway employees, and service records for military personnel of the East India Company and the Indian Army. Records for the regular army in India are at the TNA (see Using army records, pages 208–11).

The Society of Genealogists (see DIRECTORY) also holds a collection of material from India, including copies of church registers and monumental inscriptions from Indian cemeteries.

Ancestors in the Caribbean Islands The plantations of the Caribbean proved a magnet for emigrants, both as free settlers and as indentured servants. A few people were transported there. See records in *Tracing Your West Indian Ancestors* (G. Grannum, Public Record Office, 2nd ed., 2002).

The TNA has some 17th-century registers of passengers to Barbados (class E 157) and a collection of early colonial papers in class CO 1, which includes detailed information on property owners, their families, slaves and servants for the years 1678–80. A census of white inhabitants in 1715 can be found in CO 28/16. Names of slave-owners and some

The Company fights back
In the early 18th century, the Compagnie des Indes, a French trading rival, challenged the Company's hold on Madras and laid siege to the barracks at Trichinopoly (above). The Company's subsequent victory confirmed it as the pre-eminent European force in the region.

India under the rule of the Crown
Although the East India Company's forces resisted the Indian Mutiny of 1857, the bloody confrontation forced the British government to impose Crown rule in India. The new British administration included many English civil servants such as the district officer (above) dispensing justice in Mudanapalle in 1900. India Office records to 1947, when India gained independence, will help you to trace the lives of ancestors who, like the family in Safiabad (below), flourished under the Raj.

Britons abroad

KEY SOURCES OF INFORMATION
♦ Oriental and India Office Collections at the British Library.
♦ Records related to emigration at the TNA and at the Society of Genealogists.
♦ National archives in individual countries.

SEE DIRECTORY ➤

slaves appear in records of surveys carried out in the West Indies from 1812 to 1846 in class T 71 at the TNA. A number of private papers from West Indian plantations can be found in the Chancery Masters' Exhibits (classes C 103 to C 114).

Britons colonising Canada British settlement of Canada began with small outposts of the Hudson's Bay Company in the mid 17th century. By 1763 Britain controlled the whole of eastern Canada. The population remained relatively small but was boosted after 1776 by some 70,000 Loyalists fleeing from the newly independent USA.

From 1815, migrants arrived from England, Ireland and especially Scotland. Around 750,000 Britons settled in Canada between 1837 and 1867.

The TNA holds microfilm copies of the Hudson's Bay Company records, from its founding in 1670 to 1904. The Society of Genealogists also has some material, including an index of Alberta's civil registration records (1870–1905) and trade directories.

SOURCES IN CANADA Most of the records that will help you to trace British emigrants are in Canadian archives. *In Search of Your Canadian Roots* (A. Baxter, Macmillan, Canada, 2nd ed., 1994) is a useful guide. Extensive ship passenger lists for people arriving from 1865 can be found in the National Archives of Canada (see DIRECTORY).

The National Archives also holds census records for the whole of Canada (1871–1901) and other local census material. Civil registration began in 1864 in Nova Scotia, followed by other provinces. You may only be able to see early records, as in most provinces they are closed for up to 100 years.

Many of the indexes to the available civil registration records can be ordered on microfilm through Family History Centres (see DIRECTORY).

Settlers in New Zealand The first Britons went to New Zealand in about 1790, but there was little immigration before 1840, when the country became a Crown colony. Many of the emigrants arrived via New South Wales, rather than directly from Britain, so you may be able to trace them in early Australian records as well as in British sources.

From 1839, many emigrants were recruited by the New Zealand Company, whose records are held at the TNA in class CO 208. The names of assisted emigrants whose passage was paid, often in return for labour, are recorded (up to 1888) in the National Archives of New Zealand (see DIRECTORY).

Muck and brass in the Canadian outback
Attracted by the lure of gold, British prospectors arrive at the Bitter Creek landing stage on their way to Stewart during the Yukon gold rush of 1910. In the 19th and early 20th century, Canada was where enterprising Britons went to seek their fortunes; and often made them. Land was cheap or given away to British emigrants who were willing to work it. Records of land-holdings may be found in the archives of the province where your ancestor lived. Those for Ontario include details of land grants and settlers' petitions for grants, dating from the 18th century.

The National Archives also holds large numbers of passenger arrival lists: see *National Register of Shipping Arrivals, Australia and New Zealand* (A.G. Peake, Australian Federation of Family History Organisations, 1993). For ships that left British ports you can also consult the passenger lists from 1890 onwards at the TNA, class BT 27.

CIVIL REGISTRATION Official registration of New Zealand's births, marriages and deaths began in 1848. Microfilm indexes of these records up to 1920 are available at the Society of Genealogists. For further information, contact the New Zealand Society of Genealogists (see DIRECTORY).

Emigration to South Africa

Britons began to settle in South Africa from 1806—the year in which Holland formally ceded the Cape of Good Hope to Britain. In 1843 Natal was declared a British colony and by 1902 Britain had gained control of the former Boer republics of the Orange Free State and Transvaal. All four provinces were brought together in 1910 as the Union of South Africa, and they all attracted British immigrants.

Civil registration for the whole of South Africa began in 1923, and earlier in its provinces, but the records are not open. For further information and details of sources contact the Genealogical Society of South Africa (see DIRECTORY).

Elsewhere in the British Empire References to British emigrants occur in numerous TNA documents, mainly among Colonial Office, Home Office, Board of Trade and Treasury papers, with calendars (indexed listings) for certain classes. (See TNA leaflet 'Emigrants' for details.)

In class RG 36, you will find records of births, marriages and deaths between 1895 and 1965 in former British protectorates of Africa and Asia such as Kenya, Malaya and the Sudan. *The British Overseas* (G. Yeo, Guildhall Library, 3rd ed., 1995) lists registers of births, marriages and deaths abroad.

Missionary ancestors The records of some missionary societies can be consulted, including those of the Church Mission Society and the Baptist Missionary Society (see DIRECTORY). A number of other societies have donated archives to the School for Oriental and African Studies. To use its library (see DIRECTORY), you may need a letter of recommendation from the society concerned.

TAKING IT FURTHER

♦ 'Essays on African-Caribbean Genealogy' (G. Grannum) and 'South Asian Genealogy' (A. Hussainy) in *The Oxford Companion to Family and Local History* (ed. D. Hey, Oxford University Press, 2nd ed., 2010).
♦ *Migration Records for Family Historians* (R. Kershaw, The National Archives, 2009)
♦ *Handbook for Genealogical Research in South Africa* (R.T. Lombard, Institute for Historical Research, Human Sciences Council, 3rd ed., 1990).

Information on the Internet
♦ www.CyndisList.com has individual pages for each of the countries to which British people emigrated.
♦ www.nationalarchives.gov.uk/records/research-guides/calendar-state-papers-colonial.htm
♦ www.worldgenweb.org

new Britons
in search of a better life

The mass of paperwork generated by the arrival of immigrants in Britain provides a starting point for tracing ancestors from distant lands and even distant times

For centuries foreigners have come to Britain seeking work or to escape religious or political persecution. The earliest documented immigrants were European merchants who appeared in the 13th century. Three hundred years later, Protestant Huguenots escaping violent oppression in Roman Catholic France were the first religious refugees to arrive in any number, while the 19th and 20th centuries saw the influx of hundreds of thousands of Jews (see Freedom and faith, pages 262–5). Since the 1950s similar numbers from the British colonies and the Commonwealth have come to these islands to find work (see Commonwealth migration, pages 270–1).

Records of incomers occur in a wide range of documents. Although there was no registration of foreigners, or 'aliens', until the 19th century, some documents exist from the 14th century onwards.

KEY SOURCES OF INFORMATION
♦ Subsidy rolls and port records, passenger lists, certificates of arrival, and naturalisation and deportation records at the TNA.
♦ Accounts of aliens, alien registration cards and quarter session records at county record offices.
♦ *Immigrants and Aliens* (R. Kershaw and M. Pearsall, National Archives, 2nd ed., 2004).
SEE DIRECTORY ➤

Tax records The earliest references to foreigners in Britain occur in customs and taxation records, which are held at the TNA (see DIRECTORY).

SUBSIDY ROLLS The Exchequer Subsidy Rolls, in class E 179, record taxes raised between the 12th and 17th centuries. Tax raised on movable property was used by parliament to grant money (known as subsidies) to the Crown. Foreigners paid double the standard rate and were taxed separately from 1440 to 1487. Returns are arranged by county, year of the monarch's reign, administrative sub-divisions called 'hundreds', and finally by town or village. Many of the returns contain lists of names, but they are not indexed, so it is helpful to know where your ancestor lived. Some subsidy rolls have been published by local history societies.

PORT RECORDS The Particulars of Customs' Accounts (class E 122) date back to 1272 and record the customs payable on goods at port. The rolls give not only the names of ships and their masters but also those of the merchants whose goods were being carried. The records are annotated to say whether the merchant was an alien, denizen (an alien

permitted certain privileges of citizenship—see page 261) or Hanse (a merchant who belonged to the Hanseatic League, a group of German towns bound together for trade purposes). These rolls are superseded from 1565 to 1799 by port books (class E 190), which record duty paid on goods. They also give the names of merchants and whether they were aliens (often abbreviated to 'Al'). Passengers who brought in goods liable to duty were also recorded. Bear in mind that there are no name indexes, and foreign names may have been Anglicised or misspelt (see Regional & foreign names, pages 302–3). No port books survive for London after 1697.

Records of arrival Arrival records of individuals date from the Revolutionary and Napoleonic Wars against France (1793–1815), when legislation was introduced to monitor immigrants.

ALIEN PASSENGER LISTS The Aliens Act of 1816 required masters of vessels to declare the number of aliens on board, along with names and descriptions, to the Inspector of Aliens or Officer of the Customs. These alien passenger lists are at the TNA in class HO 3, arranged chronologically but not indexed. Most lists from 1836 to 1869 survive (with the exception of 1860–6), although they are far from comprehensive: it is estimated that by the 1850s almost half the foreigners arriving in Britain went unrecorded. Because of this lack of accuracy, from 1869 onwards the lists were destroyed.

The melting pot of Britain

The Chinese chefs working in the 1950s at the Old Friends Restaurant (left) in Limehouse, East London, were part of a large Chinese community dating back to the 1890s that still thrives in this part of the city. Inset is a certificate of arrival for a teacher who landed from France in 1837. The political philosopher Karl Marx arrived at the Port of London in 1849, one of many Germans to come to Britain in the 19th century; his name appears on the list of aliens (right) that the ship's master was legally bound to make.

A LIST OF ALIENS.

I, the undersigned, being Master of the *City of Boulogne*
bound from *Boulogne* to the Port of London do, in compliance with the Provisions of an Act of Parliament, passed in the 6th William IV. Cap. 11, hereby declare, that the following is a full and true Account, to the best of my knowledge, of all Aliens who are now on board my said Ship or Vessel, or have landed herefrom in this Realm with their Names, Rank, Occupation and Description.

Book's Name *Whifson*   Master's Name *Wm June*

No.	Christian and Surnames. Prénoms et Noms.	Quality. Profession.	Native Country Pays de Naissance
	C. de Jarnowski	Professor	Poland
	Lartigue	Gentleman	France
	Frospak Fafin	Cordonnier	France
	Angel E de Elia		Buenos Ayres
	Charles Marx	Dr.	Prusse
	Vincenzino's	artiste to theatre	Grece
	Ercevor	Renter	Paris

ALIENS' CERTIFICATES OF ARRIVAL On entering Britain immigrants were issued with an alien's certificate of arrival. Unless a servant, the foreigner had to present this certificate to a magistrate or justice of the peace who, along with the port authorities, sent the details to the Home Office. These certificates are held at the TNA in class HO 2. They are indexed by name for the period 1826–49 (in HO 5/25–32) and are arranged by port of arrival, month and year. Most certificates from 1836 to 1852 have been preserved. After 1852 returns were destroyed.

INWARD PASSENGER LISTS From 1878 records were made of all passengers entering Britain, although British nationals were listed separately from foreigners. A large collection of inward ships' passenger lists dating from 1878 to 1960 is held at the TNA. These lists exist only for vessels whose journeys began outside Europe and the Mediterranean, although passengers picked up en route at European ports are included. Passenger lists are in class BT 26, arranged by port of arrival and date. There are no name indexes to these records.

If your ancestor's port of arrival is unknown, but you know the name of the ship and date on which he or she arrived in Britain, the Registers of Passenger Lists (class BT 32) will reveal it. The information in these registers, covering the period 1906–51, varies and often includes ages, occupations and occasionally a proposed address in Britain.

From 1960, when air travel became popular, lists were no longer centrally preserved, but shipping archives, such as the one kept by P & O Ferries, may hold copies of lists made after this date.

Registration of aliens
From the late 18th century, a series of Aliens Acts was passed as various wars, at first in Europe and then worldwide, led to widespread suspicion of foreigners. This prompted the authorities to monitor not just the arrival of aliens, but also their movements within Britain.

A natural star
Entertainment tycoon Lew Grade was born Louis Winogradsky in Russia in 1906. Six years later his family emigrated to Britain. Grade became a dancer and with his brothers went on to dominate British show business, making a huge impact on his adopted land. In 1937 Grade successfully applied for naturalisation and in 1976 he became a peer. Baron Grade died in 1998.

ALIENS ACT 1793 The first Aliens Act required new immigrants to register their names, ranks and occupations with a justice of the peace. The Act also obliged anyone with whom immigrants lived to register details with the parish overseer (see Poor & destitute, pages 150–1). These accounts of aliens, householders' notices and overseers' returns are held in county record offices with quarter sessions records.

ALIENS ACT 1905 With the passing of the 1905 Aliens Act pauper or criminal aliens could be expelled and courts could deport convicted foreign nationals. Records of petty, borough and quarter sessions, and magistrate courts, are held at county record offices. The TNA holds registers of deportees in class HO 372. Some personal files and individual orders can be found in classes HO 45 and HO 144. Information on deportees usually includes full name, nationality, date of conviction and offence.

ALIENS REGISTRATION ACT 1914 This called for the registration of all aliens over the age of 16 with the police, and for their re-registration if any of their personal details changed. For the first time, the government obtained accurate information on the age, nationality, profession and address of aliens in Britain.

Although no central register survives, police copies of alien registration cards are held in county record offices and in police archives across Britain. Many include a photograph. In most cases only a sample batch of cards survives and access varies, with some cards being kept in closed files. By 2002 all surviving alien registration cards held by the Metropolitan Police will be available at the TNA.

becoming a British citizen

Aliens who wanted to settle in Britain could apply for naturalisation, which granted full citizenship.

Naturalisation before 1844 Prior to 1844 naturalisation could only be acquired by a private Act of Parliament. This was an expensive business, as applicants had to pay for lawyers to draft the legislation.

The case was more likely to be successful if the applicant had influential friends.

In the 17th and 18th centuries there were cases of multiple naturalisations, often for groups of Huguenots and other refugees (see Freedom and faith, pages 262–5).

Naturalisation after 1844 In 1844 the Naturalisation Act made it easier and cheaper for aliens to become naturalised Britons. As a result, far more people applied for naturalisation and in the latter half of the 19th century the Home Office introduced a number of restrictions. Aliens now had to be self-supporting and speak English; in addition, a British-born householder had to vouch for an alien's respectability and all applications had to be approved by the police.

Background papers, applications, police reports and resident references are held at the TNA in classes HO 1, HO 45 and HO 144. Certificates of naturalisation are subject to the 30 year closure rule (see page 23). Certificates issued before 1870 are in class C 54, those issued after this date are in HO 334. A surname index at the TNA provides the full name of all aliens who applied for and received naturalisation, their country of origin, town of residence and the certificate and background paper file numbers. These numbers can be used to find the individual case files and certificates.

Denization Early immigrants who were unable to afford naturalisation could petition the Crown to become denizens, which gave them most of the rights enjoyed by a citizen. Children born after the denization of their parents were classed as native subjects. The Patent Rolls, held at the TNA in class C 66, record denizations. Those before 1509 can be found in *Calendar of Patent Rolls Preserved at the Public Record Office*, published by HMSO. Individuals are not listed separately in the indexes; you will need to look under 'Denizations' or 'Indigenae'. Indexes of denization after 1509 have been published by the Huguenot Society (see DIRECTORY). Copies of these are held at the TNA and larger reference libraries.

new Britons

freedom and faith

Britain has often played host to people fleeing tyranny in other parts of the world. Those that settled here were free to practise their religion without fear

In 16th-century Europe a desire to rid the Church of corruption led to the Reformation and, ultimately, the separation of the Protestant and Roman Catholic churches. This prompted the persecution of Protestants by the Roman Catholic authorities on the Continent, and the resulting tide of refugees, at first unwelcome in Britain, settled in the Low Countries. During the reign of Edward VI (1547–53), however, English Protestantism became more firmly established and many exiles found a new home in Britain.

Records of Protestants in exile In 1571 two surveys of aliens living in London were taken. These listed the names of immigrants and, sometimes, their place of origin and occupation. This information has been published in calendar form and is held at the TNA in classes SP 10 and SP 12; it is also available at reference libraries.

the arrival of the Huguenots

The Huguenots were French Protestants who fled to Holland and Britain in their thousands in the 16th and 17th centuries. There were two main influxes: in 1572, after the St Bartholomew's Day Massacre, when as many as 70,000 Huguenots were killed by order of Charles IX; and then in 1685, after the revocation of the 1598 Edict of Nantes, which had granted religious toleration to Protestants.

a Huguenot family: the Garricks

When the Huguenots came to Britain in the 16th and 17th centuries, they brought their trades and capital with them. Skilled craftsmanship coupled with sound business sense soon led to the development of thriving industries, which greatly benefited Britain's economy. The Garricks were one of the Huguenot families who built a new life in Britain: within three generations they had found a firm place in the English establishment, and produced one of the world's finest actors.

David Garric
David Garric was a Huguenot refugee from Languedoc who came to London in October 1685. The following March he was granted denization, and in 1695 he was naturalised by Parliament.

m. Jane Sarrazin
Jane followed her husband to London in 1685, with her infant son Peter.

Peter Garrick
The four-month-old Peter survived a perilous boat journey to England in 1685; in 1688 he received a grant of denization. Huguenot names were usually Anglicised within a generation, and a 'k' was soon added to his surname. Peter joined the British army in 1706.

m. Arabella Clough
Peter's wife Arabella, mentioned in his will, was the daughter of the vicar of Lichfield Cathedral.

Huguenot records Huguenot immigrants are listed in a series of State papers in classes SP 10, SP 12, SP 31 and SP 32 at the TNA. These lists have been published in calendar form, and there are copies at the TNA and larger reference libraries.

More information on Huguenots is held at the TNA in the Privy Council Miscellaneous Unbound Papers (class PC 1), mainly dating from 1700, and Privy Council Registers (class PC 2), dating from 1540. These papers include notes on applications for denization (the granting of limited privileges of citizenship—see page 261) and policy papers on matters such as the raising of money to assist refugees. The registers are indexed and Huguenots are listed under 'French Protestants'.

DENIZATION RECORDS Huguenot applications for denization in the 17th century (see page 261) can be found in Paper Entry Books at the TNA in classes SP 44 to SP 47.

NATURALISATION RECORDS In 1708 the Naturalisation of Foreign Protestants Act allowed all

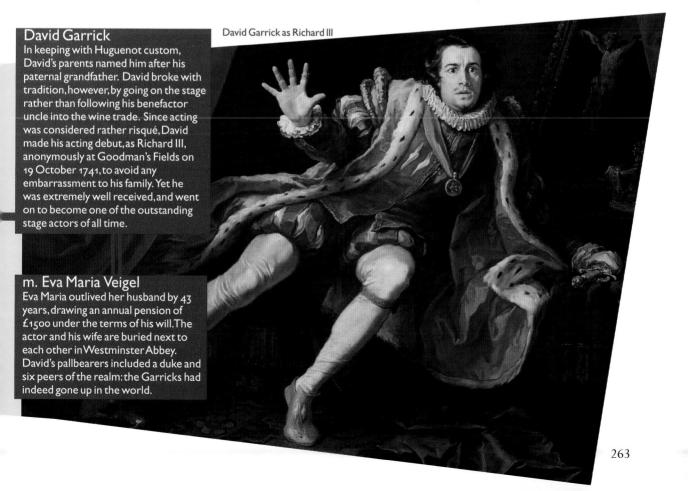

David Garrick as Richard III

David Garrick

In keeping with Huguenot custom, David's parents named him after his paternal grandfather. David broke with tradition, however, by going on the stage rather than following his benefactor uncle into the wine trade. Since acting was considered rather risqué, David made his acting debut, as Richard III, anonymously at Goodman's Fields on 19 October 1741, to avoid any embarrassment to his family. Yet he was extremely well received, and went on to become one of the outstanding stage actors of all time.

m. Eva Maria Veigel

Eva Maria outlived her husband by 43 years, drawing an annual pension of £1500 under the terms of his will. The actor and his wife are buried next to each other in Westminster Abbey. David's pallbearers included a duke and six peers of the realm: the Garricks had indeed gone up in the world.

French Protestant refugees to become naturalised British subjects without having to obtain a private Act of Parliament. Naturalisation was conditional on their swearing allegiance to the Crown in court, and proving that they were Protestants by receiving the Holy Sacrament in a Protestant congregation. A list of aliens who took this oath of allegiance in the Court of Exchequer appears on an oath roll in the TNA (class E 169/86); the accompanying sacrament certificates, signed by the officiating clergyman, also survive (E 196/10). Both have been published, in Huguenot Society Publications volumes xxv and xxvii. The surviving records of other courts are few: oaths taken in the Court of King's Bench may be found in class KB 24/2, and there are some surviving sacrament certificates for the Court of Chancery in class C 224. Records of oaths taken at quarter sessions can be found in quarter sessions records, held in county record offices (see DIRECTORY).

foreign Protestant churches

The registers of foreign Protestant churches in England are a useful source of biographical information about members of the congregation. Records of Walloon (French-speaking Belgians) and French churches, and the Dutch, German and French Chapels Royal at St James's Palace, are held at the TNA in class RG 4 (see DIRECTORY). The archive of the Russian Orthodox Church in London from 1721 to 1927, written mainly in Russian and Greek, is in TNA class RG 8.

Transcripts of Huguenot registers have been made by the Huguenot Society (see DIRECTORY); most are available in major libraries.

The library of the French Protestant Church of London in Soho Square (see DIRECTORY) keeps its own registers (which are not open to the public).

Refugees in Ireland Huguenot churches in Ireland were either part of the Church of Ireland or were Nonconformist. The Nonconformist churches kept their own records. Some Irish registers have been published by the Huguenot Society.

In 1709 there was an influx of Protestants from the Palatine area of the Rhine, in Germany, to Ireland. The Palatines largely became followers of Charles Wesley's Methodist movement, and records of the communities they established can be found in the registers of the Church of Ireland (see Parish records, page 87) or in records of the Methodist Church (see Nonconformists, pages 102–5).

other European emigrés

French emigrés Records of emigrés from the French Revolution (1789–99) can be found at the TNA in Treasury records for the French Refugee Relief Committee (class T 93) and also under Miscellanea (class T 50). There are also references in the Bouillon Papers (classes HO 69 and PC 1).

Polish and Spanish refugees The British government paid allowances to some Polish and Spanish refugees in the 19th century. References to these payments can be found at the TNA in class PMG 53.

Jewish immigration Jews began to settle in Britain in significant numbers from 1656 (see The Jewish faith, pages 110–11) when Oliver Cromwell agreed not to enforce the 1290 Edict of Expulsion, which had expelled medieval Jewry from Britain.

Religious persecution in Poland, Russia and the Baltic states under the Russian Tsars Alexander III and Nicholas II sparked a wave of Jewish emigration towards the end of the 19th century. The United States was the main destination but Britain became a staging post. The decision of many migrants to remain in Britain is evident in census returns for the East End of London. These can be consulted at the TNA (see The census, pages 62–71). Metropolitan Police correspondence and papers in TNA class MEPO 2 also provides information on the landing and settlement of immigrants.

Nearly half a million Jews relocated to Britain between 1880 and 1905, when the flow was curbed by the Aliens Act (see page 261). Many more arrived in Britain from Nazi Germany in the 1930s (see Displaced by world war, pages 266–9).

Following their faith
Jews the world over celebrate passover, or Pesah, every spring. Traditionally, this ancient festival is held for eight days and commemorates the escape of the Israelites from Egypt, described in the Bible. As a reminder of the hardships suffered on the journey from Egypt, the head of the household invites travellers to join the feasting. Many Jews who suffered persecution in their native lands in modern times settled in Britain, where a more tolerant society allowed them to follow their way of life. This picture shows a family celebrating passover in the 1950s in Whitechapel, in the East End of London, where many Jews originally settled. Today the Jewish faith is strongest in north and north-west London, Manchester, Leeds and Glasgow.

TAKING IT FURTHER

♦ *Immigrants in Tudor and Early Stuart England* (eds. N. Goose and L. Luu, Sussex Academic Press, 2005).

Information on the Internet
♦ www.CyndisList.com/huguenot.htm
♦ www.nationalarchives.gov.uk/records/research-guides/immigrants.htm
♦ www.nationalarchives.gov.uk/records/research-guides/naturalisation.htm

new Britons
displaced by world war

War was the main reason for the large-scale movement of people during the 20th century. Many of those displaced by fighting in their homeland found a safe refuge in Britain

Home from home

Polish troops fought alongside the Allies during the Second World War after their country was invaded by Germany in 1939. After the war Poland was occupied by the Soviet Union and many thousands of Poles chose to stay in Britain rather than live under a Communist regime. These children, living at a hostel in Fairford, Gloucestershire, proudly show off their national costume. Despite efforts by the Polish government to entice the Poles back home, most remained in their adopted land.

KEY SOURCES OF INFORMATION

◆ Personal records of European refugees and lists of internees and prisoners of war at the TNA and the Home Office.

SEE DIRECTORY ➤

As hostilities in Europe in the first half of the 20th century spiralled into worldwide conflict, civilian lives were often affected just as much as those of military personnel. The First and Second World Wars led to the mass displacement of peoples right across the continent of Europe, with many thousands of refugees finding a safe haven and eventually a new life in Britain. Others less fortunate found themselves in internment or prisoner of war camps on British soil.

Jewish refugees

The personal records of Jewish immigrants who fled from Nazi persecution in Germany in the 1930s are gradually being transferred to the TNA from the Home Office (see DIRECTORY). Only a sample of files, however, will be preserved, in class HO 382, in order to show how the Home Office handled the large numbers of refugees entering Britain during this period. Until all the selected files have been transferred and opened, the Home Office will continue to respond to enquiries from researchers. It will be many years before all the selected files are available to the public.

Local Jewish records A number of records relating to Jewish refugees are also held locally. Large numbers of Jews, en route from Tilbury Docks where they landed, settled in or around London. Many of them passed through the Jewish Temporary Shelter, which had been established in 1895 at Leman Street, Whitechapel. The London Metropolitan Archives (see DIRECTORY) holds the Shelter's records; they include files on Jewish immigrants, giving their name, age, town of origin, trade and destination after leaving the shelter.

In addition, the personal files of approximately 400,000 Jewish refugees are kept by the Jewish Refugees Committee (see DIRECTORY). These are especially rich in family information, and often provide details such as an immigrant's date and place of birth, nationality, profession, home address, date of arrival and new address in Britain.

Further information on Jewish immigrants is available at the Hartley Library at the University of Southampton, and at the Jewish Genealogical Society of Great Britain (see DIRECTORY). It is advisable to contact them first in writing, as access to the records is restricted.

Polish refugees

During the Second World War more than 160,000 Poles fought alongside British forces in Europe. Many of these Polish men did not want to return to a post-war Poland dominated by the Soviet Union, and the majority were allowed to stay in Britain. The soldiers' wives and dependent relatives joined them here, bringing the total number to around 200,000.

The Polish Resettlement Corps (PRC) The PRC helped to smooth the transition from Polish military to British civilian life. Their records are held at the TNA in class WO 315, and although the files relate mainly to administrative and policy matters, names of refugees can be found in PRC army lists.

Making them feel at home The Polish Resettlement Act of 1947 helped Poles to settle in Britain. Records relating to the setting up of camps are in Assistant Board files (classes AST 7 and AST 18) at the TNA. There are also education files at the TNA concerning the efforts made to assist Poles to learn English. For example, class ED 128 includes records of awards made to successful Polish students.

Welfare matters relating to Polish housing estates and social clubs can be found at the TNA in class LAB 26. Additional information on Polish refugees can be found in county record offices.

Czechoslovakian refugees

In 1938 Britain received refugees who had fled from Czechoslovakia. The following year some of them helped set up the Czechoslovak Refugee Trust. Files relating to the administration of the fund, together with specimen personal files of refugee families, are held in class HO 294 at the TNA. The index to personal papers is open, but many of the papers themselves are closed for 50 or 75 years, depending on the personal or national sensitivity of their contents.

Belgian refugees

Shortly after the outbreak of the First World War in 1914, Britain took in about 2000 refugees from Belgium. Refugee camps were established across Britain to accommodate them, and the Ministry of Health and the Local Government Board joined forces to deal with matters such as registration, hospitality, employment and repatriation. The history cards of individual refugees and their families are held in class MH 8 at the TNA; these include name, occupation, age and any allowances paid. County record offices also hold records for refugees housed in regional camps and hostels.

Hungarian refugees

Some personal records relating to the Hungarian refugees who entered Britain at the end of the Second World War are gradually being moved to the TNA from the Home Office. As with the files of Jewish refugees (see previous page), only a sample selection of files is being preserved, and until these files have been transferred, the Home Office will deal with enquiries from researchers.

Soviet invasion In 1956 Soviet Union forces entered Hungary to suppress anti-Communist demonstrations and uprisings. After the invasion, as many as 200,000 Hungarians fled to the West; approximately a tenth of them came to Britain. Little information has been released concerning these refugees. Around 13,000 of them remained in Britain, while 6000 went on to Canada and almost 2000 eventually returned to their homeland. Information on the admission, residence and

The caged birds sing

Some prisoners of war made creative use of their captivity during the Second World War. Many Italians were interned in camps on the Orkney Islands, where they built causeways linking Orkney's Mainland with some of the smaller islands, including Burray, where the band members above were imprisoned. The photograph, in Orkney Archives, is a rare record of such captives.

employment of the Hungarian refugees is held in class HO 352 at the TNA. The documents, however, are concerned mainly with policy matters and contain limited personal detail.

internee records

During both the First and Second World Wars, suspicion and hostility directed towards foreigners in Britain led to the policy of detaining enemy aliens in internment camps.

researchers may only see the fronts of the slips, as details about the internment are contained on the reverse and this information remains closed.

Also held at the TNA, in class HO 214, are a very small sample of internment personal files. These give details of the daily life of internees and most are now open without restriction.

Lists of internees Lists of internees' names can be found in class HO 215. The records are arranged by the name of the camp and list the internee's name, date of birth and date of release. Records of the camp administration often survive in county record offices; for example, the Manx National Heritage Library in the Isle of Man (see DIRECTORY) holds many records of internment camps set up on the island in both world wars.

prisoners of war

Little information survives at the TNA on individual enemy prisoners of war for either of the world wars.

The International Council of the Red Cross in Geneva (see DIRECTORY) keeps lists of prisoners of war of all nationalities for both wars. Searches are made only in response to written enquiries, and an hourly fee is charged.

First World War prisoners Two specimen lists of German servicemen who were interned as prisoners of war during the First World War are held at the TNA in classes WO 900/45 and WO 46. In addition, references to individuals may be found among Foreign Office records, notably in classes FO 371 and FO 566. Detailed indexes to both classes are in the Research Enquiries Room at the TNA.

Second World War prisoners There is no index to enemy prisoners of the Second World War, but lists of names survive among the war diaries of selected hospitals and prisoner of war camps in TNA classes WO 166 and WO 177. Also, nominal lists of prisoners of war who were temporarily interned in the Tower of London are held in class WO 94/105.

First World War internees Few personal records of internees survive for the First World War, but lists of enemy aliens submitted to the Home Office by commandants of internment camps are held at the TNA in classes HO 45 and HO 144.

Second World War internees During the first two years of the Second World War some 8000 enemy aliens, including many refugees who had fled Nazi Germany, were interned in camps. Enemy alien internment tribunal slips or cards can be found at the TNA in class HO 396. The front of these slips normally includes the alien's date of birth, address, nationality (usually German, Austrian or Italian), occupation and details of any employers.

Slips concerning aliens who were declared exempt from internment by the tribunal are open for inspection. If a decision was made to intern,

new Britons
Commonwealth migration

Documents such as certificates of nationality can tell you much about your family if your relatives were among the many thousands who flocked to Britain from the colonies in the post-war years

Taking that first step
A ship from the West Indies docks at the port of Southampton in 1961 and hundreds of new immigrants disembark. They were among the last of the colonial newcomers to enjoy easy entry before immigration was restricted in 1962.

The shortage of workers in Britain at the end of the Second World War, together with economic hardship in the West Indies, resulted in large-scale immigration from the colonies.

The newcomers' arrival at British ports can be charted in passenger lists (to 1960) held at the TNA (see DIRECTORY) in class BT 26. For example, the passenger list for SS *Empire Windrush* (BT 26/1237) records the 492 immigrants from Jamaica who came to London in June 1948 to look for work.

To search for ancestors, you need to know the port of entry and roughly when they came, as the lists are arranged by port, then year, and are not

'I came from such a bright place, so much sunshine, so much colour, it was very depressing that time of year… Some people ask you where you came from. Jamaica. And you could have come from the moon.'

Jamaican immigrant Tryphena Anderson

indexed by name. Registers of passenger lists in class BT 32 give, under the different ports, the names of ships and date of arrival up to 1951.

Processing a colonial workforce Original correspondence between the British government departments responsible for immigration and the individual colonies are among Colonial Office records at the TNA in various CO classes. Files relating to the recruitment, employment and welfare of colonial migrants are in Ministry of Labour classes LAB 8, LAB 13 and LAB 26.

emigrating with ease

Between 1948 and 1962 workers from the colonies could migrate to Britain without restriction. Under the British Nationality Act 1948, citizens of British colonies or British protectorates could simply apply to the Home Office for registration of British nationality and were issued with certificates.

The Home Office kept duplicates recording the applicant's (and spouse's) name, address, date and place of birth, the applicant's father's name and the nationality of the applicant. Sometimes referred to

as 'R' certificates, they are closed to the public for 30 years. They are held in class HO 334, arranged by certificate number rather than by name. The name indexes to the certificates are still held by the Home Office Immigration and Nationality Directorate (see DIRECTORY). If you do not know the certificate number, you should write to the directorate to obtain it before visiting the TNA.

restrictions on later immigrants

By Home Office estimates, between 1955 and 1960 some 160,000 West Indians and more than 50,000 migrants from India and Pakistan had come to live in Britain. The government favoured some control of numbers and the Immigration Acts of 1962 and 1968 increased the restrictions. To secure entry from 1962, Commonwealth immigrants with passports not issued in Britain needed a work permit. Some applications and vouchers issued for permits from 1962 to 1972 are at the TNA in class LAB 42. Though subject to the 30 year closure rule, most are now open; many include a photograph of the applicant.

The future Records relating to Ugandan Asian refugees expelled by Idi Amin in 1972, and refugees of the Vietnam War, are available at the TNA. Background information on Commonwealth migration to Britain is available at the Institute of Commonwealth Studies (see DIRECTORY).

KEY SOURCES OF INFORMATION
♦   Passenger lists, nationality certificates, work permits and background records at the TNA.
♦   Name indexes to nationality certificates at the Home Office Immigration and Nationality Directorate.
♦   *Tracing Your West Indian Ancestors* (G. Grannum, Public Record Office, 2nd ed., 2002).
SEE DIRECTORY ➤

medieval roots

If you succeed in tracing a family line as far back as
the 16th century, there is every chance that you may find
some medieval ancestors mentioned in **early records**. Much has
survived, including land records, Crown and State papers and
local manorial documents. Through the colourful pictorial language
of **heraldry** you may discover that part of your family is descended
from men who bore arms during the Crusades or the Wars of the
Roses. In the same period people began to acquire a second name,
based on occupation, geography and parents' personal names.
Your surname may provide clues to your family's earliest roots.

Work on the Royal coat of arms in 1953

early records
before parish registers

Ancient documents stored in the archives of national and local record offices in Britain can tell you much about your medieval ancestors' lives

Documents at a deathbed scene

An allegorical picture from the 15th-century work Ars Moriendi *depicts a dying man surrounded by grieving family, while a rapacious heir scours the old man's books in a bid to find evidence of his inheritance. Some wills survive from the late 14th century and you can also find many early medieval documents recording property transactions and land ownership.*

In 1538 Thomas Cromwell, chief minister to Henry VIII, ordered each parish in England and Wales to keep a register of 'every weddyng, christening and bureying' within its bounds. The event marks a watershed in the way ordinary people were recorded. In family history, records before that date are often described simply as 'early'.

It should be possible to trace at least one of your ancestral lines back to the medieval period. Your ancestors may be named as tenants or landowners in early manorial records. They might even have been granted lands and privileges in a royal charter.

how to start a search

When you begin working with medieval records, it is worth following a few basic guidelines:

☞ Be prepared to abandon the normal policy of working backwards. People often discover the fascination of early records while doing other research.

☞ Do some background reading on how medieval governments functioned and the content and context of their records. *Some Medieval Records for Family Historians* (P. Franklin, FFHS, 1994) is a clear guide to documents in print. *British Archives: a guide to archive resources in the United Kingdom* (J. Foster and J. Sheppard, Macmillan, 4th ed., 2002) lists major medieval archives.

☞ Be prepared for national and local records to overlap. The power of the Crown and State in medieval society was such that records on Bedfordshire, for example, are as likely to be held in the TNA as in that county's record office.

☞ Find printed English transcriptions of medieval records at the TNA and major reference or university libraries. Some are parallel texts that show you the form of the original. *Latin for Local History* (E. A. Gooder, Longman, 1978) explains many of the terms used.

☞ Look for documents that relate to a geographical area that interests you, such as your ancestors' town or village of origin. Some documents are indexed by both place names and surnames.

☞ Be precise. A search for information about one Geoffrey Swinscoe who lived in a particular village in Derbyshire in the mid 15th century is more likely to succeed than a general trawl for anyone with the surname Swinscoe.

☞ Do not assume that people with similar names are related. In very early works such as Domesday Book almost everyone is listed by a given name only. In parts of Wales, sons were named after their fathers well into the 19th century, which resulted in a confusion of similar names and often a change of family name every generation. As English surnames developed (see Your surname, page 298), people were often named after the place in which they lived, so that many unrelated individuals might share a name such as York.

☞ The early records of Wales, Scotland and Ireland can be very different from those of England. Although influenced by English administration at various periods in history, they had their own administrative systems, generating different types of records, often written in a native language as well as legal Latin (see pages 280–1).

KEY SOURCES OF INFORMATION

♦ English Crown and State records at the TNA.

♦ English manuscripts at the British Library.

♦ English early wills, family papers, church accounts and borough, town, corporation and guild records, at county and city record offices.

♦ Welsh wills, estate papers and other documents at the National Library of Wales and the TNA.

♦ Early Gaelic records at the National Archives of Ireland, the National Library of Ireland, the Royal Irish Academy and Trinity College, Dublin.

♦ Records of British administration in Ireland at the TNA, British Library, Lambeth Palace Library and Bodleian Library.

♦ Scottish Crown and government papers at the National Archives of Scotland.

♦ Scottish pedigrees, family papers and other early records at the National Library of Scotland.

SEE DIRECTORY ➤

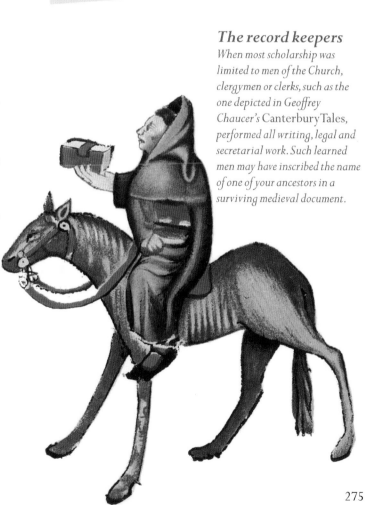

The record keepers
When most scholarship was limited to men of the Church, clergymen or clerks, such as the one depicted in Geoffrey Chaucer's Canterbury Tales, *performed all writing, legal and secretarial work. Such learned men may have inscribed the name of one of your ancestors in a surviving medieval document.*

records of Crown & State

A wealth of records, stretching back to Domesday Book of 1086, shows the workings of the English State. Most are held at the TNA and other national repositories

Most records that will help your search for medieval forebears were created by the central-ised bureaucracy of the State. Many surviving docu-ments are held at the TNA (see DIRECTORY).

Much has also been transcribed and indexed by place and name, and copies of some of the calendars (detailed listings of the records), transcripts and indexes can be found in larger reference libraries, and at the Society of Genealogists (see DIRECTORY).

The National Archives

Finding your ancestors in the TNA's vast holdings requires careful preparation. The best way to start is to become familiar with the archive through guides such as *Tracing Your Ancestors in the National Archives* (A. Bevan, National Archives, 7th ed., 2006). The indexes to the various series of records in the Court of Chancery are now available on-line through the catalogue at www.nationalarchives. gov.uk. At present, the records of the courts of Exchequer, Requests and Star Chamber are less well-indexed.

Understanding the system The various types of documents you will find illustrate the form of gov-ernment that developed after the Norman Conquest. At first the king's council (known as the curia regis) was the central government body and had administrative, financial and judicial functions. By the 14th century the functions had become separated into the Chancery, the Exchequer and various courts. The National Archives has a series of on-line research guides that include aspects

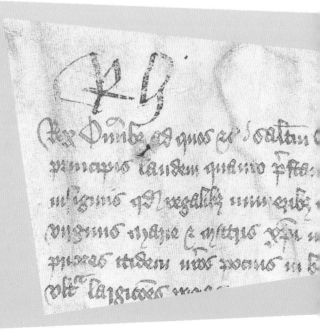

A grant of arms to Eton College
In a royal charter of 1449, Henry VI made a grant of arms to the newly built Royal College of St Mary of Eton. The flowery language is typical of its age and, after a preamble, begins: 'We assign, therefore, for arms and ensigns of arms On a field Sable, three lily-flowers Argent, bearing in mind that our newly founded College enduring for ages to come, whose perpetuity we wish to be signified by the stability of the Sable colour, will bring forth the brightest flowers redolent of science of every kind, to the honour and most devout worship of Almighty God, and the undefiled Virgin and glorious Mother, to whom as in others, so in this our foundation most especially, we offer with an ardent mind, a hearty and most earnest devotion...'. The details of royal charters were entered on Charter Rolls, which date from 1199 to 1516, when Patent Rolls took over their function.

of medieval government. See www.national archives.gov.uk/records/research-guides.

Records in print There are transcripts (many translated from the original Latin), descriptive lists and indexes for a number of the TNA's medieval records. Useful sources to start with are:

☞ *Dictionary of Genealogical Sources in the Public Record Office* (S. Colwell, Weidenfeld & Nicolson, 1992).

☞ *Guide to the Contents of the Public Record Office*, vol. I (HMSO, 1963). Copies are held at the TNA and major reference and university libraries.

☞ *British National Archives* (HMSO Government Publications, Sectional List 24, 1981) lists published finding aids, transcripts and calendars. Copies can be consulted at the TNA.

☞ The List and Index Society, based at the TNA. The society has published more than 280 volumes of indexes to, or facsimiles of, records at the TNA. Enquiries should be addressed to the society's secretary at the TNA, who can supply a list of all available material. The TNA notes the lists and indexes in its on-line catalogue.

records of the Chancery

By around 1200 the Chancery was a powerful arm of government, generating vast numbers of records, mostly in Latin, including:

CHARTER ROLLS Royal charters granting lands, rights, titles or privileges.

PATENT ROLLS Public documents, from State records to licences for the election of bishops.

CLOSE ROLLS A huge collection of private instructions from the king to officers of the Crown.

FINE ROLLS or OBLATA ROLLS Records of offers of goods or money to the king in return for privileges. A large part of the king's income derived from these 'fines'.

REGIONAL RECORDS

In the Middle Ages, the lords of Chester, Durham and Lancaster had separate judicial and administrative jurisdictions, or palatinates, which generated their own groups of archives; these records can now be found in the TNA. The Duchy of Lancaster had property and influence in nearly every county in England and Wales. There are also separate records in the TNA for the Duchy of Cornwall from 1299.

Chancery equity proceedings

From 1386 the Chancery had its own court, which applied 'equitable' principles of natural justice to cases for which the formalities of common law denied a fair outcome.

It was the busiest of such 'equity courts' and its proceedings, which are mostly in English, record a huge number of ordinary people who went to law over issues such as land ownership or marriage settlements.

Tackling the records Guides to help you find your way around Court of Chancery records include:

☞ See the TNA web sites www.nationalarchives. gov.uk/records/research-guides/chancery-equity-before-1558.htm and from-1558.htm.

☞ Appendix X of *Ancestral Trails* (M. D. Herber, Sutton, revised ed. 2000), which lists the records by class, noting indexes, transcripts and calendars.

☞ The Bernau Index at the Society of Genealogists (see DIRECTORY), which lists the first-named plaintiffs and defendants in early Chancery proceedings from 1386 to 1538.

Most Chancery records are indexed by the surname of the plaintiff only. Some depositions recording written testimony have survived.

records of the King's Exchequer

The Exchequer dealt with the state finances, both income and expenditure. It also developed its own court of law to judge cases affecting the rights and revenues of the Crown. Exchequer records include:

England brought to book

The oldest and most famous of all English public records is Domesday Book, a place-by-place survey of the land and economic resources held by the king's subjects. Covering almost the whole of England, it was made on the orders of William I and completed by Michaelmas in the year 1086. Most of the thousands of people who feature in Domesday are not named. The exception are those who held land direct from the king. The original is bound in two volumes but the way to consult it is in the 38 volume edition with original text alongside a full translation, by J. Morris, published by Phillimore, 1975–92.

PIPE ROLLS So-called from their long rolled shape, pipe rolls, written in abbreviated Latin, were annual returns of income and expenditure made by sheriffs to the Exchequer from 1155 to 1835.

KNIGHT'S FEES These were records of the land held in exchange for funding knights for the king's service. A man holding land by one knight's fee could be called upon to provide and equip one knight to serve the Crown. In England there were 60,215 knight's fees, each of about 100 acres.

SUBSIDY ROLLS These are records of a tax levied from the end of the 13th century on the

movable property of householders. They are held to 1690 in TNA class E 179 and catalogued on-line.

Exchequer equity proceedings From the late 15th century, the Court of Exchequer, like the Court of Chancery, had its own equity jurisdiction, handling matters such as land rights, and tithe and probate disputes. The website www.national archives.gov.uk/records/research-guides/equity-court-of-exchequer.htm explains how to search the records, most of which are in English.

Poll tax records These have been published as *The Poll Tax Returns of 1377, 1379 and 1381* (C. Fenwick, ed., The British Academy, 3 vols, 1997–2005).

other courts of law

The TNA also holds records of courts such as the:

COURT OF KING'S or QUEEN'S BENCH The court had jurisdiction over criminal matters on what was known as its 'Crown side', but also heard civil actions on its 'plea side'. Records of both are held in the Coram Rege Rolls, class KB 27.

COURT OF COMMON PLEAS This court had very wide jurisdiction but dealt particularly with disputes over debts and land; its records are held in group CP. The most accessible are the Feet of Fines (pedes finium), the final agreement at the end of a law suit that entitled someone to a piece of land. The TNA has feet of fines (the bottom part or 'foot' of the document was filed with the court) from the 12th century, arranged chronologically by county, with separate records for the palatinates of Chester, Durham and Lancaster.

COURT OF REQUESTS The court was established in 1483 to provide royal justice for the poor. It attracted many suitors, particularly women, and dealt with a variety of cases, including property disputes, forgery, perjury and marriage contracts. Most case papers are in class REQ 2. See www.nationalarchives.gov.uk/records/research-guides/court-of-request.htm.

COURT OF STAR CHAMBER Established in the late 15th century, the court took its name from the starred ceiling of the chamber in Westminster Palace where it sat. Its records are in English and describe cases such as riot, corruption of public officials, fraud and assaults. See www.nationalarchives.gov.uk/records/research-guides/star-chamber.htm.

special collections

The TNA also holds 15 classes of medieval documents in Special Collections (group SC). The most important are:

HUNDRED ROLLS These are investigations conducted in 1274–5 on behalf of Edward I into tenants-in-chief who sublet Crown land without licence while he was fighting in the Holy Land.

Coming before the Court of Exchequer
An ancestor who owed money to the king in the Middle Ages might have ended up facing the Court of Exchequer. Its name derived from the chequered cloth that would be laid on a table to make it easier to count out coins. Throughout the Middle Ages the Exchequer and its court was the hub of the Crown's financial administration, receiving and issuing money and hearing disputes. Increasingly, its court dealt with cases that had a bearing on royal revenues. The Exchequer's administrative role was gradually taken over by the Treasury from the 17th century, but its court continued to deal with equity cases up to 1841.

early records in Wales

The legal and administrative framework of Wales was different from that of England in the earliest medieval period because the country did not come under English rule until the late 13th century.

From that time, its legal records were much the same as those for England, although in many cases, especially in the Marches, Welsh pre-Conquest law was applied where it was of advantage to the king.

Well-documented families A major advantage for those with Welsh ancestry is that many of the Welsh were small freeholders (see Property records, pages 176–82). The tradition of inherited property extended from the later Middle Ages to the 19th century, and the pedigrees of land-owning families are often well documented in books such as *Welsh Genealogies, AD 300–1400* (P.C. Bartrum, National Library of Wales, 1988, microfiche 1980) and *Welsh Genealogies, AD 1400–1500* (P.C. Bartrum, National Library of Wales, 1983).

Anyone who can trace Welsh forebears before the Acts of Union with England of 1536 and 1542 may find they are connected to one of these families, and may even discover Welsh nobility in their ancestry.

For an overview see 'An Approach to Welsh Genealogy' (F. Jones in *Transactions of the Honourable Society of Cymmrodorion*, 1948). *The Dictionary of Welsh Biography* (Honourable Society of Cymmrodorion, 1959) lists eminent figures from pre-medieval times. Estate papers from the 12th and 13th

MINISTERS ACCOUNTS Officials such as reeves and bailiffs submitted annual returns to the king, which set out the names of tenants on various Crown lands, including some in Wales and Ireland. The records in 'Ministers' and Receivers' Accounts' are held in class SC 6 and date from the reign of Henry III (1216–72) onwards.

MANORIAL DOCUMENTS The TNA holds a significant collection of manorial documents dating from the 13th century to 1925, including those that relate to manors once held by the Crown. Most of the documents can be found in class SC 2.

centuries for some areas of Wales are noted in the catalogues of the National Library of Wales (see DIRECTORY), county record offices and major reference libraries in Wales and England.

early records in Ireland

From early medieval times the Gaelic Irish chronicled their history and genealogies in manuscript form. Among the best known are:

☞ *The Annals of the Kingdom of Ireland from the earliest time to 1616* (De Búrca Rare Books, 3rd ed., 1990). Written in 1636 by four monks, known as the 'Four Masters', it was first translated and published in 1856. Copies are held in major Irish reference libraries.

☞ *The Great Book of Lecan*—a listing of Irish genealogies, housed in the Royal Irish Academy (see DIRECTORY), which has been translated by the Irish Manuscripts Commission.

The Commission (see DIRECTORY) surveys and reports on historic manuscripts and papers and has published a number of documents about important Irish families. Its periodical *Analecta Hibernia* is of interest to family historians and sometimes carries reports on early documents held in private hands.

Early Anglo-Irish records Records of British administration in Ireland exist from the late Middle Ages. From the 16th century, collections of papers of various English administrators in Ireland are held at Lambeth Palace Library (see DIRECTORY) and the Bodleian Library (see DIRECTORY). Irish State Papers from 1509 to 1782, held at the TNA in London, are available on microfilm at the National Library of Ireland.

You may be able to find some record of material that was destroyed when the Public Record Office in Dublin was burnt down in 1922 in earlier copies of the 'Annual Reports of the Deputy Keeper of the Public Records in Ireland'. The reports are held in major Irish record offices and reference libraries.

early records in Scotland

Scotland's medieval records are quite separate from those of England; it was not until 1603 that the two countries were united, when James VI of Scotland also became James I of England.

The most comprehensive source of early records is the Register of the Great Seal, although much of this is available only in Latin. It dates from 1306 and includes all grants of land by the Scottish Crown, charters, letters of pardon and some birth briefs or certificates of descent. It has been published and indexed from 1306 to 1668 in 11 volumes with an English translation for 1652–68. Other early government documents are in the Register of the Privy Seal, published in seven volumes (1488–1580).

Property deeds dating from the 16th century can be found in the National Archives of Scotland (see DIRECTORY). The National Library of Scotland (see DIRECTORY) holds many pedigrees and family papers, mainly in Scots-English, and other early documents relating to all aspects of Scottish life.

WELSH, IRISH & SCOTTISH SOURCES

♦ *A Catalogue of the Manuscripts Relating to Wales in the British Museum* (E. Owen, Cymmrodorion Record Series no. 4, 1900–22).

♦ 'Reading Old Documents' (S. J. Davies in *Second Stages in Researching Welsh Ancestry*, J. and S. Rowlands, FFHS, 1999).

♦ *Manuscript Sources for the History of Irish Civilisation* (R. J. Hayes, Hall & Co. 1965).

♦ *Calendar of the Carew Manuscripts 1515–1624* (ed. J. Brewer and W. Bullen, Longman, 6 vols, 1867–73).

♦ *Guide to the Public Records of Scotland* (M. Livingstone, HM General Register House, 1905).

♦ *Scottish Texts and Calendars* (D. and W. Stevenson, Scottish History Society, 1987).

♦ *Green's Glossary of Scottish Legal Terms* (A. G. M. Duncan, 3rd ed., 1992).

early records
looking at documents

The structure, language and spelling of early documents can seem daunting at first. But as you acquire new skills, you will be surprised by the amount of material you can understand

Handling your first medieval manuscript should be an exciting experience. Most people never get to touch anything so old or so precious. Every manuscript is unique, for even if it was copied several times, each copy was handmade and slightly different from other versions. Reading such documents can be difficult. But if you are methodical, patient and precise, much can be achieved.

identify your document

You need to know what kind of document you are dealing with and its purpose in order to understand its structure. Official documents such as manorial court rolls usually had a fixed structure and often employed a standard form of words, with just the names and details changed in each case. This makes it relatively easy to pick out the interesting individual information from the set phrasing. Specialist guides to specific documents such as *Old Title Deeds* (N. W. Alcock, Phillimore, 2nd ed., 2001) are useful.

If you are consulting a manuscript in an archive such as the TNA or British Library, you will know from the way you traced it, and from the way it is catalogued, what it is. Documents not kept in Crown or State archives generally fall into one of the categories listed on page 287.

establish a date

The next step is to date the document, and for this you need to know how medieval dates were written. The year is usually given by reference to the reigning monarch (rather than using 'anno domini' as a dating mechanism), with days and months indicated by means of a saint's day. A typical example might read something like this:

> *… on Monday next after the Feast of St Thomas the Apostle in the 11th year of the reign of King Edward the Third after the Conquest.*

In this example, you would calculate as follows:

STEP ONE Edward III reigned from 25 January 1327 to 21 June 1377; so the eleventh year of his reign would be 25 January 1337 to 24 January 1338.

STEP TWO The annual date of the feast of St Thomas the Apostle is 21 December, which in this case must be in 1337. (Note that saints are often associated with more than one day in the year, so make sure that you are looking up the feast of St Thomas, and not, for example, the day of his 'translation', which was 3 July.)

STEP THREE A perpetual calendar—a chart that indicates which day of the week corresponds to any given date over a period of many years—shows that 21 December 1337 fell on a Sunday. Therefore, the following Monday would have been the next day, 22 December 1337, and that is the date referred to in the manuscript.

Both *The Oxford Dictionary of Saints* (D. Farmer, OUP, 5th ed., 2004) and *Dates and Calendars for the Genealogist* (C. Webb, Society of Genealogists, reprinted 1998) are helpful. The On-line Calendar of Saints' Days at http://members.tripod.com/~gunhouse/calendar/months.htm and the Regnal Year Calculator at www.albion.edu/english/calendar/regnal.htm may also be useful.

Reading the text Even experienced scholars can take a while to decipher some medieval documents. You will come across all manner of irregular spellings, contractions of certain words and the use of the three following languages:

ANGLO-NORMAN From the Norman Conquest of 1066 until the mid 14th century, a French dialect known as Anglo-Norman was the language of State and legal documents. Basic school French may be enough to help you through an Anglo-Norman text once you get used to the rather different spelling of many words—'ki' for 'qui' (who), for example, or 'toutz' for 'toutes' (all).

LATIN Following a statute of 1362, Latin became the legal language used in most formal documents such as land transactions, often interspersed with Anglo-Norman or English words. English names were frequently Latinised—'Guilielmus' for William or 'Humfredus' for Humphrey. For help with the vocabulary, it is worth consulting books such as *Basic Approach to Latin for Family Historians* (M. Gandy, FFHS, 1995) and *Revised Medieval Latin Word List* (R. E. Latham, British Academy, 2004).

ENGLISH By the end of the 15th century, English —called Middle English between the 12th and 15th centuries—began to re-emerge in some legal documents. But the words can be spelt in an unfamiliar way, such as 'maryde' for 'married', 'grete' for 'great', or 'speck' for 'speak'.

Perhaps the greatest difficulty, whatever language you are reading, is abbreviations. Scribes developed a system of shorthand to save time and space. Some words were reduced to the initial letter, as in A.D. for 'Anno Domini'; others were contracted, as in Mr for 'Master', or wt for 'with'. Usually missing letters were indicated by a loop or a line above the word.

Useful guides to interpreting these marks include *The Record Interpreter* (C.T. Martin, Phillimore, 1982) and *Medieval Local Records: a reading aid* (K.C. Newton, Historical Association, 1971).

reading an early private letter

Right worshipful and to me singular good lady, I recommend me unto you, praying you to send me a buck on Wednesday next coming, according to the promise that my master and you made at my last being with you; for a special friend of mine shall be married on Thursday next coming, to the which I have promised a buck; wherefore I pray you that he be not disappointed. And my service shall be the more readier to you at all times with the grace of God, which have you in keeping. Written in haste, the 18th day of July.

By your servant
William Goldwyn.
Madam, I pray you to speak to my master
for the £16 that is due unto me.

The rare surviving examples of private correspondence can provide a touching insight into everyday medieval life. In a letter from 1480, transcribed into modern English (left), William Goldwyn petitions his employer's wife for a buck (deer) for the wedding feast of a friend. The original is held at the TNA (Ancient Correspondence, reference sc 1/46/242).

Overleaf, the original letter is shown with notes to pinpoint difficulties in the text; a direct transcript indicates abbreviations used by its author.

DECIPHERING THE WORDS

1 This word contains an obsolete letter, called a 'yogh'— replaced by the letters 'y', 'g' or 'gh' as English evolved. Do not confuse it with a 'z'. The whole word is 'Ryght' (Right).

2 This symbol was used for Latin 'et', meaning 'and'. It was not the same as an ampersand (&), although this is the easiest way of representing it.

5 This word contains another obsolete letter, called 'thorn'. You should simply transcribe it as 'th', giving the word 'the'. Later forms of this letter resemble 'y', producing words that look like 'ye' and 'yat'. The sense would be 'the' and 'that'. But watch out for cases where 'ye', meaning 'you', is actually intended.

6 Note the loop behind this 'p': it indicates that the letters 'ro' are suspended. The word is 'promysse' (promise).

7 The little curl on this 't' indicates the letters 'er'. The word is 'Master'.

11 In this word ('service'), the long 's' has a loop, indicating that the letters 'er' are missing. The 'c' is only half-formed and flows directly into the finale.

The letter, word for word
This transcript preserves the original spelling and capitalisation, but has modern punctuation to make the sense clear. Omitted letters in the original document are indicated by a lighter colour.

Ryght worschypfull & to me Syngulere good lady, I recommende me vn-to yow, Prayng yow to sende me A Buck A wedynsday nexte commyng acordyng to the promysse that my Master & ye made At my laste beyng with yow; for A specyall frende of myn schall be maryde on thursday nexte commyng, to the wyche I have promysyde A buck; wherfor I pray yow that he be not dispoyntyde. And my service schall be the more redyer to yow at all tymys with the grace of god, wyche have yow in kepyng. wryttyn in haste the .xviij Day of Jule.

> By yowr servant,
> willam Goldwyn.

Madam, I pray yow to speck to my Master for the .xvj libri that ys dew vn-to me.

3 There are two suspension marks here: the writer has given his 'r' a little flourish, which represents a missing 'e'; and he has drawn a 'bar' or 'tittle' over the middle of the word to indicate a missing 'm'. The whole word is 'recommende' (recommend).

4 The letters 'u' and 'v' were usually interchangeable, and many words that are now joined were written as separate items. The word here is 'vn-to' (unto).

8 This was a common abbreviation for the word 'with', in use until the 19th century.

9 Thursday has a small 't'. There was no consistency in the use of capital letters.

10 Note that the scribe used two forms of 'r' in the same word—'wherfor' (wherefore). You will become familiar with several different forms of the same letter.

13 Numbers were usually written using Roman numerals (see Getting started, page 45).

15 The Latin word 'libri' (pounds, or £) is indicated by the letters 'li' with a flourish.

12 This is an 'i' with a loop, indicating a missing 'n'. The word is 'in'.

14 The petitioner's name is written 'willm', with a special superscript 'a'; the whole is therefore 'willam' (William).

early records
reflecting local life

Record offices close to where your ancestors lived before the 16th century may hold a range of old documents that can help you to establish medieval links

Many documents recording everyday medieval transactions have survived and are stored in local record offices. Their catalogues are listed on the web site www.a2a.org.uk For a listing of county and city record offices, see DIRECTORY.

manorial records

Manorial documents can be useful whether your ancestors were freeholders, leaseholders or held land by some other kind of tenure (see Property records, pages 176–87).

The surviving documents are scattered and are still bought and sold on the open market by manuscript dealers or at auction.

The Manorial Documents Register, for England and Wales only, is an index of manors, arranged by county, which lists the location of all manorial records that have been registered by their owners. The register is held at the TNA. Type in the name of a manor on the web site www.mdr.nationalarchives.gov.uk to find where records are held.

OUTSIDE THE REGISTERS Possibly as many unregistered documents exist as registered ones. A study of ownership of an individual manor down the generations might lead you to a collection of manorial records held by a solicitor or in a private deed box. You may also find details of local manors and landowners from the *Victoria History of the Counties of England*, a continuing project covering most of the country in more than 200 volumes and usually available from local libraries. See www.victoriacountyhistory.ac.uk.

Organising a medieval household
In the late Middle Ages, a lady would be taught to read and write by a chaplain or clerk, or sometimes at a nunnery. She had to learn how to manage a household and perhaps an estate in her husband's absence, and would have kept domestic accounts.

other local documents

You may find borough, corporation, town and guild records in a local archive, or family documents such as deeds, correspondence and accounts, deposited as a gift or on extended loan. Try to find a catalogue of the archive's contents starting with the web site www.a2a.org.uk

Other types of material that can be uncovered in a local record office include parochial records such as early churchwardens' accounts, which may list individuals such as parish officers.

A large amount of medieval probate material survives, including wills for the Prerogative Court of Canterbury from 1383 and for the Exchequer and Prerogative Courts of York from 1389 (see Tracing wills before 1858, pages 129–31).

A glossary of terms As you rummage through medieval documents you may encounter some unfamiliar terms. Early manuscripts, other than those held in Crown or State archives, are likely to fall into one of the following categories:

CARTULARY A volume, usually compiled by a monastery, containing items such as deeds or details of charitable gifts.

CHARTER Deed or transfer of property title, often an important grant made in perpetuity.

FEOFFMENT A grant of property.

FINE OR FINAL CONCORD The record made of a fictitious law suit, designed to formally record a landowner's title to property.

GIFT Any transfer of buildings or land.

GRANT The transfer of property other than buildings or land.

INDENTURE A deed made out in duplicate and cut in an indented fashion so that the two parts could later be matched to prove authenticity.

LEASE The grant of property to a tenant for a specified period of time.

MANORIAL DOCUMENT Any papers such as court rolls relating to a manor or group of manors.

QUITCLAIM A deed in which an individual renounces any right to property.

TAKING IT FURTHER

♦ *Texts and Calendars* (E.L.C. Mullins, Royal Historical Society, 2 vols, 1978 and 1983) is a useful guide to many medieval works in print.
♦ County histories such as *The History and Antiquities of the County of Somerset* (J. Collinson, Cruttwell, 1791) often include information relating to local families in medieval times.
♦ The former Royal Commission on Historical Manuscripts (now the TNA) has published detailed inventories of many private manuscripts held by individuals, colleges, cathedrals, abbeys, guilds, corporations and the House of Lords. The TNA's National Register of Archives can help you to find manorial, tithe and other property records, including Irish estate papers removed from Ireland by returning landlords.
♦ Major reference libraries may hold copies of bishops' registers and other early ecclesiastical records for various dioceses published by the Canterbury and York Society from 1906. Bishops' registers recorded local details of clergy and church affairs in various parts of England and Wales.
♦ *Welsh Manors and Their Records* (H. Watt, National Library of Wales, 2000).
♦ Ancestors of high status may be located in *The Dictionary of National Biography: from the earliest times to 1900* (L. Stephen and S. Lee, Oxford University Press, 1963–5), available in libraries; or *The Oxford Dictionary of National Biography* (Oxford University Press, 2004); or by visiting the web site www.oxforddnb.com; or by consulting *Burke's Peerage & Baronetage* (C. Mosley, Fitzroy Dearborn, 106th ed., 1999).

RECOVERY A complex record of property ownership, similar to a 'fine'.

WILL Wills that are similar in structure to those of today exist from the late 14th century. In certain parts of these wills the wording has also remained relatively unchanged.

heraldry
a family badge of honour

Heraldic insignia such as shields and crests appear on anything from graves to crockery. Before you follow up such a find, it helps to understand the history behind heraldry

The arms of Marmion Edward Ferrers

MARMION EDWARD FERRE[RS]
LORD OF BADDESLEY CLINT[ON]
BY RIGHT BARON DE FERRERS
CHARTLEY & BARON COMPT[ON]

Plate repeating heraldic crests

Georgian chair decorated with its owner's arms

Have you ever found a crested ring or an armorial bookplate among your family heirlooms? While such souvenirs often use heraldic insignia incorrectly, many people are descended from a family that has a coat of arms.

If you find a coat of arms in your family, you may be able to gather much information about your forebears, including a pedigree showing lines of descent, and information about the family itself from its insignia (see What arms can reveal, pages 292–5).

medieval origins

Coats of arms belong to a tradition going back to the 12th century. They originated when knights in battle were armoured from head to foot, and to identify themselves they adopted a range of easily recognised symbols and designs, which they displayed on their shields and on the surcoat that they wore over their armour. This 'surcoat' is the origin of the term 'coat of arms', or 'arms' for short.

Heraldic designs The designs could be simple, such as a red diagonal stripe on a silver background,

A glimpse of heraldic history
People who had acquired arms enjoyed displaying them, often ostentatiously. Personal belongings, from bookplates to silver, china and glass, were excellent sites for insignia, as were larger items such as furniture or more public commemorations such as stained glass. Family heirlooms may lead you to a new area of information about your ancestors.

or a row of black lozenges on a gold background. They could also combine different patterns in a complex array of stripes, crosses, chevrons, circles, images of animals, birds and plants—indeed almost anything that appealed to the user. The arrangement of these items on the knight's shield gave rise to the central element of any coat of arms, known as an escutcheon or shield.

Helmets and crests Helmets covered a knight's face and were fitted with a loose cloth called a lambrequin, or mantling, held in place by a wreath or coronet. Both of these became increasingly decorative, and were expanded to include an elaborate crest, which topped the whole helmet.

Crests were too unwieldy for use in battle, but knights wore them in tournaments. Their crested helmets were often lined up before the jousts so everyone could see who was present and whom to challenge.

The role of the herald It was also important for tournament officials, known as heralds, to be able to recognise knights by their arms—which were displayed on both shield and helmet. Heralds and their assistants—pursuivants (literally 'followers', who undertook duties for the heralds)—proclaimed the start of proceedings, the identity of combatants and the victor of any engagement. After checking the arms of all would-be participants, heralds would challenge people using arms that they knew were already in use by someone of status.

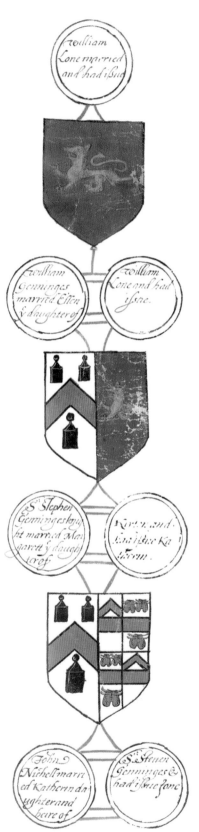

Heraldic family records
A 16th-century herald made this pedigree, going back two centuries; it includes Sir William Jennings, who became Mayor of London at Henry VIII's coronation in 1509. Heraldic records such as these can help you to trace your ancestors back to medieval times.

By the 14th century, heralds were the acknowledged experts on coats of arms and who they belonged to; heraldry takes its name from these officials, who are still its regulators.

Heralds were much more than tournament dignitaries. In battle they acted as army staff officers with responsibility for recognising commanders by their insignia. This allowed a herald to inform his master about who was fighting whom, who had withdrawn from the field, and who was yet to attack.

Rolls and armorials To assist their work, heralds drew up lists—rolls of arms, or simply rolls—of all the arms they saw at tournaments and other gatherings of fighting men. Later, the chief heralds would make a list of all who had taken part in battle and preserve this as another roll of arms. Such rolls of arms were assembled into collections called armorials, which contain invaluable information about early coats of arms and the men who used them.

Royal control In 1415 heralds complained to Henry V about the difficulty of telling some knights apart at the Battle of Agincourt because of the similarity of many coats of arms. Henry then introduced the first royal order aimed at

heraldry

Heraldic identikit in vellum
When knights arrived to fight—whether it was for honour in a tournament or for their lord in battle—their presence was recorded by the heralds. The knights depicted on the armorial roll shown above can be identified from their coats of arms as Denis (left) and Borges, who lived in Kent in the mid 15th century. If your family has a link to an old title, you might discover your ancestors in these rolls of arms.

controlling the use of arms. It was not successful, and the system remained in some disorder until Richard III established the College of Arms, led by the chief heralds (the Kings of Arms), as an incorporated body with a permanent home for the heralds' records in London.

the first records of genealogies

In 1530, Henry VIII sent his heralds throughout England and Wales to register all rightful coats of arms and eradicate the rest. In these 'visitations', everyone claiming to be a gentleman and using a coat of arms had to appear before the heralds and justify his claim. Some of these 'armigers' (people with arms) could show an official grant of arms from an earlier King of Arms; others had to prepare pedigrees of their families showing how the arms had been passed on down the centuries. Many others who had simply adopted arms in order to seem important were forced to renounce them.

Visitations continued every 20 to 30 years until 1686 and produced an incomparable collection of records (see Authorities of arms, pages 296–7). These include the pedigrees of people who could prove their rights to arms, usually going back three to five generations from the date of compilation. There are pedigrees of families from many levels of society, together with registered 'disclaimers' from those who were forced to give up their arms.

knights become nobles

Knights had social and political status, and it was out of the system of knighthood that the peerage arose—so heraldry came to be associated with titles and nobility. Some knights were called to serve on the king's council, the gathering of powerful nobles on whose cooperation the king depended, and they became known as barons. Others secured the border areas known as marches—hence the title marquis. Counts exercised control, especially in military matters, over large territories (the origin of 'county'). These men came to be known as earls, from the Anglo-Saxon word 'yarl', meaning count—so the wife of an earl is a countess. At the top of the hierarchy were dukes, so powerful that their lands were almost autonomous countries.

Most peers, when their title was created, were given particular responsibilities for attending Parliament to offer advice and assistance to the king. Usually both title and parliamentary duties were handed down from father to eldest son, a system that became the basis of the hereditary peerage that used to operate in the House of Lords. Today the peerage consists of five ranks: duke, marquis, earl, viscount and baron. Below them is the class of baronet, created by James I in 1611, which is hereditary but has never carried a parliamentary seat.

extended to the gentry

Medieval landowners who were not part of the nobility might also use coats of arms, since they could be called on to fight in times of war. Over time such landowners have become known as the gentry, or 'untitled aristocracy', bearing the ranks of Esquire and Gentleman. Even today, new coats of arms are granted only to gentlemen—that is, people viewed by the College of Arms as having respectable positions in society.

are you entitled?

In principle, only one person is entitled to use a particular coat of arms. When the armiger dies, the arms are passed on first and foremost through sons; a daughter is entitled to inherit arms only if she has no brothers or they and their children are dead. Finding a coat of arms in the family does not necessarily mean that you are entitled to use it. If you think you may be, the first step is to work out a

family pedigree that traces your origins to an established armiger. You then need to submit this with supporting documentation to the appropriate authority for England and Wales, Ireland or Scotland (see Authorities of arms, pages 296–7).

CHANGES TO A COAT OF ARMS   You must also notify the armorial authorities of any change to a coat of arms, for example, because of marriage or through descent. This is to make sure that the arms are correctly used and to enable the authorities to update their records. In many cases, official permission is needed before a change can be made, especially in Scotland, where it is an offence to use arms without proper authorisation.

APPLYING FOR A NEW GRANT   Even if you are not entitled to arms by descent you may be able to have a new coat of arms created for yourself. Having a coat of arms specially designed is a lengthy and expensive process, and you will need to prove your 'gentility' as described above.

A heraldic perk of celebrity
People today can apply for arms. Elton John's arms incorporate piano keys and discs, referring to his musical and recording successes, and are in red, yellow and black—the colours of Watford Football Club, which he supports ardently. The motto means both 'Elton is good' and 'the tune is good'.

heraldry
what arms can reveal

Finding an ancestral coat of arms is a prospect family historians look forward to. But you need to be able to 'read' the arms in order to find out what they tell you about your family's past

You need to know the basic components of a coat of arms and how to describe them in order to be able to look up the arms of your ancestor. Heraldic terminology was devised by heralds in the Middle Ages, when French was the 'official' language of chivalry, so it is based largely on Norman French. There is a large and complex vocabulary for describing precisely every element in a coat of arms, and you will need to consult a reference book such as one of those on page 295 for a comprehensive guide to the significance of the different symbols.

what is a coat of arms?

A full coat of arms is called an 'achievement of arms', or an achievement, for short. It includes the shield with its colours, design and images; the helmet above, and its wreath, crown or coronet, and its mantling and crest; the 'supporters' (often heraldic animals such as the lion and the unicorn) beside the shield; and the motto.

For most purposes, coats of arms are simplified to just the escutcheon, or shield, and the crest. This is

unlocking the past

If you find a coat of arms on a tomb or a letterhead it will probably be clear who it belongs to. You then check the details in the *General Armory of England, Scotland, Ireland and Wales* (B. Burke, repr. Heraldry Today, 1984).

It is more complex if you find insignia not associated with a particular person. Suppose you found this bookplate in an old volume, without any inscribed name.

The first step to finding the owner of the coat of arms is to create a 'blason', or description. This always starts with the shield.

The shield is divided down the middle, indicating a marriage between two armigerous families. It is thus said to be impaled: you can find more on each side as detailed opposite. The blason then covers the crest, which consists of a spotted (Pied) greyhound, in its natural colours (proper) and wearing a gold collar (collared Or), sitting (sejant) on a green mound (mount Vert).

what you will see on tombs, bookplates, crockery and silverware. Even this simpler form is enough to tell you much about the possessor. The most important part is the shield's description, its 'blason' (see Unlocking the past, below). Then you can find your ancestor (see Looking up the arms, pages 294–5).

The escutcheon, or shield This is the heart of a coat of arms. The background is known as the field and it can take on many different colours and designs, including the emblems, known as ordinaries.

HOW MARRIAGE CAN CHANGE ARMS

If an armiger's daughter marries a man with his own arms, her husband may place his father-in-law's arms beside his own on a divided shield—'impalement' (see below). If a wife has inherited her father's arms, her husband may put them on a small shield on his shield—an 'escutcheon of pretence'. Their children can combine the arms by 'quartering' them—thus arms show family developments.

1. The wife's arms are the fleur-de-lys ordinary (emblem) on an Azure (blue) field (background).

2. The husband's arms comprise the ordinary known as the cross, on a field of Or (gold).

3. The husband can put a smaller version of his wife's arms onto his—an 'escutcheon of pretence'.

4. The children 'quarter' the arms—father's 1st and 4th quarters, mother's 2nd and 3rd quarters.

THE HUSBAND'S ARMS

His arms are quartered (quarterly) from an earlier union of two families. The 1st and 4th quarters, top left and bottom right, are silver (Argent), with a black (Sable) chevron between three black martins (Martlets) —'Argent, a chevron between three Martlets Sable'. The 2nd and 3rd quarters have a red (Gules) background, with a bar (Fess) and six gold (Or) blocks (Billets) and a square of Ermine on the top left (Canton Ermine) —'Gules, a fess between six Billets Or, and a Canton Ermine'. There is also a crescent 'for difference' as the arms belonged to the armiger's second son.

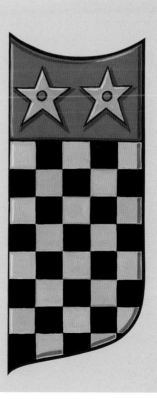

THE WIFE'S FAMILY ARMS

Her section is gold and black check (Chequy Or and Sable), and the upper part (the chief) is a red (Gules) background with two gold stars (Mullets Or) with holes (pierced)—'Impaling Chequy Or and Sable, on a chief Gules two Mullets pierced Or'. The full blason is: 'Quarterly and a crescent for difference, 1 and 4 Argent, a chevron between three Martlets Sable; 2 and 3 Gules, a Fess between six Billets Or, and a Canton Ermine; impaling Chequy Or and Sable, on a chief Gules two Mullets pierced Or. For the Crest: 'On a mount Vert a Pied greyhound sejant proper collared Or'.

Colours in heraldry These have their own special names. Gold (Or) and silver (Argent), often shown as yellow and white, are called metals. There are five other colours (tinctures): blue (Azure), red (Gules), black (Sable), green (Vert) and purple (Purpure). In addition, the field may be patterned with a fur such as Ermine or Vair—stylised images of ermine's tails and a patchwork of squirrel skins.

Designs and images These are referred to on a shield as charges, and the shield is 'charged' with that object or pattern. The principal charges, or ordinaries, are essentially geometric patterns.

Other charges include heraldic animals such as stags, and flowers such as thistles and the fleur-de-lys—a stylised lily. Sometimes the charge puns on a family name, when the arms are said to be 'canting' —the Breakspears displayed a broken spear.

Marks of cadency If an armiger has several sons, they may use their father's arms while he is alive, provided that each uses a 'mark of cadency'—something to distinguish their arms from their father's, such as a three-pointed 'label' for the eldest son or a crescent for a second son (see box, right). When the father dies, the eldest son inherits his arms, but the other sons, in theory, continue to use marks of cadency that become a permanent part of their arms. In practice, space limitations make it difficult to add marks of cadency in succeeding generations, so younger sons of younger sons often applied for their own arms or reverted to the original ones.

SCOTTISH CADENCY MARKS Because junior members of Scottish families who bear arms are legally required to matriculate (register) their arms to use them, the Scots have a more elaborate system for adaptation (see page 297).

looking up the arms

Once you have constructed a blason for a coat of arms you need to consult a reference book (called an ordinary, from the term used to describe the basic designs on shields). The most comprehensive is *Papworth's Ordinary of British Armorials* (J.W. Papworth and A.W. Morant, Heraldry Society, 1874/Tabard Press, repr. 1961). This is arranged by the nature of the ordinaries, and the objects with them. For this shield, starting on the left-hand side:

1 Look up 'chevron between', then locate 'three Martlets Sable'; this will tell you that this section of the arms belonged to the Proctor family.

2 Turn to 'Fess between' and locate 'six Billets', which identifies the Beauchamp (pronounced Beecham) family.

3 Look up 'chief', with 'a Chequy field' and 'two Mullets (stars) pierced Or', and you should be able to find the Palmer family.

Heir or first son	*the label*	
Second son	*the crescent*	
Third son	*the mullet*	
Fourth son	*the martlet*	
Fifth son	*the annulet*	
Sixth son	*the fleur-de-lys*	
Seventh son	*the rose*	
Eighth son	*the cross moline*	

Colours in black and white

As coats of arms may be printed in black and white, there is a convention for showing the tinctures (colours), right. Gules (red) is vertical stripes—as blood drips downwards—and Azure (blue) is horizontal stripes—like the blue horizon.

Or *Gold*

Azure *Blue*

Argent *Silver*

Sable *Black*

Purpure *Purple*

Gules *Red*

Vert *Green*

Ermine

Vair

Ermines

CounterVair

Erminoir

Potent

TAKING IT FURTHER

♦ *The Wordsworth Complete Guide to Heraldry* (A. Fox-Davies, Wordsworth Editions, 1996).
♦ *The Oxford Guide to Heraldry* (T. Woodcock and J.M. Robinson, Oxford University Press, 1988).
♦ The Heraldry Society publishes two journals, *The Heraldry Gazette* and *The Coat of Arms*: PO Box 32, Maidenhead, Berkshire SL6 3FD.

Information on the Internet
♦ www.college-of-arms.gov.uk
The official web site of the College of Arms.
♦ www.heraldica.org/topics/britain
Links to various heraldic web pages.
♦ www.digiserve.com/heraldry/pimbley.htm An on-line version of *Pimbley's Dictionary of Heraldry*.

NEXT STEPS

You now have the names of the families whose arms are combined on this shield: Proctor, Beauchamp and Palmer. You also know that the husband's arms represent a combination of the arms of Proctor and Beauchamp. To find out more, you would check in the following books.

Fairbairn's Book of Crests (1905, repr. Heraldry Today, 1983) says the seated greyhound crest was used by the Beauchamp family. The *General Armory of England, Scotland, Ireland and Wales* (B. Burke, repr. Heraldry Today, 1984) records that the Proctor arms were first granted in 1761, and that there was a family called Proctor-Beauchamp of Langley Park. *Burke's Genealogical and Heraldic History of the Peerage, Baronetage and Knightage* (Fitzroy Dearborn, 1999) gives more information on the Proctor-Beauchamps, as does *General Armory Two* (C.R. Humphery-Smith, Tabard Press, 1973).

Tracing the names back using books such as *The Genealogist's Guide* (G.B. Barrow, Research Publishing Co., 1977) and *Burke's Family Index* (Burke's Peerage, 1976), you find that Proctor-Beauchamp was originally Beauchamp Proctor. The *Baronetage of England* (William Betham, 1805) has a pedigree with a marriage at Sunning, Buckinghamshire, on 20 October 1789, between George Beauchamp Proctor, second son of Sir William Beauchamp Proctor, Baronet, and Charlotte, eldest daughter of Robert Palmer.

The pedigree also shows that George's elder brother, Sir Thomas Beauchamp Proctor, succeeded his father in 1773 and married Charlotte's younger sister, Mary. On inheriting further estates the family was licensed to alter the name to Proctor-Beauchamp. The Beauchamp name is an ancient one in England, and this family must have decided that they preferred to be Beauchamps rather than Proctors.

Beware—you have found two brothers who married two sisters. Fortunately the crescent cadency mark on the arms identifies them as those of the second son, so they must have belonged to George rather than Thomas. If you have any doubts, you can ask the Heralds at the College of Arms to review the original records (see page 296).

heraldry
authorities of arms

When you have found a family link with a coat of arms, you need to investigate it further. The keepers of the records are the English, Welsh, Northern Irish and Scottish heralds

Once you have 'blasoned' a coat of arms (see What arms can reveal, pages 292–5), you can pursue your research with the heraldic authorities. These have archives that in some cases date back as far as the Middle Ages.

the College of Arms

Founded in 1484, the college is a corporation of the officers of arms of the royal household. It has three chief heralds, six heralds and four juniors, known as pursuivants. The principal officer, first appointed in 1415, is Garter King of Arms, assisted by Clarenceux King of Arms, and Norroy and Ulster King of Arms. The heralds are Chester, Lancaster, Richmond, Somerset, York and Windsor, while Bluemantle, Portcullis, Rouge Croix and Rouge Dragon are the pursuivants. The earliest title can be traced to 1276, but most of them were created in the 15th century.

JURISDICTION The college has authority over heraldic matters in England, Wales (looked after by Wales Herald Extraordinary, first appointed in 1963) and Northern Ireland.

The heralds have kept continuous records of British coats of arms and the genealogies of the families entitled to them, and are responsible for drawing up new arms. They deal annually with some 200 applications for arms from corporate bodies and private individuals; they also look after naval, military, airforce and civic insignia, orders of knighthood, the marshalling of new peers in Parliament, and State events such as coronations and the State Opening of Parliament.

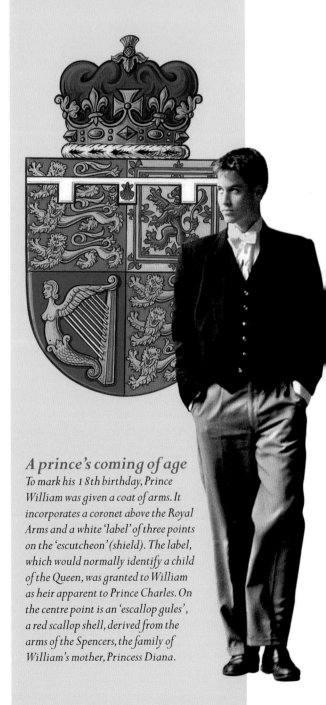

A prince's coming of age
To mark his 18th birthday, Prince William was given a coat of arms. It incorporates a coronet above the Royal Arms and a white 'label' of three points on the 'escutcheon' (shield). The label, which would normally identify a child of the Queen, was granted to William as heir apparent to Prince Charles. On the centre point is an 'escallop gules', a red scallop shell, derived from the arms of the Spencers, the family of William's mother, Princess Diana.

RESEARCH BY THE HERALDS The college is not publicly funded, so its records are not open to all, but the heralds will pursue inquiries for a fee that depends on the work involved.

the Chief Herald of Ireland

Ulster King of Arms was first appointed in 1552, with jurisdiction over the whole of Ireland, applying the same heraldic rules as in England and Wales. In 1943 the office of Ulster King of Arms was transferred to London and united with that of Norroy, and the Chief Herald of Ireland, at the Genealogical Office in Dublin (see DIRECTORY), took over for the Republic of Ireland. The Chief Herald has visitation records for Dublin (in 1568 and 1607) and for Wexford (1618).

the Court of the Lord Lyon

In Scotland the Lord Lyon, first appointed early in the 14th century, is responsible for all genealogical matters. He keeps the Public Register of All Arms and Bearings in Scotland (begun in 1672) and the Birthbrieve records, which set out the nobility of all 16 great-great-grandparents of people registered in them, with lineal pedigrees recording single lines of ancestry. He is in charge of State ceremonial, with his heralds, and he judges cases on the chiefship of clans. He can bring legal proceedings against anyone who claims unregistered arms.

RECORDS OF SCOTTISH ARMS Visitations were not generally made in Scotland, but all arms registered there before 1903 are in *The Public Register of All Arms and Bearings in Scotland* (James Balfour Paul, William Green & Sons, 1903). The Scottish Record Society (see DIRECTORY) has indexed birth briefs, and funeral entries and escutcheons.

Worth a check Even if you do not know of arms in your family, you should check the visitation records (see page 290) for the 16th and 17th centuries. Many people fell on hard times then, and your family may once have had arms recorded, or you may find 'disclaimers' from those forced to give up illegal arms. Check all the records—pedigrees often show up people from far afield. The College of Arms has the originals (see *The Records and Collections of the College of Arms*, R. Wagner, Burke's Peerage, 1952), but copies exist in the British Library and in Oxford and Cambridge college libraries. *Armigerous Ancestors* (C. R. Humphery-Smith, Family History Books, 1997) is a survey of these records with a surname index of pedigrees and arms.

THE INSTITUTE OF HERALDIC AND GENEALOGICAL STUDIES (IHGS)

The IHGS is an educational, charitable trust dedicated to studying the history and structure of families. Its 13th-century premises in Canterbury includes a library, with a large collection of original documents and many indexes, open to visitors for a small charge. Staff offer a research service (also for a modest fee), and they can give expert guidance on planned coats of arms, both personal and corporate.

The Institute runs courses on all aspects of family history—heraldry, genealogy, use of records and research techniques. There are full-time, part-time, residential and correspondence courses, leading to graded examinations, diplomas and licentiates. The IHGS publishes books, maps, indexes and collections of records (it has a bookshop), and a journal called *Family History*. The address is IHGS, 79–82 Northgate, Canterbury, Kent CT1 1BA, Tel. 01227 768664. The web site is at www.ihgs.ac.uk

your surname
how names developed

Surnames are the starting point for every family historian. Whether your name is rare or common, it will tell you something about your ancestors and help your research

Most of us have wondered at some time about the meaning and origin of our surname. Discovering a rare name in your family's past is a good 'find' and may help you to locate your ancestors in a specific area of Britain. Even common names, such as Mason and Carter, can provide clues about your forebears' roots.

the origins of surnames

It is easy to make a wrong guess at the meaning of a surname. Collier originally meant charcoal-burner, not coal-miner; Moody meant brave; and Onions came from the Welsh personal name Ennion. Some surnames have evolved over time so that Bernard has become Burnett, and Base has turned into Bayes. Others have changed out of all recognition. The Atacks were originally Etoughs and the Fretwells came from Frecheville in Normandy.

Named after a Norman English people did not have surnames before the Norman Conquest. Instead they had a wide range of personal names, such as Edgar and Harding from the Anglo-Saxon language or Auti and Ketil from Norse, spoken by the Vikings. Only a few Norman baronial families had hereditary surnames in Normandy before 1066, but after the Conquest the barons led the way in spreading the new fashion.

Norman landowners usually took the name of their chief residence as their surname. Thus the Lacys came from Lassy and the de Glanvilles from Glanville, both in Calvados. But some family names have changed so much over the centuries that they bear little resemblance to the original. The

Literary names uncovered
This selection of great writers illustrates some of the common origins of surnames. Norman names, occupational names and place names have formed many of today's surnames.

PEPYS From the Old French personal name Pepis, introduced by the Normans.

BURNS From Burnhouse, a place in Forfarshire. The family name was written as Burness until 1768, when Robert and his brother changed it to Burns.

TROLLOPE From Troughburn, Northumberland, which was formerly Trolhop, 'troll-valley'.

CHAUCER An occupational name for a maker of leggings.

BYRON An Old English name for a person who lived 'at the cattle sheds'.

Dawtrys, for example, came from Hauterive and the Sampers from one of several places called Saint-Pierre. Some Norman barons were known by nicknames that became hereditary. Giffard, for example, meant 'chubby cheeks' and Camoys 'snub-nosed'. Other men took their surname from their father, using the Norman French word 'fitz' (son of) to form names such as FitzAlan or FitzWilliam. Knights soon copied the barons and during the 12th century most Norman landowning families acquired surnames. Family coats of arms became popular at the same time (see pages 288–91).

French connections Very few people can prove that an ancestor fought at the Battle of Hastings. Many more settlers, often ordinary farming

The English population has grown tenfold since the Middle Ages but there are now fewer surnames. Many names were lost during the Black Death when a third of the population died.

families, came from other parts of northern France as a result of the victory, some of them much later. A French surname does not prove a connection with the Norman barons, and descent, even through junior lines, is hard to prove. Today's Glanvilles and Giffards are as likely to be descended from other families that acquired the surnames independently. The family names French and France were given to immigrants of lower social status.

Too few names to go around Unlike the Anglo-Saxons and Vikings, the Normans favoured a narrow range of personal names. The old names gradually dropped out of favour, though many survived long enough to become hereditary surnames—Dearing and Cade are thought to come from Anglo-Saxon, and Herrick and Swain from Norse.

A few Biblical names, such as John and Adam, were added to those brought into England by the Normans, but the choice of name was restricted and the need grew for men to be distinguished by other names. By the 14th century half the men in England were called either John or William. When Thomas,

Richard and Robert are added the proportion rises to more than 80 per cent. Using pet names, sometimes derived from rhyming forms, partly solved the problem. Dickins and Hitchcock are both pet forms of Richard, Gibbe was short for Gilbert and Hudd a variant of Hugh.

Territorial names No one knows exactly why the additional names used to identify the various Johns and Williams became hereditary. Linking a family name to property, however small, became an important factor during the 13th and 14th centuries, when manorial courts began to keep written records of property transactions and had to differentiate between individuals. Ordinary families in southern England and East Anglia were the first to follow landowners in adopting surnames. By the late 14th century the practice had spread in England and Lowland Scotland. In the Gaelic-speaking Highlands and Islands, and in Wales the old system of using only personal names continued much longer.

the meaning of surnames

Surnames developed in five main groups. Those that are commonly found may not further your research, but a rare name in your family's past will help you to restrict your research to key areas.

Local names About a quarter of English surnames are derived from particular places, and are common in areas of scattered farms and hamlets. Names such as Lobb (Devon) or Shufflebottom (Lancashire) are still found in or near their original neighbourhoods. The first bearer of this type of surname took the name from his property, usually a small farm. Surnames that developed from place names in this way often take the form preserved in local speech, such as the Brewells from the south Yorkshire village of Braithwell and the Bowsers from Bolsover.

In a few cases, bearers of names derived from towns and villages may be descended from knightly families who were the medieval lords of a manor, but most names of this kind were given to people who moved at the time when surnames were being formed. Their new neighbours called them Pickering, Rotherham or Whitchurch because that was where they had just come from.

Natural names Many surnames are derived from features of the landscape and indicate where a family lived within a parish. Some are peculiar to certain districts. The Gawkrogers, for example, take their name from a prominent rock near Halifax. Most are from common features like Bridge, Ford, Hill, Green, Marsh and Wood, or from different words for the same feature, so that a wood produces Shaw, Hirst, Firth or Holt. Other names like Bywater and Underwood locate a family more precisely.

Like father, like son A large number of surnames come from a father's and, less frequently, a mother's personal name (known as the patronymic and matronymic systems). Many Anglo-Saxon, Viking and Norman personal names became surnames when a son took a parent's name as his surname. More often '-s' or '-son' were added to the father's name. The son of William might acquire the surname Williams, Williamson, Wills, Wilson, Wilkins, Wilkinson, Wilkes, Wilcocks or Wilcockson ('-kin' or '-cock' were originally added to form pet names). The usual practice in northern England and Lowland Scotland was to add '-son', whereas '-s' was favoured in the south.

Some rarer medieval personal names have produced surnames with a regional flavour. Names such as Aslin (Nottinghamshire and Lincolnshire), or Ashwin (Worcestershire), may share descent from a single ancestor. Surnames derived from women's names, perhaps from a widow or landowner, are less common. They include some that have evolved from pet forms of names—Mogge from Margaret and Marriott from Mary, for example.

Terms of endearment Many nicknames have become surnames, including animal and bird names (Fox, Sparrow), colours (Grey, White), and physical characteristics (Short, Broad). Some refer to characteristics of the original name-bearer—Pennyfather (miserly, a 'penny-pincher') and Proudfoot (a proud manner), for example. Others are from Norman French words, such as Bellamy, meaning 'fine friend'.

Defined by work Names derived from occupations (Smith, Wright), or from holding an office (Sheriff, Constable), are among the most common in the United Kingdom. Most places had just one of these officials or craftsmen, so the name distinguished a man from his neighbours. Rare crafts produced surnames whose meanings are no longer obvious—such as Frobisher (a restorer of armour) and Arblaster (a crossbowman). Others are not what they seem: the Cowards herded cows and King, Prince, Knight, Abbot, Bishop and Pope are likely to be nicknames.

how names changed

Surnames have evolved over the centuries and, as you pursue your research, it is important to remember that an ancestor's name may be spelt differently as you work back in time.

A test of spelling Until the late 19th century most people were not literate. Surnames were spelt in various ways and successive parish clerks might record the same name differently. For example, Sheppard is the same name as Shepherd, Rumball the same as Rumbold, and Smythe is an attempt to distinguish a family from the neighbouring Smiths.

Ways of speaking Names also changed because of differences in pronunciation. Brownhill became Brownell and a few Aubreys came from Horbury, near Wakefield. Some changes were more radical. Horwich became Orange, for example, and one variant of Shemeld is Shimwell. Such changes are not always obvious at first but can be traced in parish registers and earlier records.

a Smith a Taylor
a Porter a Sadler

A new name for a new home Surnames often changed when a family moved to a new locality. New neighbours adapted names to surnames and place names that were familiar to them—when the Crook family moved to Sheffield in the 17th century, they became Crookes, the name of a village in Sheffield.

Otherwise known as Some of your ancestors may have been known by two different names, and you will need to know both. Parish registers sometimes record people with two surnames, usually in the form of an alias such as 'Thomas Smith alias Cook'. This can refer to an illegitimate birth, or an alias could be given to a stepchild or another relative and might persist for generations. In Ireland it could denote a woman's maiden name or previous married name and appears on tombstones in this way. It may also connect different forms of a name—for example, Mirfield alias Mirfin.

Changing names Common law allows people to choose any surname they like, if the change is not for a fraudulent purpose. Landowning families have often preserved family names when a male line died out by persuading a new owner (a husband or other relative) to change his name on inheriting an estate. Thus, the Sitwells of Renishaw Hall in Derbyshire are descended from Jonathan Hurt, who took his wife's name, Sitwell, in 1777.

The TNA holds records of name changes by deed poll, although there is no legal requirement to record the change. From 1851 to 1903 these are kept in class C 54, from 1903 in class J 18.

Trade names
Surnames derived from occupations, such as hunting (which formed the surname Hunter) are still widespread today. Smith—meaning a worker in metals—is a common name in many languages: Schmidt in German, Kovar in Czech, Farrari in Italian and Kowalksi in Polish.

your surname
regional & foreign names

Welsh, Irish, Scottish and immigrant influences have swelled the pool of British surnames. An understanding of their development helps to reveal their origins

Outside England, surnames evolved in different ways. In Wales, they grew from a small range of personal names, and few came from places, occupations or nicknames. This means that you may have to search through records of many people with the same surname to locate your Welsh ancestors.

Hereditary surnames were not generally used in Wales during the Middle Ages. Instead, the Welsh added 'ab' or 'ap' (son of) to personal names. They could trace several generations using this method, such as Llewelyn ap Hywel ap Gruffydd, eventually creating distinctive Welsh surnames. In time, 'ab' and 'ap' were dropped, although, in some cases, the 'b' or 'p' remained to form new surnames such as Bowen, Bevan, Preece and Pugh.

A FASHION GROWS After the Acts of Union of 1536 and 1542 joined England and Wales, wealthier

Working names

Juda and Metka Fiszer were Polish Jews who emigrated to England. When they opened their umbrella shop in Hackney in 1907, they used Fisher, the Anglicised version of their surname. Immigrants' names can be hard to trace because of the varied ways in which they were recorded.

families began to adopt English-style hereditary surnames. Welsh names were also Anglicised—Hugh was used in place of Hywel, Lewis of Llewelyn and Edward of Iowerth. Only a few old names such as Owain, Morgan and Rhys survived. Most surnames were taken from a father's first name. Sometimes this was a simple repetition such as Howell or John, but often an 's' was added—to make Evans, say.

The Scottish-Irish link Surnames in Lowland Scotland were similar to those in northern England, with many ending in '-son', such as Donaldson. In the Highlands and Islands, and in Ireland, surnames often came from Gaelic personal names, such as Neill or Brien. Scottish clan names arose in well-defined areas—the MacDonalds were linked with Skye, for example. Some Irish names can also point to regional origins— MacCarthy is associated with Cork and Kerry, and Brennan with North Kilkenny. In Ireland the system of using prefixes to denote kinship was common by the 11th century. 'Mac' meant 'son of' and 'O' referred to a grandson or later descendant of the progenitor. These prefixes were generally dropped in the late 17th century, but were adopted again during the revival of national consciousness in the 1890s.

TELLING PEOPLE APART Separating some Gaelic Irish and Scottish surnames can be hard— the Gaelic Scots are descended from Irish settlers (*scotus* is Latin for Irishman) and there were Irish settlers in Scotland throughout the 19th century. Some names, such as Kennedy, are found in both countries. Also, the Highland Scots who settled in England in the 19th century often changed their names to something the English could pronounce.

Traditional Celtic naming If you know all the children of a Welsh, Scottish or Irish marriage in order, you may also discover the first names of their grandparents. The eldest son was named after the father's father, the second after the mother's father and the third after the father. Daughters in Wales, Scotland and, less often, Ireland were also named in a set way—the first daughter after the maternal grandmother, the second after the paternal grandmother and the third after her mother.

MAIDEN FORMS Scottish women kept their maiden names after marriage and could be referred to by both surnames. If a woman married more than once, all her surnames are usually listed in indexes of parish registers and civil registration records.

Immigrants' names During the 16th century, immigrants fleeing religious persecution in France and the Low Countries settled in London, the east and south-east of England, bringing in new names. The main group, the Huguenots (see pages 262–4), Anglicised many of their names—for example,

Many families that migrated from the West Indies brought back to post-war Britain the surnames of 18th and early 19th-century slave-owners.

Hervé became Harvey. The Huguenot Society (see DIRECTORY) has published studies of their names.

A large number of Jews emigrated to Britain from 1880 to 1905 to escape persecution in the Russian Empire, and again in the 1930s to flee from the Nazis (see page 267). They brought surnames such as Cohen, Marx and Raphael with them.

The range of British surnames was increased by refugees from eastern Europe and immigration from Commonwealth countries in the 1940s and 1950s (see pages 266–71).

TAKING IT FURTHER

♦ *The Penguin Dictionary of British Surnames* (J. Titford, Penguin, 2009).
♦ *The Surnames of Wales for Family Historians and Others* (J. Rowlands and S. Rowlands, FFHS, 1996).
♦ *The Surnames of Ireland* (E. MacLysaght, Irish University Press, 6th ed., 1991).
♦ *The Surnames of Scotland* (G. Black, Birlinn, 1996).
♦ *Surnames, DNA and Family History* (G. Redmonds, T. King and D. Hey, Oxford University Press, 2011).

your surname
putting a place to a name

A rare surname in your family can help you to limit your research to certain areas of Britain. The current distribution of a name may locate its geographical origins

If you find a rare or distinctive name in your family, establishing its geographical distribution early in research may assist you in locating relatives of that name. A variety of sources are available for this purpose, but remember that a name may have changed over the generations.

Names at your fingertips If you have an unusual surname, simply looking it up in telephone directories will help you to find other bearers of your name. Counting and comparing the number of times your name appears in each of Britain's directories may take time, but will reveal an accurate geographical spread and locate areas that are relevant to your research. Collections of directories are held in local libraries, and CD versions are widely available.

Information from the census The 1881 census is surname-indexed for England, Wales and Scotland. It lists everyone in a county alphabetically and gives their first name, age, sex, relationship to the head of the household and occupation. It also refers you to the original returns, which give more information about an individual (see The census, pages 62–76). The index can be used to plot the distribution of a name county by county. Archer Software's CD, *The British 19th Century Surname Atlas*, provides distribution maps of surnames recorded in the 1881 census.

A surname sampler

British surnames are found throughout the world, but in these isles their distribution can be limited. Names are often concentrated in particular areas (see examples above). Their origins range from place names to Old Testament names that were popular among Nonconformists in South Wales.

KEY SOURCES OF INFORMATION
♦ *The British 19th Century Surname Atlas* (CD by Archer Software, 2011 edition); see www.archersoftware.co.uk. Maps of all surnames in the 1881 census.
♦ http://gbnames.publicprofiler.org. Maps based on the 1881 census and the 1998 electoral registers.

Civil registration indexes The distribution of surnames from 1837 can be plotted using civil registration indexes of births, marriages and deaths (see Civil records, pages 50–61). These are kept at the General Register Office and are arranged by surname for each year. Microfiche copies are held in some record offices and libraries.

Early registration districts were broadly similar to the census districts and so can be compared with the 1881 census returns. The indexes of deaths are best used for this purpose, as births were under-recorded in early years. The distribution of most surnames can be seen by searching indexes for a five-year period, although one year will be enough for common names. With rare names it is best to look at the period from 1837 to 1851, after which some registration districts changed.

First names Children were often named after parents, grandparents or godparents. A rare name found through several generations, such as Thurza or Clementina, may help to distinguish relatives from other people with the same surname.

It was also common to baptise children with the Christian name of a close relative, which can make it difficult to tell generations apart. The practice of giving children a second (or middle) name, which can help the family historian, began in the 18th century but was not common until the 19th century.

Hearth tax returns A surname's geographical distribution narrows as you move back in time but the records also become less complete. The best sources are the returns for the hearth tax, levied from 1662 to 1689, half-way between the period of surname formation and the present day. The original returns are kept at the TNA (see DIRECTORY), but many county record offices have copies in print or on microfiche. Surname indexes in these returns can be used to map surname distribution, although you should remember that the administrative unit (the parish or township) was not the same as a civil registration or census district.

What's in a name?
Be prepared to look for varied spellings of a surname when you search indexes for your family. Walter Vincent (right), born in 1868, used a different form of the family name from his grandmother, Hannah Vinson (below).

International Genealogical Index (IGI) The IGI (see pages 100–1) lets you access parish register entries from 1538. Data from it can be used with computer programs to plot surname ditribution. Note that IGI coverage varies widely, and some counties have few registers from the 16th century.

Medieval records Where medieval manorial court records survive, it can be possible to trace a name beyond the parish registers. Early forms of names and the places where they were first found can be retrieved from 14th-century taxation lists. Surviving lists are held at the TNA (class E 179).

TAKING IT FURTHER

♦ *Christian Names in Local and Family History* (G. Redmonds, TNA, 2004).
♦ *Family Names and Family History* (D. Hey, Hambledon and London, 2000).
♦ *Surnames and Genealogy: a new approach* (G. Redmonds, FFHS, 2002).

Information on the Internet
♦ www.genuki.org.uk/indexes/ SurnamesLists.html County surnames lists.
♦ www.one-name.org The Guild of One-Name Studies, which tracks specific surnames.

dictionary of surnames

Surnames have developed in distinctive categories (see Your surname, pages 298–305). The dictionary gives examples from each category, including many of the most common and some of the rarest British surnames. Many names have more than one origin and you may wish to consult *A Dictionary of Surnames* (P. Hanks and F. Hodges, OUP, 1989) to take your research further.

ACKROYD A surname with a single-family origin, from an oak clearing (Old English *ac*, 'oak', and *rod*, 'clearing') near Heptonstall, in Yorkshire. Akeroyd is an alternative spelling.

ADAMS 'Son of Adam', which was a Hebrew personal name.

ADCOCK A pet form of Adam.

ADDISON 'Son of Addy', a pet form of Adam. Also spelt Addeson and Adeson.

ADLARD An Old German personal name which is found mostly in Lincolnshire.

AGATE A name for someone who lived by a gate. This rare name is found in Sussex, Surrey and London and all bearers of it may be descended from John a gate, who lived in 13th-century Sussex.

AGGIS From the medieval female name Agace, derived from Agatha.

AHERN An Irish name Anglicised from a Gaelic name and most commonly found in south-west Ireland.

AINSWORTH A Lancashire surname from a village between Bolton and Bury.

AKEHURST A Sussex name from Akehurst ('the oak wood') Farm, near Hellingly.

ALBAN Originally a personal name from Britain's first Christian martyr. Most bearers of the name can be traced to a few families in south-west Wales and are concentrated there, in the Midlands and East Anglia.

ALBUTT An Old German personal name introduced by the Normans, found as a surname in the West Midlands.

ALCHIN From a lost place name in Buxted, Sussex, last mentioned in 1592. Variants include Alchon and Alchorne.

ALCOCK A pet form of a name that had been shortened to Al, such as Alan or Alexander.

ALDEN From the Viking personal name Healfdene. Other forms include Auden, Olden and Haldane. In Shropshire it may be derived from the place name Aldon.

ALDERSON 'Son of Alder', derived from one of two Old English personal names (Ealdhere or Æðelhere). It is found mostly in Yorkshire and County Durham.

ALDWINKLE From Aldwincle, a village between Kettering and Peterborough.

ALGER From a Middle English personal name. The name is found in eastern England, Devon and on the south coast of England. Also spelt Algar and Elgar.

ALLARD From Old English and Continental personal names. Found particularly in east and south-east England.

ALLEN A Celtic personal name, popularised by followers of William the Conqueror. It is often spelt Allan, especially in Scotland.

ALLEY A Viking personal name from Old Danish or Old Swedish. Found especially in the Midlands.

ALLPRESS A nickname meaning 'the old priest'. It may have a single-family origin in Cambridgeshire.

ALMAN An Old French word for a German. The variant forms of the name include Allmen and Almond.

ALSOP From Alsop-en-le-Dale, a small settlement high above the Dove valley on the borders of Derbyshire and Staffordshire.

ALVEY Derived from an Old English personal name, it is found mostly in Nottinghamshire. Elphey and Elvey are variants.

AMBLER A west Yorkshire name of uncertain origin. It may have been applied to a man in charge of horses or an enameller, or have been a nickname from a characteristic way of walking.

AMERY An Old German personal name introduced by the Normans. Numerous variants include Emery, Hemery and Imbery.

AMIS An Old French name meaning 'friend'.

ANGOVE A name derived from Cornish, meaning 'the smith'.

ANGUS A Scottish personal name of Gaelic origin. An 8th-century Pictish king gave his name to the Scottish county, from which some families may have taken their surname.

ANGWIN A Cornish nickname, meaning 'the white', probably of single-family origin.

ANKETTEL A Norman form of an Old Norse name. Ankill, Anquetil and Antell are alternative spellings.

ANNE From Ann, the place in Hampshire.

ANNEAR A Cornish nickname for a tall, thin man, common in the Redruth and Truro areas.

ANNIS A version of Agnes, a popular female name in the Middle Ages.

ANSELL An Old German personal name, popular in Norman England because of St Anselm. Found mostly in East Anglia.

ANSTRUTHER A Scottish surname from a place in Fife.

ANTROBUS Derived from a north Cheshire place name, which comes from an Old Norse personal name, Andriði, and 'bush' or 'scrub'.

ANWYL A Welsh surname from the word *annwyl* meaning 'dear, beloved'. It is a rare name, found in parts of north Wales.

ARBUCKLE A Scottish Gaelic surname from a place near Airdrie.

ARBUTHNOT A Scottish surname meaning 'confluence of the holy stream', from the parish of that name in Aberdeenshire.

ARGALL From a Cornish place name in the parish of Buddock. It means 'retreat, shelter'.

ARGENT A nickname, probably for someone with silvery grey hair. It appears to have a single-family origin in Essex or Suffolk.

ARKLE From the Old Norse personal name, Arnkell. Found mostly in northern England.

ARLOTT A nickname for a young man, often in the sense of 'rascal' or 'vagabond'.

ARMITAGE Someone who lived by a hermitage. The name originated from a west Yorkshire hermitage, commemorated by the place name Armitage Bridge.

ASHBURNER A 'burner of ash' or 'maker of potash'. Largely found in north-west England.

ASHDOWN The distribution of the surname suggests that it is derived from the place in Kent, 13 miles east of Maidstone.

ASHPLANT A rare name from north-west Devon, which has gradually changed from the personal name Absalom.

ASHURST Ashurst Beacon in Wigan is the major source of the surviving family name.

ASPINALL Originating at Aspinwall, near Ormskirk, this name assumed a variety of forms (including Asmah, Asmall and Asmold) as it spread in south Lancashire and Yorkshire.

ASQUITH A west Yorkshire surname from a place called Askwith, near Otley, which is how the surname is often spelt.

ATTREE A rare name meaning someone whose house was by a prominent tree. It is concentrated in Sussex, around Brighton and Lewes, and probably has a single-family origin.

AUSTIN A shortened form of Augustine, made popular by St Augustine of Hippo and his Canterbury namesake.

AUTY From an Old Danish personal name. Found chiefly in north Yorkshire, County Durham and Northumberland.

AVISON A west Yorkshire name, the 'son of Avice', an Old French personal name.

AYLETT From either of two Old English personal names. The name is found chiefly in Essex, Hertfordshire and London

b

BACCUS Evolved from the pronunciation of Backhouse, a name given to someone who worked at or lived by a bakery.

BACON From an Old German personal name introduced by the Normans, rather than a name for a pork butcher.

BAGSHAW A surname from a hamlet in the Peak District near Chapel-en-le-Frith. It has spread widely.

BAILEY Either a name for someone who lived in the bailey of a castle, or an occupational name for an official.

BAKER An occupational name for someone who makes bread.

BALDRY An Old German personal name introduced by the Normans, found chiefly in eastern England.

BALLANTINE A Scottish name from Bellenden, a farm in the parish of Roberton, near Hawick, in the Scottish Borders.

BALLCOCK A pet form of Baldwin, an Old German name popular among the Normans.

BALLIOL From one of two places in France.

BARKER A tanner, from the Middle English *bark*, meaning 'to tan skins'; also possibly from the French *berkier*, 'a shepherd'.

BARRACLOUGH A west Yorkshire surname from a lost place name near Halifax.

BASKERVILLE From Boscherville, a place in Normandy.

BATCHELOR From an Old French word for a young knight.

BATEMAN Servant of Bartholomew, a common medieval name. Variants are Batman, Bates and Batty.

BEADMAN A medieval bedeman was employed to pray for the souls of his benefactors.

BEAL From a Northumbrian place name; also from an Old French word for beautiful (*bel*).

BEARD A man with a striking beard, or a person from Beard in north-west Derbyshire.

BEARPARK From a village near Durham.

BEATTY A Scottish and northern Irish name from a pet form of Bartholomew or from the Anglicisation of a Gaelic personal name.

BEAUCHAMP An Old French place name for a 'fair field', from several places in France.

BEAUMONT Some places in England were named 'fair hill', as were several in northern France, so the name has multiple origins.

BEDDOW A Welsh surname from Bedo, a diminutive of Meredydd.

BEDFORD A surname from the county town of Bedfordshire and from smaller places of that name in Lancashire and Yorkshire.

BEDSER A Sussex name from a lost place name near Bexhill.

BEET A pet form of Beatrice. The surname is found in Yorkshire and the Midlands.

BEEVER Probably a nickname from a beaver. Belvoir in Leicestershire is pronounced Beever, but the name is found principally in Yorkshire.

BELCHER A nickname, meaning 'fair face', from Norman French. Also given to people of a cheerful disposition.

BELL Used as an occupational name for a bell-ringer, or for someone living near a bell. It may have evolved from a medieval name (Bel), taken from the Old French *belle* meaning 'beautiful'.

BELLAMY See page 300.

BENBOW A nickname for an archer.

BENNET From an Old French name derived from the Latin *benedictus*, meaning 'blessed'.

BENNISON 'Son of Bennet'.

BERRINGER A personal name introduced by the Normans. Bellinger is a variant.

BESWICK A northern name derived from Lancashire and Yorkshire place names.

BEVAN See page 302.

BIBBY A pet form of Isabel, found mostly in Lancashire; but Bibb is from the West Midlands.

BINNS A Yorkshire name from High Binns, near Haworth.

BIRTWISTLE A Lancashire surname from a former hamlet near Padiham.

BLACKADDER From a place of that name near Berwick-upon-Tweed, Northumberland.

BLACKBIRD Early spellings show that this was a nickname for a man with a black beard.

BLAIR A Scottish and northern Irish name derived from one of the many minor Gaelic place names for a plain or a battlefield.

BLANKSBY A rare Derbyshire name that preserves the original pronunciation of the deserted medieval village of Blingsby.

BLEASDALE A surname from a dale in the Lake District, which was named after a Viking.

BLENKINSOP A north-eastern surname from a valley in Northumberland.

BLENKO One of the spellings of a surname derived from Blencow in Cumbria.

BLIGH A nickname for a cheerful person.

BLONDEL An Old French name for someone with blond hair or a fair complexion.

BLOOMER An occupational name for an iron worker who made ingots or blooms.

BLOOMFIELD From Blonville-sur-Mer in Normandy. It is found chiefly in East Anglia.

BLOOMINGDALE An Anglicised form of a Low German name meaning 'flower valley'.

BLOOR A Staffordshire name derived from either of the two place names in that county.

BOLER A smelter of lead or iron rather than a bowl-maker. Numerous Bole Hills are named after former smelting sites on windy ridges.

BOLINGBROKE From the village near Spilsby, Lincolnshire.

BOND A small farmer who was a tenant, not a freeholder.

BONFIELD From one of three places called Bonneville in Normandy.

BONSER From the local pronunciation of Bonsall in Derbyshire.

BOON From Bohon in Normandy. Other variants include Bohun and Bowne.

BOOSIE From the local pronunciation of Balhousie in Fife, and sometimes spelt Bowsie.

BOOT A Nottinghamshire surname for a maker or seller of boots.

BOOTH A northern surname from an Old Danish word for cattle-rearing farms.

BOOTHROYD From a west Yorkshire place name near Rastrick, combining words for a cattle farm and a clearing.

BOSANQUET A Cornish name from Bosanketh; also a Huguenot name brought to England in the late 17th century.

BOSTOCK From Bostock Green, near Northwich in Cheshire.

BOSWELL A Scottish surname from Beuzeville in Normandy. The English branch of the family were called Bosville.

BOTWRIGHT An occupational name for a maker of boats. It is found chiefly in East Anglia.

BOUGHEY From Beaufour in Normandy. The surname is found mainly in Staffordshire.

BOWEN See page 302.

BOWKER One form of the Old French word for a butcher. Also spelt Boucher and Bowcher.

BOWSER See page 299.

BRACEGIRDLE An occupational name for a maker of belts that girdled breeches, found mostly in Lancashire.

BRADDEN An Irish name, Anglicised from a Gaelic personal name.

BREAKSPEAR A nickname for a warrior or a successful participant in a tournament.

BREMNER A name given by Scots to an immigrant from Brabant in the Low Countries.

BREWELL See page 299.

BREWSTER A brewer. The word was originally the feminine form, but men were described as brewsters at the period of surname formation.

BRIGHTON From Breighton, east Yorkshire. The Sussex seaside resort was known as Brightelmestone until the late 18th century.

BRISTOW From Bristol, preserving the old pronunciation of the city's name.

BROADBENT From a farm near Oldham, on the border of Lancashire and Yorkshire.

BROADHEAD A place name rather than a nickname. It comes from Broadhead Edge in the Holme valley, west Yorkshire.

BROCKLEHURST A Lancashire name from a place near Accrington, 'the badger wood'.

BROWN A nickname for someone with brown hair, skin or clothing. It is one of the most common surnames in Britain, as is one of its variants, Browne.

BROWNING From an Old English personal name.

BRUMMIT A version of Broomhead, a surname derived from a Pennine settlement.

BRUNT From Brund in Staffordshire.

BUCHANAN A Scottish surname from a place near Loch Lomond.

BUDD An Old English nickname for a plump person.

BULGER An occupational name from an Old French word for a maker of leather bags.

BULSTRODE From a place name in Buckinghamshire, meaning 'the fortified place amongst the brushwood'.

BUNKER A Norman nickname for a good-natured person, 'good heart'.

BUNTER A trade name for a sifter of flour.

BUNYAN A Bedfordshire nickname for someone disfigured by a bunion.

BURGIN An immigrant from Burgundy.

BURLINGTON The old pronunciation of the east Yorkshire resort Bridlington.

BURNEY From Bernay in Normandy.

BYATT A name given to someone whose house was by a prominent gate.

BYERS A northern English and Lowland Scottish name for someone who lived by a byre or cattle shed.

BYRON See page 298.

BYTHEWAY Literally, someone who lived by the highway. It is found mostly in the West Midlands.

C

CAGNEY An Irish name, Anglicised from a Gaelic name.

CAIRD A Scottish occupational name from a Gaelic word for a craftsman or a tinker.

CAMPBELL A Scottish clan name, originally from a Gaelic nickname for someone with a twisted mouth.

CANN From the Dorset place name; also an occupational name for a canner.

CAPSTICK A Lancashire and Yorkshire occupational name, from the Old French for a woodcutter.

CARNEGIE A Scottish surname from a Gaelic place name in Angus.

CARR Someone who lived by a marshy place covered with brushwood. It is also spelt Kerr.

CARRUTHERS A Scottish surname from lands of that name in south-west Scotland.

CARTER An occupational name for someone who moved goods.

CASEMENT Commonly found in Antrim, Northern Ireland, this is an Anglicised form of a Gaelic personal name from the Isle of Man.

CASS A pet form of Cassandra, a female name in use at the time of surname formation.

CATCHPOLE A name for a tax-gatherer or bailiff (literally a 'catcher of poultry'). The surname is found chiefly in East Anglia.

CAVENDISH From the Suffolk village in the Stour valley.

CECIL From Seisyllt, an Old Welsh personal name.

CHALLONER An occupational name for a blanket-maker.

CHAMPNEY An immigrant from the Champagne district of France.

CHANDLER A maker or seller of candles.

CHAPMAN An occupational name for a trader, ranging from a merchant to a pedlar.

CHATWIN From Chetwynd in Shropshire.

CHAUCER See page 298.

CHIPPENDALE A Lancashire and Yorkshire name from Chippingdale near Clitheroe.

CHIPPERFIELD From a hamlet near King's Langley in Hertfordshire.

CHRISTMAS In England, a nickname for someone born on 25 December. In Wales, a given name favoured by Nonconformists, which became popular in parts of south Wales.

CHUBB A Cornish nickname from the fish.

CHUMLEY From the Cheshire village Cholmondeley, west of Nantwich.

CLARKE An occupational name for a scribe. Also spelt Clark, Clerk and Clerke.

CLEGG A Lancashire and Yorkshire surname from a small place near Rochdale.

CLOTWORTHY From Clatworthy, a place name in Devon.

CLOWN Not a comedian, but from place names formed from British river names, such as Clowne in Derbyshire and Clun in Shropshire.

CLUTTERBUCK A Dutch name brought by refugees from the Low Countries in the 1600s.

COCKAYNE A nickname for a dreamer, from a Middle English word meaning 'cloud-cuckoo-land'.

COE A nickname from kay, a word for a jackdaw. It is found mostly in Essex and Suffolk.

COHEN A Jewish name meaning 'priest'.

COLLINS A diminutive of Col, a short form of Nicholas. This name is also found in Ireland, where it is an Anglicised form of Ò Coilleáin.

COOK An occupational name. Cookson—'son of the cook'—is another form.

COOPER An occupational name for a maker of wooden containers, especially barrels.

CORBETT A Norman French nickname meaning 'little crow'.

CORKER A dealer in red or purple dyes.

CORNTHWAITE One of many Lake District surnames from local place names that end in *thwaite* (the Viking word for 'clearing').

COURTENAY From one of two places in northern France; also a nickname for someone with a short nose.

COX Derived from *coke*, a Middle English word added to names to create pet forms.

CRADDOCK From the Welsh personal name Caradog.

CRANMER From Cranmore in Somerset.

CRAPPER A Yorkshire version of Cropper, someone who cropped cloth or perhaps iron.

CRAVEN From the district in west Yorkshire.

CRESWICK From a hamlet of that name north of Sheffield.

CRISP A nickname for a person with curly hair, and a short form of the Old French personal name Crispin.

CROUCH Someone who lived by a cross.

CROWTHER An occupational surname for someone who played a stringed instrument known as a crowd, or, in Wales, a *crwth*.

CRUICKSHANK A Scottish nickname for a a man with crooked legs; or from a place name in the Grampians by the river Cruick. Also spelt Cruikshank and Crookshank.

CULPEPPER An occupational surname for a herbalist or spicer, literally 'collect pepper'.

CURZON From Courson in Normandy.

CUTTS 'Son of Cutt', short for Cuthbert.

DAFT An east Midlands name, probably of single-family origin. In the Middle Ages daft meant 'meek', not 'stupid'.

DAINTREE From the local pronunciation of Daventry in Northamptonshire.

DALGLEISH A Scottish surname from a place near Dunfermline.

DANDO From Aunou in Normandy. The surname is found chiefly in Somerset.

DANGERFIELD From one of the places named Angerville in Normandy.

DANKS A short form of Dankin, which in turn is derived from a pet form of Daniel.

DANSIE From Anizy in Normandy. Variants of the surname include Dauncey and Densey.

DARCY From Arcy in Normandy; also an Anglicised version of an Irish name.

DAVIES From the Hebrew, meaning 'beloved'. Often found as Davis in England and Davies in Wales—developments from the given name David when surnames formed.

DEAKIN One spelling of a name derived from 'deacon'.

DEARING An Old English personal name.

DEATH An Essex and Suffolk name, probably from a maker of tinder, pronounced 'deeth'. There is no link with death.

DELF A quarry worker or someone who lived by a quarry.

DEMPSEY An Irish name, Anglicised from a Gaelic name meaning 'proud'.

DENCH An immigrant from Denmark.

DEVEREUX From Evereux in Normandy, a common name in south-east Ireland.

DEWEY From the Welsh personal name Dewi, 'David'.

DEWSNAP From Dewsneps, the name of a farm near Chinley, in the Peak District.

DIBBLE A name that has changed from Tibbald, the pronunciation of Theobald.

DIMBLEBY From Dembleby in Lincolnshire.

DISNEY From Isigny in Normandy. The name is found in Ireland from the 17th century.

DOBSON 'Son of Dobb', in turn a pet form of Robert.

DOCKER From small places in Cumbria and Lancashire.

DOLPHIN An Old Norse personal name. Dolfin and Duffin are alternative spellings.

DOOLEY An Irish name, Anglicised from a Gaelic personal name.

DOWNER A southern England name for someone who lived on the Downs.

DRANSFIELD From Dronfield in Derbyshire, noted as Dranfield in Domesday.

DUCKWORTH From a Lancashire place name.

DUFFY An Irish name, Anglicised from a Gaelic personal name.

DUMMER From the north Hampshire village. Dumper is a variant.

DUNCALF A nickname, possibly of single-family origin in Cheshire or Staffordshire.

DUNGWORTH From a Pennine hamlet north-west of Sheffield.

DUNLOP A Scottish surname from Dunlop, in East Ayrshire.

DWIGHT From Diot, a diminutive of Dye. Dye was a pet form of the female name Dionisia.

DYMOND An occupational name for a dairyman. The name is concentrated in Devon.

EAME A Middle English word for a maternal uncle, presumably one who acted as a guardian for an orphaned nephew or niece.

EARDLEY From Eardley Hall, Staffordshire. Local speech sometimes changed it to Yeardley.

EARP A Midlands nickname for a swarthy person.

EBBLEWHITE One form of a surname derived from Heblethwaite in Yorkshire.

EDDY From a short form of an Old English personal name, found mostly in the West Country.

EDMEAD A Middle English nickname for a humble person. Edmed and Edmett are variants. Found mostly in Kent.

EDRICH From an Old English personal name. Edridge and Etheridge are variants.

EDWARDS A common name in England and Wales that means 'son of Edward'.

ELDRED A variant of the Middle English personal name Aldred, which in turn was derived from Old English personal names.

ELKIN A diminutive of Ellis, found in Staffordshire.

ELLAM A west Yorkshire name from Ellam ('river pool') near Bingley. The name is now common in and around Huddersfield.

ELLERY A West Country version of the male personal name Hilary.

ELLIS A common medieval name, derived from Elijah, the saint's name. In Wales it came from the personal name Elisedd.

ELPHICK From a Middle English personal name, which formed other names, like Alphege and Elvidge. Found chiefly in Sussex and Kent.

ELSHAW All Elshaws are descended from William Collins, an orphan from London. His new surname was invented by the managers of the Foundling Hospital at Ackworth, Yorkshire.

EMMERSON The 'son of Emery', an Old French personal name, of German origin.

ENSOR From Edensor, the estate village in Chatsworth Park, Derbyshire, whose name is pronounced in this way.

ENTICKNAP From a small place in Surrey, now Enticknapps Copse.

ETHERINGTON From Hetherington in Northumberland.

EVANS A common Welsh surname, from the given name Evan. See page 302.

EVERARD An Old German personal name introduced by the Normans. It is often found in Ireland.

EVEREST From Evreux in Normandy. The surname is concentrated in Kent.

EYRE The heir to an estate. Variant forms include Ayer, Ayres and Hair.

FACKETT A seller of firewood or faggots.

FAIRBODY A nickname for a 'fair person'.

FAIRCLOUGH From an unidentified, lost place name in Lancashire.

FAIRFAX A nickname for someone with beautiful long hair.

FAIRWEATHER A nickname for someone with a sunny disposition.

FANSHAW From a minor place name in Derbyshire, south-west of Sheffield.

FARLOW From Farlow or Fairley, place names in Shropshire.

FARMER A tax-farmer, not a worker of the land. The farmer paid a fixed sum to collect taxes and hoped to make a profit.

FARQUAHAR A Scottish surname from a Gaelic personal name.

FARRELL From Farewell in Staffordshire; also an Anglicised form of a Gaelic name meaning 'man of valour'.

FASTOLF From an Old Norse name.

FAULKNER A falconer, the keeper and trainer of falcons for hunting.

FAUNTLEROY From Old French, meaning 'son of the king'.

FAYNE A nickname for a well-disposed person. Variants include Fane and Vane.

FAZACKERLEY A Lancashire surname from a place near Liverpool.

FEARON An occupational surname from an Old French word for a smith or ironmonger. The name Ferrer has a similar derivation.

FEATHERSTONEHAUGH From a place in Northumberland near Haltwhistle, now shortened to Featherstone. Sometimes pronounced 'fanshaw'.

FEGG From an Old Danish personal name.

FENTIMAN The servant of someone called Fenton. The name is probably of single-family origin near Stillingfleet in north Yorkshire.

FERNIHOUGH From a lost place name near Leek in Staffordshire.

FETTIPLACE An Oxfordshire surname derived from a name for an usher.

FIELDSEND Literally, someone who lived at the end of a field. The surname appears to have a single-family origin near Stillingfleet in north Yorkshire.

FIENNES From a place near Calais, recorded as Filnes in the 11th century.

FIGGES A Norman French nickname for a trustworthy person.

FINLAY A Scottish surname from a Gaelic personal name.

FISK A Norfolk name for a fisherman or fishmonger.

FLAVELL A Midlands surname derived from the Norman form of the Worcestershire place name Flyford.

FLEMING An immigrant from Flanders.

FLETCHER An occupational surname from the Old French word for an arrowsmith.

FOLJAMBE A Norman French nickname for someone with a deformed leg.

FOLKARD From an Old German personal name, found chiefly in Norfolk.

FOLLIOTT A nickname from Old French, 'to play the fool', 'to dance about'.

FORSTER A name for someone who lived by, or worked in, a forest. Other forms include Forrester and Foster.

FORSYTH A Scottish surname, Anglicised from a Gaelic personal name.

FORTESCUE A nickname from Old French meaning 'strong shield'.

FORTNUM A Norman French nickname for a strong man of little intelligence, literally 'strong donkey'.

FOX A nickname for someone displaying the characteristics of the animal—perhaps its colouring, but more likely slyness.

FRANKLIN A name of status for someone who was a substantial freeholder below the level of a knight.

FREAR From the Old French word for a friar. Freer and Fryer are variants.

FREELOVE A Bedfordshire surname from an Old English personal name.

FRISBY From one of two place names in Leicestershire.

FURSE A Devon name for someone who lived by a prominent patch of gorse.

g

GABBETT A diminutive of Gabb, which in turn is a pet form of Gabriel.

GADSBY From the Leicestershire village of Gaddesby.

GAGE An occupational name for a measurer.

GAITSKELL From Gatesgill in Cumbria, formerly Geytscales.

GALSWORTHY From a remote farm of that name in Devon.

GARBETT From one or more Old German personal names introduced by the Normans.

GARLICK A seller of garlic.

GARRICK A Huguenot name. See page 262.

GARSIDE A Lancashire and Yorkshire name from a place near Oldham.

GASKIN An immigrant from Gascony.

GAUNT From Ghent in Belgium.

GELLING A Manx name, meaning 'Guillin's servant'.

GELNER An occupational name from the Old French word for a poulterer.

GIBBS 'Son of Gibb', which in turn was a pet form of Gilbert.

GILCHRIST A Scottish surname from a Gaelic name meaning 'servant of Christ'.

GILLESPIE From a Gaelic personal name meaning 'the bishop's servant'.

GITTINGS A Welsh surname from Guto or Gutyn (pronounced 'gitto' or 'gittin'), diminutives of Gruffydd.

GLADWIN From an Old English name.

GLEDHILL A west Yorkshire surname from an unidentified place name near Halifax, meaning 'kite hill'.

GODOLPHIN From a place in the parish of Breage in Cornwall.

GOLDING From an Old English personal name; also a Jewish name from Golding, the Yiddish name for a town in Latvia.

GOODBY An abbreviation of the expression 'God be with you', probably used as a nickname for someone who used it repeatedly. The surname is found chiefly in the Midlands.

GOODER From an Old English personal name.

GOODISON From an Old English female personal name with '-son' added.

GOODWIN From Godwine, an Old English personal name meaning 'good friend'. Also spelt Godwin.

GORMLEY An Irish surname Anglicised from a Gaelic personal name.

GORSTELLO From the village near Chester.

GOSLING Sometimes a nickname from a young goose, but usually a variant of Jocelyn.

GOUGH From the Welsh word *goch* ('red').

GRAHAM A Scottish name taken from the Lincolnshire place name of Grantham, which was recorded as Graham in Domesday.

GRAY A nickname for someone with grey hair. It may also come from Graye, a Norman place name.

GREATBACH From Gradbach Farm in Staffordshire.

GREATOREX From Great Rocks Farm in Derbyshire, recorded in 1251 as Greteraches, 'a great valley'.

GREEN A name for someone who lived by a green, or a nickname for someone who played the Green Man or dressed in green.

GREENGRASS From a minor place name on the borders of Suffolk and Norfolk. The surname is of single-family origin.

GREENHALGH From one of two hamlets in north Lancashire, in Kirkham and Garstang parishes.

GREENWOOD A west Yorkshire surname from Greenwood, west of Halifax.

GRENVILLE From Grainville-la-Teinturière in Normandy.

GRICE A nickname for someone with grey hair; also perhaps an occupational name for a swineherd, from Middle English *grice* ('pig').

GRIFFIN A pet form of the Welsh personal name Gruffydd; perhaps also introduced into parts of England by Breton immigrants.

GRIFFITHS From the old Welsh name Gruffydd.

GRIMSHAW A Lancashire surname derived from one of two places in the county.

GRINDROD From a place name near Rochdale, Lancashire.

GROSVENOR A Norman French occupational name for the man in charge of the arrangements for hunting.

GRUBB A nickname for a small person.

GULLICK From an Old English or Norse personal name.

GULLIVER A nickname from the Old French word for a glutton.

GUMMER From an Old English personal name. It is scattered through southern England.

GUPPY From a minor place name in Dorset.

h

HABBERJAM All variants of this name, such as Habershon and Habershaw, evolved from Habergham Eaves (a farm name) near Burnley.

HADEN A West Midlands surname from Haden Hill near Dudley.

HAGUE From one of the west Yorkshire farms enclosed by a hedge. Hague is the preferred spelling in south Yorkshire, but Haigh is usual elsewhere.

HAILSHAM From the place of that name near Eastbourne in Sussex.

HALL A common surname for someone who lived near, or was a servant at, a great hall.

HALLIDAY A nickname for someone born on a holy day, especially at Christmas or Easter.

HAMMOND From either an Old German or Old Norse personal name.

HAMPDEN From Great or Little Hampden, near High Wycombe, Buckinghamshire.

HAMPSHIRE In southern England from the county; in Yorkshire from Hallamshire, the ancient district around Sheffield.

HANMER From the Flintshire place name.

HARBOTTLE From the place in north-west Northumberland.

HARDAKER A name from Hardacre, near Clapham, in the Yorkshire Dales.

HARDCASTLE From Hardcastle Cross near Hebden Bridge, in west Yorkshire.

HARDSTAFF From Hardstoft in the parish of Ault Hucknall, Derbyshire.

HARDY An Old French nickname for a courageous man.

HARRIS 'Son of Harry'; also the Anglicised version of various Jewish names.

HARVARD From the Old English personal name, which also developed into Hereward.

HASTED A Kentish surname from Highsted.

HAUGHEY An Irish surname Anglicised from a Gaelic name.

HAVELOCK From a Viking personal name; popularised in the Middle Ages by the romance *Havelok the Dane*.

HAWKHURST From Hawkhurst Court in Kirdford, Sussex.

HAYTHORNTHWAITE A Lancashire name from Hawthornthwaite near Lancaster.

HEALD A Lancashire and Yorkshire surname for someone who lived on a hillside.

HEBBLEWHITE One of several names that formed from Heblethwaite, near Sedbergh.

HELLIER An occupational name for a roof tiler or thatcher. Also spelt Helyer and Hillyar.

HEMINGWAY From an unidentified minor place name in west Yorkshire, near Halifax.

HENNESSEY An Irish name Anglicised from a Gaelic personal name. It is spelt in a variety of ways, including Henchey and Hinchy.

HENTY From Antye Farm in Sussex.

HERRICK From an Old Norse personal name (Eric is the modern equivalent).

HEWLETT From a diminutive of Hugh. Other forms include Howlett and Hullot.

HEY A Yorkshire and Lancashire surname from a farm ('hedged enclosure') near Halifax.

HICKS 'Son of Hick', a pet form of Richard.

HIGGINBOTTOM A Lancashire surname from Oakenbottom near Bolton.

HILL A name for someone who lived on a hill.

HINCHCLIFFE From a minor place name in the Holme valley, west Yorkshire. The second letter 'c' has often been dropped.

HINE A young servant.

HITCHCOCK A diminutive of Hich, which in turn was a pet form of Richard. Found widely in southern England.

HOBBS 'Son of Hobb', a rhyming pet form of Robert.

HOBDAY 'Servant of Hobb', found chiefly in the West Midlands.

HOBHOUSE From a minor place name in Drewsteignton in Devon.

HODDER An occupational name for a maker or seller of hoods, often found in the West Country.

HODGKIN A diminutive of Hodge, a rhyming pet form of Roger.

HOGBEN A nickname for someone with a crippled hip. The surname comes from Kent.

HOGGARD An occupational surname for a keeper of pigs.

HOLMES A name for someone who lived either on an island, or by a holly tree.

HONEYBALL A variant of Hannibal, which is not derived from the Carthaginian general but from the female personal name Amable. It is a rare name, found mainly in or near London.

HOPE From one of the numerous place names signifying an enclosed valley.

HOPKINS A diminutive of Hobbe, a rhyming pet form of Robert, with the suffix '-s', meaning 'son of'.

HOPWOOD From a Lancashire place name near Rochdale.

HORSFIELD From Horsfall, meaning 'horse-clearing', near Todmorden on the borders of Yorkshire and Lancashire.

HOSKINS The son of Hoskin, a diminutive of various Old English personal names beginning with 'Os-'. The surname is found chiefly in or near Devon.

HUBBLE From the Norman personal name Hubald, found chiefly in the West Midlands.

HUGHES 'Son of Hugh'. Hugh came from an Old French personal name brought to England by the Normans.

HUNGERFORD From the Berkshire town.

HUNTBACH From Humpidge Green in Staffordshire.

HURLBATT A nickname for someone proficient at a medieval throwing game. It is also spelt Hurlbut and Hurlbutt.

HUTCHINSON 'Son of Huchun', which in turn was a diminutive of Hugh.

HUXLEY From the village near Chester.

HUXTABLE From a small town in Devon.

IBBERSON A variant of Ibbotson, 'son of Ibbot', which in turn was a diminutive of Isabel.

IMPEY A name derived from a site enclosed by young trees or where a hedge enclosed saplings. Empey is a variant form.

INCHBALD From an Old German personal name introduced by the Normans.

INGAMELLS From Ingoldmells, the Lincolnshire seaside resort.

INGERSOLL From Inkersall Green near Chesterfield in Derbyshire.

INGOLDSBY From the place between Stamford and Sleaford in Lincolnshire.

INGRAM From an Old German personal name introduced by the Normans.

INKPEN From a village on the border of Berkshire and Wiltshire.

INMAN An occupational name for an inn-keeper, from the Old English *inn* ('lodging').

IREMONGER A diminutive of ironmonger.

IRONS From Airaines in northern France.

IVESON 'Son of Ive', which in turn derives from the Norman personal name Ivo.

JACKLIN A diminutive of Jack, which in turn was a pet form of John, or from Jacques.

JACKSON 'Son of Jack', possibly from the Old French name Jacques. The surname may have evolved from a pet form of John.

JAGGER A west Yorkshire term for a carrier of heavy loads, possibly of single-family origin.

JAMES From the New Testament name. The patronymic system created many new names, including Jameson, Jamieson and Jemison.

JARVIS From a personal name introduced by the Normans. Also spelt Gervase.

JEAVONS Either from an Old French word meaning 'young', or from the Welsh name Evan/Ieuan. Found in the West Midlands.

JEEVES A pet form of the female name Geneviève introduced by the Normans.

JEFFCOCK A diminutive of Geoffrey; it may have a single-family origin near Sheffield.

JENNER An occupational surname for a master craftsman, common in Kent and Sussex.

JENNINGS From the medieval name Janyn, which in turn was a diminutive of John.

JESSOP The usual pronunciation of Joseph in the Middle Ages.

JOHNSON A surname formed from the patronymic system meaning 'son of John'.

JOHNSTONE A Scottish surname from the place of that name in Dumfries and Galloway.

JONES A surname from the popular personal name John. It is especially common in Wales and on the English/Welsh border.

JORDAN From a personal name taken from the river and popularised by the Crusaders.

JOWETT From Juetta, a diminutive of Juliana. It is often found in or near Bradford.

JOY From the female name Joia, derived from the French, meaning 'joyful person'.

JUBB A northern version of the Biblical name Job. Also found as Jobes, Jope, Jopp and Jupp.

JUDSON 'Son of Jud', which in turn was a pet form of Jordan.

KANEEN A Manx name, shortened from the Gaelic MacCianain.

KAVANAGH An Irish name Anglicised from a Gaelic personal name. Mostly from Leinster.

KEARNEY An Irish name that formed from two Gaelic personal names meaning 'warlike' and 'victorious'.

KEAST A Cornish nickname for a fat man.

KEATING From an Old English personal name brought to Ireland by Anglo-Norman families. It is also an Anglicised form of Keaty.

KEEGAN An Irish surname Anglicised from one of two Gaelic names.

KEELER A maker of, or sailor on, a type of boat known as a keel. The name is found in Norfolk and Kent.

KEENLEYSIDE From a place of that name near Allendale, Northumberland.

KELL A shortened form of the Viking personal name Ketill. The surname is found particularly in north-east England.

KELLAM From Kelham in Nottinghamshire.

KELLETT From Kellet in Lancashire, or Kelleth in Westmorland, now part of Cumbria.

KELLY In Ireland, the name is an Anglicisation of Ò Ceallaigh, meaning 'descended from Ceallach'. In Devon and Scotland it is taken from a place name.

KEMP From an Old English word for warrior.

KENNEDY An Irish and Scottish name from a Gaelic nickname meaning 'ill-formed head'.

KENWORTHY From a place in Cheshire.

KENYON A Lancashire surname from the place near Warrington.

KEOGH An Irish surname Anglicised from a Gaelic personal name.

KERSHAW A Lancashire surname from Kirkshaw, near Rochdale.

KILBRIDE A Scottish and Irish name from either an Anglicised form of a Gaelic personal name or from various Scottish place names.

KILBY From the village south of Leicester.

KILLIGREW From a Cornish place name.

KILROY From a Gaelic name for 'servant of the red-haired lad'. Another form is Gilroy.

KINDER From the small Peak District settlement at the edge of Kinderscout.

KING A nickname, or perhaps given to someone who played the role of king in a play.

KINGSNORTH One of the many Kentish surnames formed from farms or hamlets. In this case it is from a small place in the Weald.

KINSEY From an Old English personal name.

KIPLING From one of two places in north and east Yorkshire.

KIRK A northern England and Lowland Scotland name for someone living by a church.

KITSON 'Son of Kitt', which in turn was a pet form of Christopher.

KITTO Cornish surname from a diminutive of the Celtic personal name Griffith.

KNAPP From a minor place name meaning 'hilltop'. The surname is found in southern England, from Devon to Sussex.

KNATCHBULL A nickname for a butcher.

KNEEBONE From Carnebone in the Cornish parish of Wendron.

KNUCKEY From a place name in Cornwall.

LACE Short for Lacer, a cord or string maker.

LACEY From Lassy in Normandy.

LADBROOKE From the village near Southam in Warwickshire.

LADD A servant or man of humble birth.

LADYMAN Servant of a lady.

LAITHWAITE From one of two places in north and south Lancashire.

LAKE Someone who lived by a stream, *lacu* in Old English.

LAMBERT An Old English and Old German personal name popular in the Middle Ages.

LAMBKIN A diminutive of Lamb, which in turn was a short form of Lambert.

LAMONT A Scottish and northern Irish surname from an Old Norse personal name.

LAMPLUGH From the Cumbrian village.

LANGRIDGE From several place names in southern England. It means 'long ridge'.

LANYON A Cornish surname from a place near Penzance.

LARKIN A diminutive of Lawrence.

LASCELLES From Lacelle in Normandy.

LAST An occupational name for a cobbler or a maker of cobblers' lasts (blocks).

LATIMER An occupational name for a clerk who kept records in Latin.

LAUDER From a village in the Scottish Borders.

LAVENDER An occupational surname for a washerman or washerwoman.

LAWLEY A West Midlands surname derived from a Shropshire village near Telford.

LAWSON The son of Lawrence.

LEADBETTER An occupational surname for one who beat lead into shape. It is scattered in many parts of England because the beating took place at the sites where lead was needed.

LEAVIS From an Old English personal name.

LEE A name for someone who lived near a meadow, or from place names using this word.

LEGG A West Country nickname for a person with a peculiarity of the leg, or long legs.

LEHRER A Yiddish name for a teacher.

LENNON An Irish surname Anglicised from a Gaelic name.

LENNOX A Scottish and northern Irish surname from the district near Dumbarton.

LESLIE A Scottish surname from a barony in Aberdeenshire. It is also found in Ireland.

LETTICE A nickname from the Latin word for 'joy'.

LEVERIDGE One of many variants of an Old English personal name. Others include Lefridge, Leverick and Liverock.

LEVI A Jewish name for a member of the tribe of Levi.

LEVICK A Sheffield variant of Levett, derived from an Old English personal name or from one of the places in Normandy named Livet.

LEWIN From an Old English personal name; or a variant of the Jewish name Levi.

LEWIS A personal name brought to England by the Normans. It is an Anglicised form of Llewelyn in Wales, and in Scotland comes from the Hebridean island.

LIBBY A pet form of Elizabeth. The surname is found chiefly in Devon.

LIGHTFOOT A nickname for a speedy runner or messenger.

LINDOP From a minor Derbyshire place name meaning 'lime-tree valley'.

LISTER An occupational surname for a dyer, found chiefly in west Yorkshire and East Anglia.

LITTLEWOOD From minor place names, especially one near Holmfirth in Yorkshire.

LLOYD A Welsh nickname for someone with grey hair.

LOADER From Loder in Dorset rather than an occupational term.

LOBB A nickname from Old English *lobbe*, 'a spider'. The surname is found chiefly in Devon.

LOMAX From a lost place name near Bury, Lancashire. Other forms of the name include Lomas and Lummis.

LOONEY A Manx and Irish surname from a Gaelic name.

LORIMER An occupational surname for a maker or seller of metal bits and spurs.

LOVAT A diminutive of an Old English personal name.

LOVECHILD From an Old English personal name.

LOVECOT From Lovecott Farm, Debden in Essex.

LOVELACE A nickname for a philanderer, from the Old English *lufu*, 'love', and *leas*, 'free from' or 'without'. Loveless is another form.

LOVERSALL From the south Yorkshire village near Doncaster.

LOWCOCK A diminutive of an Old English personal name.

LOWRY A northern English and Lowland Scottish diminutive of Lawrence. In Ireland it is an Anglicised form of a Gaelic personal name.

LOWTHER From the village in Cumbria.

LUCAS A form of Luke.

LUFF From an Old English personal name, found mostly in East Anglia.

LUKEY A West Country form of Luke.

LUMB There are many minor place names of Lumb, meaning 'a deep pool', in west Yorkshire and Lancashire, but the surname seems to come from the Lumb near Sowerby and Halifax.

LUND Someone who lived by a grove or small wood, close to a boundary. The name is derived from an Old Norse word *lundr*. It is sometimes spelt Lount or Lunt.

LUPSETT From a place name in Wakefield.

LUSCOMBE From Loscombe in Devon.

LUTTRELL A Norman nickname from the Old French word for an otter (*loutre*).

LYNCH An Irish surname of dual origin, from the Gaelic name meaning 'mariner', and also from the Norman *de Lench*.

MABBETT A diminutive of Mabb, which in turn was a pet form of Mabel.

MACHIN An occupational term for a mason.

MacCARTHY An Irish surname Anglicised from a Gaelic name meaning 'loving'.

MacCAULAY A Scottish surname from an Anglicised form of a Gaelic personal name.

MacDONALD A Scottish name from an Anglicised form of MacDhonhnuill, a Gaelic name meaning 'son of Domhnall'.

MacENROE An Irish surname from an Anglicised form of a Gaelic name.

MacGREGOR A Scottish surname Anglicised from the Gaelic form of Gregory.

MacINTOSH A Scottish surname Anglicised from a Gaelic name, meaning 'son of the chief'.

MacINTYRE A Scottish surname Anglicised from the Gaelic, meaning 'son of the carpenter or mason'.

McNALLY An Irish surname Anglicised from the Gaelic, meaning 'son of the poor man'.

MacTAVISH A Scottish surname which is an Anglicisation of MacTàmhais, a Gaelic name meaning 'son of Thomas'.

MADDEN An Irish surname from an Anglicised form of a Gaelic personal name.

MADDOCK From the Welsh personal name Madog.

MAGGOTT A diminutive of Magg, which in turn was a pet form of Margaret.

MAISEY From either of two Normandy place names—Maisy (Calvados) or Maizy (Aisne).

MAKIN A diminutive of May, which in turn was a pet form of Matthew.

MALLORY A Norman nickname for an unlucky person.

MALONE An Irish surname Anglicised from a Gaelic name meaning 'a devotee of St John'.

MANDEVILLE From one of several places in northern France. It is also found in Ireland.

MANNERS From Mesnières in Normandy. Menzies is a Scottish version of the surname.

MAPPIN All members of this family are descended from Derricke Mappin, an immigrant from northern France or the Low Countries, who married in Sheffield in 1593.

MARNEY From Marigni in Normandy.

MARPLES From Marple, near Stockport in Cheshire.

MARRYATT A diminutive of Mary. Other forms include Marriott and Merritt.

MARSHALL An occupational surname from the Old French word for a vet.

MARTIN From a personal name popularised by Martin of Tours, a 4th-century saint.

MARTOCK From the small town of that name in Somerset.

MASON A trade name for a stonemason.

MASSEY Either a pet form of Matthew or from one of various places in northern France.

MASSINGBERD A nickname for someone with a tawny beard. From the Middle English word *massing*, meaning 'brass', and beard.

MASTERMAN 'Servant of the master'.

MATHER An occupational surname for a mower or reaper.

MATTHEWS A Biblical name from the Hebrew word *Matityahu*, meaning 'gift of God'. Other forms include Mathew, Mat(t)hewson, Matheson and Matterson.

MAUDLING From the Middle English form of the New Testament name Magdalene.

MAXEY From the Northamptonshire village.

MAYDON From Maiden, a derogatory nickname for an effeminate man.

MAYNARD An Old German personal name introduced by the Normans.

MEADOWCROFT From a minor place name in Middleton, Lancashire.

MEDLICOTT From the small place of that name near Church Stretton in Shropshire.

MELLING A Lancashire surname from villages near Lancaster and Liverpool.

MELLOR From one of two place names in Lancashire and north-west Derbyshire.

MERCER An occupational surname for a trader, especially of expensive fabrics.

MEREDITH A Welsh surname from the personal name Meredydd.

MERRYWEATHER A nickname for someone with a sunny disposition.

METHUEN A Scottish surname from Methven, Perth and Kinross.

MICKLEJOHN A nickname, 'big John'. Meikeljohn and Mucklejohn are variant forms.

MILDMAY A nickname, literally 'gentle maiden'.

MILLER An occupational name for a miller, or for someone who worked at a mill.

MILLICHAP From Millichope in Shropshire. Millychopp and Mellychopp are variants.

MILLOM From the town in Cumbria.

MILLS A form of the name Mill, applied to someone living near, or working in, a mill.

MILLWARD An occupational surname for someone in charge of a mill.

MILNER A variant spelling of Miller.

MINGAY From a Breton personal name. Found chiefly in Norfolk.

MINSHAW From Minshull Vernon or Church Minshull in Cheshire, also spelt Minshall.

MINTER An occupational surname for a striker of coins or someone in charge of a mint.

MITCHELL From the Middle English and Old French form of Michael. A common surname in Ireland.

MOFFATT A Scottish and northern Irish name from a place in Dumfries and Galloway.

MOGG A pet form of Margaret. Found particularly in south-west England.

MOLYNEUX From Moulineaux in Normandy. Found chiefly in south Lancashire.

MOMPESSON From Montpicon in Normandy.

MOORE A nickname for someone with a dark complexion, or a name for someone who lived on or near a moor.

MORGAN From an old Celtic name.

MORIARTY An Irish surname Anglicised from a Gaelic name meaning 'navigator'.

MORREY From one of two place names in Staffordshire and Shropshire.

MORRIS From the Old French personal name Maurice, introduced by the Normans; also an Anglicisation of various Jewish names.

MORTIMER From Mortemer in Normandy.

MOTHERSOLE From Moddershall near Stone, Staffordshire.

MOTT A pet form of Matilda.

MOUNTFORD From various places meaning 'strong, fortified hill' in northern France.

MOWBRAY From Montbrai in Normandy.

MOXON 'Son of Mokoc', a pet form of Matthew. Found chiefly in south Yorkshire.

MUGGERIDGE From Mogridge in Devon. Mockridge, Moggridge and Mugridge are variant forms.

MUIR A Scottish and northern English name for someone who lived on or by a moor.

MUMBY From the village near the Lincolnshire coast.

MURGATROYD A west Yorkshire surname from a farm in Warley, near Halifax. Its literal meaning is 'clearing by the moor road'.

MURPHY An Irish surname Anglicised from a Gaelic name.

MURRAY A Scottish surname from Moray.

NADEN From a small Lancashire settlement near Rochdale.

NAPIER An occupational surname for a seller of table linen or napery.

NASH From *atten ash*, meaning someone who lived by an ash tree. Also an Anglicised form of Jewish names.

NAYSMITH A knife-smith.

NEAT An occupational name for someone who looked after a herd of cattle (Old English *neat*). It is found chiefly in north Wiltshire.

NESBITT From places in County Durham, Northumberland and the Scottish Borders. Nisbet and Nisbit are variants.

NETHERSALL From Nethersole Farm in Womenswold, Kent.

NEVE Either the nephew, probably of an important person, or an orphan who was raised by his uncle.

NEVILLE From Neuville in Normandy.

NEWBORN From Newbourn in Suffolk or Newburn in Northumberland.

NEWBOUND A variant of Newbold, derived from various places in the Midlands.

NEWDIGATE From the village in Surrey.

NEWMARCH From Neufmarché in Normandy.

NICE An Essex nickname meaning 'foolish'.

NIGHTINGALE A nickname for a singer.

NIXON 'Son of Nick', which in turn is a short form of Nicholas.

NORMANVILLE From the place of that name in Normandy.

NUNN A nickname for someone who was as meek and demure as a nun.

NUSSEY A west Yorkshire surname from Nussey Green, Burnsall.

NUTCOMB From one of the four places of that name in Devon.

NUTTALL A Lancashire surname from Nuttall near Bury.

NUTTER From the Old English word for a scribe, or the Old French for secretary.

OASTLER The keeper of a hostelry or inn.

O'CONNELL An Irish surname meaning 'descendant of Connall'. Connell was derived from a Celtic personal name.

ODDY A diminutive of the Viking personal name Oddi. A northern England surname.

ODIHAM From the Hampshire town.

O'DONOGHUE An Irish surname meaning 'descendant of Donagh'. Donagh was a Gaelic personal name.

OGDEN A Lancashire and Yorkshire name from Ogden, near Rochdale or near Halifax.

OGILVIE A Scottish surname from a town near Glamis in Angus.

OLDCASTLE From Oldcastle Heath in south Cheshire.

OLIPHANT From the Middle English word for an elephant. It might have been used as a nickname, or to refer to a trader in ivory.

OLLERENSHAW 'Alder copse'. From a farm name in the Peak District.

ONIONS Perhaps a name for an onion seller, but, more probably 'the son of Einion', a Welsh personal name. Einion also produced the more common Welsh surname Einon or Eynon.

ONSLOW From a small village near Shrewsbury in Shropshire.

ORDISH From a minor place name Highoredish, near Ashover in Derbyshire.

O'REILLY Irish descendant of someone with the Gaelic name Raghallach.

ORLEBAR From Orlingbury, south of Kettering, Northamptonshire.

ORRICK From an Old English personal name. Orridge is a variant.

OSBORN From a Norse name used by both the Anglo-Saxons and the Normans.

OUGHTRED From an Old English personal name, also written as Outred and Ughtred.

OWEN From the Old Welsh personal name Owain. See also Bowen, page 302.

OXNARD An occupational surname for a keeper of oxen.

PACEY From Pacy-sur-Eure in Normandy.

PADLEY From a Derbyshire place name.

PADMORE From the small place near Whippingham in Wiltshire.

PAISLEY A Scottish and northern Irish name from the town in Renfrewshire.

PALFREYMAN A man in charge of the palfreys, or the saddle-horses.

PALGRAVE From the places of this name in Norfolk and Suffolk.

PALLISER A maker of park pales. Often found in north Yorkshire and County Durham.

PALMER A name for a pilgrim. Named after the palm branch that pilgrims carried.

PANKHURST From the places called Pinkhurst in Sussex and Surrey, or perhaps a name for someone who was born during the church festival of Pentecost.

PAPE A nickname for someone with a bearing like the pope; or someone who took the part of the pope in a pageant.

PAPILLON A nickname from the Old French word for butterfly.

PARDOE A nickname for someone who frequently said *par dieu*, 'for God's sake'.

PARFAY A nickname for someone prone to say *par fei*, 'by faith'.

PARKER An occupational name for a keeper of a deer park.

PARKIN A diminutive of Peter. Perkin is a variant form.

PARMENTER An occupational surname for a tailor or a maker of facings and trimmings.

PARR Commonly derived from the place in Lancashire, but also from parks (from an Old English word for an enclosure).

PARROTT A diminutive of Perre, a form of Peter; sometimes from Perrott in Somerset. The name is widespread in the Midlands.

PATEL Derived from the Indian word *Patidar* meaning 'farmer', and thought to originate from Gujarat, a state in western India.

PATERNOSTER An occupational name for a rosary maker, derived from the Lord's Prayer.

PATEY A diminutive of Pate, which, in turn, was a pet form of Patrick.

PATTERSON 'Son of Patrick'.

PAWLEY From Pavilly in Normandy.

PEATE A pet form of Peter.

PELLING From Peelings, a Sussex place name.

PENHALE One of many Cornish surnames derived from places beginning with *Pen*, meaning 'headland'. This is from Penheale in the parish of Egloskerry.

PENHALIGON From the Cornish place name near Bodmin.

PENNYFATHER A nickname for a miser.

PENROSE From various places in Cornwall signifying a high ridge of moorland.

PENRY From the Welsh *ap Henry*, 'son of Henry'.

PEPYS See page 298.

PERCY From various French place names.

PERRERS From Perriers in Normandy.

PERRIN From an Old French personal name, a diminutive of Peter.

PERRY Meaning a 'dweller by the pear tree'. Found mostly in Staffordshire, where it comes from Perry Barr, now part of Birmingham.

PERTWEE From various place names in northern France.

PETERKIN A diminutive of Peter.

PETO An immigrant from Poitou.

PETTIGREW A nickname from Old French words meaning 'stunted growth'.

PETTIT From the Old French for 'little'.

PHELPS Another form of Phillips, meaning 'son of Philip'.

PHILPOT A diminutive of Philip.

PICKARD An immigrant from Picardy.

PICKERELL A nickname for an aggressive person, from the Middle English word for a young pike.

PICKLES A west Yorkshire surname from a small place near Haworth.

PICKUP From a small place near Blackburn, Lancashire, signifying a hill with a sharp peak.

PIERCE From an Old French form of Peter.

PIGGOTT A diminutive of an Old German name *Pic*, introduced by the Normans.

PINK A nickname from the Old English word for a chaffinch.

PINKEY From Picquigny in northern France.

PINNOCK A nickname from the Middle English word for a dunnock (hedge sparrow).

PITNEY From the Somerset village of Pitney.

PLANT An occupational surname for a gardener. Found in Staffordshire, Cheshire and Lancashire.

PLEASANCE From the medieval woman's name Plaisance, the Old French for 'pleasing'.

PLIMSOLL A Huguenot name from Brittany, brought into England in the late 17th century.

PLOWRIGHT An occupational surname for a maker of ploughs.

PLUNKETT From Plouquenet in Brittany.

POINTER An occupational surname for a maker of points, used to fasten garments.

POLAK A name given to a Jew from Poland.

POLLARD From Pollhard, a personal name derived from Paul; it may also be a nickname that evolved from *poll*, referring to someone with a big head or close-cropped hair.

POMEROY Found chiefly in Devon, it comes from one of many places in northern France and denotes an apple orchard.

PONSONBY From the place of that name near Whitehaven in Cumbria.

POSTAN The keeper of the postern gate of a town or castle.

POSTLETHWAITE From a minor place name near Millom in south-west Cumbria.

POTTINGER A maker or seller of pottage (broth or thick soup).

POULTER An Old French word for a poultry dealer.

POWELL The Welsh *ap Hywel*, 'son of Howell'; occasionally used to refer to someone who lived by a pool.

POWICK From a village in Worcestershire.

POYSER An occupational surname for someone in charge of a weighing machine. The name is probably of single-family origin.

PRATT An Old English nickname meaning 'cunning' or 'astute'.

PRESTNEY From an Essex farm name.

PRETTYJOHN After Prester John, the fabled priest-king of central Asia, whose fame spread throughout 12th-century Europe.

PRICE From the Welsh *ap Rhys*, 'son of Rees'.

PRINGLE From a small place near Stow, in the Scottish Borders.

PRITCHARD From the Welsh *ap Richard*, 'son of Richard'.

PRITTY A variant of Pretty, from the Old English word for 'crafty' or 'cunning'.

PROBERT From the Welsh *ap Robert*, 'son of Robert'.

PROSSER From the Welsh *ap Rosser*, 'son of Roger'.

PROVENDER From the Old French word for the man who was responsible for the provisions of a large house or castle.

PUDDEPHAT A nickname for someone shaped like a barrel, from Middle English words meaning 'round bellied' and 'vat'.

PULLEN An occupational surname from an Old French word for a horse breeder; or perhaps a nickname for a frisky person.

PURCELL From the Old French word for a swineherd. Often found in Tipperary, Ireland.

PURDOM From the Old French word for an honest man. It is also found as Purden.

PURDY A nickname for someone who frequently used the oath *pur die*, 'by God'.

QUAIFE An Old French word for a maker of coifs, close-fitting caps.

QUANT A nickname for a skilful or crafty person, or one who dressed elegantly.

QUARMBY A west Yorkshire surname from the village near Huddersfield.

QUARTERMAIN A nickname, literally 'four hands', whose exact allusion is obscure.

QUATERMASS From Quatremares in Normandy.

QUENNELL From Quenilla, a Middle English female personal name. It was derived from an Old English name with two elements, 'woman' and 'battle'.

QUILLER An occupational surname from the Old French for a maker of spoons and ladles.

QUINCEY From one of several place names in northern France.

QUIXALL From Quixhill in Staffordshire.

RABBITT A diminutive of Rabb, which in turn was a pet form of Robert; also from the Norman personal name Radbode.

RAFFLES A Scottish surname from a place so-called in Dumfries and Galloway.

RAIKES One who lived by a path up a hillside.

RAINBIRD From an Old French personal name, Rainbert.

RAINBOW From an Old French personal name, Rainbaut.

RAINGOLD From an Old German personal name introduced by the Normans.

RAMSBOTTOM From the Lancashire place of that name.

RAMSHAW From a moorland settlement in County Durham, west of Consett.

RANDALL A diminutive of Rand, a shortened form of Randolph.

RANKILL From an Old Norse or Old Swedish personal name.

RAPER A northern form of the occupational surname Roper—a maker of rope.

RASPBERRY From Ratsbury near Lynton in Devon.

RATHBONE Either from Radbourn in Warwickshire or Radbourne in Derbyshire.

RAVENSCROFT From a village in Cheshire.

RAYBOULD A West Midlands surname from the Old French personal name Rainbaut.

RAYNER From an Old German personal name introduced by the Normans.

READER An occupational surname for a thatcher with reeds, chiefly from Norfolk.

REANEY From Ranah Stones Cote, a farm in the parish of Penistone in west Yorkshire.

REARDON An Irish surname Anglicised from a Gaelic name. Also spelt Riordan.

REDDIHOUGH From a minor place name in Lancashire. Other forms include Ridealgh, Redihalgh and Reddyhoff.

REDDISH From Redditch in Worcestershire or Lancashire. Radish is a variant form of the surname.

REDFEARN A Lancashire surname from a place in the parish of Rochdale.

REDGRAVE From the village in Suffolk.

REDMAYNE From Redmain, Cumbria.

REDPATH From Redpath, near Earlston, in the Scottish Borders.

REEVE A name for a steward or bailiff. It is found mostly in East Anglia.

REGAN An Irish surname Anglicised from a Gaelic name.

REMFREY From an Old German personal name introduced by the Normans.

RENNICK From a village in Cumbria.

REVELL A nickname from an Old French word for a reveller.

REYNOLDS From an Old German personal name that was popularised by the Normans.

RHODES Someone who lived near a woodland clearing, or 'royd'.

RICHARDSON 'Son of Richard.'

RICKERT One of the forms of Richard. Rickard is particularly common in Cornwall.

RIGG From the northern England pronunciation of 'ridge'.

RIPPER An occupational surname for a maker or seller of baskets.

RIVETT An occupational surname for a maker of rivets. It is often found in East Anglia.

ROADKNIGHT From an Old English word for a mounted servant or retainer.

ROBERTS 'Son of Robert.' Robert was a Germanic name formed from *hrod* ('renown') and *berht* ('famous').

ROBINSON 'Son of Robin', a medieval name, which was a diminutive of Robert.

ROBSON 'Son of Robert.' The surname is confined largely to north-east England.

RODING From one of the group of villages with this name in Essex.

RODNEY From a lost settlement on the Somerset/Wiltshire border.

ROGERS 'Son of Roger', a Germanic name brought to England by the Normans.

RONKSLEY From a farm name in the Upper Derwent valley in Derbyshire.

ROONEY An Irish surname Anglicised from a Gaelic name.

ROTHWELL From a small settlement in central Lancashire, rather than the places in Yorkshire, Lincolnshire or Northamptonshire.

ROUND A nickname for a fat man. It has a single-family origin in or near Dudley.

ROUSE A nickname from the Old French word for red hair.

ROWNTREE Someone whose house was by a rowan tree.

RUDDOCK A nickname from the Middle English word for a robin. Sometimes derived from the Welsh personal name Rhydderch.

RUMBALL From an Old German personal name. It is also found as Rumbold and Rumble.

RUSKIN A diminutive of a personal name, probably Rose.

RUSSELL A nickname—from the diminutive form of the Old French word *rous* meaning 'red'—for someone with red hair.

RUTTER A player of the rote, a musical stringed instrument like a fiddle.

SACKVILLE From Saqueneville in Normandy.

SACHEVERELL From Sault-Chevreuil in Normandy.

SADLER An occupational name for a maker or seller of saddles.

SAFFER A Norman nickname for a glutton.

SAGAR From an Old English personal name.

SAINSBURY From Saintbury near Chipping Campden in Gloucestershire.

SALKELD From the place name in Cumbria.

SALT From the village in Staffordshire.

SAMBROOK From the place of that name near the Shropshire/Staffordshire border.

SAMM A pet form of Sampson, also spelt Sam, Samme, Sammes and Samms.

SAMWAYS A nickname for a stupid person; found chiefly in Dorset.

SANGAR From *sangere*, the Old English word for a chorister.

SANKEY A Lancashire surname from the place of that name near Warrington.

SARSON The 'son of Sara'; also from the Saracen for a swarthy man.

SAUNDERS 'Son of Sander', a pet form of Alexander.

SAVILLE From Sainville in Normandy.

SAWNER An occupational surname from an Old French word for a salter (someone who mined or transported salt). Also spelt Saunter.

SAWYER A sawer of wood.

SAYE From Sai in Normandy.

SCAIFE A nickname from an Old Norse word meaning 'crooked' or 'awkward'.

SCARF A nickname from the Old Norse word for a cormorant.

SCARGILL From the village of that name in north Yorkshire.

SCHOFIELD A Lancashire and Yorkshire surname from Scholefield, near Rochdale.

SCHOLEY From a minor place name near Hemsworth, in west Yorkshire.

SCOTT A name for someone from Scotland.

SCOULAR From the Viking word for a summer hut (or shieling) used by a herdsman.

SCRIVEN A clerk from the Old French word for a writer. Also spelt Scrivener.

SEAGRAVE From the place near Leicester.

SEARLE From Serlo, a Norman name.

SECOMBE From one of two places named Seccombe in Devon.

SEDGEFIELD From the place of that name in County Durham.

SEMPER From various places named Saint-Pierre in northern France.

SENIOR A Yorkshire nickname from Norman French *seigneur*, 'lord', or meaning 'the elder'.

SERVICE An Old French occupational surname for a seller of ale.

SEYMOUR From Saint-Mauyr-des-Fossés in Normandy; or from two places called Seamer in Yorkshire.

SHAFTOE From Shaftoe Grange and Shaftoe Moor in Northumberland.

SHARMAN An occupational surname for a shearer of woollen cloth. Also spelt Shearman and Sherman.

SHARPLES A Lancashire surname from the place of that name near Rochdale.

SHARROCK A Lancashire surname also found as Shorrocks, both of which come from Shorrock Green.

SHAW A name for someone who lived by a wood. See page 300.

SHELDRAKE A nickname from the brightly coloured duck of the same name. It may have been applied to a vain or ostentatious person.

SHERLOCK A Middle English nickname for someone with fair hair.

SHILBOTTLE From the place of that name south of Alnwick in Northumberland.

SHIRTCLIFFE From Sirecliffe, now a suburb of Sheffield.

SHOESMITH An occupational name for a maker of horseshoes.

SHOOTER A name for an archer.

SHUFFLEBOTTOM One form of the name derived from Shipperbottom in Lancashire.

SILCOCK A diminutive of Sil, which was a shortened form of Silvein or Silvester.

SIMKIN A diminutive of Sim, which, in turn, was a shortened form of Simon.

SIMPLE A nickname from the Old French word meaning 'honest' or 'straightforward'.

SIMPSON From Sim, a medieval name. Other forms are Simson, Sim(m)s and Simes.

SINCLAIR From the place name Saint-Clair found throughout France.

SISSONS 'Son of Ciss', which in turn was a pet form of Cecily.

SKEALE A Middle English occupational name for a maker or seller of wooden buckets.

SLACK From one of the minor place names of Viking origin meaning 'a shallow valley'; perhaps also a nickname for an idle person. The surname is found chiefly in the north Midlands.

SMALLCOMBE From various place names in Devon denoting a small valley.

SMALLEY From the Derbyshire place name.

SMITH See page 301.

SMOLLETT A nickname for someone with a small head.

SNAPE From various places situated on poor, unproductive land.

SNELL A nickname for a lively person.

SNODGRASS From a Scottish place name near Irvine, North Ayrshire.

SNORING From Great and Little Snoring in Norfolk.

SOWERBUTTS A Lancashire surname from a place of that name near Garstang.

SPEIGHT A nickname from *speght*, the Middle English for 'woodpecker'. It probably referred to a talkative person.

SPENDLOVE A nickname for a philanderer, someone who was free with his love.

SPINK A nickname from the Middle English word for a chaffinch.

SPRAY A nickname for a thin person, from the Middle English word for a slender branch.

SPRINGHAM From the farm of that name in Hellingly in Sussex.

SPUFFORD From Spofforth in Yorkshire.

STACY From a pet form of the name Eustace.

STAMP From Etampes in Normandy.

STANBROOK From the place so-called near Powick, Worcestershire.

STANIFORTH From a minor place name, now Low Wincobank, Sheffield.

STARBUCK A Yorkshire surname from Starbeck near Harrogate.

STEAD From one of two west Yorkshire place names, in Burley-in-Wharfedale and near Wentworth, south of Barnsley.

STEPTOE A nickname for someone who trod lightly.

STEWART An occupational name for a steward who managed a household. Also spelt Steward and Stuart.

STODDART An occupational surname for a breeder or keeper of horses.

STOKOE From Stockhow in Cumbria.

STONOR From Stonor in Oxfordshire.

STOREY From an Old Norse personal name.

STRANGEWAYS A Lancashire surname from the place so-called in Manchester.

STRICKLAND From the place of that name in Westmorland, now part of Cumbria.

STRINGER An ironworker, rather than a maker of string.

SUCKSMITH An occupational surname for a maker of ploughshares (the blades of ploughs).

SUMPTER A man in charge of packhorses.

SURRIDGE From Surridge in Devon.

SURTEES Someone who lived on the banks of the River Tees.

SUTCLIFFE A west Yorkshire surname from Sutcliff ('south cliff') near Brighouse.

SWINBURN From the place so-called north of Hexham in Northumberland.

TABERNER A drummer from the Middle English or Old French word.

TAGG A nickname from the Old English word for a young sheep.

TAINTER An occupational surname for a dyer, from an Old French word.

TALLBOY A name derived from Taillebois in Normandy, meaning 'clearing in a wood'; or an occupational name for a wood cutter.

TAMPSON 'Son of Tam', a pet form of Thomas.

TANKARD From a Norman personal name. Perhaps also a nickname for a heavy drinker or an occupational name for a maker of tankards.

TARBUCK From Tarbock in Lancashire.

TARDEW A nickname meaning 'slow' from an Old French word, which has become 'tardy'.

TART A nickname from an Old English word meaning 'sharp' or 'rough'.

TASKER An occupational name for someone who took on piece work such as threshing.

TAWYER An occupational surname for one who prepared white leather.

TAYLOR An occupational surname, and one of the most common in Britain.

TEAR A Manx name, which is a shortened form of McIntyre.

TENNYSON 'Son of Dennis.'

THACKERAY From Thackray, now under Fewston reservoir, near Otley in Yorkshire.

THIRKHILL From a Viking personal name used in England and Normandy. Other forms include Thurkettle, Thurkell and Thorkell.

THISTLEWOOD From Thistleworth, near West Grinstead in Sussex.

THOMAS A name of Biblical origin that became popular in the medieval period. It came from the Aramaic word meaning 'twin' and is particularly common in Wales.

THOMPSON Another form meaning 'son of Thomas'. Also spelt Thomson and Tompson.

THORNDIKE Someone whose house stood by a thorny ditch.

THOROGOOD From an Old Norse personal name. Thoroughgood, Thorgood and Thurgate are among the variant forms.

THROWER An occupational name in the south of England for a maker of silk thread.

TICKLE From Tickhill in south Yorkshire.

TIDMARSH From the village in Berkshire.

TILL A pet form of Matilda.

TIPLADY A nickname for a lecherous man.

TITCHENER Someone whose house was on a crossroads or a road junction.

TODD A nickname from the Middle English word for fox.

TOMBS A pet form of Thomas.

TOMLINSON 'Son of Tomlin', a diminutive of Thomas.

TOOKE From an Old Norse personal name.

TRANTER An occupational surname for a hawker or pedlar with a horse and cart.

TREACLE A nickname for an apothecary.

TRELAWNEY One of many Cornish names derived from tre or trev, meaning 'homestead' or 'hamlet'. Trelawny is in Altarnun parish.

TREMLETT From Les Tres Minèttes in Normandy.

TREVELYAN From the Cornish place name.

TREVETHICK From various places of that name in Cornwall.

TRICKETT A nickname from Norman French, meaning 'cheat' or 'deceiver'.

TRINDER An occupational surname for a braider or spinner.

TROLLOPE See page 298.

TROWELL From the Nottinghamshire village.

TRUMPER A trumpeter.

TUCK From a Viking personal name or a pet form of one.

TUCKER The West Country name for a fuller of cloth. Often spelt Tooker.

TUDOR The Welsh form of Theodore.

TUNNICLIFFE From Tonacliffe, a minor place name near Rochdale in Lancashire.

TURBERFIELD From Thouberville in Normandy.

TURNER An occupational surname for someone who made objects by turning wood on a lathe.

TURPIN From the Norman form of an Old Norse personal name.

TURVEY From the village west of Bedford.

TWIGG A nickname for a thin man.

TWYCROSS From the village on the border of Leicestershire and Warwickshire.

TYAS An immigrant from Germany.

TYLDESLEY From the place in Lancashire near Leigh.

TYRWHITT From Trewhitt in Rothbury parish in Northumberland.

TYSON From an Old French word meaning firebrand.

UNDERWOOD Someone who lived at the edge of a wood.

UNSWORTH From the place north of Manchester.

UNTHANK From various places of that name in northern England, denoting a squatter's settlement.

UNWIN From Unwine, an Old English personal name.

UPJOHN From the Welsh ap John, 'son of John'.

URQUHART A Scottish surname from the place on Loch Ness in the Highlands.

URRY From the Norman pronunciation of the Old English personal name Wulfric. Other forms include Hurry, Orrey and Oury.

UTLEY A west Yorkshire surname from a place near Keighley.

UTTING From an Old English personal name. The surname is found chiefly in Norfolk.

VAISEY A Norman French nickname for a cheerful person.

VANDERVILLE A Dutch immigrant surname, from van der veld, 'of the field'.

VARNEY From Saint-Paul-du-Verny in Normandy or similar French place names.

VAUGHAN From the Welsh words bychan or fychan, meaning 'junior' or 'smaller'.

VAUNTNER From the Old French word for 'braggart'.

VAVASOUR The Old French word for someone immediately below the rank of baron.

VENABLES From Venables in Normandy.

VERITY A west Yorkshire surname, meaning 'truth', perhaps from a pageant name.

VERNON From the place in Normandy.

VERRIER From the Old French word for a glassmaker.

VESSEY From the Normandy place name.

VICKERS 'Son or servant of the vicar.'

VINTNER A wine merchant.

VURLONGER Also written as Furlonger, 'a small farmer'. The surname probably has a single-family origin in north Sussex.

WACE From a Norman personal name; also from the Welsh word for a servant.

WADDELL A Scottish surname from Wedale, now Stow, near Edinburgh.

WADE From an Old English personal name; also perhaps for someone who lived by a ford.

WADLEY From the place so-called in Great Faringdon parish in Berkshire.

WAINWRIGHT A maker of wains, two-wheeled vehicles. The surname is found mostly in Yorkshire and Lancashire.

WAKELIN From a Norman diminutive of an Old German name.

WAKEMAN The town watchman.

WALDEGRAVE From Walgrave near Brixworth, Northamptonshire.

WALDRON An Old German personal name introduced by the Normans. The surname is found chiefly in the West Midlands.

WALKER A fuller of cloth.

WALKLATE A diminutive of an Old German personal name introduced by the Normans; also in the form of Walklett.

WALLACE A name for a Celt, from the Norman French word for a foreigner. Also an Anglicised version of some Jewish names.

WALLOP From Over and Nether Wallop in Hampshire.

WALPOLE From either of the two places in Norfolk and Suffolk.

WALSH From the Old English word for a foreigner, which was applied to the Welsh and others.

WANTLEY From Wantley Farm in Sussex.

WARBOYS From the Norman French word for a forester; and also from the place in Cambridgeshire.

WARD A name for a watchman, from the Old English *weard* ('guard').

WARDLE From the places of that name in Cheshire and Lancashire.

WARDLOW From the place of that name in the Peak District.

WARK From the place on the River Tweed.

WARNER An Old German name introduced by the Normans; sometimes perhaps a corruption of Warrener.

WARSOP From the place of that name in Nottinghamshire.

WASTENEY One of the forms of a surname derived from Gatinois, south of Paris. Other forms are Wastnage, Wastenay and Westnidge.

WATKINSON 'Son of Watkin', a diminutive of Walter. Also spelt Watkins.

WATSON 'Son of Wat(t)', a diminutive of Walter. Another variant is Watts.

WAVELL From Vauville in Normandy.

WEATHERILL From Wetheral near Carlisle. The surname is spelt in a variety of ways.

WEBB An occupational name for a weaver.

WEDGWOOD From a small place in the parish of Wolstanton in north Staffordshire.

WEEKLEY From the place so-called near Kettering in Northamptonshire.

WELCOME A nickname meaning 'well-combed' or 'well-kempt'.

WESTMACOTT From Westmancote near Tewkesbury in Gloucestershire.

WHARMBY From Quarmby, west of Huddersfield.

WHITBREAD An occupational surname for a baker of wheaten bread.

WHITE A nickname for someone with pale skin or white hair.

WHITGIFT From a village in east Yorkshire.

WICKENDEN From a lost place name in Crowden, Kent.

WILBERFORCE From the place name Wilberfoss, near Hull in east Yorkshire.

WILDGOOSE A nickname for a shy, elusive person. It is found in Derbyshire and neighbouring counties.

WILDING From an Old English personal name. It is found mostly in Lancashire.

WILKINSON 'Son of Wilkin', a diminutive of William.

WILLIAMS 'Son of William', from an old French name introduced by the Normans. It gained popularity after the Conquest and is especially common in Cornwall and Wales.

WILMOT A diminutive of William.

WILSON 'Son of Will', a diminutive of William. See page 300.

WIMBUSH From Wimbish in Essex.

WINSER One of the forms from Windsor, west of London.

WINSTANLEY A Lancashire surname from the place near Manchester.

WONTNER A mole catcher.

WOOD See page 300.

WOODHATCH Someone who lived by a gate into a wood.

WOODWARD An occupational surname for a forester.

WOOFINDEN From Wolfenden in Rossendale, Lancashire.

WOOLER From the place name in Northumberland.

WOOLISCROFT From Wooliscroft Farm in Staffordshire.

WOOLRICH From an Old English name.

WOOSTER From Worcester.

WORDSWORTH From Wadsworth near Halifax in west Yorkshire.

WORSNAM A Lancashire surname from Wolstenholme in Rochdale parish.

WORTHY From the places of that name in Hampshire and Devon.

WRIGHT From the occupational name for a maker of objects, often in wood. See also Wainwright.

WRIGLEY A Lancashire surname from Wrigley Head.

WYATT A shortened form of an Old English personal name. The Normans also used it as a diminutive of Guy and William.

WYMAN From an Old English or an Old Norse personal name.

YEO Someone who lived near a stream in Devon or Somerset.

YORATH From the Welsh personal name Iorwerth.

YOULE A name for someone born at Christmas, or Yuletide.

YOUNG A name to distinguish two people with the same name, often when a son had taken his father's name.

directory of sources

The directory lists sources of information mentioned in the book and other useful addresses. They are arranged alphabetically, including county and city record offices, except for London boroughs, which appear under 'L'. Overseas addresses are listed under the country name as are those for Guernsey, the Isle of Man and Jersey. Always check opening hours in advance.

a

Aberdeen City Archives
Town House, Broad Street
Aberdeen AB10 1AQ
Tel. 01224 522513
and
Old Aberdeen House
Dunbar Street
Aberdeen AB24 3UJ
Tel. 01224 481775
www.aberdeencity.gov.uk/archives

Adoption Section
General Register Office
Trafalgar Road, Birkdale
Southport PR8 2HH
Tel. 0151 471 4830

Airborne Assault
(Formerly Airborne Forces Museum)
Building 213, North Base
Imperial War Museum, Duxford
Cambridge CB22 4QR
Tel. 01223 839909
www.airborneassault.org.uk

Anglesey County Record Office
Shire Hall, Llangefni LL77 7TW
Tel. 01248 723958
www.anglesey.gov.uk

Angus Archives
Montrose Library, 214 High Street
Montrose DD10 8PH
Tel. 01677 673256
www.angus.gov.uk/history/archives

The Archive Office of the Chief Rabbi
735 High Road, Finchley
London N12 0US
Tel. 020 8343 8989
www.theus.org.uk

Argyll and Bute Council Archives
Manse Brae Area Office
Lochgilphead PA31 8QU
Tel. 01546 604774
www.argyle-bute.gov.uk

AUSTRALIA ARCHIVES
National Archives of Australia
Queen Victoria Terrace
Parkes ACT 2600
Canberra
Tel. 00 61 2 6212 3900
www.naa.gov.au/

National Library of Australia
Parkes Place
Canberra ACT 2600
Tel. 00 61 2 6262 1111
www.nla.gov.au

Society of Australian Genealogists
Richmond Villa, 120 Kent Street
Sydney, NSW 2000
Tel. 00 61 2 9247 3953
www.sag.org.au

Ayrshire Archives
Watson Peat Building
SAC Auchincruive
Ayr KA6 5HW
Tel. 01292 521819
www.ayrshirearchives.org.uk

b

Baptist Missionary Society (Archives)
Angus Library
Regent's Park College, Pusey Street
Oxford OX1 2LB
Tel. 01865 288120
www.rpc.ox.ac.uk

Barnado's (Head Office)
Tanners Lane
Barkingside, Ilford
Essex IG6 1QG
Tel. 020 8550 8822
www.barnardos.org.uk

Bath and North East Somerset Record Office
Guildhall, High Street, Bath BA1 5AW
Tel. 01225 477421
www.batharchives.co.uk

1066
BATTLE OF HASTINGS

Your ancestors' lives and livelihoods were often at the mercy of war, plague and other upheavals. This timeline is a snapshot of the history of the British Isles, and includes events that directly affect family records.

FAMILY HISTORY TIMELINE

- **1066** Battle of Hastings and the Norman Conquest
- **1066–87** William I (the Conqueror)
- **1086** Domesday Book compiled
- **1087–1100** William II
- **1100–35** Henry I
- **1135–54** King Stephen
- **1154–89** Henry II
- **1189–99** Richard I (the Lionheart)
- **1190** The Julian Calendar introduced into England
- **1199–1216** King John
- **13th century** Influx of foreign merchants from Europe to England

Bayeux tapestry

Bath Central Library
19-23 The Podium, Bath BA1 5AN
Tel. 01225 463362
www.bathnes.gov.uk

Bedford Central Library
Local Studies Library, Harpur Street
Bedford MK40 1PG
Tel. 01234 350931
www.bedford.gov.uk

Bedfordshire and Luton Archives and Record Service
Riverside Building, Cauldwell Street
Bedford MK42 9AP
Tel. 01234 228833
www.bedfordshire.gov.uk/archive

Berkshire Record Office
9 Coley Avenue, Reading RG1 6AF
Tel. 01189 375132
www.berkshirerecordoffice.org.uk

Berwick-upon-Tweed Record Office
Council Offices, Wallace Green
Berwick-upon-Tweed
Northumberland TD15 1ED
Tel. 01289 301865
www.northumberland.gov.uk

Birmingham City Archives
Central Library, Chamberlain Square
Birmingham B3 3HQ
Tel. 0121 303 4511
www.birmingham.gov.uk/archives

Birthlink
21 Castle Street
Edinburgh EH2 3DN
Tel. 0131 225 6441
www.birthlink.org.uk

Bodleian Library
Broad Street
Oxford OX1 3BG
Tel. 01865 277162
www.bodley.ox.ac.uk

Bolton Archives and Local Studies
Central Library
Le Mans Crescent
Bolton, Lancashire BL1 1SE
Tel. 01204 332211
www.boltonmuseums.org.uk/bolton-archives

Borthwick Institute for Archives
University of York, Heslington,
York YO10 5DD
Tel. 01904 321166
www.york.ac.uk/library/borthwick/

Bristol Record Office
'B' Bond Warehouse, Smeaton Road
Bristol BS1 6XN
Tel. 0117 922 4224
www.bristol.gov.uk/recordoffice

Bristol Reference Library
College Green, Bristol BS1 5TL
Tel. 0117 903 7202
www.bristol.gov.uk

British Library
96 Euston Road, London NW1 2DB
Tel. 0843 2081144
www.bl.uk

British Library Newspaper Library
Colindale Avenue, London NW9 5HE
Tel. 020 7412 7353
www.bl.uk/onlinegallery/newspapers.html

British Telecom Archives
268–270 High Holborn
London WC1V 7EE
Tel. 020 7440 4220
www.btplc.com/thegroup/btshistory/btgrouparchives

Buckinghamshire County Record Office
County Hall, Walton Street
Aylesbury HP20 1UU
Tel. 01296 382587
www.buckscc.gov.uk/bcc/archives/centre_for_buckinghamshire_studies.page

Bury Archive Service
Moss Street
Bury BL9 0DG
Tel: 0161 253 6782
www.bury.gov.uk/archives

Business Archives Council
2nd Floor
48 Chiswell Street
London EC1Y 4XX
Tel. 020 7860 5762
www.businessarchivescouncil.org.uk

Business Archives of Scotland
Archive Services
University of Glasgow
77–87 Dumbarton Road
Glasgow G11 6PW
Tel. 0141 330 4159
www.gla.ac.uk/archives/bacs

C

Cambridgeshire County Record Office
Shire Hall
Castle Hill
Cambridge CB3 0AP
Tel. 01223 699399
www.cambridgeshire.gov.uk/leisure/archives

CANADA ARCHIVES
Library and Archives Canada
395 Wellington Street
Ottawa
Ontario K1A 0N3
Tel. 00 1 613 992 5115
www.collectionscanada.gc.ca

Carmarthenshire Record Office
Parc Myrddin
Richmond Terrace
Carmarthen SA31 1DS
Tel: 01267 228232
www.carmarthenshire.gov.uk/english/education/archives

1215

MAGNA CARTA SEALED

- •1215 Magna Carta sealed by King John
  - •1216–72 Henry III
    - •1272–1307 Edward I
      - •1290 Edict of Expulsion decrees that all Jews in England are to be baptised, banished or put to death
        - •1307–27 Edward II

Battle of Agincourt, 1415

- •1348 The Black Death strikes in England
  - •1327–77 Edward III
    - •1377–99 Richard II
      - •1399–1413 Henry IV
        - •1413–22 Henry V
          - •1422–61 and 1470–1 Henry VI

Catholic Family History Society
45 Gates Green Road
West Wickham
Kent BR4 9DE
www.catholic-history.org.uk

Catholic National Library
St Michael's Abbey, Farnborough Road
Farnborough
Hants GU14 7NQ
Tel. 01252 543818
www.catholic-library.org.uk

Centre for Kentish Studies
County Hall
Maidstone ME14 1XQ
Tel. 01622 694363
www.kent.gov.uk

Centre for Migration Studies
Ulster-American Folk Park
Mellon Road
Castletown, Omagh
County Tyrone BT78 5QY
Tel. 02882 256315
www.qub.ac.uk/cms

Ceredigion Archives
County Hall, Marine Terrace
Aberystwyth
Ceredigion SY23 2DE
Tel. 01970 633697
http://archifdy-ceredigion.org.uk

The Cheshire Archives
and Local Studies
Cheshire Record Office
Duke Street
Chester CH1 1RL
Tel. 01244 602574
http://archives.cheshire.gov.uk

Child Migrants Trust
28A Musters Road, West Bridgford
Nottingham NG2 7PL
Tel. 0115 982 2811
www.childmigrantstrust.com

Church Mission Society
Crowther Centre for Mission Education
Watlington Road
Oxford OX4 6BZ
Tel. 01865 787400
www.cms-uk.org

Church of England Record Centre
Lambeth Palace Library
Lambeth Palace Road
London SE17 7JU
Tel. 020 7898 1200
www.lambethpalacelibrary.org

Church of Jesus Christ of Latter-day
Saints (Mormon Church)
see Family History Centres

City of London Police Museum
Police Headquarters
37 Wood St
London EC2P 2NP
Tel. 020 7601 2328
www.met.police.uk/history/records.htm

College of Arms
Queen Victoria Street
London EC4V 4BT
Tel. 020 7248 2762
www.college-of-arms.gov.uk

Commonwealth War
Graves Commission
2 Marlow Road
Maidenhead
Berkshire SL6 7DX
Tel. 01628 634221
www.cwgc.org

COMPANY REGISTRIES
Companies House
(England and Wales)
Crown Way
Maindy
Cardiff CF14 3UZ
Tel. 0303 1234 500
www.companieshouse.gov.uk

Companies House
(London)
21 Bloomsbury Street
London WC1B 3XD
Tel. 0303 1234 500 (Cardiff link line)
www.companieshouse.gov.uk

Companies House
(Scotland)
Fourth Floor, Edinburgh Quay 2
139 Fountainbridge
Edinburgh EH3 9FF
Tel. 0303 1234 500 (Cardiff link line)
www.companieshouse.gov.uk

Registry of Companies and
Friendly Societies
Second Floor, The Linenhall
32-38 Linenhall Street
Belfast BT2 8BG
Tel. 0303 1234 500 (Cardiff link line)
www.companieshouse.gov.uk

Cornwall Record Office
Old County Hall
Truro TR1 3AY
Tel. 01872 323127
www.cornwall.gov.uk

Corporation of London Records Office
40 Northampton Road
London EC1R 0HB
Tel. 020 7332 3820
www.cityoflondon.gov.uk/lma

Court of the Lord Lyon
HM New Register House
Edinburgh EH1 3YT
Tel. 0131 556 7255
www.lyon-court.com

Coventry City Archives
Cheylesmore Manor House
Manor House Drive
Coventry CV1 2ND
Tel. 024 7683 2418
www.coventry.gov.uk

1476
FIRST ENGLISH PRINTING PRESS

FAMILY HISTORY TIMELINE

Henry VIII

- •1455–85 Wars of the Roses
- •1461–70 and 1471–83 Edward IV
- •1476 William Caxton sets up the first English printing press, in Westminster
- •1483 Edward V
- •1483–5 Richard III

- •1484 College of Arms founded
- •1485–1509 Henry VII
- •16th century Reformation begins in Germany. It quickly spreads to England and Scotland
- •1509–47 Henry VIII

Caxton's imprint

Cumbria Archive Centre, Carlisle
Petteril Bank Road
Carlisle CA1 3AJ
Tel. 01228 227285
www/cumbria.gov.uk/archives

Cumbria Archive Centre, Kendal
Kendal County Offices
Kendal LA9 4RQ
Tel. 01539 773540
www/cumbria.gov.uk/archives

Cumbria Archive and
Local Studies Centre, Barrow
140 Duke Street
Barrow-in-Furness LA14 1XW
Tel. 01229 407377
www/cumbria.gov.uk/archives

Cumbria Archive and Local Studies
Centre, Whitehaven
Scotch Street
Whitehaven CA28 7NL
Tel. 01946 506420
www/cumbria.gov.uk/archives

d

Denbighshire Record Office
46 Clwyd Street
Ruthin LL15 1HP
Tel. 01824 708250
www.denbighshire.gov.uk

Deptford Forum Publishing
2 Osberton Road
London SE12 8AH
Tel. 020 8692 7115
www.dfpbooks.co.uk

Derby Local Studies Library
25B Irongate
Derby DE1 3GL
Tel. 01332 642240
www.derby.gov.uk

Derbyshire Record Office
County Hall
Matlock DE4 3AG
Tel. 01629 539202
    01629 538347 (search room bookings)
www.derbyshire.gov.uk/leisure/record_office

Devon Record Office
Great Moor House
Bittern Road
Exeter EX2 7NL
Tel. 01392 384253
www.devon.gov.uk/record_office.htm

Divorce Registry
see Principal Registry of the Family Division

Dorset Record Office
Bridport Road
Dorchester
Dorset DT1 1RP
Tel. 01305 250550
www.dorsetforyou.com/archives

Dr Williams's Library
14 Gordon Square
London WC1H 0AG
Tel. 020 7387 3727
www.dwlib.co.uk/dwlib

Dublin City Library and Archive
138-142 Pearse Street
Dublin, County Dublin 2
Tel. 00 353 1 6744800
www.dublincity.ie

Dumfries and Galloway Archives
Archive Centre, 33 Burns Street
Dumfries DG1 2PS
Tel. 01387 269254
www.dumgal.gov.uk

Durham County Record Office
County Hall
Durham DH1 5UL
Tel. 0191 383 3253
www.durhamrecordoffice.org.uk

e

Edinburgh Central Reference Library
7-9 George IV Bridge
Edinburgh EH1 1EG
Tel. 0131 242 8060
www.edinburgh.gov.uk/libraries

Edinburgh City Archives
Level 1, City Chambers
253 High Street,
Edinburgh EH1 1YJ
Tel. 0131 529 4616
www.edinburgh.gov.uk/info/428/archives

Essex Record Office
Wharf Road, Chelmsford CM2 6YT
Tel. 01245 244 644
www.essex.gov.uk/libraries-archives/
record-office/pages/record-office.aspx

f

Family History Centres
The Mormon (LDS) Church's Family History
Centres are branches of its vast library in Utah,
USA. Its British headquarters and distribution
centre for products are also listed below.

The Genealogical Society of Utah
185 Penns Lane
Sutton Coldfield B76 1JU
Tel. 0121 384 9921
www.gensocietyofutah.org

LDS Distribution Centre
399 Garretts Green Lane
Birmingham B33 0UH
Tel. 0121 785 2200

Aberdeen Family History Centre
North Anderson Drive
Aberdeen AB15 6DD
Tel. 01224 692206

1536

**FIRST ACT OF UNION BETWEEN
ENGLAND AND WALES**

- **1534** Church of England (known in Wales as the Church in Wales) is established

- **1536** Act of Union between England and Wales

- **1536–9** Dissolution of the Monasteries

- **1538** Parish registers introduced into England and Wales

- **1547–53** Edward VI

- **1553** Errol in Perthshire keeps Scotland's first parish register

- **1553** Lady Jane Grey (nine days)

- **1553–8** Mary I (Bloody Mary)

Protestants burnt on the orders of Mary I

Aldershot Family History Centre
LDS Chapel
St Georges Road
Aldershot GU1 2 4LJ
Tel. 01252 321460

Alness Family History Centre
Kilmonivaig, Seafield
Portmahomack IV20 1RE
Tel. 01862 871631

Ashton under Lyme Family History Centre
Patterdale Road
Ashton under Lyme
Tel. 0161 330 3453

Ayr Family History Centre
Orchard Avenue, Mossgiel Road
Ayr
Tel. 01292 610632

Barrow Family History Centre
Abbey Road
Barrow-in-Furness LA13 9JY
Tel. 01229 820050

Belfast Family History Centre
403 Holywood Road
Belfast, County Antrim BT4 2GU
Tel. 028 9076 9839

Billingham Family History Centre
The Linkway
Billingham TS23 3HH
Tel. 01642 563162

Birkenhead Family History Centre
Reservoir Road
Prenton
Birkenhead
Tel. 0151 608 7723

Blackpool Family History Centre
Warren Drive
Blackpool
Tel. 01253 863868

Bristol Family History Centre
721 Wells Road
Whitchurch
Bristol BS14 9HU
Tel. 01225 838326

Cambridge Family History Centre
670 Cherry Hinton Road
Cambridge CB1 4DR
Tel. 01223 247010

Canterbury Family History Centre
Forty Acre Road
Canterbury
Tel. 01227 765431

Carlisle Family History Centre
Langrigg Road, Morton Park
Carlisle CA2 6DT
Tel. 01228 526767

Cheltenham Family History Centre
Thirlestaine Road
Cheltenham GL53 7AS
Tel. 01242 523433

Coleraine Family History Centre
8 Sandelfields, Coleraine
County Londonderry BT52 1WQ
Tel. 028 7032 1214

Cork Family History Centre
Sarsfield Road
Wilton, Cork
County Cork
Tel. 00 353 21 4897050

Coventry Family History Centre
Riverside Close
Whitley
Coventry CV3 4AT
Tel. 024 7630 3316

Crawley Family History Centre
Old Horsham Road
Crawley RH11 8PD
Tel. 01293 516151

Dereham Family History Centre
Yaxham Road
East Dereham
Norfolk NR19 1HB
Tel. 01362 851500

Douglas Family History Centre
Woodsid, Woodburn Road
Douglas
Isle of Man
Tel. 01624 675834

Dublin Family History Centre
Ireland Dublin Mission
The Willows
Finglas Road
Dublin
Tel. 00 353 1 4625609
www.mission.net/ireland/dublin

Dumfries Family History Centre
36 Edinburgh Road
Albanybank
Dumfries DG1 1 JQ
Tel. 01387 254865

Dundee Family History Centre
Bingham Terrace
Dundee DD4 7HH
Tel. 01382 451247

Edinburgh Family History Centre
30A-32 Colinton Road
Edinburgh EH10 5DQ
Tel. 0131 337 3049

Elgin Family History Centre
Pansport Road
Elgin
Morayshire IV30 1HE
Tel. 01343 546429

Exeter Family History Centre
Wonford Road
Exeter
Devon EX2 4UD
Tel. 01392 250723

1588

SPANISH ARMADA

Globe Theatre, 1598–9

FAMILY HISTORY TIMELINE

- •1558–1603 Elizabeth I
    - •1559 The Acts of Supremacy and Uniformity make it illegal to celebrate a Catholic mass in England and Wales
        - •1572 First Huguenots arrive in Britain from France, following the St Bartholomew's Day Massacre
- •1585 First English settlement in America, at Roanoke Island—it was a failure
- •1588 Spanish Armada defeated by English fleet
    - •1600 Gregorian Calendar introduced into Scotland
    - •1600 A group of London merchants forms the East India Company
        - •1601 Poor Law Act consolidates system of poor relief in England and Wales

Elizabeth I

Forest of Dean Family History Centre
Holcot Road
Wynols Hill
Queensway
Forest Of Dean
Gloucestershire GL16 7JB
Tel. 01594 832904

Gaerwen Family History Centre
Holyhead Road
Gaerwen
Anglesey
Tel. 01248 421894

Gillingham Family History Centre
2 Twydall Lane
Gillingham, Kent
Tel. 0163 438 8900

Glasgow Family History Centre
35 Julian Avenue
Glasgow G12 0PW
Tel. 0141 357 1024

Grimsby Family History Centre
Linwood Avenue
Waltham Road
Grimsby DN33 2PA
Tel. 01472 828876

Harborne Family History Centre
38-42 Lordswood Road
Harborne
Birmingham B17 9QS
Tel. 0121 686 2253

Harrogate Family History Centre
10 Wetherby Road
Harrogate
North Yorkshire HG2 7SA
Tel. 01423 886537

Hastings Family History Centre
2 Ledsham Avenue
St Leonards-on-Sea
East Sussex TN37 7LE
Tel. 01424 754563

Helston Family History Centre
Clodgey Lane
Helston
Cornwall TR13 8PJ
Tel. 01326 564503

High Wycombe Family History Centre
743 London Road
High Wycombe
Buckinghamshire HP11 1HQ
Tel. 01494 459979

Huddersfield Family History Centre
12 Halifax Road
Birchencliffe
Huddersfield
West Yorkshire HD3 3BS
Tel. 01484 454573

Hull Family History Centre
725 Holderness Road
Hull
North Humberside HU8 9AR
Tel: 01482 794250

Inverness Family History Centre
13 Ness Walk
Inverness IV3 5SQ
Tel. 01463 231220

Ipswich Family History Centre
42 Sidegate Lane West
Ipswich IP4 3DB
Tel. 01473 723182

King's Lynn Family History Centre
Reffley Lane
King's Lynn
Norfolk PE30 3EQ
Tel. 01553 670000

Kirkcaldy Family History Centre
Winifred Crescent
Forth Park
Kirkcaldy
Fifeshire
Tel. 01592 640041

Leeds Family History Centre
Vesper Road
Leeds
West Yorkshire
Tel. 0113 258 5297

Leicester Family History Centre
Wakerley Road
Leicester, Leicestershire LE5 4WD
Tel. 0116 273 7334

Lerwick Family History Centre
South Road
Lerwick
Shetland Islands
Tel. 01595 695732

Lichfield Family History Centre
Purcell Avenue
Lichfield
Staffordshire
Tel. 01543 414843

Limerick Family History Centre
Doradoyle Road
Limerick, County Limerick
Tel. 061 309442

Lincoln Family History Centre
Skellingthorpe Road
Lincoln LN6 0PB
Tel. 01522 680117

Liverpool Family History Centre
4 Mill Bank
Liverpool L13 0BW
Tel. 0151 252 0614

London Family History Centre
64-68 Exhibition Road
South Kensington, London SW7 2PA
Tel. 020 7589 8561

Lowestoft Family History Centre
165 Yarmouth Road
Lowestoft, Suffolk NR32 4AB
Tel. 01502 573851

1620

PILGRIM FATHERS LAND IN AMERICA

- 1603–25 James I (James VI of Scotland)

  - 1605 Gunpowder Plot

    - 1607 First successful
      English settlement in
      America, at Jamestown

      - 1611 Authorised
        Version of the Bible
        published

- 1617 Transportation of convicted criminals
  to America and the West Indies begins

  - 1620 The *Mayflower* sets sail from
    Plymouth for New England

    - 1625–49 Charles I

      - 1634 Parish registers start in Ireland

        - 1642–51 Civil Wars—
          Charles I executed 1649

Pilgrim Fathers take their first steps on American soil

327

Macclesfield Family History Centre
Victoria Road
Macclesfield, Cheshire SK10 3JE
Tel. 0162 542 7236

Maidstone Family History Centre
76B London Road
Maidstone ME16 0DT
Tel. 01622 757811

Manchester Family History Centre
Altrincham Road
Wythenshawe
Manchester M22 4BJ
Tel. 0161 902 9279

Mansfield Family History Centre
Southridge Drive
Mansfield
Nottingham NG18 4RT
Tel. 01623 26729

Merthyr Tydfil Family History Centre
Nantygwenith Street
George Town
Merthyr Tydfil CF48 1NR
Tel. 01685 722455

Newcastle-under-Lyme Family History Centre
PO Box 457
The Brampton
Newcastle-Under-Lyme
Staffordshire ST5 0TV
Tel. 01782 630178

Newport, Isle of Wight Family History Centre
Chestnut Close, Shide Road
Newport
Isle of Wight
Tel. 01983 522833

Northampton Family History Centre
137 Harlestone Road
Northampton NN5 6AA
Tel. 01604 587630

Norwich Family History Centre
19 Greenways
Eaton
Norwich NR4 6PA
Tel. 01603 452440

Nottingham Family History Centre
Stanhome Square
West Bridgford
Nottingham NG2 7GF
Tel. 0115 914 4255

Orpington Family History Centre
Station Approach
Orpington
Kent BR6 0ST
Tel. 01689 837342

Paisley Family History Centre
Glenburn Road
Paisley
Renfrewshire PA2 8PN
Tel. 0141 884 2780

Peterborough Family History Centre
Cottesmore Close
Peterborough
Cambridgeshire PE3 9TP
Tel. 01733 263374

Plymouth Family History Centre
Hartley Chapel
Mannamead Road
Plymouth, Devon PL3 4SR
Tel. 01752 668666

Pontefract Family History Centre
Park Villas Drive
Pontefract
West Yorkshire WF8 4QF
Tel. 01977 600308

Poole Family History Centre
8 Mount Road
Parkstone
Poole, Dorset BH14 0QW
Tel. 01202 730646

Portsmouth Family History Centre
82 Kingston Crescent
Portsmouth
Hampshire PO2 8AQ
Tel. 023 9269 6243

Preston Temple Family History Centre
Temple Way
Hartwood Green
Chorley, Lancashire PR6 7EQ
Tel. 01257 226145

Reading Family History Centre
280 The Meadway
Tilehurst
Reading, Berkshire RG30 4PE
Tel. 0118 9410211

Redditch Family History Centre
321 Evesham Road
Crabbs Cross, Redditch
Worcestershire B97 5JA
Tel. 01527 401 543

Romford Family History Centre
64 Butts Green Road
Hornchurch
Essex RM11 2JR
Tel. 01708 620727

St Albans Family History Centre
Buckthorne Avenue
Stevenage
Hertfordshire SG1 1TX
Tel. 0143 835 1553

St Austell Family History Centre
Kingfisher Drive
St Austell
Cornwall PL25 3AZ
Tel. 01726 69912

St Helier Family History Centre
Rue de la Vallee
St Mary
Jersey JE3 3D
Tel. 01534 482171

1666

GREAT FIRE OF LONDON

Great Fire of London

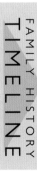

- **1653–8** Oliver Cromwell governs most of the British Isles as Lord Protector

- **1656** Jews enter England freely after Cromwell ends the enforcement of the Edict of Expulsion

- **1659** The Census of Ireland lists those with title to land and the total number of residents in each townland

- **1660–85** Charles II

Oliver Cromwell

- **1665–6** Great Plague of London

- **1666** Great Fire of London

- **1670** Hudson's Bay Company established— early settlers in Canada

- **1685–8** James II (James VII of Scotland)

- **1688–9** Glorious Revolution ends reign of James II, who flees to France

Great Fire of London

Scarborough Family History Centre
Stepney Road
Scarborough
North Yorkshire YO12 5BN
Tel. 01723 507239

Sheffield Family History Centre
Wheel Lane
Grenoside
Sheffield S35 8RL
Tel. 0114 245 3124

Staines Family History Centre
41 Kingston Road
Staines
Middlesex TW18 4LH
Tel. 01784 462627

Sunderland Family History Centre
Queen Alexander Road
Sunderland
Tyne and Wear SR2 9BT
Tel. 0191 528 5787

Sutton Coldfield Family
History Centre
187 Penns Lane
Sutton Coldfield
West Midlands B76 1JU
Tel. 0121 386 1690

Swansea Family History Centre
Cockett Road
Swansea SA2 0FD
Tel. 01792 585792

Telford Family History Centre
72 Glebe Street
Wellington, Telford
Shropshire TF1 1JY
Tel. 01952 257443

Thetford Family History Centre
Station Road
Thetford
Norfolk IP24 1AH
Tel. 01842 755472

Trowbridge Family History Centre
Brook Road
Trowbridge
Wiltshire BA14 9DL
Tel. 01225 777097

Watford Family History Centre
Hempstead Road
Watford
Hertfordshire WD17 3HF
Tel. 01923 816 540

Wednesfield Family History Centre
63 Linthouse Lane
Wednesfield, Wolverhampton
West Midlands WV11 3EF
Tel. 01902 724097

Weymouth Family History Centre
396 Chickerell Road
Weymouth
Dorset DT4 9TP
Tel. 01305 787240

Worcester Family History Centre
Canada Way, Lower Wick
Worcester
Worcestershire WR2 4ED
Tel. 0190 542 0341

Worthing Family History Centre
Goring Street
Goring-by-Sea, Worthing
West Sussex BN12 5AR
Tel. 01903 241 82

Yate Family History Centre
Wellington Road
Yate
Bristol, Avon BS37 5UY
Tel. 01454 323004

Yeovil Family History Centre
Lysander Road
Forest Hill, Yeovil
Somerset BA20 2PE
Tel. 01935 426817

York Family History Centre
Acomb Road
York
North Yorkshire YO24 4HA
Tel. 01904 786784

The Fawcett Library
see The Women's Library

Federation of Family History
Societies (FFHS)
The Federation is the umbrella body for around
200 family history societies throughout Britain
and overseas. Contact details for each society
are available from the Federation's web site.

Federation of Family History Societies
PO Box 8857
Lutterworth
Leicestershire LE17 9BJ
Tel. 01455 203133
www.ffhs.org.uk

FFHS Services Ltd
PO Box 673
Rochdale
Greater Manchester OL16 9JQ

The Federation of Synagogues
65 Watford Way
Hendon
London NW4 3AQ
Tel. 020 8202 2263
www.federationofsynagogues.com

Flintshire Record Office
The Old Rectory
Rectory Lane, Hawarden
Flintshire CH5 3NR
Tel. 01244 532364
www.siryfflint.gov.uk

French Protestant Church of London
8–9 Soho Square
London W1D 3QD
Tel. 020 7437 5311
www.egliseprotestantelondres.org.uk

1745

FORTY-FIVE JACOBITE REBELLION

- •1689–1702 William III and Mary II (d.1694)
  - •1702–14 Queen Anne
    - •1707 Act of Union between England and Scotland
      - •1708 Protestant refugees allowed to become naturalised without a private Act of Parliament
        - •1714–27 George I
          - •1727–60 George II

- •1732 The use of Latin in English parish registers is discontinued
  - •1745 Bonnie Prince Charlie proclaims his father (James Stuart) the king of Scotland in the Forty-five Rebellion
    - •1752 The Gregorian Calendar is introduced into England and Wales

Bonnie Prince Charlie

g

Genealogical Office of the Republic of Ireland
The National Library of Ireland
Kildare Street
Dublin 2
Tel. 00353 1 603 0213
www.nli.ie

General Register Office
PO Box 2, Southport
Merseyside PR8 2JD
Tel. 0845 603 7788
www.direct.gov.uk/en/governmentcitizens
andrightsregisteringlifeevents/familyhistory
andresearch/index.htm

General Register Office (Northern Ireland)
Oxford House
49–55 Chichester Street
Belfast BT1 4HL
Tel. 028 9151 3101
www.nidirect.gov.uk

General Register Office (Republic of Ireland)
Government Offices
Convent Road, Roscommon
Tel. 00 353 90 6632900
www.groireland.ie

General Register Office for Scotland
General Register House
2 Princes Street
Edinburgh EH1 3YT
Tel. 0131 314 4300
www.scotlandspeoplehub.gov.uk

Glamorgan Archives
Clos Parc, Morgannwg, Leckwith
Cardiff CF11 8AW
Tel. (029) 2087 2200
www.glamro.gov.uk

West Glamorgan Archive Service
Civic Centre
Oystermouth Road
Swansea
West Glamorgan SA1 3SN
Tel. 01792 636000
www.swansea.gov.uk

Glasgow City Archives
The Mitchell Library
201 North Street
Glasgow G3 7DN
Tel. 0141 287 2910
www.mitchelllibrary.org

Gloucestershire Archives
Clarence Row
Alvin Street
Gloucester
Gloucestershire GL1 3DW
Tel. 01452 425000
www.gloucestershire.gov.uk

GUERNSEY

Ecclesiastical Court of the Bailiwick of Guernsey
Constable's Office
Lefebvre Street
St Peter Port
Guernsey GY1 2JS
Tel. 01481 721 732

Island Archives Service
St Banabas
Cornet Street
St Peter Port
Guernsey GY1 1LF
Tel: 01481 724512

Office of the Registrar General
HM Greffier
General Register Office
The Greffe
Royal Court House
St. Peter Port
Guernsey GY1 2PB
Tel. 01481 725 277

Priaulx Library
Candie Road, St Peter Port
Guernsey GY1 1UG
Tel. 01481 721998
www.priaulxlibrary.co.uk

Guildhall Library
Aldermanbury
London EC2V 7HH
Tel. 020 7332 1868/1870
www.cityoflondon.gov.uk

Gwent Record Office
County Hall
Cwmbran NP44 2XH
Tel. 01633 644886
www.torfaen.gov.uk

Gwynedd Archives and Museums Service
Caernarfon Record Office
Swyddfa'r Cyngor
Caernarfon, Gwynedd LL55 1SH
Tel. 01286 679095
www.gwynedd.gov.uk

h

Hampshire Record Office
Sussex Street
Winchester SO23 8TH
Tel. 01962 846154
www.hants.gov.uk/archives

Herefordshire Record Office
Harold Street
Hereford HR1 2QX
Tel. 01432 260750
www.herefordshire.gov.uk/leisure/archives

Hertfordshire Archives and Local Studies
County Hall, Pegs Lane
Hertford SG13 8EJ
Tel. 0300 123 4049
www.hertsdirect.org/services/leisureculture/
heritage1/hals

1776
AMERICAN DECLARATION OF INDEPENDENCE

FAMILY HISTORY TIMELINE

- **1754** Marriages solemnised in the Church of England become the main form of legal marriage in England and Wales (Lord Hardwicke's Marriage Act 1753)

- **1760s** James Watt's perfection of the steam engine gives impetus to the Industrial Revolution

- **1760–1820** George III

- **1770** Captain James Cook lands at Botany Bay

- **1775–83** American War of Independence

- **1776** Declaration of Independence in America

- **1778** Catholic Relief Act ends the persecution of Roman Catholics

- **1779** Abraham Darby completes the first iron bridge, across the Severn at Coalbrookdale in Shropshire

- **1785** *The Daily Universal Register* is printed for the first time. In 1788 it changes its name to *The Times*

Captain Cook—explorer and navigator

Highland Council Archive
Genealogy Service
Highland Archive
Highland Archive Centre
Bught Road
Inverness
Inverness-shire IV3 5SS
Tel. 01463 256444
www.highlandarchives.org.uk

North Highland Archive
Wick Library
Sinclair Terrace
Wick
Caithness KW1 5AB
Tel. 01955 606432
www.highlandarchives.org.uk

HM Land Registry
Trafalgar House
1 Bedford Park
Croydon CR0 2AQ
Tel. 0300 006 0004
www.landregistry.gov.uk

Home Office
Departmental Record Officer
50 Queen Anne's Gate
London SW1H 9AT
Tel. 0207 273 3000
www.homeoffice.gov.uk

Home Office Immigration and
Nationality Directorate
Central Freedom of Information team
5th Floor East
Whitgift Centre Block C
15 Wellesley Road
Croydon CR9 3LY
www.homeoffice.gov.uk

House of Lords Record Office
Houses of Parliament
Westminster
London SW1A 0PW
Tel. 020 7219 3074
www.parliament.uk/archive

Huguenot Society of Great Britain
and Ireland
The Huguenot Library
University College London, Gower Street
London WC1E 6BT
Tel. 0207 679 5199
www.huguenotsociety.org.uk/library-and-
archive.html

Human Fertilisation and Embryology
Authority
Paxton House, 30 Artillery Lane
London E1 7LS
Tel. 0207 377 5077
www.hfea.gov.uk

Huntingdonshire Archives and
Local Studies
Huntingdon Library and Archives
Princes Street, Huntingdon
Cambridgeshire PE29 3PA
Telephone: 01480 372738
www.cambridgeshire.gov.uk/leisure/archives/
visiting/HLAC1.htm

i

Imperial War Museum
Lambeth Road
London SE1 6HZ
Tel. 020 7416 5320
www.iwm.org.uk

Imperial War Museum Duxford
Duxford
Cambridgeshire CB2 4QR
Tel. 01223 835000
http://duxford.iwm.org.uk

Imperial War Museum North
The Quays
Trafford Wharf Road
Manchester M17 1TZ
Tel. 0161 836 4000
http://north.iwm.org.uk

Institute of Commonwealth Studies
University of London
2nd Floor
South Block
Senate House
Malet Street
London WC1E 7HU
Tel. 020 7862 8844
http://commonwealth.sas.ac.uk

Institute of Heraldic and
Genealogical Studies
79-82 Northgate
Canterbury
Kent CT1 1BA
Tel. 01227 768664
www.ihgs.ac.uk

Irish Baptist Historical Society
The Association of Baptist Churches in Ireland
The Baptist Centre
19 Hillsborough Road, Moira
County Down BT67 0HG
Tel. 028 9261 9267
www.baptistsinireland.org

Irish Genealogical Research
Society
The Irish Club
2-4 Tudor Street
London EC4Y 0AA
Tel. 020 7427 5801
www.igrsoc.org

Irish Manuscripts Commission
45 Merrion Square
Dublin 2
Tel. 00 353 1 676 1610
www.irishmanuscripts.ie

ISLE OF MAN
Isle of Man Public Record Office
Unit 40a Spring Valley Industrial Estate
Douglas
Isle of Man IM2 2QS
Tel. 01624 693569
www.gov.im/registries/publicrecords

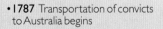

Battle of the Nile, 1798

1801

PARLIAMENTS OF GREAT BRITAIN AND IRELAND UNITE

- • **1787** Transportation of convicts
  to Australia begins

  - • **1789–99** The French Revolution

    - • **1790s** Whalers and traders
      begin settling in New Zealand

      - • **1790s** Free settlers
        leave for Australia

        - • **1793–1815** Revolutionary and Napoleonic Wars

- • **1798** Irish Rebellion

  - • **1800–50** The Highland Clearances in
    Scotland reach a peak

    - • **1801** The first official census takes
      place in England, Scotland and Wales

      - • **1801** Act of Union incorporates
        Ireland and Britain into the
        United Kingdom of Great Britain
        and Ireland

Isle of Man Civil Registry
Registries Building
Deemsters Walk, Bucks Road
Douglas, Isle of Man IM1 3AR
Tel. 01624 687039
www.gov.im/registries/general/
civilregistry

Manx National Heritage
Manx Museum, Kingswood Grove
Douglas IM1 3LY
Tel. 01624 648000
www.gov.im/mnh/heritage/museums

Isle of Wight Record Office
County Archivist
26 Hillside, Newport
Isle of Wight PO30 2EB
Tel. 01983 823820/1
www.iwight.com/library/record_office

j,k

JERSEY

Jersey Heritage
The Weighbridge
St Helier, Jersey JE2 3NF
Tel. 01534 633300
www.jerseyheritage.org/places-to-visit/
jersey-archive

Judicial Greffe
(probate and other legal documents)
Royal Court House, Royal Square
St Helier, Jersey JE11 1JG
Tel. 01534 441300
www.gov.je/judicialgreffe

Lord Coutanche Library
(genealogical and photographic archive)
Société Jersiaise
7 Pier Road
St Helier, Jersey JE2 4XW
Tel. 01534 730538
www.societe-jersiaise.org

Superintendent Registrar
10 Royal Square
St Helier, Jersey JE2 4WA
Tel. 01534 441335
www.gov.je

**Jewish Genealogical Society of
Great Britain**
33 Seymour Place
London W1H 5AU
Tel. 020 7724 4232
www.jgsgb.org.uk

Jewish Museum
The Sternberg Centre
80 East End Road
Finchley, London N3 2SY
Tel. 020 8349 1143
www.jewishmuseum.org.uk

Association of Jewish Refugees
Jubilee House
Merrion Avenue, Stanmore
Middlesex HA1 ORL
Tel. 020 8385 3070
www.ajr.org.uk

Kent *see* Centre for Kentish Studies

l

Lambeth Palace Library
Lambeth Palace Library
Lambeth Palace Road
London SE17 7JU
Tel. 020 7898 1200
www.lambethpalacelibrary.org

**North Lanarkshire Archives and
Records Centre**
10 Kelvin Road
Cumbernauld
North Lanarkshire G67 2BA
Tel. 01236 638980
www.northlanarkshire.gov.uk

South Lanarkshire Council
Council Offices
Almada Street
Hamilton
South Lanarkshire ML3 OAA
Tel. 0303 123 1015
www.southlanarkshire.gov.uk/info/427/
libraries_and_archives

Lancashire Record Office
County Hall, Fishergate
Preston
Lancashire PR1 8XJ
Tel. 0845 053 0000
www.lancashire.gov.uk

The Land Registers of Northern Ireland
Lincoln Building
27–45 Great Victoria Street
Belfast BT2 7SL
Tel. 028 9025 1555
www.landwebni.gov.uk

Land registers (for Scotland)
see Registers of Scotland Executive Agency

**The Record Office for Leicestershire,
Leicester and Rutland**
Long Street, Wigston Magna
Leicester LE18 2AH
Tel. 0116 257 1080
www.leics.gov.uk/index/community/
museums/record_office.htm

Library and Archives Canada
395 Wellington Street
Ottawa
Ontario K1A 0N4
Tel. 00 1 866 578 7777
www.collectionscanada.gc.ca

Lichfield Record Office
The Friary
Lichfield WS13 6QG
Tel. 01543 510720
www.staffordshire.gov.uk/leisure/archives/
contact/lichfieldrecordoffice

1815
BATTLE OF WATERLOO

FAMILY HISTORY TIMELINE

- **1804** Richard Trevithick demonstrates the first steam locomotive
- **1805** Battle of Trafalgar
- **1806** First colonists leave Britain for South Africa
- **1807** Slave trade abolished
- **1813** Parishes have to record baptisms, marriages and burials in books and on printed forms
- **1815** Battle of Waterloo
- **1819** Peterloo Massacre in Manchester
- **1820–30** George IV
- **1821** First census in Ireland
- **1823** Houses of correction and county gaols are amalgamated and called prisons

Trevithick's steam locomotive

Lincolnshire Archives
St Rumbold Street
Lincoln LN2 5AB
Tel. 01522 526204
www.lincolnshire.gov.uk/archives

North East Lincolnshire Archives
Municipal Offices
Town Hall Square
Grimsby DN31 1HU
Tel. 01472 313131
www.nelincs.gov.uk

Liverpool Record Office and Local
Studies Service
Unit 33
Wellington Employment Park
Dunes Way
Liverpool L5 9RJ
Tel. 0151 233 5817
www.liverpool.gov.uk/libraries-and-
archives/archives-local-and-family-history

LONDON BOROUGHS

London Borough of
Barking and Dagenham
Valence House Museum
Becontree Avenue
Dagenham
Essex RM8 3HT
Tel. 020 8227 5222
www.lbbd.gov.uk/museumsandheritage/
valencehousemuseum

London Borough of Barnet
Hendon Library
The Burroughs, Hendon
London NW4 4BQ
Tel. 020 8359 3960
www.barnet.gov.uk/archives

London Borough of Bexley
Local Studies and Archive Centre
Townley Road, Bexleyheath
Kent DA6 7HJ
Tel. 020 3045 3369
www.bexley.gov.uk

London Borough of Brent
Brent Archives
Willesden Green Library Centre
95 High Road, Willesden Green
London NW10 6SF
Tel. 020 8937 3541
http://www.brent.gov.uk

London Borough of Bromley
Local Studies Library and Archives
Central Library, High Street
Bromley, Kent BR1 1EX
Tel. 020 8461 7170
www.bromley.gov.uk

London Borough of Camden
Camden Local Studies and Archives Centre
Holborn Library
32–38 Theobald's Road
London WC1X 8PA
Tel. 020 7974 4001
www.camden.gov.uk

London Borough of Croydon
Croydon Local Studies Library
Level 3, Central Library
Croydon Clocktower, Katharine Street
Croydon, Surrey CR9 1ET
Tel. 020 8760 5400 Ext. 1112
http://www.croydon.gov.uk

London Borough of Ealing
Local History Library and Archives
Central Library
103 Ealing Broadway Centre
London W5 5JY
Tel. 020 8726 6900
www.croydononline.org/history/places/
lslibrary.asp

London Borough of Enfield
Enfield Local Studies and Archive
1st Floor, Thomas Hardy House
39 London Road
Enfield EN2 6DS
Tel. 020 8379 2724
www.enfield.gov.uk

London Borough of Greenwich
Greenwich Heritage Centre
Artillery Square
Royal Arsenal
Woolwich
London SE18 6ST
Tel. 020 8854 2452
www.greenwich.gov.uk

London Borough of Hackney
Hackney Archives
43 De Beauvoir Road
London N1 5SQ
Tel. 020 7241 2886
www.hackney.gov.uk/ca-archives.htm

London Borough of Hammersmith
and Fulham
Hammersmith and Fulham Archives
and Local History Centre
The Lilla Huset, 191 Talgarth Road
Hammersmith
London W6 8BJ
Tel. 020 7332 382
www.lbhf.gov.uk

London Borough of Haringey
Haringey Archive Service
Bruce Castle Museum
Lordship Lane
London N17 8NU
Tel. 020 8808 8772
www.haringey.gov.uk

London Borough of Harrow
Civic Centre Reference Library
Station Road
Harrow HA1 2XY
Tel. 020 8424 1056
www.harrow.gov.uk

London Borough of Havering
Local Studies Library
St Edward's Way
Romford, Essex RM1 3AR
Tel. 01708 432 393
www.havering.gov.uk

1832

FIRST REFORM ACT

- **1829** The Metropolitan Police, Britain's first statutory police force, is founded by the Home Secretary, Robert Peel

- **1829** Catholic Emancipation Act passed, allowing Catholics to participate in British public and political life

- **1830–7** William IV

- **1832** Reform Act heralds the start of the democratic system of voting

- **1832** In Scotland sheriff courts are allowed to grant probate on wills (previously the role of ecclesiastical courts)

- **1834** The Poor Law Amendment Act makes radical changes to the system of poor relief— the Union Workhouse is introduced

- **1835** William Henry Fox Talbot produces the first negative image—of a window. In 1839 in Paris Louis Daguerre takes probably the earliest photograph of a person

The first policemen, Peelers

London Borough of Hillingdon
Hillingdon Heritage Service
Uxbridge Library
14-15 High Street
Uxbridge, Middlesex UB8 1HD
Tel. 01895 250702
www.hillingdon.gov.uk

London Borough of Hounslow
Chiswick Library
Duke's Avenue
Chiswick, London W4 2AB
Tel. 020 8994 1008
and
Hounslow Library
CentreSpace
Treaty Centre, High Street
Hounslow, Middlesex TW3 1ES
Tel. 0845 456 2800
www.hounslow.info/libraries/
localstudies/index.htm

London Borough of Islington
Islington History Collection
Central Library
2 Fieldway Crescent
London N5 1PF
Tel. 020 7527 6900
www.islington.gov.uk/leisure/libraries/
local/central.asp
and
Finsbury Local History Collection
Finsbury Library
245 St John Street
London EC1V 4NB
Tel. 020 7527 7960
www.islington.gov.uk/education/
libraries/local/finsbury.asp

Royal Borough of Kensington & Chelsea
Local Studies Department
Kensington Central Library
Phillimore Walk
London W8 7RX
Tel. 020 7361 3038
www.rbkc.gov.uk

Royal Borough of Kingston upon Thames
Kingston Local History Room
North Kingston Centre
Richmond Road,
Kingston
Surrey KT2 5PE
Tel. 020 8547 6738
www.kingston.gov.uk/leisure/museums/
local_history_and_archives.htm

London Borough of Lambeth
Lambeth Archives
Minet Library
52 Knatchbull Road
Lambeth
London SE5 9QY
Tel. 020 7926 1000
www.lambeth.gov.uk

London Borough of Lewisham
Local History and Archives Centre
Lewisham Library
199-201 Lewisham High Street
Lewisham
London SE13 6LG
Tel. 020 8314 8501
www.lewisham.gov.uk

London Borough of Merton
Local Studies Centre
Merton Civic Centre
London Road
Morden
Surrey SM4 5DX
Tel. 020 8545 3239
www.merton.gov.uk/leisure/history-
heritage/localstudies.htm

London Borough of Newham
Archives and Local Studies Library
Stratford Library
The Grove
Stratford
London E15 1EL
Tel. 020 8430 6881
www.newham.gov.uk

London Borough of Richmond upon Thames
Local Studies Collection
Old Town Hall, Whittaker Avenue
Richmond, Surrey TW9 1TP
Tel. 020 8734 3309
www.richmond.gov.uk/
local_studies_collection

London Borough of Southwark
John Harvard Library
211 Borough High Street
London SE1 1JA
Tel. 020 7525 0232
www.southwark.gov.uk/info/200161/
local_history_library

London Borough of Sutton
Archives and Local Studies
Central Library, St Nicholas Way
Sutton, Surrey SM1 1EA
Tel. 020 8770 4747
www.sutton.gov.uk

London Borough of Tower Hamlets
Local History and Archives Library
277 Bancroft Road
London E1 4DQ
Tel. 020 7364 1290
www.towerhamlets.gov.uk

London Borough of Waltham Forest
Waltham Forest Archives and
Local Studies Library
Vestry House Museum, Vestry Road
Walthamstow, London E17 9NH
Tel. 020 8496 4381
www.walthamforest.gov.uk/
archives-local-studies

London Borough of Wandsworth
Wandsworth Heritage Service
Battersea Library
265 Lavender Hill
London SW11 1JB
Tel. 020 8871 7753
www.wandsworth.gov.uk

1838
PUBLIC RECORD OFFICE FOUNDED

FAMILY HISTORY TIMELINE

- **1837–1901** Queen Victoria
- **1837** The civil registration of births, marriages and deaths in England and Wales is introduced
- **1837** Permitted age for men and women to make a will is raised to 21
- **1838** The first Public Record Office is established
- **1840** New Zealand is declared a Crown colony
- **1841** For the first time, the census in England, Wales and Scotland contains personal information such as names, ages and addresses
- **1844** Legislation empowers the Home Office to grant naturalisation, making it easier and cheaper for aliens to become naturalised Britons
- **1845** Isambard Kingdom Brunel launches the *Great Britain*—the first propeller-driven iron-hulled big ship

Queen Victoria

London Borough of Westminster
City of Westminster Archives Centre
10 St Ann's Street
London SW1P 2DE
Tel. 020 7641 5180
www.westminster.gov.uk/services/
libraries/archives/visitor-information/
contact

The London Library
14 St James' Square
London SW1Y 4LG
Tel. 020 7930 7705
www.londonlibrary.co.uk

London Metropolitan Archives
City of London
40 Northampton Road
London EC1R 0HB
Tel. 020 7332 3820
   www.cityoflondon.gov.uk/corporation/
   lgnl_services/leisure_and_culture/
   records_and_archives

m

MAGAZINES
*The principal magazines devoted to family history
include the following titles:*

Family History Monthly
Diamond Publishing
140 Wales Farm Road
London W3 6UG
Tel. 020 8579 1082
www.familyhistorymonthly.com

Family Tree Magazine
ABM Publishing
61 Great Whyte
Ramsey
Huntingdon
Cambridgeshire PE17 1HL
Tel. 01487 814050
www.family-tree.co.uk

The Genealogists' Magazine
Society of Genealogists
14 Charterhouse Buildings
Goswell Road
London EC1M 7BA
Tel. 020 7251 8799
www.sog.org.uk/genmag/genmag.shtml

Greater Manchester County
Record Office
56 Marshall Street
New Cross
Manchester M4 5FU
Tel. 0161 832 5284
www.gmcro.co.uk

The Manchester Room@City Library
City Library
Elliot House, 151 Deansgate
Manchester M3 2HN
Tel. 0161 234 1979
www.manchester.gov.uk/libraries/arls

Manx National Heritage Library
see ISLE OF MAN

Merseyside Record Office
Central Library
William Brown Street
Liverpool L3 8EW
Tel. 0151 233 5817
www.liverpool.gov.uk/libraries-and-
archives/archives-local-and-family-history

Metropolitan Police Service
Historical Archives
Room 517
Wellington House
67–73 Buckingham Gate
London SW1E 6BE
Tel. 020 7230 7186/6940
www.met.police.uk/history/archives.htm

Middlesex
for records of the former county see London
Borough of Westminster *and* London
Metropolitan Archives

Midlothian Local Studies and Archives
Library Headquarters
2 Clerk Street
Loanhead EH20 9DR
Tel. 0131 271 3976
www.midlothian.gov.uk/info/427/libraries/
138/libraries_local_collections

MINISTRY OF DEFENCE
Army Medal Office
Building 250
RAF Innsworth
Innsworth
Gloucester GL3 1HW
Tel. 01452 712612 ext 8149 (enquiry line)

Ministries of Correspondence Unit
Room 6140, Main Building
Whitehall
London SW1A 2HB
Tel. 020 7218 9000
www.commonwealthministers.com/
ministries/ministry-of-defence-
ministerial-correspondence-unit-
united-kingdom

Ministry of Defence Service Records
Veterans Advice Unit
Service Personnel and Veterans Agency
Norcross, Blackpool FY5 3WP
Tel. 0800 169 2277
www.mod.uk/defenceinternet/
contactus/servicerecordsenquiries.htm

Naval Secretary
Victory Building, HM Naval Base
Portsmouth
Hampshire PO1 3LS
Tel. 023 9272 7433
www.royalnavy.mod.uk

Royal Navy Medal Office
Room 3105, Centurion Building,
Grange Road, Gosport,
Hampshire PO13 9XA
Tel. 023 9270 2174
www.mod.uk

GREAT EXHIBITION 1851

- **1845** Civil registration of non-Catholic marriages begins in Ireland

- **1845–51** Repeated failures of the potato crop in Ireland causes the death of 1 million in the Irish Famine

- **1846** 'Railway mania' as parliament approves the building of 273 new lines

- **1851** The only national census of religious worship is taken in England, Wales and Scotland

- **1851** The Great Exhibition is held in Hyde Park, London

- **1853–6** Crimean War

- **1855** Civil registration of births, marriages and deaths begins in Scotland

- **1855** Repeal of stamp duty on newspapers leads to a cheaper press

Great Exhibition

335

Modern Records Centre
University Library
University of Warwick
Coventry CV4 7AL
Tel. 024 7652 4219
www2.warwick.ac.uk/services/library/mrc

Mormon Church *see* Family History
Centres

n

National Archives
Kew
Richmond
Surrey TW9 4DU
Tel. 020 8876 3444
www.nationalarchives.gov.uk

National Archives of Ireland
Bishop Street
Dublin 8
Tel. 00 353 1 407 2300/2333
www.nationalarchives.ie

National Archives of Scotland
HM General Register House
2 Princes Street
Edinburgh EH1 3YY
Tel. 0131 535 1314
www.nas.gov.uk

National Army Museum
Royal Hospital Road, Chelsea
London SW3 4HT
Tel. 020 7730 0717 (switchboard)
       020 7881 6606 (information line)
www.nam.ac.uk

National Federation of
Women's Institutes
104 New King's Road
London SW6 4LY
Tel. 020 7371 9300
www.thewi.org.uk

National Library of Ireland
Kildare Street
Dublin 2
Tel. 00 353 1 603 0213
www.nli.ie/en

National Library of Scotland
Department of Manuscripts
George IV Bridge
Edinburgh EH1 1EW
Tel. 0131 623 3876
www.nls.uk

National Library of Wales
Department of Manuscripts and Records
Aberystwyth
Ceredigion SY23 3BU
Tel. 01970 632800
www.llgc.org.uk

National Maritime Museum
Park Row, Greenwich
London SE10 9NF
Tel. 0871 971 5948
www.nmm.ac.uk

National Monuments Record Centre
The Engine House
Fire Fly Avenue
Swindon
Wiltshire SN2 2EH
Tel. 01793 414600
www.english-heritage.org.uk/daysout/
properties/national-monuments-record-
centre

National Monuments Record of Scotland
see Royal Commission on the Ancient and
Historical Monuments of Scotland

National Organisation for the Counselling
of Adoptees and Parents (NORCAP)
112 Church Road
Wheatley
Oxford OX33 1LU
Tel. 01865 875000
www.norcap.org.uk

National Register of Archives
see National Archives

NEW ZEALAND
Archives New Zealand
10 Mulgrave Street
Thorndon
Wellington
Tel. 0064 4 499 5595
http://www.archives.govt.nz

(for correspondence)
PO Box 12-050
Wellington

New Zealand Society of
Genealogists Inc.
Level 1, 159 Queens Road
Panmure
Auckland 1741
Tel. 064 9 570 4248
www.genealogy.org.nz

(for correspondence)
PO Box 14036
Panmure
Auckland 1741

Norfolk Record Office
The Archive Centre
Martineau Lane
Norwich NR1 2DQ
Tel. 01603 222599
www.archives.norfolk.gov.uk

Northamptonshire Record Office
Wootton Hall Park
Northampton NN4 8BQ
Tel. 01604 762129
www.northamptonshire.gov.uk

North Ayrshire Heritage Centre
Manse Street
Saltcoats
North Ayrshire KA21 5AA
Tel. 01294 464174
www.north-ayrshire.gov.uk

1857

INDIAN MUTINY

FAMILY HISTORY TIMELINE

• **1857** Divorce becomes obtainable through the civil
courts in England and Wales (Matrimonial Causes Act)

• **1857–8** The Indian Mutiny

• **1858** Britain declares India a
Crown possession. The Raj begins

• **1858** Civil Court of Probate has jurisdiction
over wills in England and Wales (previously
the role of the ecclesiastical courts)

• **1859** Charles Darwin publishes *On The Origin
of Species by Means of Natural Selection*

• **1864** Civil registration of births, deaths and all
denominations of marriage begins in Ireland

• **1867** Canada becomes a Dominion

• **1869** Church of Ireland
disestablished

• **1872** Secret ballot introduced

Charles Darwin—and ape

North Devon Library and Record Office
Tuly Street
Barnstaple EX31 1EL
Tel. 01271 388607
www.devon.gov.uk

North of Ireland Family History
Society (NIFSH)
(correspondence address only)
School of Education
69 University Street
Belfast BT7 1HL
www.nifhs.org

Northumberland Archives
Woodhorn
Queen Elizabeth II Country Park
Ashington NE63 9YF
www.northumberland.gov.uk

Nottinghamshire Archives and Southwell
and Nottingham Diocesan Record Office
County House
Castle Meadow Road
Nottingham NG2 1AG
Tel. 0115 958 1634
www.nottinghamshire.gov.uk/home/leisure/
archives/visitingarchives.htm

o

Office of the Chief Herald of Ireland
Genealogical Office
2 Kildare Street
Dublin 2
Tel. 00 3531 603 0311
www.nli.ie/en/services-heraldry.aspx

Office for National Statistics
see General Register Office
www.statistics.gov.uk/hub/index.html
(The government's statistics agency, known as
UK National Statistics, is an umbrella
organisation for other bodies, including the
General Register Office.)

Orkney Archive
Orkney Library and Archive
44 Junction Road
Kirkwall
Orkney KW15 1AG
Tel. 01856 873166
www.orkneylibrary.org.uk/html/archive.htm

Oxfordshire History Centre
St Luke's Church
Temple Road
Cowley
Oxford OX4 2HT
Tel. 01865 398200
www.oxfordshire.gov.uk

p, q

Pembrokeshire Record Office
The Castle
Haverfordwest SA61 2EF
Tel. 01437 763707
www.pembrokeshire.gov.uk

Perth and Kinross Council Archive
AK Bell Library
2–8 York Place
Perth PH2 8EP
Tel. 01738 477012
www.pkc.gov.uk

Plymouth and West Devon Record Office
Unit 3 Clare Place
Coxside
Plymouth
Devon PL4 0JW
Tel. 01752 305940
www.plymouth.gov.uk/archives

Post Office Archives and Record Centre
British Postal Museum and Archive
Freeling House
Phoenix Place
London WC1X 0DL
Tel. 020 7239 2570
www.postalheritage.org.uk

Powys County Archives
County Hall, Powys County Hall
Spa Road East, Llandrindod Wells
Powys LD1 5LG
Tel. 01597 826088
www.powys.gov.uk

Presbyterian Historical Society
of Ireland
26 College Green
Belfast BT7 1LN
Tel. 028 9072 7330
www.presbyterianhistoryireland.com

PROBATE OFFICES

Birmingham District Probate Registry
The Priory Courts, 33 Bull Street
Birmingham B4 6DU
Tel. 0121 681 3400

Brighton District Probate Registry
William Street
Brighton BN2 0RF
Tel. 01273 573510

Bristol District Probate Registry
The Civil Justice Centre, 2 Redcliff Street
Bristol BS1 6RF
Tel. 0117 366 4960

Cardiff Probate Registry of Wales
3rd Floor, Cardiff Magistrates Court
Fitzalan Place
Cardiff CF24 0RZ
Tel. 029 2047 4373

Ipswich District Probate Registry
Ground Floor, 8 Arcade Street
Ipswich IP1 1EJ
Tel. 01473 284260

Isle of Man General Registry
Isle of Man Courts of Justice
Deemsters Walk, Bucks Road
Douglas, Isle of Man IM1 3AR
Tel. 01624 685265
www.gov.im/registries

1876
QUEEN VICTORIA MADE EMPRESS OF INDIA

- **1872** Public Health Act establishes urban and rural sanitary authorities

- **1873** First national Ordnance Survey

- **1873** Return of Owners of Land, the 'Modern Domesday', is made, listing owners of more than one acre of land in Britain and Ireland

- **1875** After the Births and Deaths Act of 1874, civilians are legally obliged to register births and deaths

- **1875** Benjamin Disraeli takes a 40 per cent stake in the Suez Canal for Britain

- **1876** Royal Titles Act proclaims Queen Victoria Empress of India

- **1879** Zulu War

- **1882** Suicides are allowed to be buried in consecrated ground

Zulu War

Leeds District Probate Registry
3rd Floor
Coronet House
Queen Street
Leeds LS1 2BA
Tel. 0113 386 3540

Liverpool District Probate Registry
Queen Elizabeth 11 Law Courts
Derby Square
Liverpool L2 1XA
Tel. 0151 236 8264

Manchester District Probate Registry
Manchester Civil Justice Centre
Ground Floor, 1 Bridge Street West
PO Box 4240
Manchester M60 1WJ
Tel. 0161 240 5700

Newcastle District Probate Registry
1 Waterloo Square
Newcastle-upon-Tyne
Tyne and Wear NE1 4DR
Tel. 0191 211 2170

**Northern Ireland Probate
and Matrimonial Office**
Royal Courts of Justice
PO Box 410
Chichester Street
Belfast BT1 3JF
Tel. 028 9072 4678

Oxford District Probate Registry
Combined Court Building
St. Aldates
Oxford OX1 1LY
Tel. 01865 793 055

Principal Probate Registry (London)
Principal Registry of the Family Division
First Avenue House
42-49 High Holborn
London WC1V 6NP
Tel. 020 7947 6939

Republic of Ireland Probate Office
Courts Service
5-24 Phoenix Street North
Smithfield, Dublin 7
Tel. 00 353 1 8886000
www.courts.ie

Scotland
Probate in Scotland is handled by individual
Sheriff courts. A full list can be found at:
www.scotcourts.gov.uk/locations/index.asp.

For probates prior to 1985:
The National Archives of Scotland
HM General Register House
2 Princes Street
Edinburgh EH1 3YY
Tel. 0131 314 4300

Winchester Probate Office
4th Floor, Cromwell House
Andover Road
Winchester
Hampshire SO23 7EW
Tel. 01962 897029

Public Record Office
see The National Archive

**Public Record Office of
Northern Ireland (PRONI)**
2 Titanic Boulevard
Belfast BT3 9HQ
Tel. 028 90 534800
www.proni.gov.uk

Quakers *see* Religious Society of Friends

r

Registers of Scotland Executive Agency
Meadowbank House
153 London Road
Edinburgh EH8 7AU
Tel. 0845 607 0163 and 0131 659 6111
www.ros.gov.uk

Registry of Deeds
(Republic of Ireland)
Henrietta Street
Dublin 1
Tel. 00 353 1 8716533
www.landregistry.ie

Religious Society of Friends (Quakers)
Friends House
173-177 Euston Road
London NW1 2BJ
Tel. 020 7663 1000
www.quaker.org.uk

**Religious Society of Friends (Quakers)
in Ireland**
Quaker House, Stocking Lane
Dublin 16
Tel. 00 353 1 495 6888
www.quakers-in-ireland.ie

Representative Church Body Library
(Church of Ireland records)
Braemor Park, Churchtown
Dublin 14
Tel. 00 353 1 492 3979
http://ireland.anglican.org

**Romany and Traveller Family
History Society**
6 St James Walk
South Chailey
East Sussex BN8 4BU
www.rtfhs.org.uk

Royal Air Force Museum London
Grahame Park Way
London NW9 5LL
Tel. 020 8205 2266
www.rafmuseum.org.uk/london

Royal British Legion
Royal British Legion Village
Aylesford
Kent ME20 7NX
Tel. 01622 717172
www.britishlegion.org.uk

1885
FIRST MOTOR CAR

FAMILY HISTORY TIMELINE

- **late 19th century** Influx of Jews from Eastern Europe into London's East End

- **1882** An Act allows married women to own property

- **1885** Karl Benz tests first motor car

- **1899–1902** Boer War

- **1901** Australia joins the Commonwealth

- **1901–10** Edward VII

- **1902** The Cremation Act enables public burial authorities to provide and maintain crematoriums out of the rates

- **1905** Aliens Act limits immigration

- **1910–36** George V

- **1911** Founding of the Society of Genealogists

Benz motor car

Royal College of Physicians
The Library
11 St Andrews Place
Regent's Park
London NW1 4LE
Tel. 020 7935 1174
www.rcplondon.ac.uk

Royal Commission on the Ancient and Historical Monuments of Scotland
National Monuments Record of Scotland
John Sinclair House
16 Bernard Terrace
Edinburgh EH8 9NX
Tel. 0131 662 1456
www.rcahms.gov.uk

Royal Commission on Historical Manuscripts
see The National Archive

Royal Irish Academy
Academy House
19 Dawson Street
Dublin 2
Tel. 00 353 1 1676 2570
www.ria.ie

Royal Marines Museum
Eastney Road
Southsea
Hampshire PO4 9PX
Tel. 023 9281 9385
www.royalmarinesmuseum.gov.uk

Royal Naval Museum
Visitor Centre
Victory Gate
HM Naval Base
Portsmouth
Hampshire PO1 3LJ
Tel. 02392 728060
www.royalnavalmuseum.org

Rutland
see Leicestershire, Leicester and Rutland, The Record Office for

S

The Salvation Army's Family Tracing Service
101 Newington Causeway
London SE1 6BN
Tel. 0845 634
www2.salvationarmy.org.uk/familytracing

School of Oriental and African Studies (SOAS)
(incorporates missionary records)
Library Archives
Thornhaugh Street
London WC1H 0XG
Tel. 020 7637 2388
www.soas.ac.uk/archives

Scottish Borders Archive and Local History Centre
Heart of Hawick
Kirkstile
Hawick TD9 0AE
Tel. 01450 360699
www.heartofhawick.co.uk/heritagehub

Scottish Genealogy Society
Library and Family History Centre
15 Victoria Terrace
Edinburgh EH1 2JL
Tel. 0131 220 3677
www.scotsgenealogy.com

Scottish Jewish Archives Centre
129 Hill Street
Garnethill
Glasgow G3 6UB
Tel. 0141 332 4911
www.sjac.org.uk/archives.html

The Scout Association
The Scout Information Centre
Gilwell Park, Chingford
London E4 7QW
Tel. 0845 300 1818
http://scouts.org.uk

Sheffield Archives
Local Studies, Central library
Surrey Street
Sheffield S1 1XZ
Tel. 0114 203 9395
www.sheffield.gov.uk/libraries/archives-and-local-studies

Shetland Museum and Archives
Hay's Dock, Lerwick
Shetland ZE1 0WP
Tel. 01595 696247
www.shetland-museum.org.uk/archivecollections

Shropshire Records and Research Centre
Castle Gates
Shrewsbury SY1 2AQ
Tel. 01743 255350
www.shropshire.gov.uk/archives.nsf

The Signet Library
Parliament Square
Edinburgh EH1 1RF
Tel. 0131 225 0651
www.thesignetlibrary.co.uk

Society of Friends
see Religious Society of Friends

Society of Genealogists
14 Charterhouse Buildings
Goswell Road
London EC1M 7BA
Tel. 020 7251 8799
www.sog.org.uk

SOFTWARE SUPPLIERS
The following suppliers sell a range of genealogy software and provide expert advice:

S&N Genealogy Supplies
Manor Farm
Chilmark
Salisbury SP3 5AF
Tel. 01722 716121
www.genealogysupplies.com

1926

GENERAL STRIKE

• 1914–18 First World War

  • 1914 The Aliens Registration Act calls for the registration with the police of all aliens over the age of 16

    • 1914 Britain houses 200,000 homeless war refugees from Belgium

      • 1916 Easter Rising erupts in Dublin as Irish nationalists demand Home Rule

First World War

• 1918 Women over the age of 30 win the right to vote

  • 1922 Partition of Ireland creates Northern Ireland and the Irish Free State, later renamed the Republic of Ireland

    • 1922 Fire destroys Public Record Office in Dublin

      • 1926 General Strike

        • 1927 Adopted Children Register begins in England and Wales

TWR Computing
Unit G4 Mexborough Business Centre
College Road
Mexborough
South Yorkshire s64 9JP
Tel. 01709 580066
www.twrcomputing.co.uk

Somerset Heritage Centre
Brunel Way
Langford Mead
Norton Fitzwarren
Taunton
Somerset TA2 6SF
Tel. 01823 347459
www.somerset.gov.uk/archives

SOUTH AFRICA
**Genealogical Society of
South Africa**
The society comprises 10 regional
branches. Local details can be found at:
www.eggsa.org

National Archives of South Africa
Private Bag x236
24 Hamilton Street
Arcadia
Pretoria 0001
Tel. 00 27 12 441 3200
www.national.archives.gov.za

Southampton Archives
Civic Centre
Civic Centre Road
Southampton
Hampshire so14 7LY
Tel. 023 8083 3000
www.southampton.gov.uk/s-leisure/
artsheritage/history/archives/

**Spanish and Portuguese Jews
Congregation (Bevis Marks)**
Heneage Lane
London EC3 5DQ
Tel. 020 7626 1274
www.sandp.org

Staffordshire Record Office
County Buildings, Eastgate Street
Stafford ST16 2LZ
Tel. 01785 278379
www.staffordshire.gov.uk/leisure/archives

Stirling Council Archives Services
5 Borrowmeadow Road
Stirling FK7 7UW
Tel. 01786 450745
www.stirling.gov.uk/index/services/libraries/
archives/archivevisiting.htm

Stoke On Trent City Archives
City Central Library, Bethesda Street
Hanley, Stoke on Trent
Stafford ST1 3RS
Tel. 01782-238420
www.staffordshire.gov.uk/leisure/archives/
home.aspx

SUFFOLK
The county archives are in three locations
with a shared web site: www.suffolk.gov.uk/
leisureandculture/localhistoryandheritage/
suffolkrecordoffice/wheretofindus.htm

Suffolk Record Office
77 Raingate Street
Bury St Edmunds IP33 2AR
Tel. 01284 741212 (search room)

Suffolk Record Office
Gatacre Road
Ipswich IP1 2LQ
Tel. 01473 584541 (search room)

Suffolk Record Office
Clapham Road
Lowestoft NR32 1DR
Tel. 01502 405357 (search room)

Surrey History Centre
130 Goldsworth Road
Woking GU21 1ND
Tel. 01483 518737
www.surreycc.gov.uk

East Sussex Record Office
The Maltings, Castle Precincts
Lewes BN7 1YT
Tel. 01273 482349
www.eastsussex.gov.uk/leisureandtourism/
localandfamilyhistory/esro/visit

West Sussex Record Office
County Hall, West Street
Chichester PO19 1RQ
Tel. 01243 753600
www.westsussex.gov.uk/leisure/explore_west_
sussex/record_office_and_archives.aspx

Sutton Publishing
The History Press
The Mill, Brimscombe Port
Stroud, Gloucestershire GL5 2QG
Tel. 01453 883300
www.thehistorypress.co.uk

Teesside Archives
Exchange House
6 Marton Road
Middlesbrough TS1 1DB
Tel. 01642 248321
www.middlesbrough.gov.uk/ccm/navigation/
leisure-and-culture/local-history-and-heritage

Trinity College Library
Trinity College Dublin
College Green
Dublin 2
Tel. 00 353 1 896 1000
www.tcd.ie/library

Tyne & Wear Archive Service
Discovery Museum
Blandford Square
Newcastle upon Tyne
Tyne and Wear NE1 4JA
Tel. 0191 277 2248
www.twmuseums.org.uk/archives

1936
ABDICATION OF EDWARD VIII

FAMILY HISTORY TIMELINE

- **1928** Women over 21 are allowed to vote
- **1929** Legal age of marriage with parents' consent is raised to 16 (from 12 for girls and 14 for boys)
- **1930s** Jews flee to Britain from the spread of Nazism
- **1936** Edward VIII
- **1936–52** George VI

- **1939–45** Second World War
- **1947** India gains independence
- **1948** National Health Service established
- **1948** Registrations of British nationality are issued to citizens of British colonies
- **1948** SS *Empire Windrush* brings first large-scale influx of immigrants from West Indies

Second World War

u

Ulster Historical Foundation / Ancestry Ireland
49 Malone Road
Belfast BT9 6RY
Northern Ireland
Tel. 028 9033 2288
www.ancestryireland.com

UNITED STATES OF AMERICA

Immigrant Genealogy Society (IGS) and Library
PO Box 7369
Burbank
California 91510-7369
USA
Tel. 00 1 8188483122
www.immigrantgensoc.org

National Archives and Records Services
(American military records)
700 Pennsylvania Avenue, NW
Washington DC 20408
USA
Tel. 00 1 866 325 7208
www.archives.gov

National Genealogical Society
3108 Columbia Pike, Suite 300
Arlington, Virginia 22204-4370
USA
Tel. 00 1 703 525 0050
www.ngsgenealogy.org

v, w

Valuation Office
Irish Life Centre
Abbey Lower Street
Dublin 1
Tel. 00 3531 817 1000
www.valoff.ie

Warwickshire County Record Office
Priory Park
Cape Road
Warwick CV34 4JS
Tel. 01926 738959
www.warwickshire.gov.uk

The Victoria and Albert Museum Theatre Collection
(former Theatre Museum collection)
Cromwell Road
London SW7 2RL
Tel. 020 7942 2723
www.vam.ac.uk/page/a/archives

Westcountry Studies Library
Devon Studies Centre
Castle Street
Exeter
Devon EX4 3PQ
Tel. 01392 384216
www.devon.gov.uk/localstudies

West Lothian Council Archives
Archives and Records Centre
9 Dunlop Square
Deans Industrial Estate
Livingston EH54 8SB
Tel. 01506 773770
www.westlothian.gov.uk/tourism/libservices/ices/ves

Westmorland
see Cumbria Archives Service

Wiltshire and Swindon History Centre
Cocklebury Road
Chippenham
Wiltshire SN15 3QN
Tel. 01249 705500
www.wshc.eu

The Women's Library
London Metropolitan University
25 Old Castle Street
London E1 7NT
www.londonmet.ac.uk/thewomenslibrary

Worcestershire Record Office
Headquarters Branch
County Hall, Spetchley Road
Worcester
Worcestershire WR5 2NP
Tel. 01905 766351
http://www.worcestershire.gov.uk/records

Note: Record Office relocation to The Hive, Worcester from Summer / Autumn 2012.

y

York City Archives and Local History
York Explore Centre
Museum Street
York
Yorkshire YO1 7DS
Tel. 01904 552800
www.york.gov.uk/archives

East Riding of Yorkshire Archives and Local Studies
The Treasure House,
Champney Road
Beverley
East Riding of Yorkshire HU17 9BA
Tel. 01482 392790
www.eastriding.gov.uk/cs/culture-and-information/archives/archivesloc

North Yorkshire County Record Office
Malpas Road
Northallerton
North Yorkshire DL7 8TB
Tel. 01609 777585
www.northyorks.gov.uk/archives

West Yorkshire Archive Service
Wakefield Headquarters
Registry of Deeds
Newstead Road
Wakefield WF1 2DE
Tel. 01924 305980
www.archives.wyjs.org.uk/archives-visit-us.asp

2000
THIRD MILLENNIUM BEGINS

- **1950–3** Korean War
- **1952** Accession of Elizabeth II
- **1962** Commonwealth immigration restricted to skilled workers and dependants
- **1969** Voting age reduced to 18
- **1969** ARPANET, the predecessor of the Internet, is created in the USA

- **1973** Britain joins the EEC
- **1975** Adopted people over the age of 18 in England and Wales (over 17 in Scotland) gain the right to apply for their original birth certificate
- **2002** 1901 census records are released to the public
- **2003** Creation of the National Archives at Kew
- **2009** 2011 census returns are released to the public

A laptop computer

index

IMMIGRATION

INTERNET

acknowledgments

The position of photographs and illustrations on each page is indicated by letters after the page number: **l** left **r** right **t** top **tl** top left **tr** top right **b** bottom **bl** bottom left **br** bottom right **c** centre **cl** centre left **cr** centre right. Every effort has been made to trace copyright holders of the illustrations but this has not always been possible. To make a claim, contact the Picture Resourse Manager, Reader's Digest Books, Vivat Direct Limited, 157 Edgware Road, London W2 2HR

Spine: Family, The Bridgeman Art Library/Gavin Graham Gallery, London, Frame, Corbis/Tetra Images; **Cover Main image (tree):** Getty Images/Derek Croucher, **T** ShutterStock, Inc/Kompaniets Taras, **TR** ShutterStock, Inc/Michael Stejskalova, **TL** iStockphoto.com/Hulton Archive, **CL** Getty Images/Retrofile, **C** Getty Images/H. Armstrong Roberts, **CR** Getty Images/Stuart McClymont, **BL** Getty Images/Michael Blann, **BC** iStockphoto.com/Joshua Hodge Photography, **BR** Getty Images/Image Source; **2-4** Getty Images; **6 BL** Getty Images, **BC** Getty Images/Douglas Miller, **BR** Getty Images; **6-7 B** Getty Images; **7 C** Getty Images, **BC** Getty Images/Fox Photos, **BR** Getty Images; **10-16 CL** © Reader's Digest/Jon Bouchier; **18** V&A Images, Victoria and Albert Museum; **19** © Reader's Digest/Jon Bouchier; **20 T** Family Tree Magazine/ABM Publishing Ltd, **L** Diamond Publishing Limited, **R** Future Publishing Limited; **22** Family Tree Magazine; **24** Hugh Alexander; **26-28** © Reader's Digest/Jon Bouchier; **32 L** © Reader's Digest/Jon Bouchier, **B** Duncan Harrington; **33 TL** Duncan Harrington, **R** The London Library; **34-37 TL** © Reader's Digest/Jon Bouchier; **38 incl gatefold** O.P.Rilett; **39 incl gatefold** O.P.Rilett; **39 CB** Photolibrary.com/OSF; **40** © Reader's Digest/Jon Bouchier; **42 BC** Calico Pie Ltd./www.family-historian.co.uk, **BR** Ancestry.co.uk; **43** © Reader's Digest/Jon Bouchier; **46 CL** © Reader's Digest/Helen Holmes, **CA** Richard Stanton; **46-47** By permission of the National Museums and Galleries of Wales; **47 TR** © Reader's Digest/Helen Holmes; **48-49** Getty Images; **50 C** Fine Art Photographs/Ralph Hedley (artist) 1851-1913, **BL** © Reader's Digest; **53 C, BC, BR** Getty Images, **CB** © British Library Board. All Rights Reserved; **54** Hugh Alexander; **55 CL** www.ntpl.org.uk/©NTPL/Andreas von Einsiedel; **56 T** Getty Images, **C** V&A Images, Victoria and Albert Museum, **BL** The Family Records Centre; **59** © Reader's Digest/Jon Bouchier; **61** Getty Images; **62** Mary Evans Picture Library; **63** The National Archives; **65** © Reader's Digest/Jon Bouchier; **68** The Jewish Museum/from George R.Sims, 'Living London' 1902; **70-71** The Williams Family/Sandra Williams; **70-71 C** The National Archives; **72-73** The National Archives; **74-75** © Museum of London/Ian Galt; **75** The National Archives; **76 TL** Getty Images, **TR** Robert Longdon Archive/Sonia Rolt, **C** The National Fairground Archive (NFA), **CR** The National Archives, **B** Kingston Museum & Heritage Service; **77 T** Getty Images; **79 CL** Getty Images, **BC & BR** Les Davis; **80-81 TC** Getty Images, **81 B** © Reader's Digest/Neil Holmes; **82-83** Getty Images, **83 BR** Mary Evans Picture Library; **84-85** Getty Images; **86** Getty Images; **88 TL** © British Library Board. All Rights Reserved, **TR** Suffolk County Record Office/Neil Holmes; **90 BL** Surrey History Centre; **90-91** The Bridgeman Art Library/Bristol City Museum and Art Gallery, UK, **91** City of London/London Metropolitan Archives/A.E.Harvey, Barnsbury Team Ministry and Corporation of London; **92 T** West Yorkshire Archive Service, Bradford District (Archive reference 51D81/5)/Bradford/Rev'd Peter Mayo-Smith, **B** © Reader's Digest/Jon Wyand; **95 R** City of London/London Metropolitan Archives/Rector of Stepney and Corporation of London, **Inset** Guildhall Library, Corporation of London; **97** www.jasonhawkes.com; **98** The National Archives; **99** The Bridgeman Art Library/Christopher Wood Gallery, London, UK; **100-101** The Church of Jesus Christ of Latter-Day Saints; **102** The Bridgeman Art Library/Ken Welsh; **103 BL** The Bridgeman Art Library/English School, (19th century), **BR** The Bridgeman Art Library/Hamilton, William (1751-1801) (after); **104** Getty Images; **106 T&L** Sue Lumas/Jon Bouchier, **CR** The National Archives, **BR** The National Archives; **107** Mary Evans Picture Library; **108 T** By kind permission of the House of Lords Record Office, **B** Mary Evans Picture Library; **110 TR** Dr.Anthony Joseph, **BR** The Jewish Museum, London, **R** Dr. Anthony Joseph; **112 BL** Ecclesiastical & Eccentricities Picture Library, **BC** TopFoto.co.uk; **113 T** © Reader's Digest/Simon McComb, **TR** Penny Mortimer, **BL** Archie Miles; **114-115** Sheila & Oliver Mathews; **117** robertharding.com/Christopher Nicholson; **118-119** Getty Images; **120** Ronald Grant Archive/Mary Evans Picture Library; **123 BL** The National Archives, **BR** By Courtesy of the National Portrait Gallery, London; **124** © British Library Board. All Rights Reserved/John McLenan 1861; **125 TR** The National Archives, **B** Geffrye Museum, London; **126-127** © Reader's Digest/Jon Bouchier; **129** The National Archives; **130-131 R** By Courtesy of the National Portrait Gallery, London, **L** The Bridgeman Art Library/English School/Royal Society, London, UK; **130-131** The National Archives; **132-4** Getty Images; **135 BR** Whitgift School; **136** © Reader's Digest; **138** St.Andrews University Library; **139** Bedfordshire and Luton Archives and Records Service (Andrew Underwood); **140-141** © 1993 Arthur Ingram & Roundoak Publishing:The Story of Pickfords, **141 CL** © Reader's Digest/Jon Bouchier/Pickfords; **142** © Reader's Digest/Neil Martin; **143** © Reader's Digest/Andrew's Family; **T** Guildhall Library, Corporation of London, **L** © British Library Board. All Rights Reserved;**144** The British Postal Museum & Archive; **145 BR** © Reader's Digest/Simon McComb, **Inset** Church of England Record Centre; **146** North Yorkshire County Record Office; **147** By permission of the Houghton Library, Harvard University; **148** V&A Images, Victoria and Albert Museum/Theatre Museum; **149 CR** Surrey History Centre/Byfleet Cricket Club, **BL** © Reader's Digest/Jon Bouchier/Oxshott Cricket Club; **150** Getty Images; **152-153** Mary Evans Picture Library, **152** Courtesy of the Wiltshire & Swindon Record Office, **BR** Courtesy of the Director, National Army Museum, London; **154** Courtesy of the Wiltshire & Swindon Record Office; **156 TL** Documentary Photography Archive, **TR** Manchester Central Library-Local Studies Unit, **BR** Powys County Archives Office; **157** The Picture Desk; **158** Courtesy of the Wiltshire & Swindon Record Office; **159** The National Archives; **161** Mary Evans Picture Library; **163-164** The National Archives; **165** Image Library, State Library of New South Wales; **166-167** Getty Images; **168-169 B** © British Library Board. All Rights Reserved; **170** Shropshire County Council, **TR** © British Library Board. All Rights Reserved, **R** Getty Images; **173 CL** Guildhall Library, Corporation of London, **BR** Guildhall Library, Corporation of London; **174 L** Guildhall Library, Corporation of London, **BC** The Bridgeman Art Library/Bibliotheque des Arts Decoratifs, Paris, France/Archives Charmet; **176-177** © Reader's Digest/J.Gordon Davies; **178-179** Courtesy of the Wiltshire & Swindon Record Office; **181 TR** David Sheppard, **B** © Reader's Digest/Neil Martin, **B** © Reader's Digest/Ian Atkinson; **183 TR** By Courtesy of the National Portrait Gallery, London, **BL** Courtesy of the Wiltshire & Swindon Record Office; **184** Getty Images/Topical Press Agency; **186 BC** © National Archives of Scotland/Crown Copyright, National Records of Scotland, **BR** The Scottish Record Office; **188** The Francis Frith Collection, Salisbury, Wiltshire SP3 5QP, **BR** V&A Images, Victoria and Albert Museum; **189** Science and Society Picture Library; **191 TR** Dorothy Wise; **192 T** Guildhall Library, Corporation of London, **B** The Francis Frith Collection, Salisbury, Wiltshire SP3 5QP; **194-195** Tower Hamlets Local History Library & Archives; **195 TR** The National Archives; **196 T** © Reader's Digest/Cleveland County Council Archives Dept./Middlesbrough Estate; **197** Middlesbrough Reference Library; **198 C** © Reader's Digest, **B** Science and Society Picture Library/Science Museum Pictorial; **199** From the Tennyson Research Centre, Lincoln by permission of Lincolnshire County Council; **200** David Hey; **201 TC** Hampshire Record Office, **BL** Ordnance Survey/ © Crown Copyright, **BR** Hampshire Record Office; **203 T** The London School of Economics and Political Science, **BR** Mary Evans Picture Library; **204-205** Getty Images; **206** Courtesy of the Director, National Army Museum, London/Giuseppe Chiesa (attrib); **208** Getty Images; **209** The National Archives; **211 BR** Fine Art Photographs/James Shaw Crompton; **212 TL** The National Archives, **BL** Professor J.Duncan; **212-213** Mary Evans Picture Library; **213 BR** Professor J.Duncan; **214-217** Imperial War Museum; **218-219** Imperial War Museum; **218 C** © Reader's Digest/Jon Bouchier, **BR** © Reader's Digest/Jon Bouchier; **220** Imperial War Museum; **222-223** © Reader's Digest/Jon Bouchier/Medals supplied by Imperial War Museum & Spink & Sons Ltd; **223 CL & 224** Imperial War Museum; **225 BL** The National Archives, **BR** Imperial War Museum, London; **226-227** Imperial War Museum; **227 TC & CL** Paul Blake; **229 CL,CR,C** The National Archives, **BL** National Maritime Museum, London; **231 P & O; 233 CL** Guildhall Library, Corporation of London, **BC** National Maritime Museum, London; **234 B** The National Archives; **236-237** Getty Images; **238 L** Bibliotheque Royale Albert 1er, Brussels, **CL** The Bodleian Library, Oxford, **CR** The Bridgeman Art Library/English School, (19th century), **R** © British Library Board. All Rights Reserved; **239 L** National Galleries of Scotland, **CR** Getty Images; **241 CR** The Picture Desk/Eileen Tweedy; **242-243** © Reader's Digest/Philip Hepworth; **245 L** The Bodleian Library, Oxford; **246-247 TR,CL,CR** Sharon Floate, **BR** Sharon Floate/Robert McDougall Romany gypsies photographic collection; **248-249** Getty Images/Topical Press Agency; **250 TL** The Bridgeman Art Library, **BL** Envision; **252 CL** The Picture Desk/Mitchell Library Sydney, **R** Image Library, State Library of New South Wales; **254 BL** National Maritime Museum, London; **254-255** By permission of the British Library; **256-257** Getty Images; **258** © Museum of London, **Inset** The National Archives; **259** The National Archives; **260** Camera Press, **B** The National Archives; **263** Board of Trustees of the National Museums & Galleries on Merseyside (Walker Art Gallery, Liverpool); **264-266** Getty Images; **268-269** The Orkney Library; **270** Corbis/Hulton-Deutsch Collection; **272-273** Getty Images; **274** ©Photo SCALA; **275** The Bridgeman Art Library/English School, (15th century) (after); **276-277** The National Archives; **278-279 TC** The National Archives, **B** © British Library Board. All Rights Reserved; **280** The Picture Desk/Honourable Society of Inner Temple London/Eileen Tweedy; **283** The Bodleian Library, Oxford; **284-285** The National Archives; **286** © British Library Board. All Rights Reserved; **288** V&A Images, Victoria and Albert Museum; **289** Cecil R. Humphery-Smith; **290** The Bridgeman Art Library/English School, (15th century); **291 CR** Royal College of Arms, **BR** Getty Images; **292-295** artist, Tom Meek; **296 CR** artist, Tom Meek, **BR** Photograph by Tim Graham; **297 BL** By Courtesy of the National Portrait Gallery, London; **298 BL** The Bridgeman Art Library/Nasmyth, Alexander (1758-1840)/Scottish National Portrait Gallery, Edinburgh, Scotland, **BC** By Courtesy of the National Portrait Gallery, London, **BR** The Bridgeman Art Library/English School, (16th century)/Photo © Philip Mould Ltd, London, **BR** By Courtesy of the National Portrait Gallery, London; **301** Getty Images; **302 R** © Museum of London; **305** © Reader's Digest/Neil Martin; **322** The Picture Desk/Musée de la Tapisserie Bayeux/Gianni Dagli Orti; **323** The Picture Desk/Victoria and Albert Museum London/Harper Collins Publishers; **324 BC** © British Library Board. All Rights Reserved, **BR** By Courtesy of the National Portrait Gallery, London; **325 BR** Mary Evans Picture Library; **326 BC** By Courtesy of the National Portrait Gallery, London, **BR** Mary Evans Picture Library; **327** The Granger Collection; **328 BC** V&A Images, Victoria and Albert Museum, **BR** The Bridgeman Art Library/Verschuier, Lieve (1630-86)/Museum of Fine Arts, Budapest, Hungary; **329** Dundee City Council, Arts and Heritage Dept.; **330-331** National Maritime Museum, London; **332** © British Library Board. All Rights Reserved; **333** Mary Evans Picture Library; **334** The Royal Collection © 2011, Her Majesty Queen Elizabeth II; **335** The Bridgeman Art Library/Guildhall Library, City of London; **336** The Bridgeman Art Library/English School, (19th century)/Archives Charmet; **337** The Picture Desk/National Army Museum London; **338** Science and Society Picture Library/Science Museum; **339-340** Getty Images; **341** Alamy Images/Frankie Angel.

The publishers would also like to thank the following for their help in the preparation of this book: John d'Arcy, Principal Archivist of the Wiltshire and Swindon Record Office; Mrs Daphne Barnett; Professor James P.Duncan; Louise Flaig; Polly Goldman; Putney Library; Anthony C. Rilett; Arthur L. Rilett; Dr Jill Roberts; Surrey History Centre.